Vital Issues

Vital Issues.

Edited by Charlotte Perkins Gilman.

[Mrs. Gilman is solely responsible for what appears in this department.]

The recurring headnote to Gilman's column in the Boston *Woman's Journal*.

Vital Issues

Charlotte Perkins Gilman in the Boston *Woman's Journal*, 1904

Edited by Gary Scharnhorst

UNIVERSITY OF NEW MEXICO PRESS | ALBUQUERQUE

© 2024 by University of New Mexico Press
All rights reserved. Published 2024
Printed in the United States of America

ISBN 978-0-8263-6653-5 (cloth)
ISBN 978-0-8263-6654-2 (paper)
ISBN 978-0-8263-6655-9 (ePub)
ISBN 978-0-8263-6740-2 (webPDF)

Library of Congress Control Number: 2024941547

Founded in 1889, the University of New Mexico sits on the traditional homelands of the Pueblo of Sandia. The original peoples of New Mexico—Pueblo, Navajo, and Apache—since time immemorial have deep connections to the land and have made significant contributions to the broader community statewide. We honor the land itself and those who remain stewards of this land throughout the generations and also acknowledge our committed relationship to Indigenous peoples. We gratefully recognize our history.

Cover illustration: Charlotte Perkins Gilman ca. 1900 (Library of Congress, LC-USZ62-106490)
Designed by Felicia Cedillos
Composed in Alegreya

For Emily and Rebecca, Imani and Catalina

Contents

Introduction   1

A Note on the Text   7

Column 1. January 2, 1904   9
Column 2. January 9, 1904   17
Column 3. January 16, 1904   23
Column 4. January 23, 1904   37
Column 5. January 30, 1904   43
Column 6. February 6, 1904   51
Column 7. February 13, 1904   59
Column 8. February 20, 1904   67
Column 9. February 27, 1904   75
Column 10. March 5, 1904   83
Column 11. March 12, 1904   91
Column 12. March 19, 1904   99
Column 13. March 26, 1904   109
Column 14. April 2, 1904   117
Column 15. April 9, 1904   127
Column 16. April 16, 1904   135
Column 17. April 23, 1904   143
Column 18. April 30, 1904   151
Column 19. May 7, 1904   159
Column 20. May 14, 1904   165
Column 21. May 21, 1904   171
Column 22. May 28, 1904   179
Column 23. June 4, 1904   185

Column 24. June 11, 1904   189
Column 25. June 18, 1904   195
Column 26. June 25, 1904   201
Column 27. July 2, 1904   207
Column 28. July 23, 1904   211
Column 29. July 30, 1904   219
Column 30. August 6, 1904   227
Column 31. August 13, 1904   231
Column 32. August 20, 1904   237
Column 33. August 27, 1904   245
Column 34. September 3, 1904   253
Column 35. September 10, 1904   259
Column 36. September 17, 1904   265
Column 37. September 24, 1904   271
Column 38. October 1, 1904   277
Column 39. October 8, 1904   283
Column 40. October 15, 1904   291
Column 41. October 22, 1904   297
Column 42. October 29, 1904   303
Column 43. November 5, 1904   311
Column 44. November 12, 1904   317
Column 45. November 19, 1904   323
Column 46. November 26, 1904   329

Column 47. December 3, 1904   335
Column 48. December 10, 1904   343
Column 49. December 17, 1904   351
Column 50. December 24, 1904   359
Column 51. December 31, 1904   367

Afterword   375

Notes   377

Index   401

Introduction

The socialist and sociologist Charlotte Perkins Gilman (1860–1935) was "the leading intellectual in the woman's movement in the United States during the first two decades of the twentieth century."[1] So declared Carl Degler over half a century ago in his introduction to Gilman's feminist classic *Women and Economics: A Study of the Economic Relation Between Men and Women as a Factor in Social Evolution* (1898). Gilman was also a prolific poet and author of the oft-anthologized short story "The Yellow Wall-Paper" (1892) and oft-reprinted utopian novel *Herland* (1915). In 1904, at the height of her career, she contributed a total of over a hundred thousand words to the Boston *Woman's Journal*, "a paper which holds a unique place of its own making" and "the only Voice of the Woman's Movement in this country, if not the world," as she put it in 1912.[2]

Established by the activist Lucy Stone (1818–1893) and her husband, Henry B. Blackwell (1825–1909), in 1870, the *Woman's Journal* since its founding had been devoted to advancing the cause of women's suffrage in the United States. Gilman had been a regular contributor to its pages since 1884. "The Blackwell family were among my most honored friends, brave progressive people," she reminisced in her autobiography. Lucy Stone was "one of the first—and sweetest—of our suffrage leaders, in days when speaking for that cause meant real danger as well as abuse."[3] The paper was not formally affiliated with any suffrage or women's rights organization until 1910, however. That is, for the first forty years of its existence it depended entirely upon income from subscriptions, advertising, and occasional gifts to meet expenses. And with only about two thousand subscribers who paid a mere five cents a week or $2.50 a year in 1904, the editors were sometimes forced to underwrite its production costs.[4]

Gilman did not focus her columns in 1904 exclusively on voting rights. As she once conceded, "suffrage pure and simple . . . never did interest me."[5] Instead, she hoped to transform the *Woman's Journal* into a paper that embraced "the whole woman movement."[6] In her view, suffrage was a necessary but insufficient goal. Her weekly department, titled Vital Issues, presumed that "the woman's movement is larger than the suffrage movement and includes it; and that the very cause to which this paper is devoted will be most advanced by a more inclusive treatment." She became "of her own free will, without solicitation," an unpaid contributing editor of the paper for an entire year, a gift "of time and labor equal to about three thousand dollars" had she sold the material at the prices her writing commanded at the time.[7] But she wanted both to broaden the appeal of the paper and determine whether "enough people care" to enable it to be "at least self-sustaining." If the paper earned a profit, Gilman was "to have a share in it." She promised to supply weekly "installments of original work" and she enjoyed the writing "immensely," or so she professed, because "I am free to let out the little things that flock so thickly." She even vainly hoped that some of these articles would "be reprinted later."[8] Unfortunately, though published at the height of her fame and popularity, almost none of this material—no more than a few dozen words—has ever been reprinted.

Gilman was as good as her word in her treatment of a variety of topics. In addition to her support for woman's suffrage, she lauded women's clubs and argued for passage of the Pure Food and Drug Act. A nascent ecofeminist, she decried air and water pollution and promoted clean and renewable energy sources, especially wind and hydroelectric power, long before climate change became an environmental issue. As in her book *The Home: Its Work and Influence* (1903), she envisioned kitchenless apartments, food delivery services, professionalized housekeeping, and child-care centers—proposals that in effect reinvented the home and abolished the role of housewife. And as in her book *Human Work*, published in May 1904, she endorsed the labor theory of value, opposed hazing, lauded labor unions and workers' rights, and condemned cheap (immigrant) and child labor. In still other essays she supported women's dress reform, recommended cremation instead of interment, proposed the teaching of home economics to both boys and girls, ridiculed the political ambitions of the newspaper baron William Randolph Hearst, and scorned tattooing, debutante parties, and corporal punishment of children as survivals of savage traits. She detailed the inconveniences of rail travel and even first-class transatlantic cruises, reminisced about the "rest cure" for neurasthenia she underwent in 1887, and recorded her impressions of women's conferences in Washington and Berlin and her holidays in Lilydale and Chautauqua, New York. She commented on such events as the Russo-Japanese War, the deadly Iroquois Theater fire in Chicago, the organization of a servants' union, and the dismissal of women teachers who married, often quoting from the New York daily papers she routinely read: the *Sun*, the *Times*, and *Evening Post*. All the while she disparaged, sometimes with bitter invective, "the popular mind" with its "mountainous prejudices" or "the prejudices of the huge slow-minded inert majority" as an arbiter of virtue and truth.

On the other hand, Gilman's social analysis was sometimes egregiously flawed by her Lamarckianism, her belief in "hereditary habits" or the transmission of acquired traits. She thought, for example, that a woman who became a skilled musician before bearing children was more likely than an untaught peasant woman to pass along her musical talents to her offspring. Or as she bluntly asserted in her treatise *Concerning Children* (1900):

> If you were buying babies, investing in young human stock as you would in colts or calves for the value of the beast, a sturdy English baby would be worth more than an equally vigorous young Fuegian. With the same training and care, you could develop higher faculties in the English specimen than in the Fuegian specimen because it was better bred.[9]

Nowhere is Gilman's embrace of this false notion more apparent than in her essay "Brain Growth" published in the November 12, 1904, issue of the *Woman's Journal*. There she pleads with every prospective mother "to do all she can for the race" by "selecting always the best of the race to wed and by a conscientious self-development before marriage."[10] In effect, she believed that all peoples except Anglo-Saxons had become debased stock. Or as she declared in *Women and Economics*, "Anglo-Saxon blood" is "the most powerful expression of the latest current of fresh racial life from the north."[11]

Inspired by this nativist idée fixe, Gilman constructed ethnic and racial hierarchies crowned by "Aryans," exhibited class biases, defended eugenics or selective reproduction, betrayed an ethnocentric view of the United States, and lambasted the "greasy" (i.e., nonwhite) immigrants to its shores. She denigrated the "ignorant, low-grade hired servants" employed by the leisure class, especially "colored girls or 'mammys,' young Irish or German peasants—persons such as we should never think fit company," and mimicked their dialects. A proponent of the theory of "race suicide," Gilman feared that "the lower the grade" or class or race of the mother "the more children" she produced and, in contrast, "the higher the grade, the less children"; then she identified exactly the type of mother she meant: "The American woman does not have enough children! Now the African woman does. The Italian woman does." In fact, she stigmatized "the prolific negress bearing and burying her babies with the unprogressive profusion of fruit trees." Gilman was likewise an ardent apologist for American exceptionalism: The United States was "a Christian country," she averred, ahead "in the international competition for race superiority," the result of the "development of those free institutions for which our ancestors [i.e., white northern and western Europeans] so sternly fought."[12] She routinely deployed racial stereotypes ("the Chinese brain, so simple, so subtle"), used racial slurs (e.g., "Fuzzy Wuzzies," "Kaffirs," "savages," "primitives," "squaws," etc.), and termed persons with disabilities "deformed," "degenerates," "idiots," or "defectives." She even called for "a strong sentiment of condemnation for any mother" who bears a "deformed or idiot child."[13] Little wonder that in her utopia "unfit" women liable to conceive such progeny "are not allowed" to reproduce.[14] Or that in her late essay "Is America Too Hospitable?" (1923) she lamented the influx of "swarming immigrants" to the American strand:

> They like an established nation, with free education, free hospitals, free nursing, and more remunerative employment than they can find at home.... The amazing thing is the cheerful willingness with which the American people are giving up their country to other people, so rapidly that they are already reduced to scant half of the population. No one is to blame but ourselves.[15]

In all, she rationalized that people of color inherited inferior traits through generations of oppression and so, like the offspring of feral animals, they were born wild.

Simply considered as brief lectures or moral exhortations, Gilman's collection of essays displayed her rhetorical skills. For this reason alone they deserve to be resurrected from the morgue of the *Woman's Journal*. She freely punctuated these pieces with allusions to the works of such British and American authors as Shakespeare, Charles Dickens, Elizabeth Barrett Browning, Lincoln Steffens, Herbert Spencer, Rudyard Kipling, Robert Burns, Emerson, Longfellow, Tennyson, Byron, and John Ruskin. She sometimes cited *Aesop's Fables* or the *Arabian Nights*, but more often the Bible, as might be expected of a grandniece of Henry Ward Beecher and Harriet Beecher Stowe. In her columns she coined such neologisms as "humaniculture" (the development and management of humanity), "matriolator" (mother worshipper), "homelings" (homebound mothers), and "kitchenmindedness" (the traditional domestic devotion to cooking). She repeatedly deployed the literary devices of analogy and hypothesis in her diagnoses of social problems and frequently ended her articles by addressing readers in imperative mood and admonishing them to action. As befitting a popular poet, she was even fond of alliteration (e.g., "pathos, patience, pride," "primal power and purity," "defined, discussed, defended," "blundering bee butting," "brand the bride with a conspicuous costume") and rhapsodic prose.

To be sure, Gilman sometimes wrote in the tone of a scold, as when she referred derisively to "ignorant persons" or "the poor, confused, stupid, unhappy people the world is full of." She overworked some catchwords, such as "splendid," "beautiful," "strong," and "wise," and occasionally penned such awkward or empty phrases as "precisely similar" and "associate action is required by differing entities." She used some gender-specific and what today would be considered sexist language, such as "the fair sex" for women, "mankind" for humanity, and "cowed" for the intimidated. She attributed consciousness to bees at one point but failed entirely to mention in her analyses any family structures that differed from the norm, including same-sex relationships or so-called Boston marriages and single, adoptive, or foster parenting, and she repeatedly insisted that "every normal woman should marry, should be a mother" (all the while carefully avoiding use of the word "pregnancy," lest it offend).[16]

Still, Gilman's essays in the *Woman's Journal* silhouette the foundations of her feminism and foreshadow by several years some of her better-known writings. Above all, she repudiated the androcentric theory of masculine superiority and championed throughout these pieces, especially in "Apropos of Prof. Ward's Theory" in the April 16 issue, the "gynaecocentric" theory Lester F. Ward outlined in his essay "Our Better Halves" (1888) and elaborated in his book *Pure Sociology* (1903). According to Ward, the female of a species is the "race type"[17] and the male merely a "sex type"; that is, females transmit those traits that ensure progress, whereas males merely assist in the process of fertilization. In a word, that is, "life begins as female" and the male is "a mere afterthought of nature."[18] In the fall of a prehistoric matriarchate and its succession by an androcentric stage, women became slaves. However, this subjugation of women by men is but a temporary aberration in the social evolution of humans, according to Ward. The female of any gendered species, not the male, should exercise the prerogative of sexual selection. Or as he explained:

> Woman is the unchanging trunk of the great genealogic tree; while man, with all his vaunted superiority, is but a branch, a grafted scion, as it were, whose acquired qualities die with the individual, while those of women are handed on to futurity. Woman *is* the race, and the race can be raised up only as she is raised up.... True science teaches that the elevation of woman is the only sure road to the evolution of man.[19]

Gilman wrote Ward personally less than a month after launching her Vital Issues page in the *Woman's Journal* that she considered his gynaecocentric theory "the most important contribution to the 'woman question' ever made" and she mentioned Ward's theory a dozen times in these essays. She assured him two years later that she had "done my humble best" to promote his ideas "in lecture book and article these many years."[20] In her autobiography, written early in the 1920s, Gilman declared Ward "quite the greatest man I have ever known" and "his Gynaecocentric Theory . . . the greatest single contribution to the world's thought since Evolution."[21]

A Note on the Text

The present volume reprints verbatim transcriptions of all the original columns Gilman published in 1904 in the Boston *Woman's Journal* except for some poetry, which has been reprinted elsewhere over the years.[1] This edition also omits two articles printed in the *Woman's Journal* over Gilman's signature while she was in Germany in spring 1904. Both originally appeared in the *Pacific Rural Press* more than a dozen years earlier and, were they inserted here, would disrupt the sequence of the columns Gilman contributed from Europe. In the issue for July 9, 1904, 218, appeared her "Time to Read for the Housekeeper," originally published in the *Pacific Rural Press*, August 1, 1891, 90–91; and in the issue for July 16, 1904, 226, appeared "The Shape of Her Dress," originally published in the *Pacific Rural Press*, January 2, 1892, 6.

To judge from some typographical errors, in particular some misplaced punctuation, Gilman's articles in the *Woman's Journal* were typeset from her manuscript and were not proofread or revised by the author. I have silently corrected these mistakes.

COLUMN 1

January 2, 1904

In her initial Vital Issues column Gilman strikes an optimistic note. She downplays her Lamarckian views ("Hereditary habits are malleable"), outlines her plans for the department, and introduces Lester Ward to her readers.

A New Year's Letter

To the optimist at large, there is something deeply exhilarating in the New Year. Even the pessimist in his chilly cell feels a vague sense of possible betterment creep through him. Prove as he may the unbroken horrors of the past, he cannot be so cocksure of the evils of the future.

The future is each man's personal property as well as our common heritage. Everyone can speculate on what the future will give him and can with far more assurance make up his mind as to what he will give to the future. "This year," he solemnly decides, "I will become a more agreeable member of society." And then he plans with lavish generosity scores of new and noble habits with which to gratify his astonished family and admiring friends.

There is a wasteful splendor in these good purposes when we are young and a comparable economy not to say penuriousness as we grow older.

Two delusive views of life are responsible for this conduct of ours; one, the innocent assumption that man can scale giant heights simply by applying force of will to his bootstraps; and the other, that worm-of-the-dust theory which treats us as a kind of eternal baby,

> "An infant crying in the night,
> And with no language but a cry."[1]

Worthy preachers are all too apt to foster this condition of helplessness with its vocal accompaniment by painfully reminding us in the New Year services of our last year's shortcomings. I heard a minister once in one of those prayers which are apparently meant to bring to the Lord's mind what He had else forgotten,—prayers in which "Thou knowest" takes the place of our colloquial "You know,"—discourage his hearers as follows:

"Thou knowest," said the pious man, "how many good resolutions we recorded a year ago today and how miserably we have failed to keep them! How many noble determinations we made and how we have failed to carry them out!"

The congregation was very properly smitten with hopeless remorse and impressed with the uselessness of further effort.

But I longed to rise up in my seat and protest that there was at least one person present who had made certain determinations a year ago that day and had not failed to carry them out, who had recorded a few carefully selected resolutions and kept them everyone.

It all depends on the selection.

We should emulate the cautious wisdom of the pretty society girl who announced that she had decided what she would go without during Lent.

"What is it?" inquired her friends.

And she replied sweetly: "My rubbers!"

She knew her limitations and respected them.

Character-building has its limitations, varying with the individual, of course, but having certain general restrictions.

Some people there may be who can grow a foot in an hour like a new cut banana stump, but most of us take time for becoming models of virtue.

We should not expect too much even of the New Year. If a woman is so careless of time as to have to pay double dentist's bills for broken appointments, she does not look forward to becoming a supreme type of punctuality by the middle of February.

And if she sets punctuality before her as one year's goal, she should not also endeavor to acquire "repose" in the same year.

We all have years behind us on which to figure, in which we can count the rate of our progress, whether from within or without, and if that record seems discouraging let us start in with a "minimum rate" and take just one resolution for one year.

If that is an enviable success, if one becomes "a changed man" or "a new woman" in that time, it is then safe to try as many as two for the year following; and so, in arithmetical progression, sainthood comes on apace.

Perhaps a good one to begin with would be the convenient habit of self-control—a capital foundation for further efforts.

It is an amusing study and one not calculated to enlarge our self-esteem to see how few of our acts are the result of personal choice and will. Sharp consciousness of this is forced upon us sometimes when we do decide for ourselves upon some course of action and find dozens of inferior ancestors protesting dumbly within us and unlimited superior friends and relatives objecting loudly outside.

Living is quite difficult when you try to do it yourself.

If we used personal initiative oftener, it would be easier to handle and more to be relied on when we want it badly, and that is why it is worthwhile to start in on a course of gymnastics to bring up the desired faculty. The method is easy enough, though we need some professional trainer to write a book on "How to Get Good and How to Stay So."

If you want to shoot, you do not begin to practice on charging elephants or lions in mid-spring; that is an expensive method and liable to discourage the beginner. No, you set up a target and practice early and often, advancing to glass balls and released pigeons with small hunting expeditions now and then, till you are well-prepared for the "big game."

Many a man who meets the big game of life without previous practice on small deer of some sort finds himself in the unfortunate position of the well-known "young lady of Niger,"

> Who went out to ride on the tiger.
> They came back from their ride
> With the lady inside,
> And a smile on the face of the tiger.[2]

There is plenty of target-practice in everyday life, no end of little immaterial things whereof one may say, "I will" or "I will not" and do it.

Hereditary habits are malleable, after all; a defunct grandfather is no match for a living man. The impulses we are born with, the habits that were trained into us, we can supplant with new ones of our own selection. It takes time but that is what time is for.

The beautiful thing about the days before us is their inviolable uncertainty. It is like going to the theater—a "continuous performance" outrivaling the longest Chinese play. We do not all have front seats, to be sure, but a few are in the boxes; but boxes have their own disadvantages, as the occupants well know. Our seats are as uncertain as the scenes to come. We never know how quickly they will change or, for that matter, how long we shall occupy them. Good, bad, or indifferent, change it must; and there is the ceaseless interest of the thing.

In our own little sideshows it is stirring enough, but the main attraction, the great "central ring," is enough to compensate for poor performances of ours.

The shifting scenes and new actors on the American stage today, the stirring situation in this year's performance, and the flaming posters which herald "unprecedented attractions" for the coming year—these are enough to keep any man awake. The uneasy child who has not looked on for very long is grieved as the plot thickens and fears the worst; but the old playgoer knows better—it will all come right in the end.

And to descend from soaring simile to plain fact, how comforting a thing it is to count on, that clear, strong, ethical sense in the commonest public, which demands of its plays, its novels, and its life as far as it can handle it, that it shall "come right in the end"! The best promise which each New Year brings is this steady, solid gain in the inherent qualities of the people.

It is not, after all, these roseate hopes and transcendent aspirations which are most truly valuable; it is the everyday goodness which is born in us now which we never notice because we are used to it. What we are trying to be with pain and toil our children easily will be and take no credit to themselves for being; and what we so naturally are—civil, patient, cheerful, helpful, reasonable, wise, and kind—is fruit of many and many a New Year's resolution in the long centuries behind us.

We can rub our hands serenely over the accumulated good behavior of the race and, with paternal foresight and clear American common sense, set ourselves to lay by a little, one year after another, to add to the inheritance of our children and our children's children.

Vital Issues

Here is the world. Its general condition is thus and thus—here civilization, there savagery; here education, there ignorance; here peace, there war. Are the women of the world satisfied with it?

Here is our country, as we believe, leading the world. Its general condition is thus and thus—here wealth, there poverty; here honesty, there corruption; here good people, there the immense numbers of inferior people, sick, crippled, defective, degenerate, diseased, criminal; with all the dragging expenses from which we must suffer in carrying these evils. Are the women of our country satisfied it? That women are women and men men, instead of our being clear human with no distinction of sex, is because we are parents. Woman, *per se*, is mother.

To the human world, mostly men, the general appeal is made for help and service in all human progress, and some women answer. But most women are so satisfied in personal relation, so occupied in personal affairs, so personally happy or personally miserable as women that the general appeal does not reach them and the mother goes unmothered. We are not satisfied with the world about us but we see no way to help and do nothing, or we see one way to help and do that, losing sight of all others.

Of all factors in human progress, none is more important than the position of women. Of all movements in that progress, none is more important than the movement of women. This movement, so distinctive of our age, of our race, of our own country—yet to be discerned in varying degree in other times and now spreading so rapidly in other lands—is a much more radical change in human history than even its staunchest advocates realize.

It has a biological aspect of fundamental importance, which is just dawning upon us through the great work of Prof. Lester F. Ward.[3]

Its physical, ethical, aesthetic, and economic aspects as well as the political need all to be kept in mind if we are to awake to the most vital issue of our times.

While all faithful workers in any field of social service must, in taking hold of the part, lose their grip on the whole, it becomes increasingly necessary that some should constantly labor so as to relate the parts and so present the relation that we shall have our necessary fractional labors strengthened and vivified by feeling the splendid force of the entire movement.

It is the purpose of this department so to coordinate the facts and principles in this vast world movement and so to bring them to the perception of the individual woman that, instead of the discouragement of blind and solitary effort, she may share the great light, the great power, of an irresistible current of world progress.

Five Million Women

Here are seventy-six millions of people in our United States of America, half female, a fifth grown women—seven million women. Most of them are wives and mothers. Most of them are Christians. Most of them can read and write. Let us say there are five million who are more or less educated, religious, loving women. What kind of a country would these women like to have? How would they like to have their government carried on? Are they satisfied with the school system which so touches all their children? Do they like their work? Are they satisfied with their clothes, their physical health and beauty, their intellectual and moral growth? Five million women ought to be able to accomplish a great deal. That is, taken collectively, in some sort of organization, acting together. Taken separately, there is only one woman. One woman can't do much.

The World's Mother

Humanity is above sex.

When women are as human as men, there need be no women's papers, women's pages, women's departments; both, as human creatures, will read with equal interest of the progress and the needs of their world.

The excuse for the woman's paper at present is that women hold a peculiar position. Their lives are limited and modified *as women* and therefore they must be appealed to as such. Now the real meaning and purpose of womanhood is motherhood. Special appeal to the woman must be special appeal to the mother. Man and woman are the father and mother of the world. So far, what has been done for the world, little or much, good or bad, has been done by the father. Its mother has neglected it. The world is a half-orphan. The woman has been all the mother she knew how to be to her own children at home and has never dreamed she had a duty to any other children, be they babies or youths or grown people.

Yet the safety, health, morals, education, general prosperity, and advance of our children depend far more on the kind of country they live in, the kind of government they live under, the kind of institutions which touch them on every side than on the unaided influence of never so good a mother.

What can the mother do under a despotic government, a savage soldiery, a false and corrupt church, crippled industry, and deficient education? When the father has established a free government, replaced warfare with commerce, liberalized religion, developed education—then you find safe and beautiful homes, and therein the mother can do much. But why does she not help in providing for her child these larger civilized institutions on which his very life depends? Because she thinks it is not her duty. How does she know?

The world needs mothering.

But my child, my own child, is more to me than all the world. Very good. Then learn that you cannot give the best conditions to your own child till all children have them.

From Now On

A new year opens before us and, if we choose, a new life, a new heaven, and a new earth. Now is always new.

It does matter what lies behind—yesterday or last year or farther back. Whatever has happened is now merely part of the environment. Here are you and this is now and we are to go on.

Drop the sense of time, of too soon or too late, especially too late. It is never too late for the real train. Life goes right on. A dozen Neros might burn a million Christians but Christianity goes on. A dozen churches may prevent and restrict religion but religion goes on. Humanity is a continuance and whatever you have done that you shouldn't is already past.

See here. You don't imagine that your good deeds are of such transcendent importance, do you? Then why put so large an estimate on the bad ones?

We—the great, strong, pushing, growing Human Life—can assimilate all the evils of the past, all the lessening evils of the future, and still grow.

Drop all clinging memories of the past and begin as fresh as if you were just born but born grown up.

There is no past—life is from now on. The world has got thus far for all its sins. It is here, lots of it, and full of business. There are floods of love and power abroad among us; there is knowledge, great knowledge at command; and that concrete accumulation of human energy—money. We need but to see clearly the field of action—to realize our splendid power to start in and lift the world along—from now on.

COLUMN 2

January 9, 1904

This column may serve as a baseline against which to measure some of Gilman's later, more conservative views. She remained a staunch defender of the home as an institution even as she argued for its reform. As late as 1920, for example, she published a piece in *Woman Citizen* titled "Whatever Else We Lose, We Must Keep the Home."[1] On the other hand, whereas in 1904 she encouraged young women to sow their "wild oats," she was appalled a generation later by the flappers, their access to birth control, and the sexual revolution of the Twenties.[2] Her remarks at the time engage even our contemporary debates over women's reproductive rights and bodily autonomy. She also mused in this column on the cultural differences between the United States and Bermuda, though there is no evidence that she ever visited the West Indies.

The Home of Tomorrow

Facts change faster than our ideas, far faster than our feelings.

This is most true in those matters wherein we think little and feel much, and therefore it is that the swift cumulative forward movement in the homes and home-life of our times is so little observed, so little understood where it is observed, and so little liked where it is understood.

Yet any student of present-day questions, if broadly conversant with the facts, must be impressed with the wide uneasiness, the stir and noise and discontent in that once so quiet life-center, the home. A life-center it is and one of supreme necessity to human living. And it should be quiet; it should be above all a place of rest. The more swift and varied the steps of world-life, the more perfect should be the peace and comfort of home-life. This is surely true, but it is also true that the home is part of the world and if the world is moving the home must move, too. Here we have the cause of all this trouble in the home-life of today; the world rushed on, it grows, it changes, it has moved forward with all its blended good and ill to this, the Twentieth Century of Christian life, but the home has not kept pace with it, the home is lagging behind, far, far behind. In many cases it dates from several centuries B.C.

Now we know how wearing it is to have our homes too far from our places of business. A home in the country is sweet, restful, and wholesome when you get to it, but the life of the commuter is by no means such.

The remoteness is well-known to us as a question of space but we have not thought that it was also an important question of time; that for a man to come from a twentieth-century office back to a tenth-century home is a strain to the nerves; and that for a woman born and educated in the twentieth century to be immured for life in an institution proper to the tenth century is also a strain on the nerves—and worse. What then is the line of progress proper for the home? Among the changes that are already forced upon us and those crying for adoption, which lead forward to greater peace and comfort? In what way must our homes differ from those of the past in order to be harmonious with the time we live in?

We must, while recognizing the home as infinitely dear and absolutely necessary to the family, also recognize it as a vital part of society, and society is in rapid evolution. Basing ourselves firmly on the essential facts of home life, of family life, holding fast to every principle of essential good in that life, we should be willing to open a free field of study and discussion to the investigators of this department and in especial encourage such lines of observation and suggestion as lead onward in accordance with the orderly laws of social progress.

There are the lines of mechanical improvement, of sanitary improvement, of artistic improvement, and of ethical improvement, all spread wide before us; and we shall find that there is no home so crowded in our densest city but that has still one large, unoccupied room—the room for improvement.

The home circle of today consists too often of a man overworked in the effort to maintain his family in the style they demand, of a woman overworked in the effort to take care of the family in the manner they demand, of children constrained and coerced to the supposed necessities of the home or else rudely interfering with it, and of servants—no word need be said as to the discord here.

The home circle should show us these things: A man finding complete rest and comfort in a home well within his means; a woman—*mirabile dictu!*—finding in her home complete rest and comfort, too; and children understood and provided for, happy, healthy, and harmonious so as to become in this wonderful new century actually desirable tenants!

To ends like these, to the maintenance of all that is truly good in the past, and to the advocacy of all that is safely good in the future, we should fearlessly study all sides of the common domestic questions of today in hopes of soon attaining the better homes of tomorrow.

Girls' Wild Oats

A new problem has arisen in many families of late—how to deal with the earnest, sanguine girl who longs for a career.

This career is usually of an artistic nature, literature, music, or the drama; few young women are consumed with ambition to go into business; still fewer wish to labor with their hands.

In some cases, however, the working impulse is so strong that they are willing to do almost any work so that they may get out—be free—and use their power. Loving parents usually refuse this demand *in toto*. They have many reasons, some worth considering and some not, but behind all prejudice and tradition lies the conviction that marriage and motherhood are the best "career" for any woman and that the girl will probably miss these if allowed to go to work independently in early life.

On this very ground they should reconsider their judgment. It is true that marriage and motherhood should belong to every woman unless she is debarred by some radical unfitness, but a girl with this strong working impulse is far likelier to come to her woman's heritage in due season if she is allowed to "sow her wild oats" first. It will often prove but a light crop, quickly sown and harvested without too much difficulty.

Few young girls are geniuses—if they are, woe to the hand that checks them! Few of them would care to carry on the much desired business or handicraft all the long years of a lifetime. This healthy desire to work in large modern lines is new to women yet and rather transient. Let it work out freely and be satisfied, the younger the better.

A healthy, well-educated girl will be none the worse for a year or two among strangers, alone, dependent on herself.

If hers be really a special calling, if she develops unusual power in her position, this proves how unwise it would have been to check the impulse. But in most cases the year or two would be quite enough and the girl be more than willing to return to the old home shelter or accept a new one.

The fulfillment of her strong desire for free human work will leave her satisfied as she could never have been without the trial. Satisfied that such a life is not for her and that she is better off in the old lines, or satisfied that it is her life and worth the keeping. Then going on in her proper work, her marriage will take place duly with someone who loves her, profession and all, and there will be no morbid "might have beens" to haunt her if some little domestic jars occur. She will know work and marriage both and value them highly.

The sifting processes of freedom and experience are necessary to us all. Girls should have their "Wanderjahr"[3] and profit by it. If they come back, meeker and more content, no harm is done.

If they prove nobly useful to the world and carry on a broader life, marriage and all, great good is done.

Let the girls go—they have a right to try.

"Woman's Work" in Bermuda

A beautiful cluster of green islands set in the clearest of blue seas, charming white houses of concrete and coral rock, and I, wandering about, chance upon a "Woman's Work" Exchange.

Intelligence and good will shine from the eyes of the middle-aged woman who is in charge, so I rest awhile, examine the stock, ask questions.

I ask about working women here. Are there any—except house servants? No, the good lady tells me. There is no class of working women;

there is, one might say, no poverty in Bermuda, no problem of poor classes that is. Indeed, she adds sadly and lowering her voice, those who feel it most are the ladies. She shows me the pretty things, beautiful work, much of it, some excellent watercolors in particular, and I sigh as I regard it.

Below, along the waterfront, in a poorer shop I had seen in the window "Boer Toys"—things made by the Boer prisoners, many of whom are still here.[4] I thought of those big brave men and then looked at the absurd little gimcracks which seemed to be all they could make under their restricted conditions. Free men, skilled, educated, trained to a trade do not have to whittle wooden napkin-rings.

There is a pathetic comparison between the products of the exiled prisoners and the impoverished ladies. The ladies are not exiles, perhaps, or if they are just that—being unable to get home—it does not affect their work, for the exhibit of the most indigenous of woman's exchanges is of the same superfluous prettiness, futile little sideshows compared to the real work of the world.

In a sense they are all exiles, being shut out from that world, the real living practical business world, and similarly they are all prisoners. The hopeless life imprisonment of ladies behind the barriers of prejudice and mountain walls of ancient falsehood is as absolute as that of any victim languishing in the fortress of St. Peter's and St. Paul's.[5]

They are taught from infancy that a lady, however valuable as an ornament or *gage d'amour*,[6] should on no account be of use. As the world lives by the exchange of services, real services of a highly specialized sort, it has no openings for the amiably ornamented. So when the lady—temporarily "embarrassed" or finally "reduced"—puts out her little hands to help herself, she has nothing to offer but these dainty extras and no one wants them except her fellow-ladies. They do not want them much—but they want to help a lady in distress. A delicate rarified charity. A highly-refined and round-about way of concealing the deeds of the kindly left hand from the knowledge of the futile right.

Something of the difference in economic development between men and women may be learned by comparing these woman's exchanges, wherever they may be, with their pathos, their patience, their all-unfounded pride, with man's exchange—the market of the world.

COLUMN 3

January 16, 1904

In this potpourri of columns Gilman drafts an inclusive platform for the woman's movement, discusses obstacles to the movement and the roles that could be assumed by various women, and satirizes the social debut of a debutante. Her advocacy for women's dress reform here presages the twelve-part "The Dress of Women" she serialized in the *Forerunner* in 1915. In addition, she recommends the adoption of stricter fire codes in public buildings, especially theaters.

A Platform for the Woman's Movement

There is need for some definite position for those who are interested in the woman's movement as a whole, which shall include and relate the various lines of advance in that movement, which may be clearly defined, fairly discussed, and ably defended.

Here is a proposition to that end:

> Whereas: 1. The preeminent duty of human beings is to serve and improve humanity,
> This duty is fulfilled both individually and collectively, individually through the highest personal development, physical, mental, and moral, and the transmission of this development to the race through heredity and association, collectively through specialized social functions by which humanity is defended, protected, fed, clothed, sheltered, taught, and in all ways cared for.
> Throughout history the position of woman relative to man has been

such as to prevent her best fulfillment of the above duty in either line, her environment tending to arrest and distort her individual development with mischievous consequences through both heredity and association and cutting her off almost entirely from participation in those specialized social functions through which humanity is best served.

The last century has witnessed the beginning of a world movement which this century is rapidly carrying on wherein women are changing their position relative to men.

The general direction of the movement is this: from a condition of arbitrarily-enforced feminine development and arbitrarily-arrested social development toward a normal condition in both lines, therefore,

Resolved, that every change in the environment of woman and in her range of activities which tends to reduce an excessive femininity to its normal place in life and to develop the general human characteristics is to the best interest of the human race and calls for universal approval and assistance.

Masculine, Feminine, and Human[1]

The confusion of mind on the above distinctions is so general and so extreme as to call for special definitions if we are ever to come to clear understanding on the subject. Let us define.

That is masculine which belongs to the male sex as such, to any and all males *without regard to species*. Throughout the entire animal kingdom and somewhat in the vegetable, we find distinctive masculine characteristics. As animal species develop we find certain prominent and unmistakable traits common to all males, peacock and turkeycock, bull and boar, stag and stallion. Some of these traits are still perceptible in the male of our species. That is feminine which belongs to the female sex as such *without regard to species*. Again, we find distinctive feminine characteristics throughout organic life, more and more marked and specialized as we go upward, in peahen and turkey hen, cow and sow, doe and mare, and these traits are still not only perceptible but dominant in the female of our species.

That is human which belongs to the human species as such *without regard to sex*. Through all organic life we find the distinction between species steadily increasing as we rise till in our own we find such marked differences as have enabled us to become long since the dominant race on earth. It is this race distinction that every thought of humanity inheres. Every step of social development, every art, craft, and science, all trade and commerce, the great professions, the fine arts, education, politics, religion—these have to do with humanity as such and have nothing to do with sex.

For instance: To beget children is a masculine function; to suckle children is a feminine function; to teach children is a human function.

The one great wrong in the position of woman has been and still mainly is that they have been confined to the feminine function and debarred from the human, and the collateral wrong in the position of man is that he has arrogated to his *sex* alone those powers and practices which belong to his species in common.

Once we can clearly understand these basic distinctions, the work of advancing woman's conditions will be easier. No woman has any wish to assume masculine functions and she could not, no matter how desirous; that great division of biological law is not to be bridged at this date. But she does wish to assume her full share of the human functions so long denied her and is doing so in steadily increasing range.

Present Obstacles

There are many obstacles in the path of woman's development and those which look the biggest are not always the most difficult to overcome. The first struggles, now matters of historic accomplishment in many places and of imminent success in others, were for full freedom in education. Another tremendous path of advance is that in which this paper has so steadily held the standard—equality before the law.

Again, we find a great and growing change in the industrial freedom of women, a steady enlargement of their range of activities, until now there is scarcely a field of human action wholly closed to them and there are some in which they outnumber men, as in school teaching. Yet still, those who are working most persistently to promote the general advance find women as a whole heavily bound and handicapped, still dully indifferent to any change or, if they see and desire it, hopeless of its accomplishment.

A certain close-knotted group of very old ideas with the heavy inert mass of sentiment and emotion thereto attached is the nucleus of the opposition. The prominent conditions which confront us are those of alleged "maternal disabilities" and of the deeply venerated duties of the housewife, but back of these conditions lie the concepts on which they rest. While people feel and think as they do about these things, they will largely remain as they are. Some change is being made, it is true, by the ceaseless force of social evolution. Even while we most stoutly uphold our idols, their pedestals of fact are passing away from beneath their feet—and so in time they must fall. But meanwhile, and to relieve the strain of forcibly upholding a foundationless ideal, it would be a great help if people would change their minds a bit.

There are two points in especial on which we need light: two points which, if clearly understood, would form a base for large and beautiful progress.

One of these is in social economics and the other in domestic economics. The first is this: We generally believe the work of the world now done by men is done as a means to support the family—that it is man's share of this business of supporting the family and that he ought to do it. This conviction is buttressed by another to the effect that the work of the world is limited—(when we say work in this connection we mean pay—wages—not work), that there is only enough work, i.e., wages, in the world for men and that for women to join in the world's work would not only be an assumption of man's share in the duty of supporting the family but would really add nothing to the family income—merely dividing the existing stock of wages.

The second is this: We generally believe that the work of the house, now done by woman, is done in the best way to maintain the healthy and happiness of the family—that it is her share of duty to the family and that she ought to do it. Conversely, that if she worked elsewhere in other ways and introduced a different system in the performance of "household duties," she would injure the family. Now suppose it can be shown, as against these common errors of thought, that in the first place the work of the world is primarily for the benefit of the world and only secondarily for the individual or family, and therefore that the woman's joining in this world work would not be taking from man his service to the family but adding her share of their common service to the world.

Also that, so far from the work being limited—i.e., the wages—wealth is created by labor and that to bring the productive industry of woman into action as well as man's would be to double the wealth of the world. Then her coming out into full industrial equality has no terrors but rather vast advantages. Again, if it can be shown that the present method of performing household duties is not only not the best for the family but that it constitutes a distinct injury and hindrance to it, and, conversely, that it is the most instant duty of an enlightened womanhood to alter and improve this antiquated system of living for the sake of the family and the child in especial; if, further, it can be shown that this ancient, inadequate, wasteful, and increasingly mischievous system of "domestic industry" is directly responsible for much of the evil and danger affecting the home today—then indeed we shall have gone far on the way to freedom, to progress, to a full, smooth social development.

There is more beyond—much more—but these things confront us immediately. Let us get at them as fast as possible without any fear. What is good will bear examination. What is bad we can afford to lose, though we love it as a heathen his idol.

"Successful Women of America"

The *Popular Science Monthly* for January has an article under the above title by Amanda Carolyn Northrup.[2]

It is compiled from *Who's Who in America* and gives some interesting figures. Out of a total of 11,551 persons sufficiently "successful" to be in this book, 977 are women, 1.11 2/3—little more than one in a hundred.[3] Of this number more than half are authors—a pretty clear proof that woman's principal choice in art is literature. Next come artists of the other sort, 103;

then educators, including lecturers, 91; journalists, 65; actresses, 59; musicians, 43; social reformers, 27; physicians, 21; scientists, 17; ministers, 13; philanthropists, 12; librarians, 9; miscellaneous, 3. Miss Northrup wisely eliminated from the list six who were "ladies of social prominence, wives of distinguished men," that sort of vicarious eminence not necessarily indicating any real distinction.

We are then led to moralize on the melancholy fact that hardly more than half of these successful women are married—only 54 per cent.

The least married are the educators—only 26.3 per cent of them—and we are offered the suggestion, among others, that perhaps it is due to "the acquisition of knowledge and possibly the instructive habit that makes this kind of woman less attractive to men."

There are tables of figures as to schooling, college graduation, and such matters; but the most noticeable feature in the article to my mind is that out of this list of superior women only 69 per cent gave their age. Thirty-one women out of a hundred, among such exceptionally able ones as these, are still under that pitiful and shabby tradition of the past—an assumed youth.

The percentages are very funny. There was one financier—and she gave her age—100 per cent of her. One lifesaver—she gave hers. One seed-grower—she gave hers. But out of nine lawyers three refused to give up this precious secret; even of the clergywomen, one would not tell! Perhaps worse than that, among the scientific women, out of seventeen six concealed their age! Two librarians out of nine, five physicians out of twenty-one, five social reformers out of twenty-seven, twelve musicians out of forty-three, twenty-six actresses out of fifty-nine (one does not wonder so much at this—a matter of direst professional importance), nineteen out of sixty-five journalists, twenty-two out of ninety-one educators, forty out of one hundred and three artists (now what difference could it make to an artist!), and one hundred and forty-two out of four hundred and eighty-seven authors—all these refused to give the date of birth. Largest per cent, actresses of course. Next largest, artists. Why? Except for the actress for obvious business reasons, why should any woman outside a harem object to telling her age? Can it be for business reasons with all these?—even with the ministers?

Or is it not rather a part of that mass of inherited habits and superstitions under which women suffer more than men because of many reasons? One reason for this one thing is large and plain—and very disagreeable to consider. There was a time when women had but one market for one ware and the age of the article seriously affected its market value. Can it be possible that that time is not past? If it is past, let us make haste to show that we have fully outgrown it.

Speaking of Skirts

Let us never lose sight of broad, unavoidable proofs of social development or the lack of it shown in woman's dress.

Spencer showed long ago how decoration with the low savage precedes and supersedes all idea of comfort or of decency.[4] Wherever in modern life we find dress regarded in this order of importance, there is proof of lingering savagery, of a lower type of social development, a rudimentary type.

Believing firmly that the woman's movement will never go on as smoothly and swiftly as it should until she knows where she is moving from and what she is moving toward, I mean continually to exhibit and insist upon as many of these illustrative points as appear in common life. There is no need to go hunting for them. The life of women in general is heavily encumbered with these rudiments, and they should be clearly explained and held up to scorn.

A modern, civilized being should be ashamed to manifest characteristics of past ages—low, blind, brutal ages. Human traits go in groups. You cannot maintain some savage traits in a widespread flourishing condition without finding a strong crop of others pushing up. Now we women are continually objecting to the savage traits in man—the love of slaughter and gross self-indulgence. Let us take note that our delight in extravagant personal decoration belongs to the same date. When you see a woman of our race and time, educated, cultured, amiable, and pious though she be, dragging her clothing through the foul dust and fouler slime of our streets because she thinks it looks well, you see the mental attitude of a strutting savage. She looks down with scorn on the drunkard, glutton, and murderer—but it is all of the same grade in social evolution; it is all one savagery.

Intelligence, education, civilization, culture call for wise and noble clothing, beautiful with the beauty of perfect adjustment to use; but the savage calls for personal exhibition of supposed charms, personal decoration, though it be by the torture of tattooing—and the savage calls loudest. When we know more of sociology, when we understand how we have grown thus far, how we are growing and what keeps us back, then there will be room for several new kinds of shame among those now most complacent, also room for swift and splendid growth.

Progress in New Jersey

In Orange, New Jersey, a woman's club discussed plans for an organization in the interests of employers of domestic servants, and the servants forthwith took time by the forelock and organized a service girls' union to protect their interests.[5]

These are both good steps. Anything which brings women together, which shows them their common interests whether as employers, employees, or anything else is a good thing.

The helplessness of women is in their utter disconnection. The position of a wife is purely individual and rightly so; the position of a mother is not—children have needs in common which should be met by common action, and the business of "housekeeping" is as open to the general course of organization as any other business.

Women are beginning to see this, here and there, a few of them, while the great mass, contented as Chinamen in their mere numbers and the sacred antiquity of their methods and customs, ridicule and ignore the few.

Let us therefore warmly welcome all such steps as this in Orange.

Ministers' Wives

Here is Bishop Huntington of Central New York complaining of ministers' wives! He charges them with "the radical and comprehensive fault or sin" of "worldliness of mind."[6]

"Accomplishments," he continues, "energy, tidy housekeeping, general efficiency will not atone for that sin. The clever woman must be more than that if she is to fill honorably the sacred place or calling that she has accepted. Let the wife learn to find her satisfaction where her duties are."

The duties of a wife, as we have been told by many bishops and other dignitaries for long, long years, are of a purely feminine and domestic nature. She is to be a helpmeet at home, a comfort and solace to weary man; she is to confine her interests and ambitions to keeping house and above all to tending baby. It has never been required of her that she share the masculine duties of her husband in his world work. Must the soldier's wife be martial, the sailor's nautical, the lawyer's legal?

That has never been required of us. Indeed, any effort to such end has been deplored and forbidden. And now here is this reverend man talking about "the sacred place or calling" of the minister's wife as if it were more sacred than that of any other man's wife.

The minister is "called" by his congregation, it may be, but he calls his wife to himself; she is not selected by the committee. The service, the honor, the effort, and the salary belong to the minister. Why should the minister's wife be expected to share this labor—without any emoluments thereto attached? If she is a minister, it is another matter. If she is a minister's assistant—as some of their wives are—that too is another matter.

But the duties of a wife and the duties of a minister are not identical, and if the lady's general attitude of mind is incompatible with the profession, Mr. Minister should have considered that before choosing her. Meanwhile, as a matter of fact, most ministers' wives do a large amount of tedious and wearing labor over and above that of other men's wives. It is far easier and more honorable to have one's own profession than to be an irregular, unpaid, over-taxed adjunct to one's husband's.

Wholesale Drugs and Foods

An important fact as to drugs and food in the large department stores has been established in New York. An investigation by the State Board of Pharmacy, following upon charges made by the retail druggists that the big stores sold cheap drugs that could not be pure, has shown not one instance of the violation of the law in these great establishments. Similarly, the retail grocers charged that the canned goods and other standard goods were too cheap to be good, and an investigation was made by experts retained by the retailers—a fair test, surely. It was found that the big stores take the utmost care in buying, exercise a rigid discrimination, and maintain laboratories with competent chemists to test and examine.

The testimony as to the advantage of large management over small is what might have been expected, and the further inference ought not to be lost upon women. We fondly assume that the best guarantee of purity and excellence in cooked food is in the last extreme of private management. How can we maintain this in the face of the general facts of public business and the personal facts of private disease?

It is by association and specialization that human progress has been made, and nowhere is it so lacking as in those departments of human labor yet left to women.

Two Kinds of Prevention

Since the fearful tragedy in Chicago—a horror such that the civilized world is shocked and grieved[7]—our papers are full of suggestions for future prevention and city officials are coming forward magnificently to "shut the stable door." Their new severity in enforcing the law (which no one seems to have thought of doing before) is not to be made light of, for even the sacrifice of this half-thousand lives would have some excuse if it saved the millions of people similarly exposed every night in our great gathering places.

But in the complaint and outcry and the sudden energy with which new preventive measures are being hurried forward and old ones violently enforced, only one party to the disaster is being considered—the owners and managers of the theaters; nothing is said about the possibility of preventive measures as affecting the party of the second part—the public.

Never so fireproof a theater would save the lives of the trampled little children, the girls and boys, the women and men who are crushed underfoot in the conscienceless struggle for life.

And scarcely so dangerous a place could be pointed out but that some lives might be saved if they were those of clear-headed, self-controlled people. Here is a breakdown of a hall in a New Jersey town, reported here Jan. 4, in which many lives were lost—not by the accident to the building but by being knocked down and trampled to death by the men whose brute terror was stronger than any human feeling.[8] The reputed superior courage of the male does not show well in sudden danger which is not a matter of fighting. Combativeness is not courage. The most pugnacious Irishman that ever wore chip on shoulder is liable to rush for safety over screaming women in a time like this.

Some may protest, in defense of the dead or of the living, who need it more, that courage to be calm in face of death by fire is beyond the average human being.

This defense will not hold. In the first place we find such courage, risking life and often losing it, in our common firemen, plenty of them. Are they a picked band of heroes and martyrs or are they simply men trained to this particular danger and therefore meeting it calmly? The latter, of course. Then the defender of the panic-stricken will say, "Yes, but you cannot expect the general public to manifest the courage of the expert."

To which, in the second place, we reply that there are plenty of instances of the mere general public as well as many an unexpected hero amongst them, who do meet sudden shock and danger with wise courage.

School children even, used to fire drill, have marched quietly out of burning buildings with no sign of that animal struggle for one's own life which is so destructive to the life of others. And can anyone forget who ever heard of it the splendid calm of those New England mill girls who were hopelessly cut off from rescue, and instead of tumbling over each other with insane shrieks of terror died calmly, singing to the last. "Nearer, My God, to Thee" that little portion of the public sang until they died.[9] No special training here, no special drill even, like that of the school children—just calmness and courage.

And in this particular paper, and on this particular page, the further questions—what has such a catastrophe as this to do with the movement and what special responsibility have women toward public protection?

One obvious answer is this: that if women were doing their share as citizens in framing and enforcing public ordinances, it is probable that our public would be better cared for. Women are natural caretakers, being mothers; and if they applied that faculty where it best belongs—to the care of the public—we should all be better safeguarded. But so far we prefer to keep our mothering at home, to take care of no one but our own families, and then when public disaster befalls, our families as well as others perish.

It is easy to say that if the men of Chicago had done their duty in enforcing proper laws, this would not have happened. It is as easy and quite as true to say that if the women of Chicago had done theirs, it would not have happened. The men had done something, however negligently; the women had done nothing in this matter of provision for public safety. So even on the line of prevention from the side of the theater, this sorrow comes home to the woman who refuses to accept her public duties. On the other side, there is an even stronger charge against her.

Right here let the relation of the woman's movement to the world's movement, as it will be steadily urged on this page, be shown. The main movement of the world is toward better people—the development of humanity. The best development of humanity needs to be advanced through both father and mother by physical heredity and through our general public progress in the ever-strengthening stream of social heredity.

The movement of women is from a position of arrested social development toward that of the fully-developed social status of our time, from a solely and excessively domestic relation into a normal social relation. In this special case we see the need of the woman's care in providing for public safety through civilized measures of civic legislation; and, further, we see the need of her progress in that improvement of public character which is needed as much as the improvement of public buildings—a fireproof character!

It is admitted that in many cases women show courage and men cowardice under such danger, but it remains true that the vast majority of women do not cultivate courage as much as men do. They do not do their share in building up the standard of courage for the human race.

Men are often cowards—and are ashamed of it. Women are often cowards—*and are not ashamed of it.*

Take this mouse performance. I have known exceptionally intelligent women not in the least ashamed of being afraid of a mouse. "They are such slimy things!" says one, adding absurd inaccuracy to causeless terror. A mouse is no more slimy than a chinchilla. "It is not fear," says another. "It is nerves." Now a man may and often does have the same nervous antipathy to a snake or spider, sometimes even to a mouse, but he would think he was a contemptible coward to screech and run because of it.

There are already many women who show courage and calmness, fine "womanly women," too. This proves that it is not a masculine quality and not injurious to womanhood. What we want is to see the spread of this courage, the recognition of it as a virtue, the rapid growth of a public sentiment that shall despise a female coward as much as a male one.

Women in their general position as wives, mothers, and house servants and keepers can do much, very much, to raise the standard of public courage. Whatever they are most afraid of they can begin to practice on till they no longer fear it. To love courage, to admire courage, to strive for courage, to pity and scorn the lack of courage in women—this is what we want to see. This will give us braver sons as well as daughters, helping the world through the woman's most essential function, and will do more to save life than all external measures can do, while our people are stampeded like sheep at false alarms as well as real ones.

So there are two sharp practical lessons for women "as women" in this great public sorrow. First, let us leave no civic duty undone that protects the citizen; second, let us leave no personal duty undone that shall improve the citizen.

"Dance for Miss Twombly"

"Given by her aunt, Mrs. William Douglas Sloane,[10] at the Fifth Avenue residence."

—NEW YORK TIMES, JAN. 5, 1904.[11]

In commenting upon events of universal importance as they touch on the position of women, the above performance surely needs mention. It holds half a column of space in the *New York Times* on the page of foreign news, half a column among those devoted to the imminent war between Russia and Japan with all its tremendous implications,[12] to the safety of the Jews in Russia,[13] the Venezuela award,[14] and little matters like that.

Therefore, the importance of Miss Twombly, Her Dance, Her Aunt, and the Fifth Avenue Residence strike the eye as equal to these other issues. We are given further details in eagerly running down the page of how Miss Twombly's Aunt had trimmed up the Fifth Avenue Residence for the occasion, with careful notice as to ferns, flowers, and fish—goldfish. Food was also provided, and favors, which last were furnished—donated, it appears, by a Mrs. Collins. The rest of the space is a thrilling list of names of those present.

This is but one instance, truly, but as an instance a good one of the position of women. Here is a modern American girl, cultivated and educated it is to be supposed, with no better sense of proportion than to let her name head a column in a page of world news, with no better contribution to that news than that she danced, that she possessed an Aunt, and that either she or the aunt or some of the family possessed the Fifth Avenue Residence.

That any set of women of sufficient numbers to form a reading public rate an evening of private amusement of a most commonplace character as "news" is as good an evidence of this stage of civilization as could be given. Only a few of the wealthy or in some way notorious can get this much space for their little merrymakings, but there are many more who care about it, are interested in it, would be glad to do the same if they could, and who eagerly search that list of names.

It shows how near the harem many women are yet, the harem and the nursery—mere children in the measure of world progress. To wear pretty clothes and to dance about, to invite people to see you do it and help you do it—this only shows childishness and lack of any real use in the world; but to publish it, to proclaim to thousands upon thousands of relentless readers just how childish and how useless one is!—that shows a position so far removed from the healthy human life of this great century as to make us grieve indeed for our belated little sisters. Poor relics of an age long past, going on with the same trivial amusements that satisfied them in the hanging gardens of Babylon and innocently publishing their pitiful deficiencies to this great, live, rushing, modern world!

COLUMN 4

January 23, 1904

Gilman first punctures the notion that men, even if breadwinners, are the sole support of families, then underscores the vulnerability of married women in a man-made world by raising the possibility that they may be deserted by their husbands.

"Supporting the Family"

Our ideas of the nature and purpose of life and labor are not abreast of the times.

We formed them at an early period, a very early period, and have never given them any revision.

Many honest and intelligent persons, indeed most persons, still believe that the whole business of life is to maintain one's own family, somewhat checkered by occasional efforts to save one's soul. If there is any conflict, the soul must stand aside.

Such trifling minor phenomena as the development of industry, manufacture and commerce, of art and science, of education and religion, of forms of government and other organizations are to be noticed and judged only as they affect the family. The man must spend his life in "wrestling with the world" for the wherewithal to support the family and the woman must spend hers as a house servant, catering to the immediate needs with her own hands.

With this general background of belief, all questions of advance for women are measured by their effect, real or supposed, on the family; either in her direct relation as servant or as any change in her position might affect the man's as "provider." We need to rearrange in our minds the "order of exercises" in human life.

God has not been nursing up this universe for all these ages merely to develop a race of women with dishcloths and men with market baskets. The main push and purpose of life—all life—is Growth. The main push and purpose of human life is Growth. The development of better people—that is what we are here for. The family is an early group from wherein people are *begun*—but not finished.

You can find families all the way down the line of historic progress and far back of it, but the real distinctive growth of humanity comes in with the development of the social institutions, such as the church, the school, the government. In the long, glorious work of human improvement, the family has been a constant source of love and power, but a source is not a goal. We are to live *from* the family, *for* humanity.

The great governing force of life is the human love, which we learned first of the mother but which, if we had never followed any further than she has, would have kept the world in its cradle forever. That human love, which is at once the mainspring of our religion and the most practical basis of life, finds its expression in all kinds of mutual service. The work of the world is the mutual service—people in every land doing all manner of things for the maintenance and improvement of all people. Now this seems frankly absurd to most of us.

The women—most of them—never work for anyone but their own family and never dream that they ought. Duty to family is all the duty they know. The men in reality do work for each other all over the world, and through their intricate labors society does develop, but *they think* all the time that they are doing their farming or plumbing or painting or doctoring "to support the family," and as a man thinketh so is he.

Consider for a moment some of the great names of history—Columbus, Washington, Luther, Beethoven, Pasteur, Newton, Stevenson, Angelo, Lincoln.[1] By the work of such as these is the world lifted onward. Would you say that George Washington's main duty was to support his family? Or Michelangelo's? Or Luther's? Would not you rather say of any of these great men that their first duty was to mankind—and after that to the family?

Statesman, minister, artist, poet, composer, discoverer, inventor, these are given us to serve the world, to promote the best interests of mankind. Do we assume then that certain men are to serve the world while others serve only their own families? That certain kinds of work or certain grades of work are for the world and the rest only for the family? Is the painter of pictures a world-servant and the painter of houses only a family-servant? Is science for the benefit of the race and trade for the benefit of the family only? In point of fact—plain sociological fact—every kind of human work is world-service, the only difference being in the grade of development in that work.

The printing press, for instance, is an engine to promote social progress—not an engine to promote the interests of the family of the inventor or of the families of those who use it except incidentally. With this position in mind, the work of woman takes on new significance.

The question is not only Does she do her duty to her family? but also Does she do her duty to the world? Is her work such as best to serve both these ends? Or is she allowing an antiquated and cumbrous method of working to prevent her serving either to the best advantage?

It is a matter of serious importance whether the members of society are working in such ways as shall develop their full powers and do the most service.

We are members of society as well as members of the family and the larger claim includes the less.

In the day of "labor troubles," when the wheels of industry are clogged continually, when the super-abundant wealth of our splendid country is so ill-distributed, so wasted, so misapplied, our thinking women should lift their heads above the level of their own affairs and bring their best gifts to bear on the world's needs. The conditions of the day are surely not such as commend themselves to civilized women. The increase in insanity, the increase in suicide, the increase in crime, the persistence in war, the many crying needs of our time, these are things that cannot be met by burying oneself in a never-so-exalted devotion to the family.

But it will be said—if everyone did his and her duty to the family, there would be no trouble! This is just where we mistake—putting the less before the greater—the part before the whole.

If every man and woman did their duty by the State, by one another, the world over, then the family would be far better cared for than it is now.

The family suffers everywhere from poverty, from disease, from vice, from ignorance, from public wrongs which cannot be righted save by public action. And this public action, while finding its voice in the ballot, its expression in the law, must be primarily taken in the underlying fields of business and industry.

The family fares ill when "supported" by a mistaken selfishness in the world-work of the father and a mistaken devotion in the housework of the mother. She gives her family a primeval martyrdom in place of the organized efficiency of modern life.

Wife-Desertion

This Iowa decision wherein Governor Cummins[2] refuses to extradite the New Jersey man that he may be properly punished at home brings up again the peculiar economic position of the married woman. When a husband deserts a wife, she may submit brokenheartedly, proudly, and uncomplainingly, or she may not submit at all but apply for divorce from the evidently dissatisfied partner. Either position is defensible but to seek to have the deserter chased, brought back, and punished is eminently undignified.

When men do this to their wives nowadays, applying for "restitution of their marital rights," there is prompt condemnation and opposition on the part of the progressive women. The wife is not the property of the husband, they say; she is not a slave; he cannot enforce duties evidently hateful. They are quite right. But is the husband the property of the wife? Is he a slave? Can she enforce duties evidently hateful?

Here it will be urged that there is a radical difference in the demands—he is claiming her love or what he considers an equivalent; she is only claiming his money. Exactly. It is the business end of the relation she is looking after and the courts support her claim.

A most amusing case was reported recently where a woman kept a store and her husband worked in it, receiving wages from her. She applied for divorce *with alimony* and got it. In the account it was facetiously suggested that she was sure of her alimony for she could stop it out of his wages!

There are those who honestly believe that women are not supported by their husbands on the ground of the large amount of work done by the women at home. If they are not supported by their husbands, if this large amount of work supports them, why do they not go on doing it and support themselves when he is gone? Why chase the poor man and call upon the law to make him pay the bills as before?

This is the most practical proof of the fact which men know well enough—that women are economically dependent upon them.[3] They like to have it so. They make laws and enforce laws to compel themselves to support their wives and they do not approve of the alarming proposition that women should be economically independent. And most women prefer to share the income earned by a man's trained, specialized skill rather than depend on the less amount they could earn or to undertake the serious work of training themselves to earn more.

They are justified in this position by public opinion, but they ought to hold it honestly and not depend on the income of a banker and yet claim that they earn it by ordering the meals and presiding at the table.

The Increase in Suicide

According to the annual record collected by the *Chicago Tribune*, suicide is increased in what we believe to be the best country on earth at this rate: In 1899 there were 5,340; in 1900, 6,755—a year's gain of 1,415! In 1901, 7,245; in 1902, 8,291; in 1903, 8,597.[4] We are supposed to be growing in intelligence, in wealth, in power, in "the diffusion of Christianity"—why is it that life is so hard to so many that they cannot endure it?

No other kind of animal commits suicide. No other kind of animal has the capacity for suffering we have. But our capacity for suffering is nothing to our capacity for loving, helping, taking care of one another.

How then does it come about in the land of a people proverbially kind, proverbially generous, proverbially energetic and resourceful that so many of us somehow get trodden underfoot in the path of progress? To the big, sudden, conspicuous disaster, the heart of the people responds at once. Why does not the heart of the people notice the accumulation of troubles that crushes and maddens till the end is reached?

Because our hearts are so universally content with the supposed sacred duty of minding our own business. Did Christ ever issue any commands or suggestions to that end? Or even the Hebrew Scriptures?

When the most loving, patient, careful half of the people begins to open its mother heart to the needs of the world, there will be fewer neglected lives.

COLUMN 5

January 30, 1904

Gilman foregrounds here a recurring subtext of her department: Suffrage should be a plank but not the entire platform of the woman's movement. She considered voting rights inextricably linked to such issues as women's education, childrearing, and the progress of women in the industrial workplace.

Shall Suffrage Clubs Work for Anything Besides Suffrage?

It has become a matter of discussion in suffrage clubs whether their years of patient, monotonous labor for something they do not attain might not be varied to advantage with now and then laboring for some special issue which they could attain.

Much is said on both sides, the main objection in feeling being a deep-rooted, religious sense of devotion to a cause which must have no rivals and the main objection in fact being the difficulty of finding work they could agree on. It is always difficult to combat feeling with reason, as suffragists know to their long and heavy cost, but as they are accustomed to reason it may have more weight with them than with—Antis,[1] for instance.

The long centuries of unflinching devotion to "one religion" have built into the human mind a strong tendency to exclusiveness in belief, and the long centuries of devotion to one man have given women an extra intensity in this mental habit. They have been always accustomed to passionate, life-long attachment to "this one thing" regardless of results, and the custom holds.

As a plain matter of fact, the right of suffrage as a principle of belief even is not a religion—it is only one of the good steps for mankind to take, and when considered not as a principle of belief but as a practical measure to be advanced it calls not so much for devotion as for achievement.

Would not suffragists achieve more if—well, if they achieved more? That is, if the suffrage work, pure and simple, could be visibly associated in the popular mind with the support of good measures and with their successful attainment?

Some reply that this is open to suffragists as individuals, and that they do, in that capacity, belong to other clubs which work for other things and attain them.

Yes, they do, and the other clubs get all the credit for "doing things" while the suffragists get none. The suffrage work proper remains dim and remote in the public mind because it confines itself to the advancing of principles which cannot be denied and the begging for concessions which can be and generally are. So when the ballot is attained, the good work continues to be done by the group previously doing it, and the suffrage gains small honor for the results following it.

Now, without asking all members of our great body to unite on all points, surely even the National Association[2] could from time to time find one great public service it could agree to identify with and each State one more local question, and in city clubs there are surely matters of civic improvement on which they could unite.

We keep on saying, "Give us the ballot and we will do good things." If we could say, "See the good things we have done; see the good things we are trying to do; give us the ballot that we may do more"—would not that advance our cause?

"The Ethical Training of Children"?

In the *Woman's Library*, vol. III, Lady Isabel Margesson has done excellent work under the above title.[3] Here is a woman who has read and studied and thought as well as loved and acted, and the action modified by wisdom and training is far more valuable than that based only on maternal affection.

In the blank waste of ignorance with which we face the problems of babyhood, all thoughtful contributions should be welcomed and there is much truth in this earnest study. If even the average mother can be made to see that she needs further equipment for her task than an animal instinct and family traditions, much will be done toward filling the world with wiser, stronger, happier people.

Ethics is *the* social science above all—knowledge of its laws is needed in judging every act of life, yet it is one of the least understood and most misapplied of all sciences. The confusion of ethical values forced upon the young child due to the well-meant blundering of his ignorant parents is a lasting disadvantage to the race.

We are just beginning to study these questions intelligently; the more wise and earnest women are joining together to learn more quickly and more reliably; but still the great body of people worship the brute instinct and decry a human intelligence.

And such keen satirists as Josephine Dodge Daskam[4] use their sharp weapons to defend the blind past, to hurt and check the nobler future—which is pitiable.

Schools and Mothers

In the *World's Work* for January is an article by Adèle Marie Shaw treating of manual training in schools near New York.[5] She shows that the suburban school is in advance of the city school generally, and that Montclair, N.J., is twenty years ahead of the big city. In examining the teachers' efforts, the standing evils of that class were apparent—overwork and underpay.

In Trenton, N.J., she says, "a regular teacher in the primary school receives for each of the first three months $32.50." Compare this with hired girls' wages. Suppose you hire an ordinary house servant for $4 a week. The board and lodging you give her are worth $4 more—if they are not, you do not provide decently for her. A dollar and a half for a furnished room and two and a half for food is little enough. So you really pay your servant $8 a week, only to accommodate you she takes half her pay in barter. (We always say, "and her board," as if that was additional and a piece of pure generosity!)

These primary school teachers in Trenton get fifty cents more than a four-dollar servant—and as their board has to cost them more, they really have less money.

Now where are the mothers of the school children who are willing to have them taught by this grade of labor?

It is not enough to say, "If they had the ballot, they could make this right"—no doubt they could do it much more easily but in the meantime, without the ballot, they can do much if they really care about it.

Why is it that good, conscientious, intelligent women give so little thought to conditions like these, conditions which vitally affect the whole life and progress of the nation and, incidentally, the life and progress of their own children?

Because their minds are so exclusively occupied in the daily and hourly contemplation of their own affairs that they won't stretch any wider. That is why it is so important for housework to be decentralized—to widen and limber up the minds of women, their habits of thought.

Again, Miss Shaw says, "At No. 3 in Yonkers, N.Y., a beautiful assembly hall is the work of the principal, Mrs. Bruce.[6] Parents' meetings lend dignity to the place and the programs are sensible and suggestive. Yonkers children are apparently motherless, for only fathers are heard."

Here you have the same thing—the homebound woman so tied up in trying to do her duty by her children individually that she cannot attempt to do it collectively. As far as public care goes, our children are motherless and it is not credit to their mothers.

"In the last half of the grammar school the boys have the best of it," we are told. "They keep to interesting things, study wood fiber and tree growth, make flower stands and picture frames, are divided into factory squads with foremen chosen from their own number, construct bridges of bent iron, and have a year with the machines. Beside this the girls' work seems tame. They cook and sew."

In the very time when they are free to learn something of democracy, of organization, of the principles of different kinds of work and the connection between them, back they are put into the same old ruts.

Then the narrow-minded mothers are reinforced by the narrow-minded daughters, and half the world continues to cook and sew in private and leave public duties all undone.

Woman's Industrial Progress

Among the various branches of the woman's movement, none is more vitally important than her industrial progress. Her industrial position is so far behind the stage of development reached by the more civilized sex that she finds it difficult even to see across the gulf. Industrially, women as a class have remained motionless at the bottom of the long ascent, and men have gone so far beyond them that the two have lost sight of one another. The cradle of industry is the same as the other cradle—it is the mother's care for the child. The mother's loving labor for her little ones is the foundation impulse of human industry. She is the mother of all arts and handicrafts, but so remote is her motherhood and so magnificent the growth of her long-descended family that she can no more recognize them than the ancestral Eohippus could claim the racehorse for its grandchild.[7] It is—but there are many generations between.

The mother-industry which underlies our whole world-subduing, triumph in arts, crafts, and manufactures consisted in the personal labor of the woman for her own family, and was paralleled at that time by the man's hunting and fighting for them. Between that time and this, the man's brute instinct to defend and care for mate and young has grown to such immeasurable degree that he has brought about this world of civilized living, wherein all social institutions combine to ensure and develop human life and even the sordid sins of man's other brute instincts are being gradually outgrown. The private crime and public war which still prove our lingering savagery are recognized as evils and, though still existing, are being studied and opposed by ever-growing numbers of our noblest citizens. All that we have to distinguish us from our hairy ancestors, all that makes social progress and maintains it, has come through the extension and development of man's primitive impulses and powers and their organized expression in social activities. Of late years, in a scarcely appreciable minority, some women have taken up the same line of progress and added the mother-love and mother-power to the forces that work for righteousness. But important as this movement is and rapidly as it gains headway, it is still a small percentage compared with the great mass of women throughout the world who have made no movement whatever. The world has moved—and they have shared its progress as far as they were allowed but they themselves have contributed very little to that progress.

In China the woman works at home as she has worked at home for thousands of years, and the man works in the field or the market as he has worked for thousands of years, and China stands still.

The more mobile races the men have changed and changed again their way of working, and in their onward movement the nations have grown continually. But no matter how the men changed, the women remain unchanged, industrially speaking.

The same brute instinct to care for mate and young which actuated the labors of the primitive squaw still actuates the modern woman. She works alone for her own family as she worked alone for her own family when humanity began.

She has different tools, different houses, different needs to meet because of the changes brought about by men, but her field of industry is the same, her unit of power is the same, her industrial status is the same, her range of love and duty is the same; mother-labor is more ancient than slave-labor even, and by mother-labor is the woman's share of the world's work still done.

In the great and sudden change of our own time, no feature is more impressive than this, that the women of civilized races are at last beginning to civilize their work.

They are beginning to learn to take part in modern industry on modern lines by modern standards, beginning to lift their labor from the crude helplessness of remote antiquity to the plane of today.

An increasing number of our present-day women are choosing work which allows of specialization and so develops a higher degree of skill and joy in doing, and are ever learning to organize as well as specialize—which means saving in time and strength and great gain in power.

Scarcely a business today which has not some woman in it; in some work they outnumber the men, as in school teaching; and when the Teachers' Union of Chicago joined the Federation of Labor, we saw one instance of this long-delayed co-adjutor "catching up" at last.[8]

Think of it—in a hundred years—to span the gulf between today and prehistoric time! Surely no one need think the woman's movement slow.

This shows convincingly that, although forcibly confined to a low range of action, the woman has necessarily kept pace with man through heredity and only requires equal opportunity to manifest equal ability.

But equal opportunity has never been allowed her.

Owing to the group of time-worn prejudices with which we have hedged her in, her change of industrial position is accomplished only with the greatest difficulty, and among the many obstacles looms large this objection: she should not "compete with man."

To answer that requires a little study of certain economic errors.

What We Like

The serene air of finality with which people advance the fact that they like—or dislike—such and such things is impressive. The impression lies, however, solely in the air—it has no foundation. What anybody likes or dislikes is no contribution to an argument any more than if they announced, "I am five feet four" or "My eyes are blue." Liking or disliking merely defines personality. As Ruskin says, "Tell me what you like and I will tell you what you are."[9] As a motive of conduct it has weight, especially with the young and ignorant. What they like, that they will do or have at all costs quite regardless of the reasons for and against.

But a wise man does not let his tastes and instincts govern him unquestioned. He says, "I like alcohol, but it is not good for me, therefore I will not drink it." "I like to tyrannize—it is quite natural but is not the best civilized method, therefore I will not do it."

We do not in rational life let inherited tastes and habits govern conduct unless there is also a better foundation. But we are not all rational; most of us are not; and those of us who are are not rational at all points. Our wise, reasoned conduct is but a clearing in the forest so far; the greater part of it is due to inherited tendency and the pressure of conditions. I was talking one day with a very eminent woman, a suffragist, a Christian socialist, a person of advanced ideas and strong original thought. But when it came to any proposed change in the domestic machinery—to professional cooking and nursing instead of instinctive—she resisted the idea with intensity. She could in no way deny the arguments advanced and did not try to but planted herself frankly on this great primal ground of feeling: "I revolt against it," she cried earnestly, "with every fiber of my being!" And she did—you could see her doing it. I looked at her flushed face and felt the weight of this great sea of emotion and I thought of the suffrage work for all these weary years. "That is the way men feel about women's voting," said I.

COLUMN 6

February 6, 1904

Gilman skewers the idea that the purpose of feminism is to enable women to compete with men. She also discusses death rates among tuberculosis victims and those of children in orphanages in New York, and she pleads for better prenatal training of mothers, particularly those who are impoverished.

"Competing with Men"

There is no more mischievous phrase in use in connection with the woman's movement than the above. It is a brief and pungent expression and hits two ways, seeming to involve the women in error both feminine and economic. Such a doubly-dangerous catchword should be fully and carefully examined and dismissed forever from our vocabulary when its absurd falsity is demonstrated. The "men" part of it can be most easily attended to, so we will take that first.

The proposition is that women, in pressing forward into human activities of any sort and finding men in possession of the entire field, must necessarily come into competition with them and that this is unwomanly. It is held to put her in a false relation to men, to detract from her womanly charms, to lower her standard and lessen her attractions. Being accepted and believed, it deters many otherwise sensible women from enlarging their field of activities—the all-pervading men having preempted every claim in sight.

Now the essential error in this position is the universal assumption of mankind that human activities are sex activities—male sex activities, each and all. If they were, it would indeed be unwomanly—and also impossible—for women to attempt competition. A female as such cannot compete with a male as such, their special powers and inclinations being fundamentally different. These common human industries and arts which men are following all over the world have not the faintest relation to sex.

Because women invented sewing and raised it to a high grade of efficiency, we do not therefore accuse the tailor of "competing with women" because he also practices the art. It is not a male function nor a female function but a human function, a process necessary to the development of social life and open to any member of society.

There is just one occupation on earth which is distinctively masculine and that is fighting. The business of slaughter belongs by inherent sex-distinction to the male, and there has never been any danger of women's "competing with men" in this field.

The transient condition which gives us today a man-filled business world is not essential; it gives way daily before the steady entrance of women into field after field of previously "masculine" occupations; and presently we may leave out that end of our mischievous phrase and be confronted only with the statement that "women should not compete." We can withdraw our thought from the supposed error in sex-relation and focus it on the supposed error in economic relation. Here the assumption is this: "Work is done merely to get pay. Work and pay are limited—there is not enough to go around among the people now at work. For a new lot of workers to enter the field would only throw the present workers out of employment or reduce their wages in proportion to the number of new workers."

This position is honestly and earnestly held by almost all of us; and as the present set of workers happen to be men and the new set happen to be women, it has a paralyzing effect on the industrial progress of women.

That a given proposition is false, visibly and provably false; that it is ridiculous in its shallow absurdity; that it is without base or backing when fairly studied and may be instantly overthrown—does not lessen its force in the popular mind. If the majority of the people have been taught a thing a long time and "believe" it—i.e., hold it in the mind without reason—then falsehood and absurdity and little things like that do not matter much. People do not "believe" from a process of reasoning nor are they likely to disbelieve from such a process. All suffragists know this from experience in their efforts to convince the popular mind by argument.

So it is with no glad smile of triumph that this economic absurdity is laid low—it will bob into place again the moment the weight of the argument is off and the believers will believe as before.

Here are the modest and unbelieved facts:

The work of the world is necessary to supply the wants and express the powers of the people. So long as there are any people who have powers to express and wants to be supplied, there is work to do. The product of all this work is what we call wealth—the sum of human activity in material form. So long as the earth supplies the requisite materials, the more work there is, the more wealth there is. Therefore the "pay" keeps pace with the work—people work to make things and the things are distributed in payment for the work, and the more work is done the more wealth there is to distribute in payment.

So every addition to the workers adds to the world's wealth—*they make their own payment and more.*

A hive of a thousand bees would have as much honey as a thousand bees could make. A hive with two thousand bees would have twice as much honey. Imagine the swarm objecting to an accession in numbers on the ground that there was not honey enough to pay them! The bees make the honey—they eat it, of course, but they make more than they eat.

So the working man and woman make wealth; they use some, of course, but they make more than they use.

Therefore, the entrance of the submerged half of the world on the plane of productive industry will pay itself and add to the world's wealth beside. Now some thoughtful person, unable to dispute these simple facts and yet painfully aware that in the business world of today the entrance of women has lowered the wages of men in some cases, will call the above facts "sophistries," will say "that is all true enough in theory but *practically* (how fond we are of that word!) it comes out as we say—the women compete with the men and lower their wages!"

The contradiction is admitted and is thus explained: In real economic law, the case is as I have stated it. In present economic conditions, the case is as the unthinking observer sees it. Economic laws are permanent.

Economic conditions are transient, variable, open to improvement; we arrange them and we can rearrange them when we will.

If our present economic conditions are unsatisfactory, if they are inimical to the advance of women and the best interests of society, it is for us to study and improve them—holding fast to the permanent underlying laws involved and altering the transient conditions to suit the facts.

Perhaps the entrance of the non-competitive sex upon the business world may of itself show us the way to better conditions.

Women are pouring forward to take a hand in the world's work because the world needs them and they need it, because such normal social industry develops the woman and enriches the world.

It is a question of human beings, not males and females—of contribution, not competition.

Tuberculosis and New York

The city of New York holds no patent on tuberculosis—all our cities have it and the country, too, the New England farmhouse as well as the city tenement.

But New York has a criminal amount of it as our largest and most crowded city.

Ernest Poole in a recently prepared monograph on the subject shows the enormous ratio of deaths from this one disease—10 per cent of the population, a hundred thousand in a year, one-third of all deaths to women between twenty and thirty-five, to men between thirty and forty-five 32 per cent, to young men between twenty and twenty-nine 36 per cent.[1]

"The Black Plague[2] in London," Mr. Poole says, "is ever remembered with horror. It lived one year. It killed fifty thousand. The Plague Consumption kills this year in Europe over a million and this has been going on not for one year but for centuries. It is the Plague of all plagues—both in age and in power—insidious, steady, unceasing." In the New York tenements there are today "at least twenty thousand suffering in some stage of this disease."

We have learned of late the nature of this disease, its contributing causes, its means of prevention and cure. It could be stamped out like cholera and yellow fever and smallpox. But like all human efforts, this requires concerted action.

The appeal to women, from the point of view held in this department, is this: Here is an enormous evil, present, continuous, active. It is killing us by millions. We are submitting to it as medieval Europe submitted to the Black Death, as Asia submits to the cholera, because of ignorance, apathy, and lack of organization.

It is part of the especial business of women—as women, as mothers—to care for the health of the community. They do not do it. They do not even do half of it—their share as citizens apart from their special duty as women. Why do they not? Because they have not the ballot? That is an indirect contributory cause for negligence but it does not excuse them. If they cared as they should for their public duties and did what they could without the ballot, it would go farther toward getting it than any amount of petitioning.

We say, "Give us the ballot and we will do so and so." Why not say, "Give us the ballot because we have done so and so!"

The men who refuse the right of suffrage to women are not foreign enemies. They are our immediate male relatives and know us fairly well. They know only too well the narrow range of interest in most women's lives, their scant knowledge of or care for the larger civic processes with their far-reaching results. Now we may say, "This is because women are confined to narrow limits—they are not allowed the larger range which would develop larger capacity." That is true enough but as a matter of fact there are many splendid women who have done noble work for their country and the world even under their present restrictions. We point to them with honest pride. We are always backing our claims by the increasing number of large-minded women who have accomplished something.

Nothing succeeds like success. Nothing goes so far to change the mountainous prejudices of the popular mind as the daily presence of visible facts.

If the movement of women had to wait for the ballot, it would not have made a hundredth part of the progress it has—nor would it have even obtained as much concession in the matter of suffrage as it has. The steady enlargement of the mind, of the conscience, of the range of interest and activities, this shows the advance and leads the way to more.

Now suppose the women of New York became awakened to their responsibilities in this question of life and death, this twentieth-century shame of needless waste in life and property. Is there nothing they could do about it—until they had attained the ballot?

The men of New York vote. They vote in the venal official who allows the hideous overcrowding and unsanitary conditions of tenements which promote death at this appalling rate.

If the women voted also, I believe they would be more conscientious about the public health. But this faith would be strongly reinforced if they were more conscientious now. Because we are forbidden the simplest and surest means of fulfilling a citizen's duties, we are not therefore excused from those duties. No mother would refuse to cook for her children because the father would not get her a gas range to make the work easier. Easy or hard, the children must be fed.

"In Greater New York today there are thirty thousand cases of tuberculosis," says Addison M. Baird, D.D.[3] This condition of unnecessary death is the fault of the negligent women as well as men. Duties are another name for rights. If we fulfill the duties, we shall achieve the rights inevitably.

The Home and the Orphan Asylum[4]

The *New York Times* tells us that during the last year the death rate in the Hebrew Orphan Asylum of that city was 2 1/2 per cent—as against an average of 10 per cent among the home-reared babies outside.[5] This is very encouraging. We have heard so long of the inevitable ill results of "herding" little children (these orphan Hebrews are from the newly-born infant to five years old); of the "terrible death-rate" among babies cared for in large groups; and in general of the "curse of institutionalism," that this bit of counterevidence is most refreshing.

It is an excellent instance. These children are orphans—entirely deprived of the mystic charm of "a mother's care." These are poor children and presumably of weakly constitution, inferred from the premature death of their parents; they are "herded" in large numbers in this "institution" and—they have four times the chance of living of the infant in its mother's arms.

The outside general percentage includes the children of the rich and educated, of the healthy and vigorous, of the passionately devoted parents. These poor little survivors of shattered homes have no advantages whatever except that of competent care!

Now really, prejudices aside, or rather stepping aside ourselves for the moment from the mountain of prejudice we cannot move, this is a fact, a large, triumphant fact, which ought to make an impression even upon mothers. Its inferences are more than its direct figures, for a child with a mother ought to be far better off than a child without one. If the home could but stand even with the orphan asylum, that would be a poor showing for motherhood—but to be four times worse!

The British Mother

In the *Contemporary Review* for January is an article on "The Poverty Line and Physical Degeneration" by Mrs. Bosanquet, in which the practical efficiency of the maternal instinct is brilliantly illuminated.[6] Alarming figures have been given by Booth[7] and others showing that about one-third of the British public live "below the poverty line," are insufficiently provided with the necessities of life, and grow up defective in varying degree. Mrs. Bosanquet disputes some of the figures and asserts that in most cases it is not absolute poverty which is responsible for the visible horrors of the result, not lack of money, but lack of intelligence.

She shows that in many cases the wages earned are sufficient to maintain healthy life, "hardy people have been reared on less," but that the money is wasted and misspent partly on drink, partly on improper food.

The effort which is being made to supply nourishing meals to the school children she deprecates is insufficiently radical. "The mischief begins before school years, for it begins before the child is out of its mother's arms"; and again, "Harm has been done by injudicious feeding and neglect before a child is three years old, which is never redeemed in later life."

The problem is unsolved "unless you have taught the women how to treat a baby." If the children are fed at school, "not only will the mothers become more slack, but it must be noted that feeding at school gives the child none of that practical knowledge of housekeeping and food preparation which it gets from watching and helping its mother."

Here we have again the everlasting attempt to bolster up our ineradicable position that the mothers—in the face of proven incapacity of an entire third of them—are specially fitted for the task. Have not these convicted incapables, who ruin the child's health beyond repair before he is three years old, been "watching and helping their mothers" for endless generations?

If the maternal instinct exists at all in modern human beings, it ought to come out strong in their children's infancy and be easily conspicuous in so primitive and simple a task as nursing the baby. Yet as Mrs. Bosanquet says, it is common to find babies less than six months old familiar with every form of solid food used by their parents.

It is useless to talk about educating them. Instinct has nothing to do with education unless to disappear before it. The less education a people has the more instinct—instinct being an animal safeguard far inferior to rational intelligence. Now is there such a thing as "maternal instinct" or is there not? If there is, what good does it do—how does it affect the child? In this instance we have indisputable proof that in an immense proportion of the population this devoutly worshipped instinct does not lead the mother to feed the child property *even during the nursing period!*

If instinct cannot guide a female animal in an animal function, it must be a poor reliance. Is it not time that we abandoned this claim to an outgrown faculty of the lower animals and began to make some effort toward the assumption of the human faculties?

COLUMN 7

February 13, 1904

Gilman again ponders the boundaries of "woman's sphere," pictures a wider field for rural women's clubs, and decries the blatant gender bias infecting American journalism.

Woman's Sphere

One wonders sometimes what kind of creatures women think they are—if not human. And if they are conscious of being human—one continues to wonder why they do not know it.

Why should they be so content with being female—which is no distinction of our race but a condition quite common among animals.

"I am a woman!" says she proudly. Yes, granted, anyone can see that. "I am a wife!" Certainly, all women—unless something ails them—should be. "I am a mother!" Of course—that follows naturally and is sometimes not even a matter of choice.

Well—go on—what else are you? Every kind of female animal can say "me, too" to this much. What are you that is *human*, that we, the highest race on earth, can do and that pigs and ducks cannot? Suppose you asked a man what he was and he proudly mentioned his sex as almost a sufficient excuse for being and then added in a sort of sacred ecstasy that he was a husband—and a father.

By all means, we reply—assuredly—that goes without saying, but what of it? So is a Hottentot. What are you as a civilized modern man—as an American citizen—in what capacity do you serve the world?

Are you of the laboring class? Do you do useful work that we cannot live without? Are you an artist, feeding the world with beauty? Are you a discoverer, an inventor, leading us onward to new power and comfort? Do you take part in our slow-moving legal processes? Do you share in the cumbrous but improving operations of government? Do you heal the sick, steer ships, move freight and people—what are you?

He gives you one of a thousand replies. Somewhere in the myriad wheeled enginery of the great world he has his appointed place and helps the march forward.

Now Estimable Female, what are you—besides?

"I am a housekeeper!" she answers still proudly. She has been carefully taught—since the world was—that that was her one and all-sufficient business, her only proper sphere.

But you are a civilized human being, aren't you—you belong in this century—you are man's equal—you have some education? And then she replies with real satisfaction that she is all this, that she has nowadays more education than the man and shows equal ability. Then how about your business—why is it that thirty thousand men are so many different kinds of social servants and yet from President to common laborer their thirty million wives are all housekeepers?

This touches a proper pride and she replies with a most inspiring little speech about the majestic importance of her position, about the "molding of the child's mind," "caring for the health of the family," and "the sacred influences of the home."

What could be more glorious, she cries with passionate enthusiasm, than to rear to noble manhood and spotless womanhood these tender little ones! To minister to their physical health, their mental growth, their moral vigor! To maintain a center of peace and love for man that he may be strengthened for his battle in the world!

It does have a beautiful sound. So this is what women are doing—all of them nearly—giving their whole minds to it, their whole hearts to it, their whole time to it. This is the lifework of all women for all the years since humanity had homes, is it?

They ought to be experts in the business by this time surely. Let us cease from troubling then and contentedly feast our eyes on the noble manhood and spotless womanhood with which the world is filled! On the splendid spectacle of physical health, mental growth, and moral vigor of the general public! On the perfect contentment of the average man in his center of peace and love! This housekeeping womanhood has had a fair trial.

Its results leave something to be desired.

How if our petrified primeval domestic functionary should break her shell and try her hand at world-keeping?

Here is a big, round world, rich, beautiful, capable of supporting millions and millions of happy people—*happy people*—not the kind that blunder and struggle and suffer and die shameful deaths on its face today. Is the world what it ought to be? Is the world what it might be? Is it as good as we know how to make it—to say nothing of the goodness we have yet to learn?

Is the woman half of the world satisfied with it? It is their business—theirs as much as man's. Neither God nor nature ever told them that they were eternal housekeepers and only men were to be world-keepers. Here are the women of the world today—not somebody else's world but their world, disgracefully neglecting their duty in it. Here are people starving—here are people freezing—here are people sickening—here are people sinking into hopeless degeneration—here are people overworked till they die of old age at thirty—here are people underworked till they die of fatty degeneration of the intellect—here is war going on yet, which belongs at about the level of cannibalism—and all this in woman's sphere—the world.

She cannot make the world right by keeping house any more than men could. That is her poor, shortsighted, foolish mistake. She thinks the world consists only in a number of houses as so many barnacles might think it consisted only of a number of shells.

The world has houses in it just as it has beds and stoves and other conveniences but the world, the modern, progressive, grandly growing world lives far more in its ships and locomotives, its great machines and engines, its boundless fields of action, industry, and commerce, art and science, and all the rest. If all the men kept house, too, there would be no human world. Such as it is, good and bad, men make it, and the badness is the kind that always indicates the absence of woman. This noisy, dirty, disorderly, everlastingly fighting world is just what every bachelor mining town is—it is the result of unalloyed, unbridled masculinity. When our poor, timid, ignorant women and our rich, cowardly, lazy women wake up their minds to this big, plain fact—that the world is theirs and is shamefully neglected by them—perhaps they will see that a large, intelligent, righteous world-keeping would make the problems of their individual housekeeping much simpler.

Country Women's Clubs

Among the easy possibilities for increased power and happiness among women in the country is that of establishing a local clubroom, rooms, or house in every little town and village. Say there are fifty women in the town and fifty more within a "shopping" radius—one hundred women who use that town as a business center. Let these women contribute ten cents a week each—that is not much. Ten cents extra of the week's purchases separately is a small sum. But in a year it is $5.20 and that is $520 for the club. There is usually to be found in our towns some woman in straitened circumstances yet having a good house of whom rooms could be rented for the club use and cared for by the resident at small expense.

One room for meetings—that might mean "the use of the parlor" once a week or month or whenever the club held its regular meeting. The main essential, however, is the "rest room" for the use of the women from the outlying country while in for their purchasing. A place to fix one's hair, to sit down or lie down a little, to nurse the baby, to meet one's friends. That ten cents a week from a hundred women ought to pay from the rooms, for their care, for the attendance of one person on Saturday or whatever day it was most needed, and for a number of magazines besides. One dollar a week ought to be enough room rent for the smaller places where there would be the least membership and the least use, or two in larger towns. Another dollar for the attendance of someone on the club day—possibly a member could do this without charge. There would remain on our ten cents a week and membership of a hundred plan—which is ten dollars a week income—a large sum for club use. Five cents a week with such a membership would be enough. A clubroom like this could maintain an extensive magazine exchange—all our best magazines could be taken and used by the members. "Traveling libraries" could find headquarters there and the nucleus of a local public library be formed.

The same room could be used in the evening for boys' clubs, for reading, games, and debate—a most valuable influence to counteract the temptations offered even in the smaller towns.

Girls could hold their club meetings there, too, and an associate membership of men might be added to assist in giving entertainments from time to time. Such a club of women naturally becomes an important influence in village improvement, increasing the beauty, cleanliness, and health of the town, helping toward good roads, lending its influence to lift the standard of the local schools, helping the churches in good works, adding in every way to the progress of the neighborhood.

For the isolated farmer's wife they would be of incalculable advantage and in the village itself almost as desirable, teaching the women to make common cause for the common good and to outgrow the pettiness sure to result from narrow living. When a thing like this can be done so easily, so cheaply, so instantly, and to such large and growing advantage, the wonder is that a town in the world exists without one. Some towns have them. Some towns have women's clubhouses even—whole buildings, centers of manifold beneficent activities—but there are thousands and thousands where the men's club is "the store" and the women's club is the church and the young people have none.

Let the women get together on this simple basis of neighborly association and advantage, put up their dimes, and enjoy the swift and beautiful advance in common comfort and social development so sure to follow.

Reporters' Ridicule

In Mr. Williams's exceedingly clever book of reportorial experiences, *The Stolen Story*, he refers incidentally to the "one sent out to write the funny story of the woman's convention."[1] For fifty years this has been a newspaper habit. The clear-headed, progressive papers have outgrown it largely but the journalistic mossback keep it up. The woman's movement goes on but these short-sighted papers do not go on; they stay still in the position of their grandfathers. Originally they stood in front, opposing the first steps of the procession. The procession has long since passed them, horse, foot, and dragoons, but they keep up their piping under the impression that nothing has changed. They have not changed and they forget to notice that other things have. So we feel no surprise when a young person working for the *Chronicle* of Houston, Tex., contributes one more attempt to belittle and make ridiculous a meeting of the Equal Suffrage League.

Texas is young, brave, strong, progressive, full of splendid possibilities for advance. Texas is fighting the Standard Oil Company even now—success to its battle![2] Texas is large and, as a frontier state with its overplus of men and a southern state with its traditional chivalry, ought to stand forward nobly in support of the efforts of women to improve their position.

The particular reporter who wrote the particular "funny story" in the instance which forms my present text was a woman, or so signs herself, but the animus is man's. She would not have written in that way for a woman's paper—its readers would not have found it so funny, its editors would not so willingly have paid for it. The point of view from which the progress of women appears ridiculous is the man's. His attitude dates away back to Dr. Johnson, who held that a woman speaking in public was like a dog standing on its hind legs; the wonder was not that she could do it well but that she could do it at all.[3]

Is it not worthwhile for our intelligent men to wake up a little on this subject, to get some sense of historic proportion, to see that this movement has passed its funny stage long ago? When a thing is very small and weak and makes mistakes, it is very easy to ridicule it. It costs nothing and if the thing one is ridiculing fails, then one's wisdom and foresight in jeering at it is vindicated. But when the thing one is ridiculing goes right on, gets stronger and stronger, succeeds continuously, then the person making fun of it becomes ridiculous.

These benighted scoffers do not keep up with the facts. Editor, reporter, and reader have failed to note the change in the facts since they began to laugh. From Sweden to Tasmania, from Scotland to New South Wales, from Quebec to Manitoba, from New England to New Zealand, and in twenty-three of our United States, women vote in varying degree. In four of our states they have full suffrage and in Federated Australia and New Zealand.

This is not a remote contingency but an established fact. It works and it works well. Good, plain, honest, motherly women and sweet, attractive, gay young ladies vote by the thousands even now yet remain as motherly and as attractive as before.

It is not that they want to vote—and that is so ridiculous!—but they do vote and it is not ridiculous at all.

Worthy editors who find current history such cause for laughter, do you never consider that future history will find that cause in you?

If anything is legitimately absurd, it is Mrs. Partington's mop[4]—or Mr. Partington's!

A Girl of Spirit

It is a pleasure to record that a girl of Williamsburg, N.Y., fought and put to flight a highwayman.[5] She was going home attended by a "natural protector" in the shape of one young man when two other "natural protectors" so far forgot their nature as to attack them. Instead of screaming helplessly and leaving her escort to struggle with two assailants, she promptly "engaged" with one, showing an amateur enthusiasm which he was unable to resist.

If women would only remember that they have muscles as well as emotions, that a woman is a large, heavy animal as well as a creature of light and no inconsiderable opponent when enraged, we should have a shorter record of crimes and casualties.

COLUMN 8

February 20, 1904

Gilman explains in this column the reason "why great women are few": Even very talented women are consigned domestic duties. Moreover, she contends that the American newspaper publisher William Randolph Hearst (1863–1951) was "not a woman's candidate." On the contrary, Hearst's actions were antithetical to the interests of women. The Hearst chain of newspapers had sensationalized its reports of Gilman's separation and subsequent divorce in December 1892 from the American artist Charles Walter Stetson (1858–1911). The scandal was fanned by a series of articles in Hearst's *San Francisco Examiner*.[1] "My name became a football for all the papers on the coast," Gilman remembered forty years later.[2] In addition, she ruminated on the significance of the recent meeting of the National Convention of Women Suffragists in Washington, DC.

Why Great Women Are Few

It has often been advanced as proof of the inferiority of women that there were so few great ones, even in a line where they were encouraged to work, as in music. Those who are reading the stories of the private life of Mommsen may find enlightenment on this question.[3] Mommsen was a great man, a very great man. He slept but three hours, ate his lunch in ten minutes, spilling it on his clothes as he gobbled, walked an hour a day, and worked all the rest of the time. His power of concentration was so great that it made him the extreme type of helpless absent-mindedness in all other directions. He had not sense enough to put on his hat or to get off his car when reaching his destination; his students frequently had to go after him and escort him back; and conductors were told where to drop him as if he were a child. At night he worked till 2 o'clock, eating steadily but unconsciously from enormous quantities of food placed at hand.

He had, incidentally, twelve children, but between short-sightedness (this mighty intellect was too prejudiced to wear glasses—preferred to blunder and be taken care of) and absent-mindedness he scarce knew them when they spoke to him in the street. He refused to leave his work when a Crown Princess called on him or worse when an immense band of enthusiastic students gathered to do him honor. He was beloved, revered, and salaried because of his colossal lifework, a vast amount of valuable labor which went on uninterruptedly for a long lifetime.

Now what made this work possible to such a feeble, helpless, discourteous, untidy person? His wife. A wife who bore those twelve children and reared them as she best might and waited on this learned man as a slave might wait on a baby.

Greatness in any one time requires neglect of some others, and these others have to be taken care of by someone else. A great woman as great as Mommsen, who was as short-sighted, as untidy, as helpless, as absent-minded, as inconceivably rude and inconsiderate, as unnaturally oblivious of her own children—but to go too far—she would have no husband. What man would marry such a creature? What man, even if he wanted to, could keep up a lifetime of clockwork devotion to such an unattractive genius?

Such a woman, we serenely say, must choose. She must decide between being a wife and mother or giving up that noble work for her "career." And how long does anyone suppose a man like Mommsen would have lived alone? Those twelve children show his need of the family relation—he was no celibate. He needed and we do not doubt valued the unceasing affectionate devotion of his wife. Without it he would have suffered in spirit as well as in body. But he did not have to choose. He had both.

The woman of equal genius must die. She dies, if celibate, for lack of personal love and care—no one to support her in the infinite exertion of her task, to defend her from interruption and criticism, to provide her food and clean her clothes, and tell her when to put her hat on and when to take it off.

She dies, if married, even sooner, long before the twelve children could be produced. No woman could work as Mommsen worked for nineteen hours a day—or half that—and keep home and care for children, too.

Does that mean that motherhood prohibits genius? No.

Not motherhood but nurse-hood, governess-hood, teacher-hood, and most of all *servant-hood*. Genius almost always is accompanied by a strong sex nature. That is why so many geniuses live in sin and die in sorrow. If they were happily mated, this need not follow.

The woman-genius could be a glorious mother, bearing splendid children to carry on the line of power; she could be a happy wife, gratefully and proudly rejoicing in the love that made her work more beautiful and strong; but she cannot be a general servant or a nursery-governess.

We must learn to distinguish between motherhood, wifehood, which are feminine functions, private, personal, physical, and psychic; and education, which is a social function open to any specialist. Also we must someday learn that the complicated labors now making nearly every woman a home-servant should also be relegated to the specialist and removed from the home. When these things are understood, we could have as many great women as we have great men; they could serve the world fully and nobly and yet be happy women, too; instead of having to choose, as they do now, between the terrible sacrifice of celibacy—costing so much more to woman than to man—and the other sacrifice, so common among women, which surrenders "the personal career" for what we insist on calling "motherhood" when it is really domestic service. It is a cruel choice, and its loss and pain to the woman is followed by loss and pain to the world. If she does not marry, we lose the highest quality of human stock. If she does, we lose half the world's genius. This is one reason, one of many, why intelligent women should hasten to dismiss these household industries from their contemptibly pitiful plane and raise them to the level of world industries with the others.

We should think of how bitterly the world needs its few great ones, great artists, great scientists, great teachers and thinkers and lovers of mankind. Half of them are at present lost to us, overstrained in the pitiful effort to do what they are not fit for and pining for opportunity to do what they are fit for.

When the work now done by women in this gracefully slipshod, primeval way is done as orderly world service by those most competent, we shall double the effectiveness of human effort, both in the grade of genius and all below it.

Why We Ignore Reason

Man is a reasoning being; it is his preeminent race distinction.

To "lose one's reason" is to be insane or an idiot.

To be "reasonable" is to facilitate life, to make everything go well.

To be "unreasonable" is to be a nuisance, public or private—or both.

Why then does clear, solid reasoning weigh so little with most people? They may be led or forced to recognize the connection of thought, the irresistible argument, the absolute proof, but it leaves them unmoved. Why? Because of the way we are brought up as children.

Reason is not made a cause of conduct while our habits are forming. We are persuaded or forced to act under pressure of several kinds, fear, hope, affection, and such, but seldom under pressure of clear reason.

As we grow older we learn what reasoning is. We see it done in geometry and consider it part of that abstract science. We admire it in logic and esteem it as a sort of mental acrobatics, difficult, admirable, but in no way suited to common use—mere metaphysics.

When we are reasoned with and convinced against our previous belief, we feel that it is a sort of juggling process, skillful legerdemain, that the reasoner has taken advantage of us by superior skill in his art—but as soon as he stops doing it, we return to our former position.

The daily action of our minds is not reasonable. What we do may be reasonable but we do it because we were trained to as children, because other people do it, because our hereditary tendencies lie that way—not from a process of reasoning. Therefore, it is that the "light of reason" shines so vainly on the world. We are reasoning creatures but we use our powers so little that they are sadly feeble.

If we would begin at once, at any age, and establish to our own minds the reason—or lack of reason—in a given course of action and then go on or stop because of that reason, we should develop unsuspected mental power.

Power comes with exercise. As we formed the habit of reasoning and acting from reason, as we learned to admire the persons so doing, pity weak-minded persons who could not, condemn the pig-headed persons who would not, we should become as a people open to conviction, and then all swift, ennobling, progressive thought would pour into the world and lift it to the level of true humanity, real civilization.

Not a Woman's Candidate

Among the names mentioned as would-be candidates for the Presidential nomination appears that of the yellow journalist Mr. W. R. Hearst. His claims to the position, aside from purchasing power, lie in the alleged humanitarian services of his newspaper. Without going into the general question of these services—or their patent purpose—one thing should be borne in mind by the women of America: that Mr. Hearst has used the power of the press against the advance of women. Many newspapers find a woman's convention a topic for funny stories, but this man's papers have used not only ridicule but offensive personal attack.

Not only in our efforts to secure political expression but in other progressive steps were the movements of women made subjects for contemptuous criticism. For instance, the Pacific Coast Woman's Press Association, a body of authors and newspaper writers formed in San Francisco, was a continued topic of ridicule and abuse in Mr. Hearst's newspaper in that city, both "Western chivalry" and "professional courtesy" being thus ably represented.[4]

Whatever progress was made by women was subject to the safe insults of this powerful paper—until it became popular. Then, as representing a market, it became worthy of respectful notice and got it promptly.

As women grow more successful and are treated with more consideration, they should bear in kind remembrance those who honored their early struggles and should not forget those who dishonored them with all the power of society's greatest engine, the press.

This record of contemptuous misrepresentation and opposition should be borne in mind by our women citizens, whether they have the ballot or "influence." Let them use both.

At the Convention

The most important feature of these great gatherings of women[5] is that of the association itself—the coming together of these so long isolated factors of society's life.

Human progress is psychic, not physical. Our separate bodies are no better than those of other animals in their physiology, but our collective body—society—in its sociological action is far higher in the order of evolution.

It is through association that men have grown, through lack of association that women have not grown, and now that they are coming together at last they grow so that you can fairly see it!

The dignity, the ease, the breadth of view, the thought and study and wide experience shown on the platform at these conventions are beautiful proofs of the advance of women.

There is something extremely comforting in the steady accumulation of accomplishment which so powerfully encourages our cause. The Colorado women actually *look* different. They are not supplicants nor demanders; they are not arguing and pleading and struggling and toiling—they have arrived.

So with the charming woman from Australia, Mrs. Watson-Lister.[6] She is graceful and gentle and good to look at—but so are other women. The difference is in an easy, comfortable, *peaceful* air, an air of able citizenship. They are not striving for it—they have it.

If those who find fault with the looks and manners, the words and deeds of the strugglers for equal suffrage, would but realize that it is not the suffrage *but the struggle for it* that brings out the points they object to!

As soon as this primal right and duty is granted them, they are peaceable enough. Life moves along smoothly. All the tearing and pushing stops.

We have heard of women who married men "to get rid of them"—wouldn't it be a good thing if the men who cannot abide suffragists should enfranchise them to get rid of them?

Why must we address God in Elizabethan English—or that of the pious but ignoble James of Scotland?[7] The opening prayers here—like all other prayers with their "O Thous" and "Thou Knowests"—bring up this thought again.

If we kept saying "O you!" and were profuse in our rather vulgar "you know"—that would not sound so well, would it? But this means the same thing. It is an archaism. It all helps to keep God in the background of our minds as if He were a character in ancient history, some remote foreigner who could not understand our present language, and that is a pity. We think it more respectful to use the language of our remote ancestors. Why?

It was to be regretted that Mrs. Katharine Day was prevented by illness from telling us about the Municipal Campaign in New York.[8] So many women did such good work in that effort to keep up the standard of civic efficiency and honesty in the big city, and the work was so exactly in the line of what suffragists want to do, that it would have been useful to hear about it.

It is true that we could do it much better, much easier with the ballot; it is true that it does seem asking a good deal of women to seek their help in politics while denying them their equal rights therein. But why should not much be asked of women? They have much to give. We cannot stop to quibble over points of what ought to be asked of us. The world is in trouble and needs attention. It needs its mother and needs her now.

The practical sense, the long-cultivated patience and forgiveness of women, ought to serve them here.

We know enough, thousands of us, to be of real service in the problems of the hour and we ought to serve whether we are asked or not—whether we are permitted or not!

Things need to be done in every city in our land and in the country, too. Exhausting as the suffrage work may be, it does not take every hour of the day.

Women need the ballot unquestionably and need it to help the world as well as themselves, but meanwhile there is much important work that can be done without it.

The world saw progress before men had the right of suffrage. The world makes progress even now on other lines beside that. I am not underrating the social value of democratic government, far from it, but urging that half a loaf given to people who need it is better than no bread.

―――

Miss Anthony—bless the great heart of that World Mother!—made a delightful speech on Friday evening. She was most warmly received.

Figure 1. Officers of the International Council of Women in Berlin, 1904 (Susan B. Anthony at lower right). *The International Council of Women*, ed. Mary Wright Sewall (Boston: International Council of Women, 1910), frontispiece.

The difference between this modest hall and its modest attendance and our enthusiastic, enormous crowds in New Orleans last year shows how people grow indifferent to what they hear often.[9]

Our power of unbiased individual judgment is very small. Generally, the mind of the public is swept by common tendencies which it never thinks of resisting. It would have to think to resist them, and thinking is a form of exercise; it calls for mental muscles but too often atrophied from disuse.

When a few more years of history show us a balanced democracy of men and women, how very small some people now looming large will look. In the perspective of ten or twenty years, all the considerations now weighing heavily will change places and assume new importance.

If any of our legislators are interested in the permanent dignity of their positions before the public, they had better make haste and reconsider their views on the woman question. Indeed, some of them, not interested at all in the verdict of history, might be more sensitive to the verdict of a vast body of new-made voters—with good memories.

COLUMN 9

February 27, 1904

Gilman bookends brief essays about politicians' differing attitudes toward suffrage with answers to a correspondent's questions and a piece about "cooking as a marital duty."

The Last Ditch

The chairman of the Senate Committee, after listening to the equal suffragists with what appeared to be an excellent interest, finally ensconced himself dexterously in the last ditch of the Antis—"the women do not want it."[1] He did not, however, claim that this was an argument or that he advanced it in objection to what had been said, but simply maintained that it was the shortest way to get what we wanted.

The present effort is to convince a majority of that half the people now in power, or two-thirds of them. How would it be shorter to convince the entire other half not already suffragists? They would be no nearer then than we are now, for the half in power would still remain to be convinced.

Moreover, the present voting population and especially their elected representatives are far easier to reach than the non-voting population, for they are so grouped as to be approachable collectively while the non-voting population, isolated and unorganized, require a house-to-house visitation of endless extent. Legislative bodies representing the opinions of their electors can act for them authoritatively. Women have no representatives and cannot so act.

If the Senator meant that the united opinion of the entire population of women would have such weight that the men would instantly accede to it, he is advancing a proposition impossible of proof on the one hand and, what is still worse, impossible of attainment. It is not at all likely that all women will unite in an opinion any more than all men. There are plenty of men now who do not believe in universal suffrage even for themselves. How could it be expected of all women?

This egregious demand reminds one of the attitude of unjust tyrants in old fairy tales who required of their petitioners to go and kill the Giant-with-Seven-Heads or some such trifle before they could be heard.

But these modern dignitaries require us to overcome a giant with thirty million heads as a condition of granting justice. As a matter of fact, no such condition was ever made or fulfilled in similar extensions of suffrage to other petitioners. It has been granted as a political measure without any petition at all or with that of only a small minority. In the twenty-four States and Territories where we have already some form of suffrage, no such condition was made or met. It is only a hiding place for minds unable to oppose the movement on any rational ground and unwilling frankly to admit that their real ground is emotional.

We ought to have immense patience with our opponents. The growing power of the woman movement along all lines is to the ignorant and prejudiced a portent of evil instead of sure promise of good. They are afraid and they do not like it. Fear and dislike are not worthy grounds of opposition so they are not admitted. Instead of meeting the question fairly and putting themselves on record before all history as promoters or resisters of progress, these gentlemen take refuge behind the women *a la* Adam and say, virtually, "We have no opinion on this subject. We do not say it is wrong and you shall not have it nor it is right and you shall have it, but most women do not want it; when they all do, why, then there will be no difficulty." This too is a matter of record and will be read with amazement by the sons and daughters of these obstructionists.

It is far more brave and honest to say, "I do not believe in this; I think it would do more harm than good," than to take this ridiculous proposition of waiting for a unanimous opinion from half the population.

Answer to an Inquirer

A correspondent asks these questions:

"If women have failed in housekeeping and homemaking, how can they be expected to succeed in the larger and more arduous duties of 'world-keeping'? Failure in one thing does not presage success in another, rather the reverse."

>*Answer.* Women fail in housekeeping for lack of the larger faculties gained in "world-keeping." A man—an angel—would fail in the conglomerate mass of undeveloped industries we try to carry on at home. The failure of savagery does not presage failure in civilization. A properly kept world will include properly kept houses; with the world as it is now the housekeeping must fail.

"Are you not too hard on women? Do you not expect of the woman more than of the man, namely to marry, bear children, work for a livelihood, and take part in active public work?"

>*Ans.* No. Men do all of these but bear children, and women are given the power to do that besides the common human capacity to do the other things. "To marry" is not a toilsome sacrifice but a joy and strength—if it is a right marriage. What we call "working for a livelihood" *is* public work; it is exchange of labor, specialized and organized, whereas women work in private for their families only, unspecialized and unorganized. "Public work" to the extent of ordinary citizenship—intelligent voting—is no task. When "public work" becomes official, there is usually a salary attached so that again it is the same as "working for a livelihood."

"Condensed. How can a woman compete with man industrially during the years of child-bearing?"

>*Ans.* She cannot. She does not have to. But she can easily do enough work to serve the public and maintain herself during that period, as she now does heavy housework without pay. There are many kinds of labor more compatible with child-bearing than housework but women have always been able to do that. I know of one who had nine children and never missed washing on Monday but once! When all

women work all their lives in modern, organized industry, they will arrange the conditions of labor to suit their especial abilities and disabilities as men do. One month out of a year is not so bad as fifty-two drunken Mondays!

"Will you not write an article on 'Wifehood' to teach women that it is their duty to have enough independence of mind occasionally to disagree with their husbands?"

Ans. No. That has nothing to do with wifehood in itself. It has to do with the economic dependence of women on their husbands and I have written a book on that.

"Briefly. Many women would enjoy financial independence but have not been trained to work—what should they do?"

Ans. Learn—work is no mystery.

"Many women who follow trades and professions after marriage warn other women not to follow their example and point to worthless, shiftless husbands as reasons for the warning. My experience in life has been that women are more willing to work than men. I do not understand, then, your frequent railing at women for laziness. Do you not think that men would willingly let women support them and rear families besides?"

Ans. This is a complex proposition as stated. It is true than some men would let a woman support them but most men unspeakably despise them for it. When women are economically independent—they will not marry that kind of man, so after a while there will not be any more of them. No law compels a wife to support an able-bodied husband in idleness nor ever will—neither men nor women would make such laws.

If a woman is willing—and able—to do it of her own free will, let her! She might have a very handsome husband driving around in a victoria[2] with a fat little dog in his lap. Why not? Women are not ashamed to be so exhibited.[3] The woman's power of self-support—and of child support in part—makes her independent of such parasites; nothing else does. As my questioner says, women are "more willing to work than men." They are by temperament and ability natural workers. Therefore, the position of a female parasite is more contemptible than that of a male parasite. In many primitive organisms, the male is a parasite—lives on the body of the female, a microscopic adjunct, or something larger, is carried around by her in a little pocket.

But there is no parasitic female on earth except woman. Therefore do I rail at women for laziness—it is an unnatural vice in them, far more blamable than in man.

If not satisfied, will my correspondent kindly read *Women and Economics* over again!

Cooking as a Marital Duty

From Ohio comes legal recognition of the fact that a wife is by virtue of her position a domestic servant.

One Mrs. Holsky of Coshocton, O., has filed a petition for divorce and while the case was pending appears to have "struck" in these domestic duties.[4]

The judge, being appealed to by the hungry Holsky, has granted an injunction restraining her from refusing to do the housework—she is explicitly ordered to cook the meals and make the bed for her husband. It is well to have the position of a wife clearly defined that those who maintain the angel-and-pedestal theory may be enlightened.

A series of letters from bachelors has lately been appearing in a New York paper explaining why they do not marry and generally concurring in finding fault with the girls of our day as being expensive luxuries instead of profitable servants.[5] Some sprightly answers from girls and women take exception to the position of household drudge, one saying frankly that she prefers not marrying and supporting herself by more congenial and better paid work.

It is a personal hardship and an injury to society that any healthy human being should live a celibate. If our more intelligent and progressive women prefer celibacy to housework, that leaves us to replenish the world with the offspring of contented home servants, which is a pity, too.

Two things need clear exposition in this matter. To the women: that housework has no real connection with marriage. If our women do not like their position as domestic servants, let them change the status of that field of industry, make it a business like any other business open to whatsoever women—or men—may prefer it, a business with regular hours, proper pay, and room for legitimate competition. To the men: that this private servant method of meeting the world's physical needs is hopelessly inefficient and expensive—the least competent and most wasteful method they could possibly maintain unless every man did it for himself, which would be one degree worse.

The women are quite right to object to this wholly unsuitable stage of labor, but they ought to have sense enough to distinguish between housework and matrimony.

Wifehood is a natural and beautiful relation, carrying no trade-implications whatever. Housework is an ordinary human trade at a contemptibly low stage of development.

Men have been so long accustomed to marrying a wife and having a cook thrown in that they find it hard to see the distinction. It is upon women that this illegitimate assumption works most hardship and it is for them to recognize the evil and stop it. The sooner the better for all concerned.

If this kind of labor now expected of all wives unless their husbands are rich enough to waive the demand and in this Ohio case legally enjoined upon the rebellious woman were advantageous to the world, then it would be wrong to resist it but it is not. It is distinctly disadvantageous. It is not only proven insufficient to keep the world in health but it breeds evil characteristics in all parties concerned. Women hold two positions in relation to the world: they are human beings and females. As human beings it is their duty to serve mankind in the best labor possible, developing their highest powers for this purpose.

As females it is their duty to serve mankind in that tremendous function through which the world's whole evolution of species has been mainly accomplished, in true motherhood. The unbiased selection of the best husband as the child's best father is the female's first duty. Neither direct world service in one's best trade nor direct world service in one's best motherhood can be given by this pitiful status of domestic labor.

From the *New York Times*, Feb. 20, 1904:

WHEN LOVELY WOMAN STOOPS TO POLITICS[6]
A remarkable story of frauds, ballot-box stuffing, and nefarious schemes to defeat the honest voter, carried on by women in a State where Woman Suffrage has been adopted and where women put to the blush even the most hardened of political managers and ward politicians.

A story without parallel in political history.

This is a conspicuous advertisement of a Sunday story—to cater to prejudice.

DEFENDS WOMAN VOTERS.[7]
Ex-Congressman Shafroth of Colorado Defends Them from Fraud Charges.
Washington, Feb. 19. Ex-Congressman John L. Shafroth of Colorado,[8] who resigned his seat because of election frauds in Denver, denies that these frauds were committed mainly by women. In an interview today, Mr. Shafroth said:

"Of the persons implicated, very few were women—not more than one in ten at the outside. The frauds were committed in the lowest part of Denver, where not many women live. It is preposterous to make the incident an argument against woman suffrage.

"Everybody knows there are bad women as well as bad men, but what would any good man think if it were proposed to take his vote away from him because a few bad men somewhere had cheated at an election? In Colorado the women vote as generally as the men and fraud is much rarer among them. As a rule their election methods are honorable and the influence of woman suffrage upon the State has been distinctly for good."

This is a modest position, an authoritative denial from headquarters—but it does not stand in the way of the story. Honor to Mr. Shafroth!

COLUMN 10

March 5, 1904

Gilman here offers an unconventional opinion about suffrage: that disenfranchised women should assist women who have won the right to vote in other states. She also reminisces about the recent women's right convention in Washington, DC, discusses the woman's movement in Asia, and recommends a regimen of healthy exercise for women.

Suffrage Work

Some very interesting confirmation of my views as to how best to work for suffrage—i.e., to set about doing the things we would do if we had it—has been received from two Colorado women.

Both are influential professional women, one in medicine and one in journalism.

"We have the hardest part," said one of them earnestly. "We've got to make good!" They have the ballot and it remains for them to show the use they make of it that the noble purposes of the would-be voters can be carried out.[1]

Everyone watches them; their efforts are mercilessly criticized and misconstrued, yes, and misrepresented; they do, indeed, under many difficulties have to "make good."

The unenfranchised States have begged these successful sisters to help support "the suffrage work"—i.e., the work of trying to get suffrage. How if the unenfranchised—who are so enormous a majority—should reciprocate by helping to support the other side of this effort, the work of using the ballot?

Can nothing be done without the ballot? How is it that the world managed to rise so far as it did before the day of suffrage for anybody? And how is it that the woman's movement has made such marvelous progress in so many lines, even though still so foolishly restrained on this? Here is a large number of intelligent, conscientious women anxious to help their sex and to help the whole world. They assume and quite rightly that the use of the ballot is the quickest way to carry out their good intentions. Very true. They are right but the majority does not agree with them, and in the form of government we are seeking to enter the majority must rule. It then remains, of course, to convert the majority to the views of the minority, which we are patiently striving to do.

But is that all that remains? Is there nothing else we can accomplish in the meantime? And most especially, could we not convert this amiable, evasive, intractable majority sooner if we used other weapons besides argument?

As a matter of fact, have not women without the ballot accomplished great things already in many ways, and is not that accomplishment the best argument in our armory? Is it not something too academic, too metaphysical to keep our main campaign one of argument instead of altering our line of attack to suit conditions of resistance? Are we not somewhat blinded by the undeniable truth that the use of the ballot is the best way to promote progress and so fail to see that there are others? It is as if we were beating and banging on a great locked door, a broad door, an easy door, but a strongly fastened one; and in the meantime some of us actuated by a spirit of practical opportunities had got out of the windows and were on their way already. After all, the ballot is not an end—it is a means. It is a method by which to express opinion—to exert the will. It is the fairest, the easiest, the best, but—there are others. Now it may fairly be held as a matter of policy that if these window-climbers had remained behind the door, battering fiercely, it might have been opened sooner. But it also may be held that if more had got out of the window and gone further on their way, the door would so have been opened sooner. The position of saying, "We will concentrate all our forces on this door and do nothing else till it is opened" is far too much like the position of the orthodox Socialist who refuses to take part in immediate political action because he thinks it is shorter to convert the majority to the Socialist party and then reform everything at once. He honestly believes that is the quickest way to help the world but he cannot prove it. Meanwhile, work along other lines is giving us better conditions which the ultra-orthodox condemns, holding it better to have conditions grow worse and worse, so driving all of us into Socialism. The true Socialist, wishing a better world for all of us, should study more closely the vast and intricate machinery of the society he is trying to influence and move along natural lines. Now we suffragists wish a better world also. We are not as a class a conscious or sex-conscious group seeking to benefit ourselves at the expense of men. If we were, they would be quite justified in opposing us.

We are seeking to benefit both men and women, and children, to benefit the world.

We say, "We want to help the world. The ballot is the best way. Give us the ballot!"

Men say, "We won't."

Then we hammer and hammer and hammer—trying to make or persuade them.

Suppose we say, "O, you won't, you foolish boys, you obstructors of progress! But there are other ways. We *will* help the world—and you can't stop us!"

No more they could!

An editorial in the *Evening Post* of New York speaks with warm approval of the resolution to take part in other movements for social progress adopted in our recent Convention. It gives credit to women for their successful efforts in civic reform and similar lines of social betterment and says: "For the suffragists to take no part in all this has meant complete separation from one of the most vital popular movements of the day and a consequent loss of power and influence."[2]

We may comfort ourselves with the knowledge that much of this good work was done by suffragists; that is, that many valiant workers for immediate good are also workers for suffrage or at least believers in it.

But so long as it is not done by suffrage associations officially, "the cause" gets no credit for it. Now that our National Convention has adopted this line of work, every suffragist should rise to new enthusiasm and do more, far more, than she ever did before.

If it becomes apparent that we love the whole world more than our own sex and attainment more than a comparatively barren devotion, that the good of the community is dearer to us than any "cause" alone, and that the strong and successful helpers of humanity are the very ones who persistently demand the ballot—it will bring on the day of true democracy with speed.

The New Woman in China

The great and growing reform movement in China, which is reaching the women as well as the men, ought to rouse the enthusiasm and assistance of all women the world over. When China moves![3]—there is no excuse for sloth in any place on earth. This oldest of remaining civilizations, which was rich and learned when Abraham left Chaldea to wander in Phoenician wilds,[4] which has lived on unchanged while the rest of the world rose and fell in tumult, and which up to this time has resisted by its huge inertia the encroachments of all nations that could reach it, is now wakening and stirring at last. A more magnificent tribute to the growing unity of humanity could hardly be imagined.

The human race is one race, however so far divided, and in the brain is its ground of union. Common ideals and common efforts to attain them will yet bring us peace on earth and progress nobler and more vital than we dream of yet.

Out of the confusion of many religions and the strong undertow of hereditary habits of mind, we are today at last emerging. The laws of social development are beginning to be learned, laws not dogmas, facts to be studied and lines of action open to all of us.

Here this new Plato, this great Chinaman revered by his followers as a second Confucius,[5] is working out for his country a plan of social reform of tremendous scope. And he starts true to the eternal base, the biological laws of our being, in his proposed "Ministry for the Education of the

Unborn." Men and women are to have equal rights and share in the responsibilities of the government. Think of that—for China!

American will do well to hasten her steps if she wishes to make good her place as leader of the world.

Japan has done more in proportion in the last fifty years than we, more than any nation ever did in the same time, and now if China joins the procession, we may see startling changes in the world's people.

This special ministry is to give attention and care to all prospective mothers with a view to improving and purifying the race. From six to twenty years all children are to be given equal education and, following that, training in their preferred occupation after a compulsory year spent in the "Ministry for the Care of the Sick and Aged." Legal supervision is to be exercised over marriage of all criminals. Kang Youwei, the promulgator of this great plan of reform, is a friend of the young Emperor, but the extremely able and wholly reactionary old Empress has blocked the movement so far.[6] A sad sight that—to see one of the ablest women in power in our times using that power to prevent progress.

A daughter of this great man, Miss Kang Tongwei, edits a woman's paper in Shanghai,[7] and another is now in Hartford—studying to enter Wellesley.[8]

No reformers need weary in the harness if they will but keep their eyes open to the march of events throughout the world.

Social progress is all accomplished through brain-development. As the mind opens, widens, strengthens, we see our way and are able to move. That mind of ours is one the world over, so fast as the Babel walls of language are broken down and so fast as we learn to resist ancestral thought-habits.

If the Chinese can overcome that pressure and bring their highly-developed intellect to bear on our common world problems, it will mean "an open door" to progress for the whole world.

A New York Woman's Club House

The New York City Federation of Women's Clubs is considering the purchase of the Knickerbocker Athletic Club House on Madison Avenue.[9]

It is in some ways more to be desired that women build clubhouses for themselves, but until they do that it is next best to use one already built.

In the report of the proceedings it is regrettable to see how little seemed to be thought of some of the most valuable and attractive features. "There is a swimming bath *which can be let*" and "a gymnasium *to be used for fairs and the like*" (the italics are mine); these enumerated among the assets of the proposed purchase. It may be said in passing that this swimming tank is the best in the city. This is a pity, a great pity. Women can swim as well as men and enjoy it just as much. One of the delights of a clubhouse is to have precisely these privileges—why should the women abjure them? As for the gymnasium—women need gymnastics more than men as they have less exercise ordinarily. But I may misjudge the intention from a newspaper report; perhaps these accommodations were to be let to other women part of the time and the gymnasium only rented for fairs on special occasions.

A city like New York has enough clubbable women to maintain more than one fine clubhouse, and this would be a good beginning. The Woman's University Club has its own home near Gramercy Square but that covers only a small number. The main demand at present in a club building is for rooms to hold meetings, but the further demand for real living conveniences is growing.

In London there are so many pleasant women's clubs—and men's-and-women's clubs as well—that we might be stirred to friendly emulation.

There is the new Anglo-American Lyceum Club for women writers, artists, and such professionals to open in London in June; such a club ought to have headquarters, as it has members, on both sides of the Atlantic. American women travel freely and will enjoy their new clubhouse in London, but they would enjoy having one in New York as well for themselves and for English visitors.

Such a club might temporarily make use of the generous accommodations of the Knickerbocker Athletic.

Housework and Athletics

The indifference of most women to a high standard of physical development is not so much because they are women as because they are house servants.

People who are confined to a house almost all the time, either as performers or overseers of labor, and who find in that house their principal area of expression do not care so much for physical expression.

The Greeks, who carried bodily development to its highest mark, both in strength and beauty, were anything but housebound. In Sparta, where the women had more of this culture than in the rest of Greece, they, too, were far freer from domestic labor.

Housework is not good exercise. It makes one tired, even exhausted, but it does not develop the body nobly and beautifully. Most of it is wearing to the nerves but not to the muscles, and when you have the hard work—washing, ironing, and sweeping—you have the disagreeable and really injurious concomitants of heat and dirt.

The dealing with dirt is almost constant in housework, whether dust, grease, or stains, and the kind of exertion required to remove dust, wash dishes, or launder clothes is not the kind that makes for grace and beauty. When one is through with all this, if one ever is, there is no ambition left to add the wiser and more enjoyable exercises to the previous labors.

Women get tired out doing what is not good for them and have no strength left to do what is. Those who do not do the work but who merely oversee it and who use the house to exhibit their things, their furniture, their clothes and pictures and vases, are not likely to consider the human body as a means of expression. It may be an admirable clothes-horse but not in itself that exquisitely adjusted engine which is the best vehicle of the human spirit.

Athletics needs out-of-door life; the house forbids it. And how may this be helped? It may be helped by women's changing their business. When houses are not horizons, when women work outside of them and get to where they can properly judge them as they never can from inside—then the house and its furnishings will sink to true proportion in life. The exigencies of outside work will necessitate, as has already been shown in large measure, a rational and comfortable costume; dress will become a means to an end instead of the summit of ambition. And then with the house and the dress both in their place, women can begin to see that the body is the first thing to express one's self in.

A larger, more dignified life, broader ideals, more rational habits, higher purposes—these may be expected as women come out of their little monogamous harems and take part in the world's work. Then as human beings they will want human bodies—human first, female second. And human bodies need human exercise to develop them, scientific and constant work, exhilarating and delightful play, neither of which is to be found in domestic labor.

COLUMN 11

March 12, 1904

Gilman praises a pair of advocates for women's education: Mary Mills Patrick (1850–1940), president of the American College for Girls at Constantinople from 1890 to 1924; and Sarah Porter (1813–1900), founder of the Farmington School for Girls in Connecticut in 1847. She also indicts the double standard that excuses men for moral lapses while victimizing or blaming women for the same offenses.

Opposing Currents

At a meeting of the Woman's Municipal League of New York, Riverside Branch, Dr. Mary Mills Patrick, president of the Girls' College at Constantinople, spoke on "Civic Conditions in Eastern Cities." She told us of Athens—the great peonine of its ancient days carried undying in Plato's Ideal Republic[1] and its pathetic state today, the people paralyzed by three centuries of Turkish rule and wasting their energies in devoted study of the splendid past.

Ancestor-worship, whether physical as with the Chinese, moral as with the Hebrew, or intellectual as with the Greek, never builds a live nation. Life must grow and growth does not work downward. "Let the dead past bury its dead"[2] should be taught these Eastern peoples. She told us of Sofia, the capital of Bulgaria, of its equal education for girls and boys, even co-education in one school, and of its splendid woman teacher—a graduate of this college of Dr. Patrick's, who kept on teaching even when her husband was prime minister.[3] She showed how wide a list of nationalities was covered by their students and how various students, their minds broadened and enriched, go back to their several countries and start schools there—fertile seeds from the parent tree.

She spoke especially of the influence of American thought, American scholarship, on the eastern mind as being particularly beneficial, distinguished always by a freshness, an individuality, a willingness to see new truth and follow it.

As Dr. Patrick spoke, she brought to us a breath of that vast world-service which is more important than world-politics and the intimate touch of a dozen nations and their mixed and warring race elements. We felt the difference in *time* which separates people. We live in the twentieth century—Turkey does not. Greece does not. "The age we live in" varies with the varying races of the earth; it is not measured by the passing cycles of astronomy. Across these gulfs and precipices stretches the wonderful power of social transmission, that exquisitely distinctive prerogative of humanity by which we may transfer to the lesser the gain of the greater and bridge these chasms for the common good of the world.

More and more with every step of progress we see this vast current of social transmission reaching around the world evening up the inequalities of race by education, by commerce, by personal contact, by the use of the same material instruments of progress with their inevitable practical influence.

And against this current we may see, too, in every people an opposing current, a thick, black, heavy stream welling slowly up from the unburied past. This opposing current is that of heredity, physical and social—physical heredity which tends to preserve the earlier type of body and brain, and social heredity, far more dangerous, which makes a religion of ancient ignorance and forces it relentlessly upon each new-born child.

This is one of the most dangerous forces in human life. No other animal has it to combat. They may have the errors of the past incorporated in their physical bodies but they do not have them educated into their very souls as a religion.

The mind has its inheritance as well as the body. Such and such habits of thought and feeling leave their impress on the physical brain and predispose the child to adopt similar habits. Then if the conscious effort of his parents and teachers and the unconscious effect of his whole environment is to hammer in those same old feelings and ideas, we have race heredity—one of the hardest things to resist.

The nations of the East, unmoved for centuries, convinced of the final truth of their own religions, worshipping what is old, condemning what is new, pour into the helpless minds of their children a tremendous current of feeling, personal, religious, national, and others. This stream of race heredity tends continually to refill the world with the same kind of people and resists all change and progress. Against it is rising from year to year, spreading wider and wider, faster and faster the ever-increasing force of social transmission.

The gain of the ages, embodied in a thousand forms of use and convenience and kept a living spirit in transference of language, art, and personal contact is now being distributed over the early most beneficently.

It is the stronger of the two. It is irresistible—in the end. The nations assimilating most of the gain of the ages are the dominant nations and will ultimately influence all toward that great goal of universal peace and common progress to which we are tending. Toward this end every living member of society may help, not only by promoting such prominent influences for international good as this Girls' College at Constantinople, but each in her own person by steadily combatting the current of race prejudice in herself, by resolutely turning her face from the old and toward the new.

Most of all—and no human duty is paramount to this—the educators of children should use their immense power to stand between the child and the past—to keep the past off him—not pile it on. The child should learn to know and love the life of today and the hope of the future before he studies, for avoidance, the errors of the past.

The Memorial to Miss Porter

To honor the memory of Miss Sarah Porter, founder and principal of the Farmington School, an annex to the New York Exchange for Women's Work, is to be erected. Graduates and friends contribute the money. There is to be a Dutch lunchroom, archaic and artistic, having a stone fireplace large enough to hold hewn logs. There is a parlor, a special parlor where will be exhibited the work of such Farmington girls as may contribute to the Exchange and where other Farmington girls will come and buy. Then there is on the third floor a sort of clubhouse accommodation for Farmington girls visiting New York.

To erect a memorial to a strong and useful woman, one prominent in the world's greatest work, education, is well. To put it in the form of a clubhouse for temporary use of members or graduates of a school is at least a practical comfort to the living if no special honor to the dead.

But to make a place for this particularly trivial and limited performance—the exchange of woman's work—and call that an honor to one who gave her life to grand, legitimate Human work is absurd. It may be a good and necessary thing to have these places for the benefit of women who need money and who are unable to take part in any legitimate industry, or who are perhaps not unable but so falsely proud that they prefer this limited "exchange" on a strictly lady-like basis to the real exchange of the world's market, or who prefer the extra price of wealthy or charitable purchasers to the plain market price of their products.

The Exchange for Women's Work may be a necessary step from helpless homebound lives to real citizenship, but it is difficult to see how such a place redounds to the credit of a real worker like Miss Porter. Fancy a memorial to Dr. Arnold of Rugby[4] consisting of a building for the exchange of men's work—for the private purchase of pitying friends! This whole position of making special arrangements for women's work as if it were sub-, super-, or at any rate extra-human is wrong.

"Woman's work" is the bearing and rearing of children—and is not exchangeable!

Making things, decorating things, all forms of production great and small—this is human work. Nothing could more conspicuously set forth the inferior development of women as human beings than these baby steps of theirs in the direction of "work."

It is the more pitiable because every main line of industry was begun by them in the long proto-social period, the era of the matriarchate. To work is not a misfortune forced upon the reluctant "lady" by "reverses"; it is the essential dignity of human life. Her ignominy was in not being taught to work in the first place.

Perhaps after all I misjudge the purpose of the builders of this memorial. Perhaps they do recognize perfectly the eleemosynary character of the institution and are erecting it in that spirit as one might in England erect an almshouse.

The "Double Standard"

There is one reason for the double standard of morals for men and women and for the widely varying judgment based on that standard which is not often advanced.

Why is it, we cry protestingly, that a man may sin against morality and yet remain an honored member of the community and if a woman commits the same sin, she is an outcast beyond forgiveness? Here is a very practical answer. Because a man is a useful member of society in several ways. His failure in this one relation does not prevent success in others. Society has need of his services and finds him just as useful as he was before. Therefore, he is still valued and perhaps honored, not for his chastity but for his business ability.

Now the woman, speaking generally, is not a member of society at all. She is a member of the family. She lives in relation to some man as wife, wife-to-be, or wife-has-been. She is valued and judged accordingly.

If she sins in that relation, *she has no other to fall back on*. She is disqualified in our judgment for that particular position and she has no other. Where you do find women eminent and powerful in political position, as among queens and nobles, or eminent and powerful in the arts, as great actresses or singers, there you find the same leniency of judgment as in the case of men.

We may disapprove of some of the conduct of George Sand but she is George Sand still, the great author[5]—there is something left to approve of. Similarly, on a very low industrial plane, we are not critical of the character of the charwoman or the barmaid. If a person is useful in many ways, they may err in one and still be valued in the others. If a person is useful in but one way—and has rather an arbitrary rating at that—then if they err, they are not otherwise valued.

As a matter of pure morality, chastity is a virtue for either man or woman but not more so for one than for the other. When women are strong and active in social service in as many ways as men, they can afford to be more lenient to one another in this one line of error and they can also afford to be more strict with regard to men.

"Wanted—Young Girl to Mind Baby and Do Light Housework"

Well—what is there unusual about that? Nothing. It is perfectly usual, common, universal.

The young girl is very young, in this case just an extra. She is very ignorant and of poor extraction—else she wouldn't do it.

But that is not material. She may be 13 or 14—with all a child's limitations; she may have had but little broken schooling and no other education; she may have had—probably has had—the lowest of home influences and street or shop influences as well. She may not be worth more than the $2 a week she will get—if she gets that. But she is quite competent in the mind of the divinely-endowed mother of the family "to do light housework" and to "mind the baby."

The light housework—dusting, dishwashing, setting the table, preparing the vegetables, making beds. Nothing of importance here—only the health and comfort of the family and somewhat of its prosperity.

Minding the baby—taking it out in the little carriage, watching it while it toddles about, staying in the house while the mother is out or otherwise engaged—that's all. She is not the final arbiter of the baby's health and education, that supreme power is with the divinely-endowed aforesaid; but she does have charge of that baby for a good many hours when the mother is absent from home.

And how many of those all-important first impressions, how many answers to first questions, how many strange and vivid tales, how many exhibitions of irresponsible authority does this young girl contribute to the unfolding brain she has charge of! What a comment it is on our motherhood—what a glaring, ghastly proof of our incompetence that we should think the care of a child of such small moment, a thing to be done by a "young girl" in the interval of "light housework"!

"Women in Panic in Blazing Car"

That is the way the newspaper described it.[6] It must be exciting to be penned in thickly in a car and have it blaze up under your feet and around you—you being a woman unaccustomed to active exercise and encumbered with a mass of inflammable loose clothing. But on this particular occasion there was a man, a big man, too, the paper said, who also got excited. He was trimly clad in heavy woolen goods after the fashion of his kind; he was capable of active exercise and free to make it for he was outside. Yes, this big man was on the platform, where he remained, jumping up and down and screaming with terror. He refused to get off. When a policeman tried to grab him and pull him off, he bit the policeman's finger. So great was his terror of the fire, he didn't feel that he bit the policeman who tried to rescue him.

And over a paragraph describing the performance of this jumping, screaming, biting idiot is the heading "Women in Panic in Blazing Car." If the women were in a panic, what was the man in?

COLUMN 12

March 19, 1904

When the Russian army invades Manchuria, Gilman condemns imperialism. Never a pacifist, she nevertheless opposes wars of aggression. She also extols a progressive Wisconsin politician lost to history and makes the case for wider educational opportunities for young women and the role of philanthropists and suffrage clubs in civic improvement.

Our Attitude Toward Russia

In the very general comment on the feeling of the American people toward Russia and among the various explanations of our sympathy for Japan, little importance seems to be given to the ethical values involved. We are so generally accepted in Europe as being a nation of money-getters that, when seeking to explain any national act or attitude, a commercial interest is looked for. Russia is our friend; Russia has done us no harm; why should we side with Russia's enemy? There are reasons much deeper than our desire for an open door for trade.

The last fifty years have brought the peoples of the world into an intimate acquaintance and contact of rapidly increasing extent. We know each other now as was impossible in earlier days. Governments upholding traditions and precedents and acting through military movements as they did in the time of Rameses[1] fail to recognize the new intelligence and power beneath them. But underneath the crust of precedent and ancient custom, the social consciousness grows more and more alive.

In our country, where the diffusion of intelligence is so great and the relation of the individual to the government so vital, where the press with all its crass abuses still does convey to the people such an amount of information, this social consciousness is far more awake than in a less highly organized nation.

It is this vast body of awakened people, inevitably aware of what the world is doing, that gradually accumulates a sense of approval or disapproval for the actions of the world. In the two countries now at war, a difference as of black and white is shown as judged by the standards of national progress in America. Never a nation on earth has so come forward to embrace what is good, to seek enlightenment, to find the best and to adopt it as has Japan.

There is no parallel in history for its progress. To put behind the sacred tradition of an Oriental past, to pocket the natural pride of national egotism and admit the superior methods of strangers, to be willing to learn of all peoples and to put in practice their advantages as fast as possible—this is the marvelous achievement of the world's most precocious child. We had English blood in our veins, English traditions of liberty behind us. We had a virgin continent to grow in and a flood of ambitious immigrants to do the growing—everything to help and nothing to hinder.

Japan, with the immeasurable past of the sleeping East to hold her down, with a small, crowded country and only her own well-endowed people, has "lifted herself by her bootstraps" in fifty years. Sending her sons and her daughters, too, in some cases to learn foreign languages and customs, she has selected that which was good from other lands and incorporated it in her own. Our pride is flattered by this frank admission that we have institutions worth adopting and our hearts are moved to honest admiration for the intellectual power, the courage, the patience of these, the only Orientals who have allied themselves with the future, of an Eastern land where hopes and achievements have supplanted memories and dreams.

While Japan has thus honestly won the sympathy and admiration of the civilized world, what has Russia been doing?

Her people, it is true, have done much. Brave and far-seeing novelists have drawn the veil from the national life, have shown us with ruthless accuracy how Russians live. The giant figure of Tolstoy looms across the world in protest against the evils of his beloved land.² The students pour out their flood of passionate enthusiasm in fruitless resistance to the government and in fruitful sowing among the peasantry. There is a slowly rising flood of rebellion against hoary injustice, repressed and crushed down everywhere yet seething and pushing underneath. The people of Russia are people of the world like all of us and want to grow.

But as a nation, in its action before the world's judgment seat, Russia has not won approval. One splendid deed is to her credit—the freeing of the serf.³ And then the imitation of the universal peace movement. However the purpose of this step be criticized, the step itself is toward the highest level of civilized life. But in the face of these we have the long black record of ruthless oppression, the cruel iron hand on Poland, the bloody persecution of the Jew, the peculiarly conspicuous outrages upon Finland, and the policy of brutalizing repression on her own people with its horrors of prison and exile. These are not things another government takes action on but they are things that the people of the world form judgment on.

"I have always been your friend," says a big neighbor. "I have exchanged polite visits, I sold you the lot you wanted, I came and stood in your yard when the scrap was going on, yet now I have a fight you are cheering on the other fellow—I don't understand it."

And then we explain that our large and keen-eyed family have heard the screams of his children under cruel punishment, seen the helpless ignorance in which he kept them, frequently received those who fled into our yard because of his unbearable cruelty and heard their complaints, and that our family have thus gathered some feeling against him. He does not see that these things are any of our business.

We have not made them our business to the extent of trying to govern his household for him but we cannot help the effect on our feelings.

So in this open issue of war, our government remains friendly to the Russian government—and to the Japanese—and properly neutral in official deed, but our people honestly admire the splendid progressiveness of Japan and honestly condemn the archaic despotism of Russia.

Our own misdeeds are too patent for us to take any very lofty ground. We have oppressed the Indian and the African and the Filipino; we, too, have corruption in high places; we can say little of the slaughtered Jew while we burn the Negro alive; but we do have a record of progress not yet matched, and we blame in others the very evils we have to admit in ourselves.

A Piece of the Millennium[4]

While open war and hidden crime still go on, we need to know for our soul's sake of the good and beautiful social processes that go on, too.

No better way upward is open to us than that of education, free, wholesale education, gaining every year in stock of knowledge to be shared, gaining faster yet in methods of imparting it, and gaining most of all in new appreciation of what the human creature is and how best to develop him.

For this high end "all creation groaneth and travaileth"[5]—to make better people.

The slow, blind process of evolution fetched us up as far as the human animal and since then we have complicated that useful method with our conscious efforts, more rapid but not always moving upward.

Now we are learning to combine the two, to study nature's laws and model ours upon them, and the result is better.

The education that recognizes the body as the most immediate vehicle of the soul, that trains all faculties to their fullest, that brings out in the child the power and the love and the habit of *doing* things—as well as forcing him to learn a number of facts about things—this is what goes furthest to make better people. Combine this with a wise psychology, a method which enlists the cooperation of both rich and poor, which maintains personal initiative and develops wide mutual service, and you have about as valuable a social institution as we can now imagine.

All this in singularly purity and efficiency we find in the schools of Menomonie, Wisc.

The most recent reference to this is a descriptive article in the March issue of *World's Work*, one of the series of investigations made by Miss Adèle Marie Shaw.[6] The matter is particularly interesting to my own mind because I have been there and seen these wonderful schools. For thirteen years one wise, far-seeing citizen has been working toward this beautiful end and the other citizens have cooperated with him.

Senator James H. Stout is the man, Wisconsin's noblest servant.[7] Through such improved schools as may serve as world models, through traveling libraries by means of which the stimulus and inspiration of society's great heart is pumped out into the farthest outlying districts of scanty and isolated inhabitants, through the soundest views of genuine democracy and the practical application of them, this wise man is improving the human race of his locality by the highest and swiftest of social processes.

As we read of this beautiful provision for happy growth, this greenhouse for humaniculture where health and happiness and knowledge and skill are the portion of practically every child, it seems almost too good to be true.

Manual training from kindergarten to college is the keynote, or motor-training as they are calling it now, a far better term, and a training school for manual training teachers. A "plant" of unsurpassing privileges, where they handle their wood from green lumber to finished product and make tools and machines as well as use them. A gymnasium, where instruction is given to girls and boys, to men and women, and the largest swimming tank in the world which is open to school children—80 feet by 30. They have to learn to swim; it is part of the curriculum. The County Agricultural School stands near, one of the first two in the world, and the County School for training rural teachers. Mr. Stout was the active factor in securing these.

Wisconsin also has seven State Normal Schools and the effects of this full and thorough training are visible all through the State to the remotest district school. Beyond all this—and I can give here but a small part of the spreading advantages already secured—is a further purpose to add a Trade School where the pupils may finally specialize and learn under the best influences the work of their lives.

With the full and careful record of this school life, with conference of parents and teachers, with the child's unusually well-developed personality to speak for itself, the best results of this long training will be secured to the citizens.

It is this which comes so close to the millennium—and is so far put in practice in this little city in Wisconsin. When the community intelligently goes to work to make the best possible product of its young stock—of every last and least competent citizen, no less a citizen at six or ten than at sixty—then we shall be able to tell what humanity is really worth.

And if it is so good already under terrible disadvantages, so patient and generous and loving, so brave and resourceful and gloriously productive, what will it be when every child has a full, fair chance?

The Girls' Share

It seems ungracious to find fault with so beautiful a work as that of the Menomonie schools, but one criticism is to be made—that the training is not equal for boys and girls.

This artificial distinction is already changing. Miss Shaw says: "The directors of the schools, from Mr. Stout to the youngest professor, would be glad to see any boy or girl given the best the school offers. The conditions that curtailed the girls' opportunities are fast giving way."

In the gymnasium there is full equality. Mr. MacArthur, the director, wisely says: "It is previous to her fourteenth year that a girl can best be developed and strengthened for the duties of life. Up to that time she is the boy's equal or superior in physical prowess if given an equal chance." And again: "No amount of subsequent physical training will compensate for the loss of freedom during the years from nine to fourteen."[8]

This is perfectly true and applies to all education—mental as well as physical. In the especially valuable motor-training it still holds good. All that the boy learns of wood and iron, of plan and execution, the girl should learn, too; and all that she learns of textile fabrics and food values, of management and economy, he should learn, too.

It is a serious mistake to divide trades on sex lines; if these things are taught as trades, as educational processes, there is even less excuse for dividing them.

If the girl must needs be a house servant all her life, she ought to have the fullest training in other lines of work before this limitation shuts down on her.

The crying need among women is development along human lines, not those of sex, and no better process is yet discovered than this early motor-training.

Let Menomonie lead in full and equal training for its daughters and sons and the rate of improvement in citizenship will be doubled.

Carnegie's "City Beautiful"

One of the increasingly numerous efforts to improve human life that so distinguish our time is in the plan made to make Dunfermline, Scotland, a sort of civic ideal. The beautiful project has been described at length, *Mr. Carnegie's* donation of a Park and Glen and $2,500,000,[9] and the careful plans made by the Institute for Social Services.

Beautiful buildings, model homes, all manner of provision for boys and girls, for amusement, instruction, recreation are provided, but not a word of any change or improvement in the work of women. So accustomed are we to the presence of women as life-workers in the home that we accept it as a fact of nature and never dream that it may have serious and unpleasant consequences in the workings of the body politic. Morris in his *News from Nowhere*, that graceful picture of a happy life under enlightened anarchy, represents the women as perfectly contented to sweep and clean and cook as before.[10] Anything and everything may change but this—this is an eternal as the eternal feminine itself.

That is the ground of our error. We assume these labors to be in some mysterious way feminine—to belong to the sex—and naturally fear to change that primal fact. As if we could!

As if a division established a million of years before humanity began could be altered by a change in profession!

But *human* character can be altered by such a change of profession, and nothing is more needed in the world today than a change in human character.

No "city beautiful" can be realized until it has citizens with broad minds, free souls, and full-sized consciences, and these are not bred in the kitchen.

A city where both men and women are citizens, where they share in all the work, all the honor, all the pleasure, all the pride can be beautiful as no crippled community of half-citizens may dream.

But that requires such rational development of our allotted "domestic industries" as shall bring them into line with the present work of the world—and their patient performers with them.

What Shall the Suffrage Clubs Do?

In the new purpose of our earnest workers to broaden their lives and attain their great end the sooner by taking in others as a means to it, the question of what to do is a most important one.

The easiest way, the most natural, and the one that will no doubt be most frequently followed is to take up immediate local issues. The smallest village or the largest city alike offers opportunity of this sort.

Special information can be obtained as to civic improvement, what is being done in different places and the best methods, from the Institute of Social Services, 287 4th Ave., New York. What has been done by women's clubs in this line is of very direct encouragement, and enough of our members are members of these other clubs to know what is being done—what needs to be done. The point we wish to gain is to associate public service with the suffrage movement in the popular mind. What is done by other clubs—though more than half their members may be believers in the suffrage—does not count to our credit.

If every city and town in America had a suffrage club which could say, "We have labored in the interests of the community, we have improved the schools, improved the roads, improved the buildings, improved the sanitation, helped to prevent vice and crime; give us the ballot that we may do it better and more easily"—that demand would be hard indeed to refuse.

Suppose that a suffrage club invited several representative workers to come and state their views as to what was most needed in the city. That would give a number of things to choose from.

Suppose they found there were insufficient school buildings and said, "We will work for this—the children of this city shall have schools." Then they would need to study the subject, find out about the city government, the appropriations needed, the obstacles to overcome. Even if they could not accomplish all they wished they would be that much wiser citizens, that much better fitted to use the ballot wisely when they get it.

Suppose they took up the crusade against consumption or the effort to ensure pure milk or to secure a better water supply.

The secret of successful democracy is that every citizen should act like a wise king. He should know, he should care, he should do as far as he can. "The people" is king in our country and a very careless and indifferent king he is. Simply to elect a good man to do our work and then leave him unwatched, unhelped, unpraised, and unblamed unless he succumbs to the temptation of office grossly offends—that is not good government.

A wise, conscientious, far-seeing people cannot be misgoverned for they are the government. Now we women claim our share in the government and it is denied us. Never mind. Let us do our share wisely and bravely whether we are allowed the easiest means or not. Easy or hard, there are all these things needing to be done and we can help.

COLUMN 13

March 26, 1904

Gilman again reiterates the purposes of her column: She underscores the importance of voting rights but relates it to such issues as the right of both men and women, especially women teachers, to marry at their own discretion, and of women's need for economic independence and professional childcare.

What Are Vital Issues?

I called this department "Vital Issues" because I meant to treat in it matters of fundamental importance to the world and women, to women as related to the world. The question of equal suffrage is a vital issue, surely—for which this paper stands preeminently—but there are others, not conflicting by any means, all tending to the same end of human betterment.

Every intelligent, conscientious man or woman wants to improve the conditions of life on earth. We can see that our life needs improvement—that is glaringly conspicuous; we can see that it has improved—that is comforting; and then we plunge in according to our lights and seek to improve it further.

The ground of discussion is on methods, how best and quickest to reach the desired end. An extremely primitive method is that of charity. Assuming material goods to be the desirable end and that some have these and others have not we say, Let him that hath give to him that hath not and all will be well.[1] But all is not well. Apply the constructive imagination to this process, carry it out to the full—what is the result? Owing to several causes, certain persons possess a surplus of goods and others are minus; to continually distribute these goods by charitable methods does not raise the value of the human stock receiving them but deteriorates it and also deteriorates the giver.

Charity does not improve the human race. It is at times an essential temporary measure but it is not a permanent benefit to society; it is not a vital issue. What is?

Anything which tends to preserve and improve our lives, the questions of social physiology rather than pathology.

Irrigation in the arid West is a vital issue. Immigration, education, civil service reform—we all know the vital issues before the public in general.

But the existence of a woman's paper presupposes some distinct interests for her; we wish to present here the vital issues for woman. These can apply to her only wherein she differs from man—in the essential and natural distinctions of sex and in the arbitrary and unnatural distinctions which have been forced upon her.

To woman as woman, freedom to choose the best husband, the best father for her children, is a vital issue, and that involves economic independence. No amount of political equality will guarantee independence so long as women must get their livings from their husbands.

After this primal necessity of personal independence comes the further duty of human motherhood, the complex problems of the best care and education of the child. There is no more vital issue than this—to the whole world in its results, to women in that they were responsible for the fulfillment of this great duty. Quite beyond this question pertaining naturally to woman as such come the many others which appeal to her in her unnatural position of forced objection. Here is where the right of suffrage comes in—a human right belonging to all members of a democratic government irrespective of sex, and all those minor claims for common justice, for property rights, equal education, and whatsoever liberties belonging to the people of our place and time.

The claim of women today should be first for economic independence as a condition to the right fulfillment of the primal duty of motherhood; second, for a far wiser provision for infant education—in further fulfillment of the same duty.

After these and without any regard to being women, our claim as human beings is for equal suffrage and equal rights everywhere in the field of world service. To see the justice of these claims and not only their justice as benefitting us but their value to the whole world, and then to urge them, to demand them, to secure them, and to prove our right to them—this demands a clearer, stronger view of life than most of us have today.

The harm done to the world by the long subjection of women is greatest in its effect on character. We have been forcibly confined so long to our harems or our homes that we forget there is a world outside. We have been so restricted to first-hand personal duties and interests that it is hard for most of us to recognize that there are world duties and world interests. If men had been kept at compulsory home-service for all these thousands of years, they would suffer like effects.

In the splendid awakening of today, the unfolding of crippled wings, the feeble, uncertain efforts with members long disused, we women find ourselves confronted with the confusion and pressure of the world and are ill-equipped to meet its demands. Fortunately, we are not required to do the impossible. While we press on to the beautiful things that shall be, we are still comfortably supported by things as they are. Our sense of immediate personal responsibility is bred of our domestic cares. The house-mother is the pivot on which all turns, and when she seeks to work in larger relation she feels as if she were still the pivot, as if every problem in the world was "up to her."

Men do not feel this way. The habit of organization teaches a divided responsibility. The visible interdependence of the trades shows that no man is wholly changeable with the faults and virtues of the system.

We need to acquire a sense of calmness and patience.

Here is the world—full of trouble but still gaining all the time.

Here we are, just wakening from our long sleep—or stupor, coming forward as a vast reserve force to help humanity, to bring the mother-power into full play, and to add to mother-power the long-suppressed ability of half the human race. In such a tremendous era we need not hasten unwisely but study the field before, select the wisest avenues of advance, and then move out and on—an irresistible, upbuilding force.

Marrying and Money

There has been a good deal of talk and newspaper filing of late on the question, "Should a man marry on a thousand a year?" A pretty girl reporter came to interview me on the subject. "Should bank clerks marry on a thousand a year?" she asked. "Why not?" said I. "There are two of them—two thousand dollars—they could live very comfortably on that."

"Why, no," she said, "there is only one."

"Oh! I thought you spoke of their marrying—marriage takes two," said I.

"But they are not both bank clerks!" she cried.

"Why aren't they?" I inquired politely. And she was somewhat at a loss. Then I gave her another chance. "Well, suppose she isn't a bank clerk or any other kind of wage-earner. She can do all the work. They can get a nice flat in Harlem for $300 a year, food, gas, and so on $400; that leaves $300 to dress on and for car-fares and such. They could live very comfortably on a thousand."

But my interlocutor was not satisfied. "Oh, no," quoth she, "the wife would not want to do the work. They'd have to keep a girl. The question is could a man support a wife on a thousand dollars a year?"

"If you are asking whether a man could maintain one honest working woman with wages and another idle woman who did nothing at all for her living on a thousand dollars a year—why, no. Of course not. But why should he? Surely, if a woman cannot work like other industrious mortals and be paid for it, the very least she could do is to work at home without pay!"

Nevertheless, the pretty little reporter seemed to think it quite likely and not at all improper.

It brings up a very interesting question, though not a new one. For what is the woman maintained who does not work either at home or abroad? How does she justify to herself her position in the world?

Here are all these people everywhere, working so hard to produce and distribute wealth, making all kinds of beautiful, valuable, and ingenious things, lifting, always lifting the standards of civilization, making the world wiser, safer, cleaner, healthier, better in a million ways.

And here are these women—those who do not even do the housework—taking advantage of every upward step, claiming every comfort and luxury they can secure, well-dressed, well-housed, well-fed, well-educated, and doing nothing whatever to add to the good of the world.

Of course, no poor man can keep a white elephant of that sort. The less they do the more they want. Therefore, they must needs "marry" money. They may not deliberately prefer an aged millionaire to a hearty young bank clerk; they may insist on some manly virtue besides hard cash; but no man can marry them who has not "the price."

This class of women is quite large among us, about a fifteenth of the female population—over two million. And as they are usually more influential than the rest of the thirty million as they are seen and heard and attended to while the great dumb majority toil in their separate kitchens, they count for more than numbers.

The position of women in regard to money is a "vital issue" undeniably.

A Child's Vocabulary

Prof. John J. Jegi of Milwaukee has made a most interesting study of a child's vocabulary.[2]

He kept a notebook when his little child began to talk and set down each new word as she learned to use it. When she was four years old, he had a stenographer follow her about one day and take down every word she uttered. From this and other study of older children he has summarized as follows:

A child of two years uses	1,200 *different words*
Child of four years	3,300
Child of six years	4,600
Pupil in 8th grade, fourteen years	8,000
Student of twenty, attending normal school	16,000
Man of ordinary culture	25,000
Learned man	33,000

Everything that brings to our consciousness the vital importance of these early years of human life, the dignity and ability of a little child, is of value because in time it will help us to adjust our ideas of infant education to in some ratio to the facts.

We persist in treating babies and little children as if they were not yet educable, as if all they needed was the care of a servant or of the average mother, who knows little more. We send out our little children with nursemaids as we might send out geese with a goose-herd, someone to keep them within bounds and see that the fox does not get them—that is all. The older mind we spend large sums to educate. We build great schoolhouses and greater colleges; we hire competent teachers and tax ourselves again to provide normal training schools to make them more competent. We recognize the brain in the older child and do what we know how to develop it.

But we do not recognize it in the baby.

If an animal had a vocabulary of 1,200 words like our two-year-old, we should think it had some intellect. But being a baby, we fail to recognize it. As a matter of fact, the baby brain needs the very highest kind of culture, not in the higher mathematics, to be sure, but in such exquisitely adapted environment under such expert guidance that it may be stocked with a magnificent assortment of first impressions in due sequence and arrangement. The clarity of vision, power of thought, surety of judgment, accuracy of impression which we might ensure to our little ones by wise care in infancy would make all the further problems of life far easier to them.

Married Teachers

The Court of Appeals in New York has reversed one previous decision and sustained another, deciding that a woman teacher who marries cannot on that account be dismissed by the Board of Education.[3] The court did not commit itself on the reason or unreason of the regulation forbidding women to marry.

It is not a very deadly matter, only one more of the instances showing our general conviction that a married woman "belongs" solely and wholly to her husband, that her work must be domestic, and that if a mother, she cannot be anything else. Of this particular profession—the education of children—one would think that motherhood would add greatly to a teacher's usefulness.

If motherhood is all that we claim for it—if it opens the heart, stimulates the mind, enlarges the sympathies—if above all it develops love and understanding of children—surely it must be an advantage of a teacher.

Can it be possible that we do not in our hearts believe all this, that we in reality are but too much afraid that motherhood would only mean a concentrated passion for its own children and a decrease of interest in others or ability to care for them? Or is it that we think that children have a right to the whole time and attention of their own mother—though she were a college president? Are we so sure that it is good for them?

Speaking of teachers and mothers, it is interesting to note that the Syndic of the Paris Municipal Council recently urged upon the Educational Department of the Seine[4] that they teach their children about the Franco-Russian alliance,[5] the Russo-Japanese war, and the Hague conference,[6] and that they inculcate a horror of war. Nevertheless, they must also be taught that so long as there was no Supreme Court of Arbitration their serenity required constant vigilance and in time of danger they must "fly to the flag."

This is really a very promising thing. It shows faintly but unmistakably our dawning recognition of how much can be done for human nature when we begin to get at children universally, when the most enlightened and recent feelings of humanity can be brought to the young citizen through the State machinery of education instead of leaving him wholly to the influence of tradition and intense personal feeling in the family. A sense of world-citizenship brought home to the heart of the child will lift us fast and far.

COLUMN 14

April 2, 1904

This two-part column reads like a précis of Gilman's treatise *The Home* (1903). In the first part she responds to a pair of complaints about her denigration of housework and the traditional division of labor in marriage. In the second she outlines what she considers a "model home."

As to Housework

The appeal of "L.N."[1] in the last issue of this paper goes quite to my heart. So also do others I have received by letter and by word of mouth—there are many. Thoughtful, intelligent, conscientious women cannot fail to respond energetically to so direct an attack on a time-honored institution as I am making.

As one good friend remarked, "I do not like your books. I am not going to read any more of them. They make me uncomfortable." "You do not have to believe them," said I. "Yes, I do," she answered. "That is just it. While I read them I have to believe them—afterwards I don't."

A better tribute author could not wish.

A correspondent asks, "Won't you be good enough to look at things from my point of view for a moment? Women have *not* failed as housekeepers and homemakers; on the contrary, they have achieved praiseworthy success therein. The homes of this country are generally well-ordered, the children well-trained, and the husbands happy and contented."

She goes on to say that wherein women do fall short it is owing to lack of equal power in the partnership and gives this illustration: "Suppose two men are partners in the shoe business. One attends to the outside selling and the other to the inside work of the store. The outside man, however, dictates what wages shall be paid the help; he is free to come in at any time and overrule the inside man's arrangements, to impose extra work, and in general is the recognized authority in the firm. Now if conditions in the store fall short of perfection, would any sane person hold the inside man responsible?"

This idea of a partnership is also set forth in the article by "F.M.A." in our last issue.[2] Says this writer, "If a man and a woman agreed to keep a grocery as equal partners and to an equal division of work whereby the woman should make the sales and receive the money and the man should do the packing and delivering, no power on earth could make that man believe that his work was inferior to the woman's or that he was economically dependent upon her because she took in the money and paid the expenses of the joint business."

The error in this common phrase, "the domestic partnership," becomes apparent if we eliminate the marriage. If household duties were performed by a woman other than a wife—or conceivably by a man—such an employee would never dream of claiming to be a partner. Mr. Robert Webster Jones says: "Two departments engage the energy and attention of the firm, the earning department and the home department."[3] He speaks of the earning as if it were a branch of their common business of housekeeping. A man earns in his trade, his special form of social service, in which the wife takes no part; he earns whether married or single, whether he keeps house or boards. If he loses his wife, gives up his home, he keeps right on with his earning; but if she loses him—where is her end of the business then?

If the wife is "doing just as much for the success of the firm as he is, if not more," as Mr. Jones says, are we then to assume that our few rich men are such by virtue of the special capacity of wives—or that our innumerable poor men are such for lack of it?

Is it not, on the contrary, true that we frequently see most capable women spending valuable energy and ability in managing the "home department" of poor men, and frivolous, idle, extravagant women maintained in luxury by rich men?

Partnership is a very definite business relation recognized by law.

Private housekeeping is not a business at all. To keep oneself fed, warmed, clothed, cleaned, and healthy is essential to life and happiness but it is not a trade, nor is it any more a trade for a mother to do this for her children. When you do it for other people—for pay—it becomes a business, and if two people do it together, sharing the profits and losses, they may be partners. But for one person to engage another *to do it for him* is not a partnership.

A French couple keeping an inn where the husband is cook and the wife is cashier are partners in a common business—they work with each other—not one for the other.

A husband and wife are partners in a sense in one function—that of rearing children; the husband usually contributes the capital required and very little else; the wife doing the rest according to her lights. But this has nothing to do with housekeeping and nothing to do with the woman's claim for "support"—they work together for their common end and he should no more pay her for the labor than she should pay him for the capital. Moreover, if marriage is a partnership as alleged, on what ground does a divorced woman sue for alimony or a widow claim a share in her deceased husband's fortune? There is no fortune made in housekeeping. Does *she* claim to be a partner in *his* business as well as in hers? In this earning department, which Mr. Jones speaks of as if it were merely a subsidiary branch of housekeeping, the husband performs some kind of work for the general market, he serves mankind at large in some branch of industry, and receives from his employer, customers, pupils, or whatever section of mankind at large he touches a return in money. This return represents, justly or unjustly, the amount of their product they give him for what he has given them. "F.M.A." says with what seems a touch of satire, "The man who labors in the 'special and highly organized industry' of digging up paving stones under the imprecatory direction of his 'boss' believes in all sincerity that his day's work of eight hours is superior in itself and of far greater commercial value than that of his wife who, during the sixteen hours of work and care for her home and children, crude as it may be, has combined the knowledge and skill to some extent of a dozen trades and professions."

It is. The man is quite right. Only our lack of knowledge of industrial evolution prevents our seeing it.

The fact that he only works eight hours is one proof of superiority. Organized labor has reduced by half the time spent in its tasks—an advance which means gain for all the world.

The fact that he does one thing well enough to get a dollar and a half a day for it is another proof.

She is still doing parts of many things as man did when he made his own canoes and weapons. A savage can do far more things than a street laborer but that does not show his work to be in advance of or equal to that of the laborer but quite the contrary.

As to the paving stones, it is a very happy instance of high social development. Roads are always a mark of progress; all civilization depends on them.

The devoted wife and mother was doing all she is now—yes, and more—at a period before roads were built, but her ceaseless labors did not advance humanity particularly.

What the devoted housemother confined to the home from the beginning of history utterly fails to see is that while she works tirelessly for her mate and young, he works for something more. She does not go outside except when allowed for amusement. She gives her life to the service of her family and honestly believes that he is doing the same thing. That is why she thinks their work is equal, is a partnership.

If she will but lift her eyes beyond the narrow rim of physical relationship and look abroad over the great, wide, suffering world, if she will study it, care for it, learn to know how it has come thus far toward peace and plenty and how it has failed, if she will honestly recognize how the work of the world has changed and grown and risen and carried the world with it and how the work of the home has not changed and not grown and not risen and not carried anything with it—then she can see the essential distinction between paving a road for the feet of all people and cooking a dinner for her own children. Try to follow this line of development in one industry.

Here is the early savage mother making garments for her young out of hides or woven cedar bark. Follow this as far as you can where only mothers work for their own and you find small progress.

Now follow the growth of textile industries through all the spreading centuries to the infinite variety of fabrics and designs made for us today by innumerable mills—the brocades and velvets and exquisite veilings, the rich and heavy woolens, the sturdy linens like canvas with all that canvas means to the world!—and compare that magnificent development of a great social function with the homespun still made by the housewife in some remote quarter of the backwoods.

"The homespun will wear just as long!" protests the defender of domestic industry.

Yes. A Navajo blanket will wear longer. A shirt of deerskin longer yet—and one's own skin longest of all! The difference is in the degree of development and that is what is so hard to explain to minds accustomed for all the ages to a kind of work in which the only development is in its utensils—made by men outside.

As to liking housework—that proves nothing. I like it myself, always have. No thrill of joyous pride so intimate and sweet as that of the successful cook! And the calm satisfaction of a clean, well-ordered home—when you know that the very backs of the bureau drawers have been scoured and the uttermost rag in the piece-rag is rolled smooth!

What people like—as I have frequently observed before—merely proves what they are used to and brought up to enjoy.

The stagnant races of Asia are profoundly contented; that is what ails them.

Men like to hunt, to go out and kill things, when they have no faintest use or enmity for the victim of their sport. They like it because it is an old, old racial habit, deep-builded into their very bones.[4]

And women like housework for the same reason—because it has been their main occupation for thousands and thousands of years.

As to its being "a healthy stimulus to the whole feminine constitution—if not overdone,"[5] it cannot compare with the healthy stimulus of exercise in the open air. Most of its good effect in this line is due to the inherited conscience which still lulls us with the sense of inherent right in a business which modern reason shows is almost wholly wrong.

Instances are given of the good and great things written by, here and there, a woman in the intervals of housework—a sad, short list! When you think of the splendid work of the great writers of all the world and how much of it would never have been if the scholars and authors had been doing their work in rare moments stolen from cooking and sweeping, and then think not of what a few wonderful women have done in spite of housework but of what the whole great world of women have not done because of it!—then it looks differently.

It is not that we should all write books—Heaven defend us!—but that we should all develop our special ability and use it for the good of the world.

Someone will answer: "Men don't care any more for the good of the world than women do." No? Suppose all the men retired to their several homes and devoted their energies to the assiduous service of their houses and families—where would "the world" be then? There would be no world. Only the earth and savages. The civilized world is the result of extra-domestic efforts, of the extension of great social functions wherein men work together for our common welfare.

Human life does not consist merely in family duties. The main duties of life are social and include the familiar.

A civil engineer plans canals or railroads for many people and from what they give him in return he maintains an expensive and wasteful group of primitive industries in which his wife labors and enjoys. But he is not a partner in her business nor she in his. She contributes no suggestions to the railroads he plans—he contributes none to the management or labor of the house. If she were not there to do it for love, he would hire a servant to do it for money.

A servant is not a partner—neither is a devotee.

"Housework," "domestic industry," is a very old, very inadequate, very exhausting, very wasteful and expensive method of serving the physical needs of the world.

And I might as well spare my readers more repetition and beg them, if they want my full views, to read *The Home: Its Work and Influence*, McClure, Phillips & Co. (with apologies for advertising).

The Model Home

I am asked to give my idea of a model home. Certainly. It is in a small, beautiful, simple house in a fair garden. One's private grass is almost as necessary as one's private room—a home of sunlight and starlight and sweet air. In the home is a separate room for each member of the family and one or more gathering rooms, meeting the twin needs of human life, union and privacy. The house is supplied with perfect plumbing, plenty of conveniences for bathing for all the inmates, thus minimizing labor.

The beauty of the home is first in its own proportion, color, and decoration—a house one would make a picture of with delight or sit in a shaded garden and look at—because it was so beautiful. There would be very little cloth in the home. Cloth is animal or vegetable tissue, dead, and gradually adding dust to the air. Smooth surfaces made soft by color and rich with noble decoration would satisfy the eye, and a system of exhaust sweeping would make it antiseptically clean.

Each bedroom would express the nature and tastes of the occupant and its own main purpose of rest and retirement, and the common rooms have that large, simple beauty necessary to the happiness of a mixed group. The main effect of this home to a visitor would be its distinct expression of the family living there; to the inhabitants it would be to each an intimate personal expression and a common joy. Here young lovers would find their shelter and separation; here baby souls would learn the rudiments of life in peace and concord; here the aged would have that quiet, that aloofness, that enjoyment of long habit they so need; here friends would be welcome. Sounds rather vacant, does it? Nothing going on; what would they *do* in such a house?

Do? Rest and recuperate for the day's work, to be sure—what is home for? Enjoy their own close companionship apart from the rest of the world—the sweet, primal, restful family ties which are so essential a part of life. Invite their own chosen friends to share that aloofness. All that belongs to the physical basis of life, all the close, tender, original ties; these have their place in the home. Perfect fitness, ease, comfort, quiet, privacy, rest, and all sweet family affection and intimacy—these would be ours in such a home—what more do you want?

As to what they would do there—rise in the morning vigorous and happy, dress perfectly for what tasks lay before them, go out gaily and perform those tasks, come back for seclusion and rest and resumption of family ties. And in the hours of absence?—I am talking of a model home, not of a model world. But the babies—the children—where would they be? Asleep in their own rooms or awake in the common rooms or the garden while at home. And where would they be when not at home?

In school: baby garden, kindergarten, school, and college—"models," too, while we are at it. And the mother, the wife, where is she? At home with her family while her family is at home. And where else? In the "model world" I am not describing. But—but—where is the housework? There isn't any to speak of. The exhaust company sucks out the dust as often as necessary; skillful cleaners do what more is wanted when desired. There are not so many "things" to wait on in the model home.

But the dining room—the kitchen! As to the kitchen, that has no place in a model home. If the family prefer to eat at home, the food comes up on a dumb waiter and the dishes return on it.

From where? To where? From the Food Supply Company which any civilized village would maintain with its system of underground connection by which all the common needs of the separate homes were supplied—a finished network of conducts for all pipes, wires, and regular transference of food running to each home from the street mains, all underground, noiseless, safe, clean, easy to keep in repair. Above your truly private home, your private garden, your clean, smooth, tree-shaded street, never torn up but once.

Then the woman would have nothing to do at home? She would have as much to do as the man—no more.

It would be their home. They would take the same pleasure in planning and arranging and adorning it as they do now—with better results. They would have each other's society there and that of the children. They would have everything people have now in a home except care, worry, labor, noise, dirt, interruption, confusion, waste, intrusion, discord, and disease. I admit that takes a good deal out. There would be very little left in some of our homes if all that were gone.

But the model home would replace them with ease and relaxation, peace, rest, quiet, purity, privacy, simplicity, economy, harmony, and health.

"Well," says my reader dubiously, "that's all very pretty but I don't like it. It doesn't sound natural."

True. We haven't got it yet. But we shall like it when we have it.

Now if the reader, vaguely conscious of a lack, missing so much of what she has always considered home life, asks where is all the interest, the effort, the ambition, the love and pride that we now center in the home, the answer is simple and beautiful.

With home an easy, restful place, no tax at all upon our minds and hearts but just pure comfort and recuperation, we could then turn all the power we now spend there and all the tenfold more power we should have with nobler homes upon the world we live in. Interest, effort, ambition, love, and pride—all these gladly poured forth to make the smallest village and the largest city as satisfying and developing as we now seek to make our homes.

Remember that we now waste in our homes two-thirds of the money spent there and almost half the productive labor of the world, to say nothing of the anxious love and care with which we try to "save at the spigot and spend at the bunghole." We seek to make home happy and to keep people there—but people live in the world, which is far from happy and that great neglected world reacts with cruel injury on all our struggling homes.

"The model home" will give us time and strength and wealth, clear minds and overflowing hearts with which to hasten on the making of a model world.

COLUMN 15

April 9, 1904

Born Charlotte Anna Perkins in 1860, named Charlotte Perkins Stetson after her first marriage in 1884 and Charlotte Perkins Gilman after her second marriage in 1900, she allowed in her autobiography that "it would have saved trouble had I remained Perkins from the first" because "this changing of women's names is a nuisance we are now happily outgrowing."[1] Much as she objects to the practice of branding women with their husbands' surnames, she satirizes the idea that parents "own" their children.

Women's Names

"If only our artistic and literary friends of the feminine persuasion might change their domestic relationship without being obliged also to change their names, how many of us would feel that we had not lost a delightful companion! Recall the number in recent years who, for the sake of a mere husband and the meager compensation of a 'Mrs.' have partly or wholly submerged promising and brilliant careers in domesticity." Thus *Current Literature* speaking of Sara Jeannette Duncan—now Mrs. Everard Cotes.[2]

It is a very healthy and promising sign that notice is being taken of this clumsy and injurious custom of changing women's names on marriage. As with most old and general habits, we bear with it, put up with its manifold inconveniences, and either overlook its essential ignominy or absolutely enjoy it. As the devoted Jewish bride cuts off her long and lovely hair and goes ever after in a hideous wig and rejoices to do so "for his sake," as in other races women have patiently submitted to blacken their teeth, pull out their eyebrows, go through all manner of painful and belittling performances to show that they now belong to a man in marriage, so do rational, cultivated Anglo-Saxon women feel no shame but a sweet sense of devotion in "bearing his name."

It is a small enough matter compared to the wig; it is not physically painful and does not detract from personal beauty; and in the long centuries when women were nothing but belongings it caused no inconvenience. Women aforetime not being people but property had no protection save in a strong owner, and the name of the master was as valuable to his woman as to his slave or his dog.

A dog unlicensed is the prey of the dogcatcher and a woman unlabeled had no "protector." So she had first her father's and then her husband's and her only name—her first one—was only used in close intimacy. But now that women are emerging from the long period of subjection to the androcracy, now that they are beginning to be persons, human beings, distinct and useful members of society, it becomes a little awkward now and then to have them nameless.

The clever Anna Stowell Jones made a name in fiction and promptly loses it when she becomes Mrs. Roderick H. Sturgis.[3] If her good man dies and she becomes in time Mrs. Albert Y. Shoemaker, another literary reputation is sacrificed. She may, it is true, keep her "maiden name" as a writer and wear her husband's as a social distinction merely, but why this awkward divergence from the general habit of the race? Charles Dickens, known and loved by all, did not have to go about as Mr. Cordelia Havemeyer (not that that was his wife's name, by the way!); he had one name and made it an honored one and did not have to submerge it in another because of assuming a purely personal relation.

As I pointed out in an article written years ago on this subject, there are four common instances wherein people are required to give up their names—persons who inherit money with this somewhat offensive condition, monks or nuns when they renounce the world and enter the monastic shade, convicted criminals when they go to prison, and women when they marry. This is not nice company. It shows that one's name is something to be proud of and its surrender always more or less of a sacrifice.

One of the large evils of the practice is that we are slowly but surely extinguishing the names of the world. Every time there is a family with only female descendants, that family becomes extinct—so far as name goes. Keep this up long enough and we will all be Smiths and Joneses.

A good many are alarmed at any notion of changing our custom because they fear it would cause trouble and confusion in legal matters. They are perhaps ignorant of the amount of trouble and confusion caused by our present practice, of the fortunes spent every year in tracing female heirs through these transformations, and of the fortunes lost every year—completely lost—to those female heirs because this beautiful custom had hidden them forever!

If men had to submit to any such ignominy, such loss, such inevitable confusion, they would move heaven and earth to amend matters, but women are used to endurance and have not felt this yoke particularly—up to the present.

So long as they were not persons, but only females, it did not matter. Each man marked off his own lot with his own name and it did not concern anyone else. But now that women are resuming their original positions as active members of the species and becoming differentiated individuals with a use in the world beyond their general functions, names are essential to them.

Among the various steps in social progress immediately before us is that of developing a new system of naming human beings, a system which shall not rest on a mistaken theory of masculine supremacy or burden us with genealogical records, but which shall clearly and permanently distinguish individuals.

There need be no fear of sudden and ill-advised action—racial habits take long to change—but this is an important matter deserving careful study by our best thinkers.

Woman's Welfare[4]

This is a small magazine issued quarterly by working women in Dayton, O., devoted to advancing the interests of women and children throughout the industrial world. Its editors belong to the Woman's Century Club, which has been doing valuable work for eight years and is united with the State and National Federations.⁵

They send sample copies of this magazine to "the five powers—Proprietor, Pedagogue, Preacher, Press, and Politician," thus distributing information on their special line to these influential centers of social activity.

An interesting list of "What Some Women are Doing" is given in the current issue.

One instance is of an excellent arrangement between an intelligent woman and a grocer. She takes from him each evening all the fruit he has not sold during the day and makes jellies, jams, and preserves of it—which he sells for her afterward. The advantage to him is in keeping his stock of fruit constantly fresh and losing none of it. She gets special rates in purchasing and a market for her goods. This is an evident gain to both parties—as all righteous trades must be—and deserves to be followed by more women and grocers generally.

Another gives much delight to long-maligned womanhood. It has been charged against us from years immemorial that women could not drive nails. Now here is a woman admitted to full membership in the Master Carpenters' Association. She is a graduate of Vassar and N.Y.U. Law School.⁶

Two damsels making a success of a dainty but cheap lunchroom are not so much of a novelty but furnish a useful illustration of what it is to do "womanly" work as a paying business instead of doing the same thing as a gratuitous part of wifehood (which it is not).

In Michigan, however, is another step out of the usual: a woman who is a jobber and retailer in iron, steel, and heavy hardware. Still more impressive is the account of Mrs. Ira E. Tutt of Los Angeles, a mechanical and electrical engineer who is one of the leaders in her profession in that locality. She has built two big electric plants in Arizona.⁷

These instances, increasing from year to year, from day to day, are cause for deep rejoicing to all thoughtful women. Little by little, facts like these mount up against the wall of prejudice which has hemmed us in so long and will finally sweep it away.

The more thoroughly it is established that women can do good work in the broad lines of general industry, that sex distinction does not apply in the field of social service, the sooner shall we realize that our condition of universal house-service is wholly unnecessary.

What is most needed is for the successful business woman to show a better product in healthy, well-reared children than that of the domestic woman, and this is quite within her power.

The organizing ability that makes success in the world will make success in the home, too. When women realize that the rearing of the world's children *is a business* also—not a trade in the sense of commercial profit but a business-like horticulture—the raising of our most important product—people—then they will cease to consider it as a private matter of their own to be managed and mismanaged at their will.

Property in Children

Most people feel that they "own" their children. In very ancient times they did and could sell or kill them if they chose to. Parental rights have been steadily abridged, child rights are gaining ground, yet in the eyes of the average home-bound woman her child is still her own and she can cheer it, feed it, train it as she sees fit. The State does interfere to check extreme cruelty, absolute neglect, to prevent child labor and to compel education, but in all ordinary limits the idea of any authority outside the family does not cross the mother's mind. The father usually has the power of ultimate decision, but if he agrees with her, they may do what they will with the child.

What is needed here is not arbitrary interference from outside but a change in the parents' standard of judgment.

Take the one point of dressing children. Most mothers honestly feel that they have a right to put on the child whatever seems to them proper and beautiful and never dream that the child has a right—a distinct personal right of his own or her own—to be dressed in accordance with the needs of childhood.

The suffering inflicted on little children by their mothers' vanity is about as unjustifiable abuse of power as the world can show.

Where the child is taught to enjoy and share that vanity—to take pride in elaborate clothing at a period when such sentiment is revoltingly unnatural—the effect is worse. Here we have the soul—the character—ruthlessly degraded during its most impressionable years.

When women find normal expression in legitimate social activity, they will not seek it through personal decoration to such a ridiculous extent and still less will they seek to gratify themselves at the expense of a child's comfort, health, and right endowment.

We should get the *general* viewpoint—consider children as a class—an immense and predominantly important class of human beings whose best service needs our best wisdom, our collective wisdom, and cannot be trusted to the unrestricted whims of personal ownership.

"Naughty Baby," "Good Baby"

"Yes," says the weary striver after righteousness, "'be virtuous and you'll be happy, but an approving conscience is very lonesome company.'"

Then you give warm praise to his efforts and he drinks it in and becomes happier.

Among the truisms of morality is the tremendous influence of one's associates, their approval or disapproval.

We all know how we are led by the people we are with, how sheep-like is the flow of human conduct, how hard it is to be satisfied with the conviction that one has done right when everyone else thinks it wrong. And we have accepted this in our usual patient, stupid way as being "human nature."

Not in the least.

It is human nature to derive intense pleasure from the fulfillment of one's own concept or precept; the workings of one's own brain and their expression in action gives far more intimate and vivid satisfaction than exterior opinion.

It is an artificial trait or rather an artificial exaggeration of a natural trait which makes us so helplessly subservient to praise or blame.

Who forces upon us this dangerous weakness?

Our mothers.

Our dear, loving, primitive, "instinct-guided," utterly untrained mothers.

Little they know of the laws of psychic development in infancy, of how to assist the baby brain to take the reins of conduct. Their only effort is to make the child do certain things they consider advisable and their only means is to turn on the current of approval or disapproval. Ultimate disapproval is punishment, ultimate approval is reward, but they are but the full expression of "naughty baby" or "good baby." This is begun when the child is far too young to know why the parent is pleased or angry; he merely learns—and learns ineradicably—that it feels good to have mother pleased and feels bad to have her displeased. Instead of being trained in the pleasure of right action he is trained in the pleasure of suiting other people—and he never gets over it. If our babies were allowed to share in the benefits which we spare no expense to secure for our older children, then the first habits of the brain might have some chance of right formation—and the whole conduct of the world would change.

COLUMN 16

April 16, 1904

Gilman here praises the theater, particularly the work of the American actor and director Mabel Hay Barrows Mussey (1873–1931), in the education of women; and she outlines for her readers Ward's gynaecocentric theory.

Old Greece in Young America

The work of Mabel Hay Barrows in producing Greek plays has been spoken of in these pages in previous years, but that was when she was doing it for colleges. This year, in Chicago and in New York, she has been bringing *Ajax*, a tragedy of Sophocles, with a cast of real Greeks.[1]

The Chicago performance was at Hull House and Jane Addams said of it that in its purpose, method, and result it was an ideal instance of what Hull House was trying to do.[2]

Miss Lillian Wald of the Nurses' Settlement, who has been called "the Jane Addams of New York,"[3] was instrumental in the production here and it took place in Clinton Hall, the first of those people's casinos put up by the Social Hall Association of this city.[4]

The work as seen by the public consisted in the acting of a fine old play with appropriate setting and costumes by a group of modern Greeks with Miss Barrows in the part of Techmessa and I believe one gentleman who was but half Greek in blood.

It was wonderfully good acting. Ajax, who came from Chicago to take the same part that he did in the Hull House performance,[5] was especially

Figure 2. *Ajax* tableau, Hull House Chicago, "Modern Revivals of Old Greek Plays," *Chautauquan* 43 (April 1906), 156.

impressive, but the merit of the whole number was more astonishing than that of any "star."

That these commonplace mercantile men, whom we know mostly as small dealers in fruit, flowers, or antiques, should be able to recite ancient Greek with dignity and ease and to take part in so exacting a play acceptably—this was what made the presentation notable.

We do not appreciate how generally educated in the glories of their historic past are the citizens of modern Greece, how their former dignity is ever in their minds, and how they have kept alive in unbroken succession their hereditary tradition. Even the ancient rivalry between Athens and Sparta still remains vivid; Miss Barrows found herself obliged to divide the parts equally between her Spartans and Athenians or there was trouble at once.

The actors felt their parts. They admired and enjoyed the tragedy and knew the story of its characters. They were proud of the mighty past they were portraying and proud of showing it to the Americans.

Back of the representation itself with its dramatic, historic, and archeological interest lay the earnest work of the committee who helped prepare for it and the exhausting labors of Miss Barrows. It is difficult to overestimate the quality and quantity of effort required to bring together all the irregular and often warring elements involved in an amateur performance by men of different race, clan, language, education, business—different in all ways yet held together by their common pride. Hard as this work was, it was rendered many times more so by the frequent changes among the troupe, actors laboriously drilled to some degree of excellence and then dropping out suddenly as the time for the performance drew near and the quarrels and misunderstandings always imminent.

It is in such effort as this that Miss Barrows shows real genius. To reach the heart through every shell of outward distinction, to inspire, encourage, illuminate, to convey the feeling of Sophocles and something of her own enthusiasm beside—this was what she was doing through arduous weeks, under incessant disappointments and difficulties.

Still further in, behind the visible performance and all its preliminary labors, lies the large meaning of the work.

Many were the puzzled inquiries as to what it was "for." Was it a charity—to help the Greeks or what? Was it educational—to the actors, the spectators, or both? Did she make money out of it?

Its purpose was none of these. In some degree it touched them all incidentally save the last. Miss Barrows gave months of exhausting work and got nothing save indeed the admiration and esteem of friends new and old. But the real meaning of her work gives it place among the vital issues of our day, for our country in particular, but also for the world as a whole.

The great movement of our age is the unifying of human life, the outgrowing of petty limitations of race and place, and the developing of that noble international consciousness which already is making itself felt.

To this end America is doing magnificent service. This nation was founded on broad lines of human right, rights, liberties, and duties for all men. (Today we even begin to claim them for all women, too.) America in its foundation principle of union—the grouping of independent States in common purpose—has succeeded where ancient Greece in all its grandeur failed and in succeeding has established an organic principle of social life.

America opened her arms to all people and all people came—another mighty step forward toward world-ruling humanity. The push toward universal dominance which Alexander[6] and Napoleon[7] mistook for the dominance of one nation is here rightly expressed.

One people shall rule the earth—but that is when we are all one people and the mingling of races in our country is the first great historic example of such a world-blend.

Even Rome at her broadest had no such cosmopolitan blood nor sentiment. Her patricians still ruled in the one central city; here even the New England Brahmin[8] is unable to maintain supremacy. America is for the world's people and no tiny rivulet of race descent can maintain itself separately save as a small side stream—the swelling current is formed of every nation and will ultimately dominate the globe.

In this vast process we find ourselves confronted with the pressing problems of today's immigration, problems we have not yet learned to solve.

But toward solution tends every step that brings us mutual sympathy and understanding, and it is such a step that Miss Barrows takes when she unifies the spirit of Greece across two thousand years and brings Greece, new and old, to more intimate acquaintance with America.

Apropos of Prof. Ward's Theory

Are the readers of the *Woman's Journal* making themselves familiar as rapidly as possible with the gynaecocentric theory of Prof. Lester F. Ward as set forth in full in his last book *Pure Sociology*, published by Macmillan?[9] Nothing so important to the woman's movement has ever come into the world.

If the theory is finally established, and it will no doubt be combatted with violence by the mass of androcentric thinkers—namely, the world in general—it will change our whole thought as to women.

Habits of thought which have governed the human race for thousands of years are not to be altered in a day, but so great is the power of education, so wide and strong our systems of transmitting ideas today, that enormous progress can be made. The great doctrine of evolution, faintly adumbrated by earlier thinkers, has only been set clearly before us for some half a century,[10] and already the thought of the leaders of thought is changed by it and the world as a whole visibly affected.

So with this great theory upon woman, we may look to see its vast effects at least begun and help to spread them.

The theory in brief is simple enough, being to the effect that the original form of life, later called female, has continued unbroken from the beginning and is in herself capable of reproducing the species;[11] that the male sex was introduced quite late in development as a microscopic adjunct because fertilization was found to be an advantageous process; that this tiny, helpless, parasite assistant was gradually evolved to race equality through selection by the female; that equality and a perfectly free female endured until well along in the proto-social period when man—alone among all created species—subjugated his female and introduced the androcentric period which is only now beginning to pass. Professor Ward in the nature of his book does not of course go into the far-reaching social consequences—that will remain for the second volume perhaps as applied sociology—but he does point out the biological consequences and shows how terrible were the effects upon the race of this unnatural position of woman.

The woman's movement which is now taking place is not something contradictory to nature, as many of our honest opponents hold, but a simple reassumption of original place—that of full equality in race distinctions and as the main factor in reproduction.

Recently a strong argument in support of Professor Ward's theory has occurred to me and I offer it for consideration here.

It is this: That since the establishment of the full division of the sexes and the development of the male to full equality in species—such, for instance, as where oysters contribute equally to the processes of parentage and perform equally all processes proper to the life of an oyster—both have gone on together in the differentiation of species side by side. Both become vertebrate, both become warm-blooded, both become quadrupeds—whatever raised them in race distinction was shared by both alike. But while these great lines of common progress were being followed, the female alone has introduced whole stages of progress—stages of crucial importance to evolution. Through development solely confined to the female, we pass the stage of primitive fishes, birds, and reptiles—mere egg-layers—and rise to where the young are born alive—an enormous step. Highest of all, that crowning final stage in reproduction on which all the higher grades of life are based, is the last step of female evolution—order mammalia. In these world-changing processes the male has not shared at all. His part in the process is the same among mammalia, marsupialia, or ovipara. Since the early establishment of his comparatively simple mechanism, he has contributed nothing whatever toward nature's main line of race development, but he merely inherited the rudiments of the female's tremendous advance.

This certainly goes far to substantiate the claim that she is the main trunk and he the branch.

There is no danger that women become too proud. As human creatures the advance is all in the male line—and we inherit the rudiments!

But as a biological basis for our thought these things are most essential to know.

A Gentle Defender

The kind and earnest defense of the *San Francisco Examiner* published in the last issue of this paper[12] urges me to quote from the brief comment I previously made. If the gentle defender had read it more carefully it would perhaps have made her approval of the California paper's present virtues unnecessary. I stated very definite facts as to the *Examiner*—facts which this lady admits and puts even more strongly, adding that whatever progress was made by women was subject to the safe insults of this powerful paper—until it became popular. Then, as representing a market, it became worthy of respectful notice and got it promptly. As women grow more successful and are treated with more consideration, they should bear in kind remembrance those who honored their early struggles and should not forget those who dishonored them with all the power of society's greatest engine, the press. A paper may readily change its principles to suit a changing market or a political purpose, but such alteration is not like an honest reform of an individual. The point here is perfectly clear. At a time when women were a safe and easy mark for abuse and contempt, this paper gave it them with a coarseness and a gross injustice no Eastern journal could parallel. It now sees fit to treat them well—for reasons of its own.

But if a man insults and abuses you when you are weak and defenseless and then becomes respectful and admiring when you grow large and strong, do you therefore consider him a friend? A man who ten years ago was a prominent Democrat would not commend himself now as a Republican candidate,[13] no matter how swiftly and thoroughly he had turned his coat.

I make no criticism whatever of the good works of Mr. Hearst's newspapers at present—but repeat the only charge made in this paper, that he is not a woman's candidate.

COLUMN 17

April 23, 1904

In the first two parts of this column Gilman calls for judging reforms (e.g., educational improvement and increased opportunities for women) by pragmatic tests, hails a pair of advances in horticulture, and applauds the progressive turn of the *New York Evening Post* under the editorship of the liberal activist Oswald Garrison Villard (1872–1949).

What is Practical?

Most people do not consider a thing practical unless they can see it—whether with microscope, telescope, or the naked eye. It must be apparent to the senses, a thing to be weighed, measured, felt, tasted, heard, or smelled.

If it is an action they are considering, they do not find it practical unless it can be done at once—or at least within a week. If it can be done by one person individually, that is most practical. If it requires the combined action of many persons and a good deal of time, that is not practical to the general mind. Yet love is as real a thing as lumber, hate as hardware; our emotions are very practical things.

We criticize the Irish peasant for having the pig in the kitchen, the Italian or German for having the manure heap in the front yard, yet a mass of decayed opinions or a foul prejudice is just as practically disagreeable in the mind as these more outward and visible offenses. Women generally are practical in the sense of having a firm grip on small immediate issues, things personal and handmade. That is why it is so hard to rouse them to general recognition of the working value of suffrage even when they admit its position "as a principle."

The prospect of going out all together and performing an act for the public welfare does not seem to them as practical as toiling for the private welfare of their own relatives at home and alone.

Yet a thousand people—ten thousand people—are as practical as six, surely!

A better system of education for the children of a city, a State, a nation is as practical as finding a good school for Johnny, surely! But Johnny's mother does not think so. Johnny to her is a more practical fact than a million other Johnnies. One would think that all mothers were Christian Scientists in regard to other people's children and thought they existed "only in the minds" of their parents.[1]

It is a practical matter with us to increase our own incomes; it becomes vague and theoretical to increase the incomes of the world. Now why? Why is "practical" synonymous in our minds with "personal" and "immediate"?

Simply because we are so shortsighted.

The field of practical observation to our physical senses was once limited to the powers of our own lenses and retinas; now we have made lenses of glass, retinas of collodion, and enlarged our field of observation wonderfully.

We are beginning to find a knowledge of world politics as practical as that of one's own ward—it takes a somewhat larger mind perhaps to follow it but it is a real thing. Time was when no man knew much save of his own land and the rest of the world was but ground for travelers' tales.

Now with women today, why is it that the mass of them are so limited in their ideas of what is practical, so hotly interested in personalities, so unmoved by the larger issues of the day? For a reason so "practical" that it ought to appeal to every one of them—because her life work is "personal" and "immediate," a ceaseless repetition of ignominious details.

We all know this well enough but have long been bolstered up in our position by repeated assurance that it was only thus the best good of the world could be served, that if we each labored faithfully for our own all would be well cared for.

When anyone proposes to us a general scheme for social betterment, we are no more able to grasp it with our little concentrated minds than we could see a transformation scene through a reading glass. We literally cannot see it. This vagueness and blur such as confronts the victim of myopia when bereft of his glasses makes us call the larger plan "unpractical."

The unpracticality is not so much in the plan proposed as in our scale of observation.

A continent is as practical as an acre lot or an ant-heap, only you have to change your focus to get a good idea of it. The most practical issues before the world today are the large, public ones—matters of general concern, including the personal, but not to be met on any personal lines.

Let every woman who has at present interest enough in the State or the nation read Mr. Steffens' "Enemies of Society" in the April *McClure's*—there is something practical![2] The troubles and difficulties of this time are more and more those of a public nature, and what is needed beyond everything else is a generation of people big-minded enough to understand them.

Such people are not to be born or reared by women whose whole range of ideas is bounded by their family affairs and domestic labors. No mere "education" will help it, either—it needs a change in the habits of thought and that rests on a change in habits of action.

We've got to enlarge our field of work.

Those Fingers and Teacups

The present-day heroine is as skillful with teacups as her grandmother was with fine needlework.

It is no longer "the thing" to be eternally busy with embroidery or knitting; fine arms are not flying across harps as erst they were; yet we must be displaying our bodily attractions in some way.

The "frou-frou of our silken shirts" is one source of delight, and we may sit erectly and gracefully on our horses, dance well, and swing an effective club in golf, but where the masculine heart gives way is at that tea table.

It is so subtle a reminiscence of service—no longer the poor cook receiving only the bones and leavings, no longer the patient waiter eating only when the men had finished, but still the pleasant flicker of remembrance—the woman preparing refreshment for the man.

Small, dainty appurtenances, no manual labor, just the play of white hands and rosy fingertips among the egg-shell china and bright silverware—all delicately appealing to our inherited sensibilities.

There was a time when women were brutalized drudges—and they are yet among decadent savage tribes and the peasant class everywhere.

There was—not a time but a class—where women were a decorative appendage of society—and they are yet wherever that class has influence.

With the great generic term "woman," there have been associated from time to time groups of sub-ideas which have no inherent connection with her majestic place in nature. The original dignity of the major sex, the great earth mother, the upbuilder of species, has been obscured in our minds by the more recent and artificial conditions with which our human errors have overwhelmed it.

Dignity, power—there are the primal ideas to connect with womanhood. Love in the sense of eternal motherhood, the ceaseless, boundless *giving* love of the mother, this is hers naturally. Productive industry is inherently hers, too, with all its endless concomitants—accuracy, patience, skill, continuous invention—these things belong to woman as she was, is, and always will be.

But artificially imposed ideas like those of the submissive drudge, the meek, all-enduring Griselda,[3] or the fairy charmer who caters thus effectually to the man who is to maintain her in her *bric-à-brac* position—these do not belong to woman and do her no real honor.

As we slowly waken to a knowledge of our true position in the world's life, of our immense power and as great responsibility, we can so remake the world even as we have made it from the beginning.

Big, strong, vigorous, active women, skilled in all bodily exercises, with well-used intellect, special training in a chosen profession, general knowledge of the world, and the eternal mother-heart reaching its full height—in tender care for the whole world's children—these may not be so expert at twiddling teacups but they will give us a world of "sweetness and light" wherein we may find pictures of womanhood quite as attractive and more worthwhile.

A Conservative to the Front

The *New York Evening Post* is conservative and conventional enough, surely. Yet last spring that eminently respectable paper had a long editorial headed "What Are We Coming To?"[4] which so fully accepted and approved the most radical progress in domestic industry that friends asked if I wrote it! And in truth it urged every change I have, even to the married woman's working, except the scientific nursery.

Now in the issue for April 13, the *Post* has another article called "Future Housekeeping–Woman's Unorganized Work to be Done Commercially," which speaks with calmness and appreciation of the current development in this industry.[5] Where a great industrial change is in process of adoption, a change of such crucial importance as this, one which so intimately and directly affects the life of half the entire world and almost as directly that of the other half, it is a pity that some of our old-line suffragists should be found "antis" to this form of progress.

Of course a suffragist need not be expected to know everything nor to approve of every line of advance proposed to us, but on the woman question, in a matter preeminently important to us and to our movement, surely the intelligent and broad-minded women who can see far enough to approve of equal suffrage ought to be able to see thus far, also.

Why are we so timid about it? What are we afraid of? Is our creed so rigid, our view so narrow, that we wish merely to vote, to express our opinion and have our way at the polls and wish no more?

The right to vote is of deep and radical importance but it is not all. Men do much with it but there is much they do not and cannot do with it.

If men—all men—were butlers, footmen, cooks, general house-servants, their voting would fall sadly short of raising them to full development. The business in which people spend their lives is the most important thing to them.

What we do makes us what we are. If what we do is mischievous or dishonest, we can all see the evil of that, but if it is merely defective—barbaric, inefficient, crude—we do not seem able to realize the mischief of that at all.

We women, so long handicapped in a hundred ways, struggling slowly out into the light—here a loophole, there a window, there a crack—are still blind to many of the main issues even in their own lives.

This particular issue is coming now into general notice and those of us who wish to keep in front on this line will have to hurry.

Mr. Luther Burbank of California is doing great things in horticulture.[6] He has succeeded in raising a pitless plum and a stoneless prune and a new hybrid fruit from the apricot and the plum called the "plumcot."

Blessed be the man who gives us a new fruit! Someone, reading of these marvels, began to prate of what was "natural," of what "God made," and objected to man's tampering thus presumptuously with the works of nature. To which I emphatically responded that, if we had contented ourselves with what God made, we should be eating crabapples yet. We are used to our wide and varied supply of fruits and unconsciously assume that they were always there—whereas centuries of careful horticulture went to make them.

Col. Waring of New York,[7] among other deeds of beneficence, gave us the "Trophy tomato"—the big, smooth-bodied one that can be peeled so easily. They used to be all tied into the middle—deeply indented.

It is particularly beautiful, useful, valuable work and it seems a kind of work exquisitely suited to women—temperamentally and by education. Let some of us get busy and invent a new joy for human eating.

Women and French Literature

I saw a singular comment on French literature lately in an article by Emil Reich in the *Contemporary Review*[8] to the effect that the conventual seclusion of the *jeune fille*[9] robbed France both of lyric poetry and of the great novels.

The lyric, said Mr. Reich, is mainly based on a man's love for a girl, and where he never sees one save under surveillance he cannot write that kind of poetry.

Missing the society of young women who are "good," he solaces himself with that of the other kind, and though this may give rise to poetry of a sort, it is not the pure lyric. So the novel, forced to treat continually of falling in love after marriage—as there has been no chance before—is monstrous and limited. All of which is interesting in the tremendous range of influence it opens when women, with all their power to stimulate art, are fully and fairly established in human life everywhere.

In oriental nations, where the women are hidden in harems, we have only stories, Boccaccian in feeling, and poetry of a similar nature. As they come out into the open, free, intelligent, respected, we have a far nobler literature about them. "Annie Laurie,"[10] for instance, could hardly have been written in Turkey nor even in France. But far beyond every known level, beyond even Beatrice with her exalting influence,[11] lies the period we are but just entering when women will be to men more even than beloved.

No matter how high they stand in those beautiful relations of sweetheart and wife, there remains open around them the whole human world to figure in; women always, but not always regarded in the relation of sex.

Think of the literature of the world if men had held no place save that of husbands and fathers—how small and tame it would have been!

The full-grown women of tomorrow will figure more and more in the art of their time, the same grand and beautiful figure but in manifold positions hitherto unknown.

The world is but half-born in this respect and has some wonderful growing to do.

COLUMN 18

April 30, 1904

Gilman denounces a German play that, as she asserts, perpetuates "the primitive concept of woman as a creature of sex," urges a more scientific approach to sanitation, and recommends wider economic opportunities for invalids.

Wedekind's *Erdgeist*[1]

Another drama based on what some call the eternal feminine is being produced in Germany. It is a very frank and extreme expression of a common idea, an old idea, an idea which is founded on ignorance and which works continual evil.

This is the primitive concept of woman as a creature of sex and no more, a theory finding its fullest modern expression in Grant Allen's answer to Lester Ward's proposition that women are the race. Said Allen, "Women are not the race, they are not even half the race, but a sub-species told off for purposes of reproduction merely."[2]

In varying shades of delicacy, now with a religious bias, now with a scientific, now a sentimental, this view is presented all through the world's literature.

Wedekind gives it brutally; his "Lulu, the woman snake"[3] is a personification of simple animal passion to whom all men fall victims. A striking, realistic drama shows the terrible consequences of this creature's power with the seeming inference that the cause is always with us and the effect inevitable. The younger Burne-Jones in his picture of *The Vampire* has portrayed the same old idea[4]; Kipling reiterates it constantly; it appears to be all he knows about women[5]; older writers had no reserves on the subject but treated it as a foregone conclusion; and more modern ones cleanse and concentrate this primal spirit into a lifelong devotion to one man but recognize it no less as the mainspring, indeed the only spring of woman's character.

All of which serves to bring into strong relief the far-reaching revolution in the world's thought which must follow the acceptance of Ward's theory. Under this Lilith and Lulu and Vampire aspect of the case, and equally under the tenderly poetic conception of his beloved wife,

> Who, waking, guideth as beseems
> The happy house in order trim,
> And tends her babies and, sleeping, dreams
> Of them and him,[6]

lies the great androcentric assumption that men are people and women only females. Ward shows that the exact contrary was true through the whole period of the evolution of species up to a quite recent stage in social development, that the first and never-ceasing type of life was the female and that the male sex was introduced later for a specific use in the extending processes of reproduction, and that he only gradually assumed race equality with the female.

It remains indisputable that the human race throughout all its later history has reversed this position, that the human male has not reached equality but gone far beyond the human female in race development, and that he has done all that possible forcibly to detain her in an extremely primitive position.

This unquestioned progress of the man and arrest of the woman, his wide growth in all manner of human capabilities and her restriction to the purely feminine functions, is what has allowed this common view of women's crude sex-power and its ill results. To this can readily be traced the basic myths of many religions, the Eve and the Apple, the Pandora and the Box stories,[7] and others. How we came to believe all this is clear enough, but Ward shows us how to see under and over and around it and recognize at last the true relation of woman to man and to the world.

Here is the true position:

The woman of each species is the true race type—she is and does all that belongs to her kind of species. With us, in that she fails thus fully to be and do all that is human, she is an aborted type; her position is abnormal. With us, the male, in his unique position of monopolizer of race functions, has arrogated to himself the whole range of human activities as being masculine and in holding her down to one relation—that of sex—has grown to consider her as a purely sexual creature. Meanwhile, under this temporary historic aberration, a period of arrested development for women and splendid growth for men, and one no doubt essential to our progress, the major forces of life continue to work.

The male, being created originally for his special power in assisting the processes of physical immortality, is constrained from first to last to seek and serve the female—so far this *Erdgeist* theory is all right. The power of the woman *is* the primal fact and so far as biological relations hold the final fact as well.

But here is the error: The degrading and mischievous effects assumed to be inherent in the woman's power are merely inherent in her *position* and her position is in no way essential or permanent. The upward road in the evolution of species is in the constant leadership of the ever-improving female—pursued forever by the ascending male. This is not the vague assertion of what is to be in some future time when women reach equality with men but a simple statement of fact as to what has been always, except in a relatively short period of human development. The process followed by nature is exquisitely simple. The female, true type of race, carries on all race activities and develops them as well. The male, with his inherent tendency to vary, plays around the steadier female type and introduces new elements, progressive or otherwise.

The female, free to choose and surrounded by actively competing males, selects the best, and so through him as well as by her own advancement elevates the race type.

If this still held in humanity as it does in all other species, we should be writing dramas and painting pictures of a quite different sort.

Instead of a "snake-woman," we should have the true human female, a broad, fully-developed human being, intelligent, capable, variously active, all that men now are *which is not masculine,* and nothing is masculine except the specific traits shared by males of other species; yet she would still hold this innate power of sex, drawing to her with inexorable attraction the male of her species.

The reviewer of this play describes Lulu as "vile yet sinless because she knows not what she does—a creature of natural impulses, unconsciously cruel, sensual, and fascinating. She is the principle of earthly passion—the female, the eternal temptress, the woman."[8]

In a natural condition, with women in full human development, all this would be reversed. It is the male who embodies the "principle of earthly passion." He is the "eternal tempter"—if there is any. As the peasant proverb has it, "'Tis for man to try and for woman to deny." The natural relation of the sexes is for the female to go about her business as a full-grown type of species, following its activities contentedly and adding to them her own supremely important processes of reproduction. To promote these last, nature has provided the male who eternally pursues and sues, who is irresistibly impelled toward the female by the fundamental laws of his make-up.

If she is in her right place, this works only good.

She is not injured by this "temptation"—it is natural that many should seek her, natural that she should select the best and care nothing for the others.

Neither is he injured by it.

So long as the woman is in her right place, the man is in no way hurt by loving her—whether he win her or not.

All the blackness of the picture results from the peculiar morbidness of a woman who is a creature of sex and no more. That is a flat contradiction of nature's law. She is race first and most, sex afterward; he is the creature of sex originally. That he should gradually develop race characteristics is well—to that end has tended this long tragedy of the subversion of woman. That he should monopolize them is ill, and that he should make of his great race-mother a mere sex-type without human features is monstrous. Much has been said of the modern advance of women as tending to make them "usurp the position of man."

That is exactly what has been done unwillingly by this "eternal temptress" creation.

She is in the position of man, a most unbecoming position for a woman and working great evil.

It is high time that women recognized the ultra-sexual as masculine, quite harmless and orderly in its place, but that *as women* it belongs to them to be full types of race—human creatures absolute.

Scientific Sweeping

How many of you housewives are keeping pace with the beautiful invention of Exhaust Sweeping? Here is a man (not a housewife, be it observed) devising a method by which dirt may be powerfully sucked out of our houses.

A machine comes to your door, a long hose is introduced into your house, and its open end—a sort of narrow carpet-sweeper affair—played over the carpet from which every particle of dust is removed through the pipe and—O pitiful limitation of the process!—carted into the street from whence it may reenter the house. What ought to happen is to have a "dampener" to the apparatus where the dust would be wetted down to a small, easily removable quantity.

Perhaps in time they may even make briquettes of it—and so at least force service out of one of man's greatest enemies. Dust is a direct danger to life, sometimes slight, sometimes severe, but always injurious.

The patient woman, so wholly occupied in doing her duty that she never has time to study it, has been struggling with dust since the world was—or rather since the home was.

She is always wiping it off things, sweeping it up, casting it out in one way or another. By and by she will learn where it comes from—then how to avoid it—and in course of time human dwellings may be as pure as the forest—almost.

The outdoor dust comes from first the upturned soil of the farm. How is that to be avoided? Easily enough. By surrounding the dwelling homes of the farmers with areas of grass and trees away from the ploughed fields. A mechanical possibility surely and in time a social one. Second, from our dirt roads in the country and in country or city from the presence of many beasts of burden and the grinding traffic.

By and by we shall learn to make smooth, hard, dustless roads for pleasant traveling, to have all heavy traffic go on rails, in cities to have it underground. No horses anywhere except on grass—where they are happiest and do no harm.

A city could be clean as a hospital. All surface roads, smooth floors, carrying people only; every city street with its big tube below for all pipes, wires, and transfer of goods. So there would be no dust save from shoe-leather and rubber tires.

Third, in houses the dirt comes from the endless heaps of dead cloth we have about, and paper, and the like. Fewer things, all books, etc., under glass and no "hangings"; with clean, fresh, often renewed clothes, and a home would not feather off inside into a slow cloud of dangerous particles as it does now.

Fourth, and as bad as any—ashes. Wood, coal, and their ashes—these make dust for us continually.

The use of gas and finally electricity will do away with this, too. With gas, the coal and dirt can be kept in one place and the dust and smoke consumed as it is made; with electricity—from wind and water power—there need not be any.

All this is out of reach—a millennial dream? Not at all. All this is within our reach, a practical and profitable possibility—we ought to wake up and reach it. And—I would remark to the careful housewife—it cannot be reached with a dust-cloth.

An Industrial Sanitarium

Some doctors have more brains than others. Rather unscientifically put, as more of have but one, but at least some doctors use more of their brains than others. Now here is one who wants to start an industrial sanitarium. That is good sense—sound, practical sense.

It ought to mean a very long step in our treatment of invalids. To the doctor—the ordinary doctor who has necessarily specialized on the medical point of view and unnecessarily forgotten that there are other viewpoints—a patient is but "a case." He stands in the mind of his physicians as a thus and thus defective body—to be put in order like a watch or, more slowly and deliberately, to be tinkered with like a grafted tree.

Now a watch is only machinery and can be so treated. A tree is machinery of a kind and also life, but its life is simple and does not cause complications while the grafting is going on. Good Mr. Burbank has made "plumcot" without outraging the feelings of father apricot and mother plum—or scandalizing the Prunus family. If Mrs. Plum had a sensitive and conscientious nature she might have suffered keenly and the new fruit have been injured. Trees do not bother about what is being done to them nor about other matters in the meanwhile, but people do.

The "patient"—the "case"—is also an individual person full of cares and interests, and when you sharply cut off that person's activities and send him to a sanitarium to sit around and get well (or something?) it does not occupy his mind. Or hers. Now this industrial sanitarium is intended to provide occupation as well as sanitation. There are plenty of light, pleasant, interesting trades which invalids could learn and practice, thus taking their minds off the ceaseless contemplation of their own and others' diseases and furnishing health-food for thought and conversation as well as for the alimentary tract. Perhaps as the plan develops the trade unions will get after it and interfere as they have done in the case of prison industry.

Never was there a more undeniable good than productive industry for society's defectives; it is simply a resumption of normal activities—or a first introduction to them.

And here are the unions—mighty force for good that they are—making historic fools of themselves by preventing it. So no doubt they would object to the performance of any useful and profitable work by the newly-encouraged invalid, and those physically defective must perhaps content themselves with fancy work. Or fancy bookbinding.

The real trade of bookbinding has not so far taken serious steps to interfere with the ladies who practice art in leather and gilding, so maybe the invalids might do that, too. Doing something, whatever it may be, will do them good. To quote my favorite motto—anything is better than nothing.

COLUMN 19

May 7, 1904

Like her sometime mentor W. D. Howells (1837–1920), a champion of literary realism, Gilman urges female readers to shun sentimental or romantic fiction. She also condemns laws that permit women teachers to be fired if they marry on the assumption that they no longer need jobs outside the home and they should not preempt positions that might otherwise be filled by unemployed men.

Love Stories and Life Stories

Women are the reading class in America—and fiction is the class of literature they read.[1]

No harm in that.

"Fiction," original composition, is great art.

The marble gods who teach us beauty from the heights of old Greece are works of fiction. But there are other gods than Eros; other tales than that of Psyche are told in stone.[2]

Fictitious literature is or may be the most amusing, uplifting, inspiring, and magnificently instructive of arts.

But in the main our works of fiction are "love stories." We demand in them what the magazine editor calls "a heart interest" as if the heart (in itself a fictional term, that worthy pump having no more connection with love than our worthy liver!) had but one interest.

The heart beats fast when we are moved by love, that is by love of the "common or garden variety," the physical emotion, but so it does when we are mightily afraid or fiercely angry.

If you have angina pectoris, you are cautioned against anxiety, fright, and rage more than against love. Therefore, it is apparent that the heart, the real live organ, has more than one interest. But accepting the term on its face value, why are "affairs of the heart" the only affairs in which the general reader, and notably the female reader, is supposed to be concerned?

We are told that love is "the ruling passion," that it "makes the world go round," that "all the world loves a lover,"[3] and that "a fellow feeling makes the whole world kin."[4]

So we find our great common interest emotionally in this universal function as we find our medium of social intercourse in feeding—another universal function.

There is much of reason in all this. It is true that race preservation is nature's first law, that every form of life is moved in common by this primal force, and that we human animals have added an immense increment of associative idea and emotion to the original passion.

This is true and beautiful and right. So long as we live in animal bodies we are under this law and our lives depend on it; so long as the structure of society remains we must feel also a richer complex of emotion, of sentiment and passion, than the lower and simpler forms of life.

Admitting all this, it is still possible to overweight and overestimate this part of life, and we do it, we women, far the most.

We have been told so long ago that

Love is of man's life a thing apart,
'Tis woman's whole existence[5]

that we have believed it. The facts agreed with the theory, too; our whole existence was carefully limited to this field; we were dressed and educated to grace it; we bloomed out into a brief and glorious career while under inspection and selection before final surrender, and then we pursued the rest of our lives with varying devotion and satisfaction in this one department of life.

The typical woman picture is either that of preliminary or subsequent absorption in love—the maiden wooed, the woman won, the mother ever after "only mother." Some twenty years to the wedding, some twenty years of child-rearing, and then you have a woman of forty who is—what?

She is an ex—; she is a *mater emeritus* [sic]; she "lives life over again in her daughters," her own life having flowered, fruited, and withered away into that of a house-server honored for her past achievements in maternity.

The real power and importance of motherhood we have never overrated; in fact, we have never yet understood or appreciated it, taking a most inadequate and slovenly performance for the real thing.

Because we do not understand it and do not properly honor it, we have erred in restricting the woman entirely to this one function, regarding her from no other point of view, associating her always in our thought with love, marriage, and maternity, ideal, actual, or reminiscent. This is the reason that our greatest art, literature, in its ablest manifestation—the creative form—is so largely limited to love stories.

It is a pity. It hampers the writers, it distorts literature, and it steadily fosters and intensifies the mental attitude which demands it.

Human life has other and greater interests than this; and women, being human, are just as much concerned with all these as men are.

When men were all soldiers, when their whole education was martial—their ideals, ambitions, sense of duty, hopes of glory—they cared only for tales of battle; and in that period they naturally and innocently supposed that life was all war. But it wasn't. Thinking a thing does not make it so. It does to the thinker, to his misleading, but it does not alter the facts.

Human life in its rich, swift, glorious development, covering more of change and growth in a few brief thousands of years than the slow world could show in as many millions, has laws and processes of its own more vitally important to us than those of earlier stages. We constantly develop higher planes of living—without losing the lower. We still breathe—trees breathe. We digest—insects digest. We love and fight—animals love and fight. These are all interesting and valuable processes, indispensable processes—except the fighting; that is a mischievous rudiment.

But while as animals we have steadily kept on breathing, digesting, loving, and fighting, as human beings we have risen to an entirely new plane of life.

The whole field of mental development, all education, all the arts, all the sciences—these are human; these are ours alone. Have women no action and no interest in these?

The whole field of productive industry and its accompanying system of distribution, of transportation, with all the allied range of discovery, invention, and exploration—these are human exclusively. Have women no part nor lot in these?

The growth and improvement of governments, of systems of jurisprudence, of the dominant sweep of religions in their beautiful evolution—these most of all are human, wholly ours.

Where are women in these things? Are women then not human that they remain content with the functions of a sex and fail to participate in the functions of a race—the greatest race on earth?

In the last hundred years—the threshold of the future—we have lifted our heads and stepped forward, claiming place and power as members of society as well as that previously ours as members of the family. A brave, wise, patient few have so pressed forward, their numbers increasing daily, but still the greater part remain content with the position of female only, letting life go on as it will in the unaided hands of men and making the functions and feelings common to their sex, from bird to mammal, "their whole existence."

When the new intelligence, the new sense of duty rouses them; when they waken and come out of their interminable kitchens and parlors; when the vital issues of life are real and pressing to us all, we shall have a better proportioned literature.

The Married Teacher

The Board of Education in New York City has canceled its by-law prohibiting marriage of teachers and reinstated Mrs. Vandewater, who was dismissed under this regulation.[6]

They have amended the article but it still reads, "No woman principal, head of department, or member of the teaching or supervising staff shall marry while in the employ of the Board of Education." They keep the prohibition but admit that it cannot be made effectual, saying, "We are tired of fighting over this matter in the courts and the public is in favor of retaining married teachers."[7] This is a good step, important in its three parts: the recession of the Board of Education from an untenable position, the decision of the Court, and most of all the solid weight of public opinion. Right understanding of the matter calls for a very wide view of the conditions involved. This particular skirmish is but one on a very long line—the line of industrial advance for women.

So sure are we of the preeminent importance of the maternal duties (which is true) and of the incompatibility of these with any others (which is not true), that we regard the entrance of women into any extra-domestic position as necessarily involving injury to the old duties—the new ones—or both.

We have grudgingly allowed the privilege of work to single women but deny it to the married, and fearing that the woman herself will not be intelligent or conscientious enough to avoid the downward path we have sought to prevent her error by force. The position the public is gradually forsaking and that is a most hopeful proof of progress.

There remain difficulties enough of a practical nature still to prevent the working woman from marrying or the married woman from working in many cases, but these, too, are gradually being faced and removed. Here is a teacher of unusual competence and value in a high-class private school.

She wishes to marry—she wishes to keep on teaching.

But marriage means children—or ought to—and that means a break in regular work.

Now in schools of this class where every effort is made to secure the best talent, teachers are engaged or "bespoken" a year or so in advance. The principal cannot afford to have a competent teacher drop out and leave her with only the leavings of the market to choose from. In this case the married woman is less dependable than the single woman—and so at a disadvantage.

Marriage with presumed maternity is still at a discount in the market. How is this fact to be met? Simply enough. The difficulty lies in the few married teachers competing with the many unmarried ones. As soon as all teachers are married the difficulty ceases. Those few women who preferred to remain single for life could fill exceptional positions where substitutes could not be obtained and perhaps command exceptional prices as solace to their loneliness, but the great bulk of humanity prefer to be married and being teachers does not alter this natural condition.

Consider then a fully efficient teacher, college bred, having been through her normal course and her period of apprenticeship—she should be about twenty-five years old. She should by that time be married and should expect for the next ten or twenty years to be liable to occasional withdrawals.

It might be said that a rational prevision could arrange to have these events during vacation or in alternate years, but even without such arbitrary dictation to natural processes there would be in any case periods of retirement for the mother. This would be readily met by a system of substitutes and understudies—not all women being thus withdrawn from service at the same time.

And meanwhile the teacher temporarily retiring from the school could still do private tutoring for as many hours as she felt able.

When all women are engaged in industrial occupations, the conditions of industry must be compelled to suit the conditions of maternity. Why not? Surely half the people in the world can afford to arrange their share of the work to suit themselves.

Mrs. Eliza Burt Gamble writes to me that Prof. Ward's "Gynaecocentric Theory" was presented to the world by a woman ten years ago in *The Evolution of Woman*, published by G. P. Putnam's Sons, 1894.[8] In answer to which it is enough to say that Prof. Ward's theory was first published in an article called "Our Better Halves" in the *Forum*, November 1888.[9]

I should be very glad if a woman had worked out this so important proposition, but there also seems a sort of poetic justice in its being done by a man.

COLUMN 20

May 14, 1904

Gilman denounces a misleading article about women in the industrial workplace and a deceptive antisuffrage poem. She then commends in counterpoint to "Woman in Panic in Blazing Car" (column 11) the safety protocols that prevented panic among theatergoers during a fire in New York.

"The Truth (?) About Women in Industry"

Flora MacDonald Thompson has an article with the above title (without the interrogation point) in the May *North American Review*.[1] It may well be that her statements taken separately are "true." She may have carefully verified her facts, proved her allegations, and derived her statistics from reliable sources, but a number of truths put together without relation or proportion do not make "the truth."

For instance, Mrs. Thompson's assertion that the average wage of working women is less than a dollar a day may be "true" as an arithmetical result of some computation she has made, yet it has no bearing on the question whether women should teach school or be physicians. The capacity and fondness of some women for the profession of medicine and the need of other women for their services is the reason for their being, and the "truth" that any or all women are underpaid does not affect the position. If our friend had paid some attention to the increase in women's wages that follows their increasing capability, that is a "truth" which we might well consider.

No one has denied that women are grossly underpaid for their services, but we need not therefore all do our own housework.

Another great stress is laid on the feebleness of women, their inherent frailty as a sex, and the laws and regulations with which men seek to "protect" them in industrial occupations.

No such frailty is ever alleged as an excuse for avoiding fifteen hours of housework. Possibly Mrs. Thompson makes the common mistake of supposing that women in the sacred precinct of the home do not work or that housework is less exhausting than other labor. We should always bear steadily in mind that only one in sixteen of American women keeps even one servant.

The frailty of fifteen out of sixteen of our women does not prevent them from doing the work for which we hire vigorous peasants and carrying on maternal duties besides. They sicken and die under this strain in considerable numbers. Perhaps if Mrs. Thompson could give us the figures as to the health rate of the women who work at home, it might show just as much disability as that of the women who work in shops. A little more "truth" here would be enlightening.

Objects of charity she calls the wage-earning women because many charitable institutions seek to make up for the low wages by various beneficent palliatives. And what is the woman who has to ask her husband for car-fares? It is not well to live on charity ever. The working woman should have higher wages. So should the wife—and earn them.

But the charity given the wage-earner does not militate against her so earning, any more than the pitiful dependence of the wife militates against marriage.

We must have marriage, and we must have women in industry, but we need to better many accompanying conditions.

Most weight of all is laid on the interference of outside industry with woman's duty to her family. Here the author, though her profession is that of a writer and carried on at home, complains bitterly of the exactions of her employer—the editor. The article must be finished at a given time whether the baby is sick nor not. She cannot sit at the bedside of a sick child because her work must be done.

Now this may be "true."

Perhaps once, or more than once, a particularly exigent editor and an especially sick baby occurred. Or if she writes for the daily press, there must be of course this demand all the time and it would naturally prevent the mother from being a nurse as it prevents the father.

Who then will take care of the sick child? The nurse, of course. The real nurse who knows how. But "no hired nurse can make up for the mother's care—training cannot equal love"—that is what many feel. But no matter if they do feel so. It is not a fact. Ask any experienced doctor. If the child is not seriously ill, the nurse is as good as the mother. If the child is seriously ill, the nurse is better.

The mother does not object to a "hired doctor"—she hardly would maintain that mother-love was better than a doctor's training. Why is it better than a nurse's?

But the main element of confusion in this article is not to be shown by refuting its several points or showing their irrelevancy. It lies in the author's lack of historical perspective and sociological knowledge.

We are going through a stage of social development in which the position of woman is difficult, both at home and abroad. The economic problems of the world confront her as they do her brother. She is new yet to the industrial world of today, coming suddenly out of her long-preserved archaic seclusion into the light and noise and pressure of the present time.

This industry, once wholly hers, has been so wholly monopolized by men that they innocently call it "men's work." Mrs. Thompson makes this mistake, too.

In this sweeping and sudden change of position—a class immovable for thousands of years suddenly bursting forth into life and motion—with all the false starts, wrong moves, and antagonisms natural to such a beginning, women are at many disadvantages in their new situation. But these disadvantages are local and transient—they have nothing to do with the principles involved. As soon as women as a whole are calmly doing their half of the world's work, the conditions of industry must be made to suit them. Half the world has a right to dictate conditions—as well as the other half. Let those of us who wish to judge fairly of this question strive to avoid the pitfalls of immediate and personal difficulties when studying what is right for the whole world.

The Ivy and the Oak

The "man of straw" we suffragists are often accused of fighting has come to the front with renewed vitality—this time being a woman.

> To the Woman Suffragist
>
> Why all this toil for triumphs of an hour?
> Why creep and climb to reach the fireless flame
> That flashes from a frail, deluded fame?
> Why barter fruitful love for fretful power?
> Full faith in man is woman's fairest dower;
> Who doubts her would-be knight doth taint with shame
> The honor of a long-loved lineal name.
> Doth rob love's garden of its sweetest flower.
> The ivy with the oak can ne'er compare.
> Though forceful efforts make her cease to twine:
> Though she be trained as broad, as full, as fair,
> Each gustful wind will prove her still the vine.
> Let come what will, let fall what may between,
> Man's love is ever best whereon to lean.
>
> —Mary Quinlan Laughlin[2]

It is pretty good verse of its kind. "Why barter fruitful love for fretful power?" is a fine line. Why, indeed; who would, who ever wanted to? Isn't the straw man on the other side? Is it not the "anti" who so absurdly misestimates what suffragists are working for and even more absurdly distorts the facts concerned?

Take this ivy and oak simile, for instance—it is rank miscegenation. Ivies and oaks are not *mates*—not the same species. Some trees are divided in sex like animals—one mother tree, one father tree, but in such a case Mrs. Tree is quite as sturdy as Mr. and in nowise clings to him.

Similarly, if vines are thus divided they both cling—the he-vine does not stand up like a beanpole for the she-one to run on. When you come to the animal kingdom, you find no instance, not one in all created creatures, where the female clings to the male in graceful abandon.

You do find, however, among low and tiny primitive organisms, numbers of instances where the male is a tiny parasite or small, convenient article carried about in the pocket of the female.

From the small and timid mouse to the raging lion, the female not only does everything in the way of business that the male does but more, for on her falls the main burden of caring for the young. He helps—sometimes.

But laying aside these alluring studies, look at the more direct inferences of this popular point of view.

The anti-suffrage mind always assumes a choice—a required choice—between the duties of a female and the duties of a citizen; those who wish to be citizens are supposed to wish, as part and parcel of the process, to leave off being women.

In there anything to hinder leaning on man's love in the 364 days of the year wherein one is not voting? Or might it not be possible still to lean on it all the way to the polls and back again?

What has voting to do with "faith in man—woman's fairest dower"? Will she learn so much about him in her civic duties that a pleasant faith will give way to unpleasant facts? Truth is mighty and will prevail; if he is not worthy of faith, it is better to know it. But if he is, he will stand the test and she will love him all the more as she adds knowledge to faith and finds him worthy.

Would that the brain substance of the anti-suffragist could be penetrated by the large, plain, easy fact that intelligent and active citizenship is not a sex function and will no more rob women of their womanhood than it robs men of manhood. It has nothing to do with sex, absolutely nothing.

And would—O would—that the anti-suffragists might all acquaint themselves with the facts of Ward's gynaecocentric theory and see that man is the "creature of sex" by nature, not woman.

If he, in course of time, has acquired so many valuable and efficient race-characteristics, if he has well-nigh monopolized them and become so prominently human that he really believes humanity to be a masculine trait and yet has not lost his manhood, may it not be reasonably hoped that the female, originally the main type of species but in our race temporarily aborted, may re-assume her natural position and become fully human without losing her womanhood? Whatever the purblind and prejudiced may think, whatever botanical metaphors of evil connotation they may use, the ivy being a deadly enemy of the oak instead of a mate, the calm, triumphant facts remain, and the world does move.

A Theater Fire and No Panic

New York has had a chance to show the advantage of preparation—and many owe their lives to the lesson taught by Chicago's needless, awful disaster.[3]

In one of Proctor's theaters holding about 1,700 people, on the evening of May 6th a fire broke out. It was not visible from the auditorium and before the people were aware of it the ushers opened the fourteen exits and a line of policemen stood in each aisle.[4]

The manager, Mr. Brunelle,[5] then quietly announced from a stage-box that there was a fire—and no danger if they would pass out quietly.

But that was not what saved the house—this was owing to a speech by Captain McNally of the police force: "The first man that makes a disturbance or starts a stampede will be clubbed into submission," he shouted at the top of his voice. "Remember the Chicago fire! The people there were killed by being trampled on. Nobody will be hurt here if you go out quietly!"[6] And they did.

More policemen were in the right place.

A Blue Baby

Another victim of the domestic laundry! A mother—and incidentally a laundress—prepared a large tub of bluing, and while she was hanging out clothes the baby fell into it. The baby was rescued—but remains blue. What a terrible thing it is that mothers should be forced to leave their sacred duties in the home and go out into the world, neglecting their children!

But no, this was her own washing in the home—she only went out into the backyard. So it was all right.

COLUMN 21

May 21, 1904

Hardly among the first people to object to hazing—the first state antihazing law was passed in New York in 1894—Gilman considered the behavior the vestige of a savage trait.

Hazing and Child-Culture

The practice of hazing, lately arousing such strong criticism in West Point and Annapolis,[1] now crops out again in a most pious institution—St. Stephen's College.[2] An unusually intelligent father has grasped the fact that young men in college are not outside the grip of the common law and that they have no more right to commit assault and battery than have any other persons. This astonishingly clear-headed gentleman, Mr. Edwin Bedell,[3] is suing for $10,000 as damages for injuries inflicted on his son. The pocket nerve may reach where reason and civilization fail to penetrate.

In our universal ignorance of the status of childhood and our lack of any efficient system of child-culture, we fail to see the real nature and derivation of this peculiar practice. Yet one needs but a slight general knowledge of social evolution to recognize in hazing a survival of the primitive custom of initiation by torture, the system of ordeal which prevails among savage tribes to this day and may be still studied among our American Indians[4] as well as in earlier historic instances. Our Mandans have an especially revolting and painful method of initiation,[5] but the custom is as wide as the world, is found in Australia, Africa, Asia, wherever savagery remains.

The practice may have a foundation even back of humanity, as Kipling hints in the "looking over" process wherein the wolf cub is admitted to the band[6]; but however that may be, it is clearly shown in our early stages of growth and is not difficult to understand.

The rationale of the process is this: Here is a group, the existence and success of which depend on the efficiency of its members. When the new individual seeks admission to the advantage of the group life, he must first be tested to prove his efficiency.

Before that he was a member of the family, an underlying smaller group with less advantages, and in passing from family to tribal life he must pass this test of fitness for membership.

In that social period the practice has very rational grounds and works well, though often carried to excesses of needless cruelty by the callous ingenuity of the savage mind.

The remarkable fact in our present-day hazing is the survival of so primitive and brutal a practice through our centuries of civilization and, in our own case, of Christianity.

Two things are plainly evidenced by it: one, the continuity of the race habit with the persistent reversion of the young to earlier types; and the other, that however civilized the adult may be, we have not yet learned how to civilize our children.

This is the salient point and one which calls for instant and serious study. The practice of hazing often involves a brutality which leads to death—our colleges and schools have a shameful record of case where the victim of hazing came directly to a violent end.

Even within the past few years, a number of deaths have occurred directly and avowedly from hazing, and we have no means of ascertaining how many more have indirectly died or suffered in varying degrees.

Beyond this actual brutality, another and more characteristic fact is manifested: a glaring ignorance of ethical values and human rights. It is natural that we should still bear with us our brute inheritance; few of us but have felt its pressure at times; but in age-long training we have learned to control these tendencies and to recognize the larger principles of social relation which demand a higher code of conduct.

The child, by the law of reversion of the young of a species to its earlier types, is nearer to his primitive ancestors than the adult[7]; and this biological phenomenon of reversion is what earlier thinkers called original sin.

Childhood has its more than offsetting advantages, however, in embodying the progressive development of the generation behind it and in sustaining the uplifting influence of education.

Insofar as we have really gained in constitution and character, the child is born better, and insofar as education reaches him, he is not only helped over the reversionary tendencies but set before his parents in the path of progress. What then can account for this shameful persistence of savage traits in our grown children, boys who are nearly men and who are educated successfully in the external manners of civilization and in special studies of a high order?

How does it happened that a clean, decorous, intelligent young fellow of sixteen, eighteen, or twenty years stands in the forefront of human progress in some respects and in others is still a vulgar savage? If it were simply the reversionary tendency of youth which we were not able to check, he would be a savage in all ways. But he is not. He is a gentleman, a civilized American in many lines of conduct.

Education has produced tremendous results wherever applied, but we have not learned to educate the child's real nature with evenness and reliability. That a boy should reach eighteen with the earmarks of the savage still prominent upon him is a painful comment on our methods of child-culture.

Our children, reared in the family status, are taught the behavior necessary to family relation, but they are not taught really to understand the principles of human relation, the balance of human rights, the laws of human conduct.

These college boys and military academy boys are made to pass rigid examinations in mathematics but ethics is not required in the curriculum.

A series of wisely-planned questions on human rights and relations would exhibit such yawning gulfs of ignorance as would astonish the instructors—if indeed they were themselves proficient in this line.

The physical current of descent in humanity goes on, flowing in unbroken stream from the dark past to the ever-brightening future, and each new generation shows to us in endless repetition what progress we really have made and where we lamentably fail. Nowhere is failure more apparent than in our efforts to modify the "stream of tendency" in youth. We compel an extra form of improved behavior but have not reached the nature of the child.

We have never recognized the status of childhood as such. We have not seen that children are permanently with us as a distinct class, embodying our primitive tendencies and passions and also our latest gains in genuine race-development.

In this class of human beings still thrives a mass of barbaric impulses and habits transmitted down the ages not only from father to son but from child to child in their natural association.

Cannot the wisdom and love of civilized humanity, the endless wealth of material and opportunity, be turned to better account in its application to the living stock of the race during its most easily modified period? Cannot we do something to elevate childhood as a status? "Boys will be boys," but there is some difference between the boys of cave-dwelling cannibals and the boys of a decent civilization—and there should be more! Childhood needs special conditions for its best growth and surely by study and cautious experiment we can find out what those conditions are and use our enormous resources to supply them.

Childhood is visibly untrained in ethics—that is the one conspicuous fact brought out in these hazing practices. Either the boys do not know that it is wrong to inflict pain and injury upon others or they have not sufficient self-control to check a recognized evil impulse. In the first case they need ethical training—from the primer. In the second, they need to be confined in asylums for the feeble-minded.

A boy of eighteen who cannot modify his own conduct by his own judgment and will is a defective and needs the care of experts to develop his latent faculties.

There is no need of considering this second assumption. It is palpably false. The degree of self-control exhibited by the "hazee" is worthy of his savage ancestors, yet he in turn becomes a "hazer" with a clear conscience. The trouble lies in lack of effective ethical training during childhood, not lack of religious training but of practical ethics.

In our efforts to control and modify the conduct of the child, we use methods of more or less temporary efficacy but which do not educate the will and judgment. We make no analysis of the nature of given phases of conduct, no treatment calculated to alter the tendency as a whole.

The habit of teasing, for instance, a peculiarly useless and disagreeable form of rudimentary evil custom and allied to this same system of ordeal, is allowed in most families with slight check in extreme cases instead of being promptly classified as senseless and utterly wrong and met with full disapprobation. So far are we from appreciating the ethical enormity of this habit that we frequently find it imitated by the adult who finds amusement in teasing the child. Again, our methods of reprobation and punishment are not such as are calculated to teach respect for human rights and for the sanctity of the person.

We allow to go unchecked the minor exhibitions of evil impulses and are surprised and confounded by their more violent expression.

The study of the educator should be along lines of conduct following the specific act back to its general cause and so learning in time to eliminate evil tendency and modify character. Then we should not find the same difficulties appearing in each generation to be struggled with and deplored in the same futile manner but should make gradual and even progress toward a better race level. With legitimate training in ethics, even such as is now commonly known among us, a civilized boy would not more allow himself to torture a comrade then he would go naked or eat human flesh.

The Day-unto-Dooryard Theory

This is a combination of two of our common working theories of life: one to the effect that if you do right everyday, your whole life will be right, the other that if everyone sweeps his own dooryard, the city will be clean. The philosophy of the two is similar and both rest on an "if"—a word of more import than size. In the philosophy is no great error, though it is laboriously misplaced. It is like say, "If you take each step toward the north your whole course will be northward" or "If you wash your fingers, hands, arms, face, neck, head, chest, shoulders, back, body, hips, legs, feet, toes, eyes, ears, and other parts, your whole body will be clean." Equally true and simpler is the statement, "If your course is due north, your steps will be northward" or "If you wash your whole body the parts will be clean."

But the real weakness in these commonly accepted guides to action is the "if."

If you do right everyday, your whole life will be right—but how are you to know the rightness of each day's acts unless you have some clear decision as to your life's purpose? We are not inchworms. Human duty cannot be judged within half-hour limits. There are certain principles of method and manner which apply to nearly all action—as cheerfulness, courtesy, kindness, promptness, accuracy—but these have little to say as to the choice of a profession or the conflict of great duties.

Harold Skimpole was most loving and kind in his daily intercourse with fellow-mortals but the scheme of his life was wrong.[8] Mr. Micawber was an amiable man in small matters.[9] The world is full of worthy people who do everyday what they assume to be right yet whose lives as a whole give us no assurance that they chose truly.

You cannot measure a life in such short sections. Great lives are strengthened and held true by great principles, principles deep and far-reaching, based on wide study of humanity. Under such influence we can withstand temporary pressure to one side or the other and the insidious weight of hereditary habit.

The small lives of most of us, the little weary, confused lives, stumbling this way and that, finding it all so difficult and disappointing, lack this long-distance reliability because of their little tape-measure theory of conduct.

No man tries to lay out a railroad by a foot-rule. Life is too long, even one physical life, to gain any sense of its general direction by measuring from one day to the next. And the real human life which comes down unbroken from past ages needs a good reach of history to give us any wise judgment of right conduct.

So with this effort to keep one's own dooryard swept and by an aggregation of many well-swept dooryards make a clean city.

A city is more than an aggregation of dooryards.

A street cannot be kept clean in lateral sections by the efforts of abutting householders, nor yet in longitudinal sections by every man sweeping after his own horse. "If" they would do so, it would be clean, pathetically repeats the tape-measure theorist.

"If" every man taught his own children, we would need no schoolmaster. "If" every man built his own house, we should have no carpenter.

"If" every man took care of himself, we should save expense of sheriff and policeman. True enough—but of no sense or value for we do not and we cannot live that way. These two closely allied and essentially defective theories of action are to blame for much of our misconduct. We inch along from day unto day, our eyes carefully fixed on our footsteps instead of the north star. We strive ceaselessly with our own dooryard and, if ours is pretty clean, look down with scorn upon our neighbor's. His yard may be piled high with blowing papers while he strove to improve the city government and get clean streets for all. Your clean yard does not make his clean, but if you helped him to help the city, all would be kept clean together.

Every man labors to build up his own business and provide for his own family—"If everyone did so, all would be provided for," we cry approvingly.

It is not true. In the effort of each to care for his own, that common action which cares for all is neglected and many a family suffers. Every woman labors to keep her own children fed and clothed, warmed and taught, to make them pure and good and happy. "If" everyone did so, all would be cared for, we insist, and continually exhort everyone to mind his or her own business—really believing that the world is best served in this small, selfish way.

It is not true.

In their isolation and pathetic limited efforts, the child and home do not receive as much benefit as they would from service of wider range and deeper purpose.

Let us pocket that foot-rule and take a survey of the track—the whole of it. "But we cannot see the whole of it!" No, nor you cannot see an inch of it. Tomorrow is as uncertain as 2001. But you plan cheerfully for tomorrow and buy theater tickets a week ahead. Any conscientious intelligence can plan for its sixty or eighty years, not as omniscient but as one taking reasonable chances. "My mother does not wish me to work. My duty is to her. She needs me every day," says the young woman of twenty with the foot-rule theory. And at forty she is left alone with no money, no profession, no practice, aim, or interest in life. She had a right to assume that life was before her in years as well as days—scores of them—and to plan for the whole. A profession would have made her better able to care for her mother and left her rooted and growing when her mother was gone.

"My wife and children are provided for. I break no law; my dooryard is in perfect order," says the worthy citizen. And presently some disease or crime, bred by the city's neglect of its tenements and its children, destroys his family and brings him to undeserved sorrow or ruin.

Undeserved? By no means. He did not do his duty—only a fraction of it. Not until the city is clean has anyone the right to be contented with a spotless private yard.

COLUMN 22

May 28, 1904

Much as in "Two Callings," her prefatory poem to *The Home*, Gilman here frames the moral imperative to work to improve the world through social service as a type of religious duty or calling. She follows this admonition to act with a homily on cleanliness next to godliness.

With or Without Calling

"You have your work; you can do that, must do it; but what can I do? I have no calling."

This is the position of many earnest souls today who long to be at work but are not driven from within in one inexorable line.

They look with envy on the "elect person" who is pledged to some special cause or profession and call that labor easy as compared with their perplexity.

So remaining in want of some manifesto from heaven as to what they should do, fearing mightily lest they embark on what they should not do, they do nothing. A clear word needs to be said to these would-be workers.

In the first place, it is not as "easy" as the uncalled suppose to be bound to labor in one settled line. It saves perplexity, of course; to be harnessed and driven is to be free from worry as to which road to take, but it also deprives the driven one of freedom of motion. The needs of the hour cry in vain; the stretched hands of opportunity must be passed by; he who carries water may see men starve and he who carried bread may see them die of thirst.

Suppose you are born a fiddler—good at fiddling and good at nothing else, your discursive efforts at usefulness in any other direction always a failure, the one plain path before you—to fiddle till you die. Of course, it is easy in a way. You develop your musical powers to their fullest, trying to praise God like Théocrite[1]; you have pleasure in your labor and honor, too; but there are times when the fiddle does not seem to be the most needed thing on earth and you long to be more immediately useful.

Philosophy and patience and large wisdom are needed by the specialist to avoid the twin pitfalls of this life—the blind pride which thinks his instrument the main and most valuable one, and the blind discouragement which sees no use for it.

The world needs some specialists and has them, and the peeling, stripping, and uprooting which go to make their usefulness are well-described by Mrs. Browning in her wonderful "A Musical Instrument":

> Sweet, sweet, sweet, O Pan,
> Piercing sweet by the river.

That reed was under no pressure of perplexity as to what he was for when Pan had done with him! But

> The true gods sigh for the cost and pain—
> For the reed which grows never more again
> A reed with the reeds by the river.[2]

The specialist has a clear path but not always an easy one. Fortunately for us all, there is more need for the majority in less marked paths. Eyes and ears are very useful but legs and arms are larger. Most of the work of the world can be done by intelligent humanity with no more consideration than that of wise choice and careful training.

"But how choose?" demands the person on the fence. (The fences are black with them.) "Those poor men there work because they have to and maybe they are doing the wrong thing. I do not have to from outside like them nor from inside like you. How shall I choose and know I am doing the right thing?"

There are times when one is tempted to pluck these captious idlers from their top rail and cast them in with those who "have to from outside," but some are really honest and conscientious and deserve an answer.

By virtue of your exalted position on that fence, dear friends, by virtue of your freedom from "have to," either outward or inward, you can overlook the field, see what needs to be done, and do that.

The "emergency man" is useful. The "general utility man" is needful, and the man who tries to meet an emergency and make himself generally useful is likely to develop in one of two ways. Either he will discover a latent aptitude by practice and so become a specialist or he will become valuable for his general experience.

There are splendid opportunities in not being driven into one line of work. One is free—free. One can look widely and study carefully, choose the direction and moment of action, and act with great effect.

The people without a mission and without compulsion are an invaluable reserve force whence fresh supplies may be expected at any time at the points where need is greatest.

The position is mainly held by women. You seldom find a man dawdling about and asking what he ought to do. He usually has to do something which is not wholly injurious or he is more or less a specialist and he cannot choose.

But there are many women now able to work, willing to work, ashamed of their futile, idle lives yet neither led nor driven in any one direction.

The world needs just such help and needs it badly. So much of the effort on new lines is necessarily experimental, so much more is necessarily unpaid that those who "do not have to work" are the very ones to undertake it.

The very strangeness and newness of the field puts the specialist at a disadvantage and calls for exactly the general intelligence, unbiased minds, and free good will of these perplexed women.

In every village, town, or city, in the country more than anywhere else, lie the projecting handles of opportunity waiting for these untrammeled hands. The "crying needs" are easily to be heard if we will but listen. Make a list for yourself of the things most wanted where you live, the common needs of your community:

Better roads.
Better training for schoolteachers.
More schoolhouses.
Suitable employment for convicts.
A milk inspector.
A restroom for country women who come in town to shop.
Public kindergartens.
Manual training.
Good public laundries.
Trained domestic service by the hour or day.
Better laws as to the housing of the poor.
Art in the schools. Whatever happens to be a local need or a general one which you care for most.

Then begin. Just begin anyhow. You will learn how to do it right by doing it wrong as a child learns to walk. The world has done enough already for us easily to avoid humanity's more infantile mistakes but each individual still learns his place by conscientious trial. You soon find what you cannot do—and so by gentle rebuttal here and there are pushed into your own place at last.

If the detached forces of our society could be turned on at the points where they are most needed, much beautiful work could be done, work desperately needed yet inviting no one who is compelled to look for pay and waiting long for those who are called.

Let us call ourselves and rejoice in our freedom to work as we choose.

Dirt and Patience

It is said that everyone must eat a peck of dirt before he dies but no one wants to do it all at once. Neither is it desirable to have this necessary peck sifted and ground into us by force—cast stinging into our eyes, poured in our laps, powdered in our hair. But whosoever travels by rail today, in a soft-coal country especially, must endure this evil. And we do endure it with patience—sometimes a smiling patience, sometimes the immovable, calm patience of good breeding or despair. Those who can afford to dress for the occasion dress for dirt as do those who descend into a mine. Those who cannot afford special costume, a dirt-dress, sustain injury to their ordinary wear, again with patience.

Look down the long car—it is dim with smoke and dust.

Here a child, more healthy in its demands, insists on having the window open. It must have dirt and smoke but it will have fresh air also. In at the window pours the bitter smoke and a fine rattling flood of cinders. They get in the child's eyes but that is borne patiently. A stern parent insists that the window be shut and the current of fresh air ceases. But above, through the open ventilators, pours the fine cloud of smoke and cinders undeterred. The injured lungs slowly progress toward the inevitable disease produced by inhaling bits of coal. Pale and limp, sick with the heat and foul gases, the passengers lean back as best they may in every attitude of resignation. The less patient man squirms and changes his position, walks up and down, goes out to stretch his legs on the station platform.

The more patient woman, forbidden such activity and forbidden also to put her feet up and have her arms over the back of the seat, accustomed so well to sitting still as a business, continues so to sit under this affliction, trying the strength of her corset by her spineless relaxation. The anatomist marks the in-curve at the "pit of the stomach" and speculates on the evil being wrought within her by the steady pressure, sees the slow perfecting of the "corset-liver" well-known to medicine and laments it. The artist, sulky enough anyway by reason of the evils of the journey, notes instead the bad lines of the figure, the shapeless, vase-like curves of the waist and the limp shoulders and chest sitting in the embracing rim of the corset as in a dish. The restless activity of the child, the lounging of the man is better than this flaccid immobility. So they sit or squirm or lounge or walk about in the heat and noise and dirt and evil smell of coal gas, developing the virtue of patience.

Meek citizen of a civilized nation, dweller in an enlightened age, you travel much and suffer much therein. Does it never dawn on your downtrodden mind that the suffering is not essential to the traveling? Does the average traveler know that there are in existence patents not a few for the consumption of smoke and cinders by the fire that makes them? The ingenuity of man has devised ways to avoid this evil thing, the process of slow death by dirt, and still we do not see it put in practice. Why is this? If a way is known to make travel so much safer and pleasanter, how does a year pass without our using it? There are two reasons, both strong and valid. In the first place, it would cost something to use these methods of consuming smoke and cinders. It is cheaper to let them loose. In very primitive times we all lived in smoke wherever there was a fire. A mere hole in the roof let out the surplus after the inhabitants had breathed it. Our smoke-makers are satisfied with this primitive method. A hole in a pipe to let it out is all the apparatus they care for, especially as they themselves are not forced to breath it every day. Why should they introduce elaborate mechanical contrivances when simple ones will do? The new way would cost money. Those who make the smoke are wise.

In the second place, the traveling public like the stationary public are so accustomed to endure evil that most of them have never thought of the smoke-and-cinder nuisance as removable. They unconsciously assume that it must be so—because it is so.

It is to be questioned whether one in a thousand knows that there is any way to make the fire consume its smoke—or cares. And if any do know it, they never question the power of the sovereign railroad to wreck its will upon the public; they are meekly grateful for the slow concession to absolute need and demand nothing further.

They seem to think that it is very good of the corporation to allow them to travel on any terms and that the reluctant, grudging provision made for increased demands is pure disinterested benevolence. They do not know that it is their just demand which alone creates and maintains the railroad service of the country, from track-layer to president, and that they may make that service what they choose. Those who breathe the smoke are fools.

COLUMN 23

June 4, 1904

The first part of this column contains the donnée of Gilman's *The Crux* (1911), in which she rewrote the formulaic western novel from the eastern heroine's point of view. In her alternative plot, a group of eastern women migrate to the American West in search of personal happiness, economic opportunity, and better health.[1] The second part underscores this latter point, emphasizing women's need for "right physical development."

Woman's "Manifest Destiny"

Admitting that a woman's destiny is to marry, that that is what she was made for (among other things), that in this position lie duty and honor and happiness and personal profit—why does she not set about it more valiantly?

Not in a leap-year seizure of such men as are within reach—there are not enough of them to go around, in England by hundreds of thousands, in our New England states, in plenty of places where superabundant women lag uncommendably in their primal mission. Believing as they do, how in honor and conscience can they wait supinely for what never happens instead of heroically seeking opportunity? In the world as a whole, men and women are about equally apportioned, and even though the waste of men folks in our primitive wars deplete the ranks, there are still great numbers in many places.

Why do not the women who really believe that marriage is their mission go forth in bands of maiden emigration to the frontiers where lonely men grow hard and bad for lack of "women's influence"? This would not show the unmaidenly forwardness of pursuing the particular man; they could be as coy and difficult to please as they liked when fairly in the field; it would merely indicate a frank recognition of their foremost duty and a high-minded determination to fulfill it.[2]

Of course, such migration would bear upon the face of it a confession that these women wanted to be married. Well, ought they not to want to fulfill their highest duty? What is there to be ashamed of in that? Why should women be unwilling to admit a perfectly righteous purpose? Is the social maneuvering in which they spend laborious years to this one end more worthy and honorable than frank emigration?

Honest, self-supporting women have as good a right to go to Nevada or Montana or South Africa as they have to go to a summer resort. And instead of competing madly for a minority of cautious and experienced men, they would have woman's real prerogative of choice among competing suitors. Moreover, it is not only that these laggard women sin in omission of their great duty where a little laudable effort would fulfill it but that the unwomaned men suffer for lack of home and love and right living; and the frontier country suffers and waits for the refining and uplifting, the pacifying and improving which follow an established family life.

Is the historic development of America nothing to its women? If we are in truth citizens, let us get about our duties. The upbuilding of our country, the overcoming of evil tendencies, the fostering of all social improvements—these call for the increase of good people and the influence of our best civilization.

With two such calls as this—the most basic duty of the woman and the highest duty of the citizen combined—we ought to see a steady pour of good women to those places where women are most needed.

We see no such things. Unprincipled women go and prey upon defenseless men. High-principled women do not go. They would say it was due to modesty and timidity. Timidity is a mild, pretty name for cowardice—as fib is a pretty name for a lie.

Women should not be afraid to do right even if it costs some hardship. As for modesty, there is nothing immodest in fulfillment of duty—of one's great mission. Modesty is sometimes alleged to cover mere laziness.

The character of several States and territories of our country and many other places could be rapidly changed by the simple presence of numbers of intelligent, educated women. The character of the population would change, too, in rapid sequence. Politics would alter for the better, education advance more rapidly, the world's good be better served in all ways.

Let the conscientious surplus of women go West, like the young man.[3] They would carry benefit to the lands adopted and would greatly improve the position of women at home.

Educated Bodies

One of the neglected duties which stare women in the face from nearly every looking-glass is that of a right physical development.

The position of women after their long degradation is in many ways analogous to that of the freed slave.

He is refused justice on account of his inferiority. To reply that the inferiority is largely due to previous injustice does not alter the fact.

What he has to do is to build up race character and capacity under the past and present disadvantages. If he does it, he will make a splendid addition to our nation. So the woman, saddled with disabilities due in her case not to any racial difference and not to any necessary weakness of sex distinction but solely to past conditions, must prove her equality before she can expect to have it recognized.

The physical inferiority of the average woman is a needless handicap.

She forgets—if she ever knew—that the female of advanced species of animals is a strong, fine creature, quite able to keep up with the male in the struggle for existence.

His superfluous decorations in the way of antlers, mane, and tail feathers do not help him to get dinner or to escape from his enemies. Among the fierce carnivorous beasts she is if anything the better fighter of the two.

Now here are we, belonging to a species of distinct standards in physical beauty and power, possessed not only of knowledge of what that standard is but of visible types in picture and statue and yet content to go about in slovenly dog's-eared bodies instead of the crisp, clean-cut beauty, the vigorous development, that make life so much more a joy to all mankind. We are, of course, hampered by heredity, but what of that? So is and has been every form of life on earth from the beginning. Life is one continual struggle to outgrow one's grandmother.

The New Englander inherits a flat chest, a delicate digestion, and an enlarged conscience. Very well, let the conscience be exercised on the chest—we can enlarge the one and reduce the other at the same time. We need not remain as we are. Improvement is nature's first law. We strive persistently to "improve" our minds—why not improve our bodies?

Much has been done in our schools and colleges, much in outdoor athletics, games, and sports. But though the girl develops far better than she did a generation ago, the woman has not yet a proper pride in her own body.

She is concerned about her hat, her skirt, her straight-front effect, and her bustle, but the right carriage and proportion of her own body she cares not for.

This is another line of work in which women can do much with or without the ballot. To show we are strong, wise, and brave without it will go far toward getting it.

The "notion counters" array of body-deformers is a piece of damaging evidence.

COLUMN 24

June 11, 1904

In this miscellany Gilman discusses "interesting people" or celebrities and explains "man's dual nature" in Lamarckian terms, though her remarks are more ambiguous than similar comments in *Women and Economics*.[1] Never a vegetarian, she also defends the consumption of meat and the wearing of animal fur for "comfort," though not for sex decoration.

Interesting People

When Mrs. Ponsonby de Tomkyns invited the great prima donna to meet the great duchess and the great duchess to meet the great prima donna,[2] a certain social phase was most cleverly typified.

Many are the forces governing the elaborate maneuvers of our social world, some subtle, some most patent, and among them this one stands out clearly—the desire to meet "interesting people." Simply to "meet people" is not enough, though that in itself is a steady and insatiate demand; it is further requisite that the people be of a specific quality, in some way differing from the general run, marked, notable, "interesting."

For this reason English society stands so deservedly high in Europe: because therein one is more apt to meet not only the people who own things but the people who do things, and while the possessors of lands and titles differ somewhat as one star differeth from another in magnitude, those whose distinction lies not in what their fathers gave them but in what they themselves are giving to the world are necessarily more varied and impressive.

Figure 3. George du Maurier, "Killing Two Birds with One Stone," in *English Society at Home* (London: Bradbury, Agnew, 1880), no. 19.

With women in especial, those women of wealth and leisure whose only activities are social—"social" in the limited sense—this desire to associate with notable persons is intense and incessant.

The great painter, singer, writer, actor, soldier, one great in anything, is in demand far exceeding the supply, and small ones are foisted into undue prominence to fill the gap; for the uninteresting people are many and the interesting people are few. It is no wonder that anyone, set comfortably down to have everything and do nothing, grows unconsciously dull; and when large numbers of persons continually having everything in the same manner and continually doing nothing in the same manner meet together, they have small ground for entertainment—much in common, to be sure, but nothing in particular.

Hence the refreshment of looking at and talking to those whose lines are wider, deeper, more exciting and who, because of large and varied work, develop in character and become with no special effort of their own these precious "interesting people."

Two possibilities suggest themselves as offering hope of a more extensive and reliable supply of these social necessities.

One, that a bureau be established, local, national, even international perhaps, through the good offices of which a constant supply of freshly interesting people could be furnished and those of standard attractions be kept in active circulation.

With proper registers and liberal fees and with due business activity, there should be no difficulty in supplying every social function of importance with at least one interesting person.

Lists of the desirable disengaged could be circulated in advance and applications registered early; there should be no serious difficulty in making every entertainment a success to patrons.

The other suggestion is not so feasible, so practical, but has elements of attractiveness if not considered too revolutionary. It is that those who seek so earnestly for entertainment and variety should each and all take up some large and useful work and become interesting people themselves.

Why "Dual"

There has been much talk for very long on the "dual nature" of mankind. Why "dual"? Are the conflicting impulses of our complex organisms so simple as that? Is not the term "dual" merely a relic of that crude and primitive stage of thought when we labeled the world Good and Bad without shade or compromise; when our picture of life was printed in two colors? The Angel and Devil period was sharply dramatic and easy of comprehension but have we not passed it?

What are the facts in the case, considering man not as a piece of fresh clay with God and Fiend fighting for possession, but as a product of long, slow, irregular evolution from beast to human?

The habits of one age are the instincts of the next. Man still retains many of the instincts and impulses of earlier periods in his history, that is all. The instinct of hunting—one older than humanity, dating back to quadrupedal prowlings perhaps, still survives in modern humanity. It may be eliminated in time or we may see fit to retain it. But there is nothing "dual" or essentially evil about it. It is simply a survival—a slowly-disappearing rudiment—as though we secretly cherished some innocuous tail or dew-claw. Most of our objectional traits of character were useful, even admirable, in their time. They are bad now because they are out of date.

Society as it proceeds in slow development requires and produces in us new characteristics, new virtues, a "new nature." If we for various reasons fail to respond with the conduct and temperament called for in our time, if we continue to manifest the feelings and behavior long since outgrown by the world, it merely shows that we are behind the times, belated megatheriums where we should be racehorses, crabapples where we should be Golden Sweetings. But it is not a simple case of duality. There are thousands of shades and complexities involved as we slowly eliminate earlier tastes and develop later ones. Instead of this dramatic opposition of good and bad we should learn to understand the delicate processes of social evolution and spend our energies in fostering the needed qualities of our time.

Human life is not a dueling ground, a field of moral combat between two clearly defined forces acting in direct opposition; it is a garden with a large and promising crop but irregularly developed.

Mere leaves and buds in harvest time are not sinful but they are disappointing when we expect pumpkins.

We do not, however, blame the pumpkin vine or accuse it of a dual nature. We conclude that the land was not suitable or the weather. Or perhaps that we do not know how to raise pumpkins.

A Wreath of Corpses

A clever, handsome woman kindly disposed enough to be singing for a Settlement Club wears around her hat a complete wreath of smashed hummingbirds. Not only their feathers, whose beauty might for a moment make us forget their background of death, but the wretched little creatures' dislocated wings and dried heads with staring glassy eyes, so ugly in their unnaturalness as to call anyone's attention to the anomaly.

That one animal should kill and eat another is the law of nature. Only the Buddhists and some vegetarians seek to be better than God in this arrangement. To kill in self-defense is also natural; to kill for various uses of hide and tallow, sinew and bone, is like killing to eat. But to kill for ornament is a thing no creature does but man—and men have ceased to do that in civilized races.

As intelligence increases, as education extends, as the higher sympathies develop, the associative idea of death and pain becomes stronger than the sensuous effect of color.

But our women in this respect are not civilized. Their love for beads and spangles shows the true savage in his harmless weakness, and their indifference to cruelty even in its frankest exhibition shows that savage in darker colors.

Fur may be essential to our comfort; beady-eyed heads and flaunting tails of little dead beasts are not. They are not beautiful—any more than a string of scalps, and they belong to the same era.

"Burglars, Thieves, or Servants"

Here is a nice classification, reminding one of our own group of "idiots, lunatics, criminals, and women."[3] But this one has solid foundation. It means business. One of our numerous insurance companies guarantees against loss by these destroyers. The "moral" is that we should give a little more serious thought to our domestic machinery.

Is it after all the best way to live—this complicating family privacy with unknown foreigners? Here is the safety of the home—our property, the health and lives of our children—imperiled by these strangers in our midst.

If the danger were not serious and general, it would not form part of the regular risks undertaken by a big insurance business. Suppose we think about it.

COLUMN 25

June 18, 1904

Gilman attends the Quinquennial Congress of the International Council of Women in Berlin, Germany, in June 1904. Though not a formal member of the US delegation, she travels with the members and participates in many of their activities.

A Steamer Letter

FRIDAY, MAY 27, 1904.
ON STR. FRIEDRICH DER GROSSE[1]—EIGHT DAYS OUT.

My Gentle Readers, Enraged Readers, or any kind of readers interested in these columns, will be regaled for the next two months with warmed-over essays and tales and fresh letters. This first one should, however, be called salt.

As a steamer letter written at sea, it is dedicated especially to those fond, inexperienced persons who imagine "a sea voyage" to comprise all manner of balm to body and spirit.

"Take a sea voyage," says your doctor. "You need a change—you need a complete rest. Nothing is so restful as ocean travel—sleep a great deal—eat plenty—keep very quiet—get all the ozone—the pure, exhilarating sea air!"

So the confiding invalid invests her little all in a ponderous ticket and many conspicuous trunk labels and sets forth on the towering liner. The "change" is granted her. A more complete change from the comforts of civilized life could hardly be desired. But as to rest and quiet!—as to eating!—as to that much-extolled sea air! Let us suppose the lady to be seasick for a few days. That is nothing so dreadful. Some, to be sure, suffer much but ordinary seasickness is rather beneficial. One ceases to eat, which gives a rest to the internal machinery, and other causes give it exercise! Then there is a period of quiescence—nothing doing. This busy food-factory of ours is closed for repairs and more thoroughly renovated than by a course of spring medicine.

So we will not dwell upon the discomforts of seasickness but merely upon those incidental to the voyage *per se*. As to eating. If ever there is a time when one needs simple, wholesome, nourishing food, it is on a steamer. And if ever there is a time when mortal stomach—that pale and weary organ so recently outraged, so tired, so grateful for peace—was presented with a medley of ill-assorted luxuries, it is on a steamer. Heliogabalus[2] might have liked it, or Vitellius,[3] or any professional epicure, but for persons inured only to "home cooking" or what a modern purse and taste command at a restaurant, this deluge of dainties with two sets of foreign names is not what the soul craves. However, in its heavy-gorgeous way, the food is good and if one is well, it can be assimilated.

But when we come to consider that "complete rest" which was promised, for which we abandoned our beloved bed and board, our family and circle of friends, I should like to be shown where it can be found on shipboard.

Does one take to one's bed for it?

These beds are straight and narrow enough to lead to eternal life[4] and hard as the way of the transgressor.[5] Two enormous blankets, buttoned into a bag of sheeting that looks like a tablecloth, keep one warm but do not lend themselves to changes of temperature with any degree of facility. When they give you clean sheets, it is another bag put on over the first one. Pillow cases the same.

Adjusting one's self to this padded shelf, rest is then confidently expected. It is not easy for a body accustomed to be still when it sleeps to sleep while being swung and joggled about. It is not easy for a brain accustomed to quiet when it sleeps to sleep under an intermittent assault of all manner of strange noises. No one would expect to sleep at home if somebody was regularly joggling and irregularly tipping the bed and other persons were chopping wood, beating carpets, firing pistols, chapping and popping and whistling, ringing bells and tooting horns at intervals.

As a measure in therapeutics it might appeal to an Apache medicine man, but it is not a rest cure.[6]

However—you get up after a while and come on deck. This you have read about and seen pictures of. You have your rug—a Kenwood,[7] if you are wise—and your chair and a little pillow. The wide ocean is before you to gaze listlessly across. Now for that complete rest!

And you find yourself cooped up for an interminable week or more in a sort of garden party and afternoon tea. Your chair is but one of a row set thick along the crowded deck, all filled with people, all—or mostly all—talking, talking, talking the day long. That listless gazing across the illimitable waters is grievously interfered with by innumerable other people who walk. Up and down, up and down they walk between you and the sea, over your head if there is a deck above you, underneath if there is a deck below you, and right in front of you wherever you are.

They have to walk. You walk yourself as soon as you are able. It is such a relief from resting!

On a big liner in the season of travel, there is no place short of the masthead where one can be alone—and passengers find that "Zutritt verboden."[8]

And now for that trump card of good doctor—"the sea air."

Sea air is a fine thing. On many a clean-scoured sunny rock, on level yellow beaches, on warm windy downs of close turf have I lain and gloried in that strong, sweet ocean air. Clean, vivifying, strengthening, full of ozone and inspiration—too much cannot be said for sea air. Unless you are rheumatic. Sea air is apt to be damp. When you are at sea, it seems invariably damp. Your bed is damp; your clothes are damp. You never feel really dry. But the dampness is the main thing you can secure in the way of sea air—at sea. Did you expect to breathe it—poor landling? What you breathe on an ocean steamer is not so much like ozone as it is like $H.2.S.O.4$.[9] (That may not be the way to write a chemical formula but those are the letters and figures, I think. At any rate, that is the kind of smell.)

If you are warm-blooded and clad in furs and can sit or walk all day in the teeth of the wind—when there is a wind—you get sea air. But nowhere else. The air you get otherwise is not sea air but ship air—and if any animal has fouler breath than these maritime monsters, I have not met it.

If you go "forward" thinking to find sea air, you smell the steerage, which is not invigorating. If you go leeward to find shelter from the searching wind, you also find the ports and windows open and more kinds of smells pouring out of them than ever you smelled on land. Wherever you plant your chair, some blunt-nosed ventilating pipe is near you and contributes its sample of what is going on in the bowels of the ship. And if you go to the stern—misguided wanderer—you find sweeping over you in a mingled stream all the odors that drift back along the mighty creatures decks, a rich *potpourri*—the blended reek of the whole vessel. Of course, it is diluted with sea air—else would you die unpleasantly, but for the pure article give me a solitary stretch of coast somewhere above all the voyages that ever were taken. At least on steamers. Perhaps in the sailing days it was better. Soot and cinders did not mingle with your ozone nor so many kinds of cooking go on down below your stateroom.

One other thing deserves to be mentioned in enumerating the pleasures of a voyage. Surely nowhere save on an ocean steamer are the inequalities of our social life so coarsely forced upon you. It is a shock to go from Fifth Avenue to the lower East Side in New York, but it takes some little time to get there—there is a merciful distance between. But here the rank squalor of the steerage, its slouching, hopeless forms and discouraged faces, its inconvenience and visible misery, is arranged like a spectacle before you. The first-cabin passengers stand gazing down at the steerage, laughing, taking photographs, as if it were a bear pit.

The second cabin is less obtrusive, being merely fenced off in the rear on the promenade deck, and its ill-bred children daringly dodge around the barrier and visit the glories of the first. Second-cabin traveling is very popular, too, having really all the comforts of the more expensive class for about half the money. But it is a painful thing to any genuine democrat to see people thus glaringly cut in sections—financial sections—and to have to see it all the time.

To add a few personalities for the benefit of good suffragists. Our Grand Old Woman has been "on deck" every day of the trip—has not missed a meal. And her sister is with her in vigor and cheerfulness.[10]

Mrs. Blankenburg[11] and Mrs. Catt[12] have also been good sailors. The suffragists and councilors usually meet in the evening around one of the tables in the big saloon and hold all manner of informal confabulations.

A band of yellow-waving[13] sisters came to the Hoboken Pier to see the party off with beautiful souvenirs of flowers for Miss Anthony and others.

It is a happy and harmonious group having very good times together and all well-pleased, I fancy, that the voyage is so nearly over. I am!

Another "Woman's Paper"

One more of the papers supposed to be specially adapted to women has turned up. It is a cheap one, an inferior one, but in it make-up and table of contents follows the same lines as those of our biggest and most successful femininity-pleasing periodicals.[14] By what these papers offer to our women we may learn what the women like, and by what they like we may learn what they are. The predominant features of these specially prepared combinations of reading matter are fashions, fashions both for dress and for house furnishing, home-service and other kindred matters; specific directions as to the management and care of a home and family, notably as to the care of infants; fiction, of course, of the mildest; directions for preserving fruit (and beauty); and information carefully prepared in a sweetened edition.

With this goes a mass of advertising as to domestic supplies and feminine diseases and the most gentle editorials calculated to suggest without offending.

The lesson not only offered but forced upon us by all this is that "the woman reader" holds a most peculiar position in her business. Here we have "Hints to Housekeepers" ladling out the same old directions as to how to remove grease spots, to protect from moths, and the like. Offer these to any Cleaning and Renovating establishment and see what they would say. Would not the answer be, "I know my business, thank you"? There is the advice as to the care of infants. Here is offered in the paper now serving as an instance the following:

"During the first year the only suitable nourishment for an infant is its own mother's milk or that of a healthy wet-nurse. Suckling should be repeated every two hours—less frequently at night."

And again: "Avoid all those compounds which are not superior to natural foods."

When we contrast this advice with the popular superstition about the marvelous infallibility of the maternal instinct, there seems to be a mistake somewhere—perhaps two.

If the mothers have this mysterious, unerring guide to teach them what is best for their children—(and if they have it at all it ought surely to come in play in this primal function of feeding the baby!)—then why do they need directions from mere men?

Again, if they do not have it, can it be supposed that they would undertake so important a business with no better source of information than these irresponsible newspaper items? There seems to be a serious deficiency somewhere in this mother business and it does seem as if the Woman's Paper was equal to supplying it. Suppose we offer "Hints to Shopkeepers" to the managers of our big stores or "Advice on the Care of Carnations" to the florist—would not each promptly reply, "I know my business"?

Here is the core of the trouble. If a man does not know his business, he fails and has to give it up and try another. Under pressure of this law, men take their work seriously and learn what they have to do. The sifting process of failure finally brings them to what they can do—or if they can do nothing, if they are complete and proven failures, other men can learn from them what to avoid.

But if a woman does not know her business, she cannot give it up and take another—she is maintained in her capacity by Mr. Jones—who pays the freight, and very heavy freight it often is.

Thus subsidized, women do not take their business seriously, do not learn it as men learn theirs, and what is worse their failures give no useful lesson to the others—for each stands or falls alone—in "the privacy of the home."

In this position of isolated inefficiency, without previous training, and prevented by the ceaseless pressure of her duties from learning how to do them while she has them to do, the woman's difficulties can only be alleviated by some medium of information which can penetrate the privacy of the home and give these eternal teaspoonfuls of advice over and over continually.

Hence the woman's paper in its popular and successful form. Does its popularity and its success indicate the proportion of incapacity among women?

COLUMN 26

June 25, 1904

Gilman chronicles a pair of personal experiences, her visit to Germany in June 1904, and her "rest cure" while in the care of the nerve specialist S. Weir Mitchell in 1887.

From Germany

BERLIN, JUNE 8, 1904.

The National Council of Women of Germany met us at Plymouth with letters and leaflets, a cordial invitation to a reception at Bremen, and a drive about the city. They were expecting fifty and we were but fifteen all told.[1] However, we accepted unanimously and telegraphed as requested from Cherbourg.

When we reached Bremen Harbor at about 6 A.M., there on the deck were three good ladies to receive us, and big placards marked "I.C.W." made us feel quite at home.

A special compartment was reserved for us on the train and we enjoyed the two hours' ride to Bremen through a level country all green and sweet in the bright June weather. Most of our party went to Hillman's Hotel,[2] an excellent one. There we rested till eleven, when five carriages appeared and we rode in state through the interesting and beautiful old town full of shady parks and rich with flowers, stopping once to enter the great Cathedral.[3] The reception was given in the Parkhaus,[4] a stately building in the midst of the park. There were good things to eat and drink (of a strictly "temperance" nature, these last), music and singing, and addresses in both

English and German. All these German women seem to speak English with ease, which is fortunate for us.

The sense of common interests, common purpose, and goodwill was felt by us all. Our Consul at Bremen made an excellent address, the only gentleman present and seeming rather to enjoy it.[5]

We started for Berlin at eight the next morning, Tuesday, May 31st, arriving at one, and the members and delegates found plenty to do. Extra persons, mere speakers-at-large like myself, have a far easier time.

For two days the business meetings labored in several languages and the International Woman Suffrage Union was formally instituted. Eminent women from several nations were present and worked enthusiastically for the new organization.

It was a great disappointment not to have with us Mrs. A. Watson-Lister of Australia, whose sad loss compelled her sudden return, but the women voters of the new world were not without representation. Mrs. Napier of New Zealand was an impressive speaker with her story of accomplishment to encourage our aspirations.[6]

To Europe, where the closely crowded nations are so much a menace to one another, this union of women with the hope of urging on all measures that promote peace, education, and reform, is even more valuable and impressive than it is to us. It is hard for an American, safe between two oceans, with an English-speaking people to the north and only Mexico touching us in any way foreign, to grasp the international problems here.

Saturday evening, June 4, a public suffrage meeting was held with speakers from America, England, Sweden, New Zealand, Holland, and Germany. The hall was full, crowded, many standing in the aisles to our great danger had there been a fire. I rather wondered at this, having heard much of the strictness of police regulations in Germany. It was a fine audience, not only in quantity but in quality. One man spoke for us also, Dr. Breitscheid,[7] and spoke well.

Miss Rodger-Cunliffe of England[8] told how many of the local suffrage privileges of women were being taken from them by changes in form of local government, the tendency being to abolish small bodies and concentrate more and more in town and county councils; and that the result was to strengthen their feeling that they must have Parliamentary suffrage, without which they had no security in any minor concessions. She spoke, too, of how nobly the working women of England were striving for this end, seeking to elect a representative of their interests to Parliament and to pay his expenses out of their own small earnings in ten thousand sixpences! This part of the project was defeated, however, by the fall in wages to starvation limits, owing to the unchecked gambling of Mr. Sully in the cotton markets of America.[9] We have grown to see the evils of the Louisiana Lottery and others like it but are still blind to this public, international kind of gambling with its results of unearned wealth to some and undeserved ruin to others, mischievous in effect both on character and on real economic progress. This is a concrete case for suffragists to study, seeing how this speculation on the New York Exchange may have interfered with the progress of beneficent legislation in England.

A beautiful lady of Holland, speaking excellent German, made the most popular speech of the evening,[10] and our inimitable Anna Shaw closed the exercises with a short and deeply moving address.[11] The audience—very hot and crowded and lacking air, many standing—were interested to the end and applauded warmly.

I have been inquiring about the standing of the suffrage movement here and find that it is but two years old as an organization and has already about two thousand members.

This is somewhat so with us, many excellent women giving themselves heartily to far-reaching reforms, in exhausting public work, and yet fearing the simple, primal, self-evident proposition that in a democratic government the shortest way to get anything is to vote for it in predominant numbers.

Considering the newness of the movement here and the extreme radicalism it is supposed to represent, the numbers and character of those interested in it give great encouragement. Miss Anthony is greeted everywhere with loving enthusiasm.

On Sunday in the American church here,[12] a meeting was held in which she spoke with Mrs. Catt, and Miss Shaw read from the Scriptures and prayed. There are no women ministers in Germany and Miss Shaw made a great impression.

Mrs. Catt is winning all hearts. Her evident ability, her clear, strong, penetrating voice, and logical method of presentation, together with the winning womanliness of her appearance, have impressed everyone. She was promptly elected president of the International Suffrage Association without a dissenting voice, and everyone is pleased with the choice.

When the time comes for women to hold office in America, we shall have some well-prepared for such places by the labor and the diplomacy incidental to leadership in woman's organizations.

They will not be the traditional young woman with a baby in arms, as is so often feared by the anti-suffragists, but practiced and well-seasoned workers as well able to serve their country as they are now to serve the cause of women.

Their Dressmakers

"You geese!" said I. "Why don't you keep one of your own?"

This address may seem severe, but then I was an invalid and invalids are allowed to be irritable. Perhaps convalescence had "set in" and made me crosser; at any rate I quite lost my patience with those girls.

They were trained nurses, some half-dozen of them together in a fashionable rest cure,[13] fine, handsome young women and old enough to know better than to waste time, temper, and money in such idle fretting. My own nurse began it. Her dress had not come to hand when it was promised nor within three weeks of it—indeed, it was still behindhand, though she had used every means in her power to urge on the recalcitrant dressmaker. The prettiest nurse in the house happened in just then and was presently joined by another.

One of the amusing things in a rest cure is the ways the nurses congregate in the invalids' bedchambers and chatter like merry magpies. Your own friends you may not see—nor books nor papers; the doctor's calls are short and quiet; no outside influence is allowed to break the charmed silence of the sickroom; but these merry nurses, full of health and spirits, flit in and out as freely and converse as fluently as though the rest cure was an afternoon tea.

So I got quite an insight into the affairs of these damsels and they interested me.

Well-paid, well-fed, well-lodged, and doing work which, though sometimes exhausting, was often easy and always crowned with the sense of noble usefulness—they seemed to me most enviable workers. But they themselves had no such notion. Their complaints were lively and among them this upbraiding of their several dressmakers ranked high. "Why, she never got my fall dress done last year till after Christmas!" said the prettiest one, "and I sent it in September!" "I haven't a single thin dress yet," said the stout nurse with the yellow hair. "Here I'm wearing last summer's and they're all rags." "It's perfectly outrageous!" said the dark-eyed one; "you can't depend on anything they say. They promise and promise and you can wait till your clothes fall off you—much they care!"

One would have thought to hear these damsels that they were bond slaves of some awful potentate, helpless sufferers at the hands of this august being who made or rather delayed to make their dresses.

Wherefore my short stock of patience gave out and I assailed them from my pillows. They took it meekly enough for we were all good friends, but they did not grasp the idea.

"What do you mean?" said the oldest and really the shabbiest of the party.

"Just what I say!" I replied a little sharply. "Give me a pencil and paper and I'll show you."

The doctor would never have allowed this but then he wasn't due that day. So I had the pencil and paper and an extra pillow at my back and proceeded to illustrate my argument. "How many are there of you here?" I asked—"in your bureau—you girls who know each other?"

It appeared there were about twenty in round numbers, all fairly well-acquainted and all suffering under this same dereliction of dressmakers. "Now I'm going to talk business," said I, "and you must give me the facts. About how much do you girls pay these dressmakers of yours in a year?"

They fell to figuring in that profuse, self-contradictory way peculiar to the unbusinesslike mind, but out of it all I finally succeeding in extracting an average of something like fifty dollars a year which they paid for dressmaking.

It seemed a good deal to me, especially for women who really needed only their neat nurse costumes and one for street and traveling wear. But they thought differently. Far be it from them to wear a uniform—they scorned it. Even their caps they took off after the doctor had made his rounds.

They wore in the sickroom half-worn street dresses and kept their wardrobes filled from the top and filtering down constantly in degrees of increasingly shabby unfitness.

This was not my point just then, however.

"Fifty dollars a year," said I. "Twenty of you—that's a thousand dollars a year. Now why in the name of all reason and common sense don't you join your mutual necessity, get each to pledge the amount and select her dates in advance, and hire a dressmaker of your own?

"It is just about as much work as one smart woman with a machine could do in a year, and you could have a signed contract to hold her to dates or forfeit payment. Here's a crowded labor market on one hand, and you perfectly able to employ but not able to get your orders filled. It's absurd. Select your dressmaker and hire her by the year—then you'll never have any more trouble."

Perhaps my being an invalid made me weak-minded—more so than usual. Archimedes offered to lift the earth if he was furnished a leverage outside it.[14]

I daresay my plan was a good one if those twenty young women could agree on a dressmaker—and a fair division of dates.

COLUMN 27

July 2, 1904

Gilman continues to report about the Congress of Women in Berlin.

Letter from Berlin

BERLIN, JUNE 12, 1904.

It is a pleasure to hear the *Woman's Journal* warmly commended over here. One lady said, "Why, I should not have known all about this Congress, who were the speakers, and how important it was to be if it were not for the *Woman's Journal!*"

Our time is going gaily. Mrs. Catt has written of the suffrage meetings[1] and I hope Mrs. Sewall will write of the Council or some faithful "Mitglied"[2] who has been to all the meetings of that august body. Not being a delegate, not having a voice or vote, and being ignorant of many tongues, I avoided these meetings. To hear and not speak is a trial at best; but to hear and not understand—and not speak—is worse.

In these gatherings of women, speaking three languages officially and heaven knows how many actually, the wonder is not that there is misunderstanding and delay but that there is so much understood and accomplished. While men, even of one nation and in a long-established democracy, still fail of perfectly calm, clear, and brief discussion and swift accomplishment, women unaccustomed to parliamentary action and of many races make a very creditable showing. Humanity can see far ahead but can only progress gradually. The advance of women in all lines is one of the most rapid movements the world has ever seen. To the historical spectator it shows a railroad swiftness, but to those who are in it, it seems more like a canal-boat sometimes.

The beauty of Berlin in this lovely June weather—only one rainy day so far out of fourteen—is only exceeded by the hospitality of its people. The invitations come in flocks—from visiting-card size to huge, official-looking "Karten," 6 × 8. Invitations general and special, public and private, in houses, in gardens, in hotels, in museums, in the woman's club, in the parlors of the American Ambassador,[3] in a mighty building devoted to women's work of all sorts, and in the "feast room" of the Rathaus of the City of Berlin. Royalty itself is to receive a picked number—Miss Anthony always and of course, the Grand Old Woman of America; Mrs. May Wright Sewall; and Mrs. Mary Wood Swift. And every day come fresh invitations.

Fortunately, Berlin is not as vast in its distances as New York and Chicago. Fortunately, again, the cabs here (comfortable open carriages with a fine mechanical conscience set up before you, recording the distance and the price automatically) are refreshingly cheap. They start at 50 pfennigs, which is but 12 cents or so, and you can go a long way for a mark, which is a poor imitation of a quarter. The electric cars are comfortable, too, but the distracted foreigner, uncertain of her German and very certain that she must be in several places at once, rejoices in the cab.

These German women speak English almost without exception; many of them have been in America or at least in England; and most have friends and relatives in our country. So we find ourselves among friends, warmly welcomed, lavishly entertained, and very much at home.

The most impressive fact to my mind which is shown by traveling is the essential unity of human beings. The differences are superficial; the identity is deep. In the beautiful years to come, when society recognizes its children fully and gives to them, first and deepest, their heritage of world-feelings instead of leaving them as now to be continually reinforced in hereditary prejudices of family and race and only gather faint glimpses of the great world which is really theirs—then we shall recognize the big, friendly human heart in every people on earth and act accordingly.

They say that with the Oriental races it is different, that there is a veil between us and them that can never be lifted. I do not believe it. It is one of those statements, strongly made and helplessly accepted by our long-coerced minds, as so eloquently voiced by Kipling:

> Oh, East is East and West is West, and never the twain shall meet
> Till earth and sea stand presently before God's judgment seat.[4]

I haven't the book and cannot quote accurately. But the good man was trying to make us believe that nothing on earth could ever bring these longitudinal distinctions together. Being English, Mr. Kipling perhaps believes that Greenwich was foreordained and marked off distinctly on the primordial rock and little matters like east and west are always relative to it. But if one remembers that the earth is round, that it also revolves, that the Englishman's mysterious "East" is mere bald "West" to a Californian, and that England itself is "East" to a New Yorker, then we are not so sure they will never meet. In point of fact, there isn't an inch of the earth's surface that is not either east or west according to where you stand—except the poles. Our friends the Japanese are showing considerable capacity to "meet" with the Western civilization (which to them is "eastern," by the way) both in the arts of peace and those of war.

Here in Germany the people seem just like our own. More blond, perhaps, a bit stouter with fresher red in their cheeks, but far more sense of being "our own folks" than of being strangers. Even the *Grafins*[5] have the same intelligent, agreeable, familiar look, and a pleasant princess from Austria amazed me anew by being so humanly agreeable.[6]

The beauty, cleanliness, and order of the city are very impressive. These art-loving people have even managed to give beauty to their elevated railroad! Surely miracle could no further go. The big iron structure with wide supports of a soft, creamy, brown color has beneath it a graveled walk with occasional seats and grass and trees along the sides! There is a floor under the rails—nothing to drop through, and the noise is less than with us. I don't know how they manage that but wish we did.

But the beauty of the houses is what strikes me most. Not splendor and expense, not merely comfort and convenience, but beauty, the real thing. Why, even a blank wall—a big, staring wall such as we are so incessantly confronted with when our ungoverned buildings tower above one another—when these people have one, they so decorate it by a simple treatment of the color in the plaster that it gives the effect of arches and windows, string piece and cornice—of a fine house front, flat, instead of in relief. Even beyond that, in the Palast Hotel[7] court, a big blank wall is actually painted like a scene in the theater, not brilliantly, but in two colors perhaps, shaded browns—only instead of the dreary bricks you get an effect of great trees and shady distances.

When we realize what this earth might be—right here, right now, if we human beings would but wake up and set about it—it seems so splendidly good that one can hardly wait.

But one must wait. Only the young child picks open the bud to hasten its blooming.

Human life is bursting into flower before our eyes today, but that "day" is not one of twenty-four hours. How much will the good time be hastened when we, like the Japanese, are willing to go to other countries and learn, to take the best from each and yet keep our own national individuality after all!

These great International meetings of men and woman help the growth of the world most appreciably.

There is friction, of course—difficulty, of course—but the good accomplished far outweighs the incidental cost.

Our welcome in Germany ought to assure us that the people of the world are far more alike than they are different.

COLUMN 28

July 23, 1904

After visiting her daughter, Katharine, in Italy, Gilman embarks from Naples on July 4, files another report about the Berlin Congress during a Mediterranean stop on July 6, and lands in New York on July 13.[1]

Homeward Bound

SS *PRINZESS IRENE*,[2] JULY 6, 1904.

Once more at sea—and this time finding it much pleasanter. The *Prinzess Irene* is called "the lady ship" and a lady she is, serene, quiet, steady, and a little slow.

Hence we are spared the jarring of a hard-run screw and forge along as smoothly as a ferryboat. It being midsummer, there are few passengers going this way and this gives comparative quiet to the ear as well as the rest of the body. And with warm and pleasant weather, open ports, and habitable decks give us more "sea air" than is usually obtainable.

The rush and whirl of the Congress prevented my writing while it was going on, and a crowded week of traveling afterward was equally inimical to letters; but now there is time enough and a little space of removal gives a better picture in the mind.

For suffragists, the pleasantest feature of the great gathering might be found in the universal interest in the "Frauenstimmrecht"[3] among the gathered representatives of many lands, the keen interest and large attendance at suffrage meetings, and the special honor paid to our great Miss Anthony. When the Empress[4] received the presidents of each national council, Lady Aberdeen[5] the incoming and Mrs. Sewall the outgoing international president, she also received Miss Anthony on her own merits. Well has it been said, "There is nothing impossible to the steadfast determination of one human will."

When a human being absolutely and determinedly devotes a life to some one purpose, he or she grows great and that greatness is recognized sooner or later: it cannot be hidden.

To the old view that women are useful only as mothers with some additional convenience as housekeepers, the visible presence of great women who serve the world in their human capacity, if not as "females," is invaluable.

Of course, we need mothers, but there are plenty.

Of course, the fullest life should include all functions but not all of us may have all things. And in this strange, changeful, trying period of the renaissance of women, many must renounce much—in order to do more.

One woman at the Congress, a magnificent creature from Norway, young, strong, serenely beautiful, with a long, heavy, flaxen plait hanging down her back and ropes of big silver beads around her neck,[6] was also proudly carrying a sturdy child of a year or so. It was a splendid picture—the woman in all her typical, original power and beauty; the handsome, well-grown boy to prove fulfillment of all primal duty; and then the big human soul and mind—the interest in her country's progress and that of other countries; the journey from her northern home to join this meeting of the nations. In the smoother years that are coming, the alternative will not be forced upon the growing woman, and she will be able to be a full-grown, widely useful human creature and a happy woman, too. All honor to those who have served the world in these hard years of heavy cost, relentlessly demanded and so nobly paid!

This meeting in Germany was a triumphant success. The preliminary suffrage meeting was satisfactory—some coming to that who did not stay to the later proceedings; the Council accomplished much and the Congress was better than our hopes. There was a large attendance both of delegates and visitors, and the general public of Berlin filled the halls from day to day. The audiences were immense, including many men.

It must be a strange thing to a man, accustomed only to see women singly, in their private capacity or in social groups, each with an escort, to be present at these great gatherings, to see thousands of women together not "as women" but as human beings and members of society. Quite apart from argument and appeal, the impression made by the mere visible presence of such an aggregate of public-spirited women must be very great.

And it is. Many remarks were made on it by astonished German gentlemen.

Besides the public welcome, interest, and applause, we were received and entertained with all cordiality and honor by the hostess city. The beautiful houses of Berlin received us. Art museums, gardens, galleries, parks, all were open to us; royalty, nobility, and—what really counted for more than all—"der Stadt Berlin" itself magnificently entertained this organization of women united to serve the world.

The reception by the city, our great banquet in the richly decorated Rathaus, marks an epoch in the woman's movement. Here was the great public building, built by men and for men, the official home of the governing sex, open to do honor to the once only domestic sex—with Burgomeister, Oberburgermeister, magistrates, and ministers in their gold chains receiving and entertaining us. And this not as individuals, not as separate dignitaries however distinguished some of our women are, but as an organization of real value to the world.

It should be a lesson clear and convincing to those loyal but limited souls who put their chosen reform before all others and say, "We must have prohibition *first*" or "suffrage *first*" or "socialism *first*." We must have first what we can get first—and some things come together.

We do not confront a growing child and demand hair first or teeth first or bones first. We do not, or at least should not, confront a growing character, forming or reforming, and say, "We must have courage first" or "patience first." Growth is complex and gradual in individuals or in the world as a whole and needs to be studied before we can safely hasten it.

In earlier days, when less was known of the nature of man, we assumed the people could if they chose become quite different and behave quite differently. Now we are slowly and somewhat reluctantly finding out that conduct is the symptom of character and character the result of conditions. The problem of the scientific reformer is: How to change conditions so as to improve character and thus modify conduct to the desired form.

We are learning something of this problem, though but slowly.

Stealing a Servant

There is a peculiar feeling among women that it is dishonorable, mean, nasty—they have no words strong enough for it—for one woman to offer higher wages to another woman's servant and "take her away."

A better proof could hardly be asked or given of the fact that domestic service is not on the level of ordinary business employment but is a survival of an earlier stage of labor when work was not the property of the worker to be exchanged for money but was the property of the master.

The servant in the eyes of the woman is still something between part of the family and a piece of property. "She has taken 'my servant'" is the complaint—as if she owned the servant! We do not say "my butcher" and blame anyone who lures him to another city by better pay; we do not blame our minister for accepting a "call" to another church with a "wider field of influence" (and a higher salary); but we do most bitterly blame the servant who is thus "bribed" to leave us and still more bitterly the unworthy wretch who "bribed" her. "Especially," as one lady urged with passionate intensity, "especially if it is a *friend* who does it."

As the general public are not free to observe the merits of our servants and our enemies in particular are also excluded from our homes, it is difficult to see who could notice the able cook or housemaid except "a friend."

If the friend does so notice and desires to secure for herself the use of these abilities and can pay more for their use than the present mistress, why should she not make the offer?

"But it is so underhanded, so mean, to get away my servant behind my back! Why doesn't she come to me?"

Why should she come to you? You do not own the servant. Beyond the time of "warning" agreed upon in your contract, you have no more claim upon her time and strength than you have on that of a seamstress or a trained nurse.

In the business world, if a young man is doing good work for his employer and his merits are noticed by another employer and this other offers him a higher salary than the first, he announces that he wishes to leave at the end of his agreed time and leaves—with no hard feeling. Or the first employer, if he values the young man, asks him what he expects to make by the change and offers him that or more to keep him, and he stays with no hard feeling.

In the business world it is expected that the able man will rise and he does rise. In some cases his original employer offers him higher wages or gives them if demanded, but this is not frequently paralleled in the domestic world. That is a different place altogether, far more ancient, still holding the ideas and sentiments of a remote past. How is a servant to rise, to get on in the world, to develop her abilities, fill a larger place, earn more money? How indeed? We do not expect her to. It is the last thing that enters our thought. We still consider her in a vague way as part of the family ("familia," meaning domestics!), forgetting that a family is united by physical ties of birth and that an economic connection is on an utterly different plane. The wage system is an entirely different thing from the slave system and domestic service is a halting compromise between the two. Therefore do we expect "loyalty," "devotion," "respect" from servants, though why the person paid to cook should be more devoted or loyal than the person paid to fill teeth it is hard to see.

"Because she is in a position of trust!" is indignantly replied. "Because the work of caring for the family is entirely different from buying and selling. We *must* have permanent, dependable servants. The health and comfort of our families, the happiness, the very existence of our homes depends on them!" And we expect to have healthy and comfortable families and happy homes on the basis of four or five dollars a week "and found." If this work is so responsible, so valuable and important, how can we expect to have it regularly and efficiently done by these poor, ignorant four-dollar-a-week girls? Even with board and lodging added in, it amounts to only nine dollars, a dollar and a half a day and nothing on Sunday—the wages of the street laborer.

Look at the dollar-and-a-half-a-day man; would you be willing to entrust your family health and happiness to him? Is such as he fitted to hold a position of trust in the inmost center of the home? And if he is not, how can you expect it of his daughter? It is such false economy, this entrusting the most intimate and valuable work to the lowest class of labor and the worst paid! "But we could not afford to pay them more!" No, of course not, and the slaveowner could not afford to pay the slave anything. When labor is wasted, money is scarce.

Our primitive waste of labor in this business of domestic industry keeps the world poor.

So long as the women of the world are content to be house servants, whether to husbands or masters, that universal waste of labor retards our economic development.

No nation content with the spinning-wheel and handloom could keep pace in the great march of modern progress, and our hand-stove arrangement, our one-woman kitchen, is on a level with the twirling spindle of antiquity.[7]

Woman's Alleged Inhumanity to Woman

A popular writer in a current magazine has an article on the timeworn slander upon women, that they are more cruel to one another than are men.[8]

The patient acceptance of this old libel is one more proof of how little people think. Let a thing be said with some air of assurance, let it be repeated, preserved in print, stiffened by age, and the world believes it.

Now let us apply our minds in a broad and thorough way to the above proposition and see for ourselves if it is true.

The statement is a general one. It is not alleged that here and there a woman is unkind and cruel to another woman but that women as a whole are thus unkind and cruel to their sex. And it is not even as sharing in the injustice and severity which distinguishes the human race that women are blamed but as manifesting more cruelty than men to women or even than men to men.

If the statement were simply in regard to the race, none could deny it. Man—meaning the human race—is more cruel to his own kind than other beasts and also far more loving. No one disputes the poet's description, "Where every prospect pleases, and only man is vile,"[9] or the familiar charge, "Man's inhumanity to man makes countless thousands mourn."[10]

Among low savages, the women are certainly as cruel as the men to their prisoners and victims; and among fierce beasts there is choice in ferocity between the sexes unless the female be most courageous and relentless in attack. But all this is interracial and not intersexual.

We are asked to believe that in the human race one sex is more cruel than the other, and that not to the other sex but to its own kind.

Now let us look at the facts. That women have suffered much hardship and injustice in all races from the beginning of history until now is patent, but that their miseries were due to the treatment of their own sex is not so clear.

The most painful period of social evolution for women was that of the androcentric revolution which followed the long-established matriarchate. That era of decadent savagery brought more sorrow to woman than even she could bear and many a race died out from too much cruelty to its women. But the oppressor was the man.

In later ages, during the long, slow development of civilization, we find women always at a disadvantage. They were the slaves of men even when the chains were golden ones, and if they failed to please, no law protected them. Now it may well be that one slave is unkind to another, that one odalisque is jealous of another, that spite and treachery obtain in a harem, but none of these evils is comparable to the cruelty which so enslaves and degrades.

The greatest evil under which women have suffered is the loss of liberty. Did women rob them of it? They have suffered from lack of education. Did women withhold it? They have suffered from unjust laws. Did women make the laws? They have suffered from all the barbarities of war—loss of home, husband, son, loss of honor, of life. In the sack of a city, is it woman's cruelty to woman that fills the air with shrieks? Or in a modern city, rich and at peace, is it woman's cruelty to woman that sends the girl to suicide? Are the thousands of wretched prostitutes who shame our proud society the result of woman's inhumanity?

Men, says the popular writer in the recent magazine, and all others who uphold this ancient myth—men are kind to women, easier to work with, more considerate; it is far pleasanter to be employed by a man than by a woman.

The error here is mistaking gallantry for kindness or business experience for good will.

It is allied to the "natural protector" myth. Many people honestly believe that men are the natural protectors of women. So are miners the natural protectors of gold and stock-raisers of cattle. The shepherd protects his sheep from wolves and from the other shepherds—it is one of the prettiest figures in all poetry—but who shall protect the sheep from the shepherd? What in the name of reason does he want of those sheep but to fleece them and milk them and sell them and kill them? Any man protects his property if he can. But Uriah wasn't much of a protector against David when David wanted to do the protecting.[11]

It is not to be denied that women are jealous of one another and that polygamous wives or harem inmates or even a set of summer girls where men are scarce and hard to come by may do mischief to one another. But are they more jealous and cruel in this case than men similarly placed? If some matriarchal Solomoness had three hundred husbands and seven hundred (singular, but we have no masculine term for the others!) lovers, let us say, is it to be imagined that all these gentlemen would live together in unbroken peace and amity? Where the summer girl is few and men are many—at a military post, for instance—are there no machinations and rivalries? No doubt women are jealous of one another, but they do not kill their rivals as men do.

Masculine jealousy and sex-combat is [sic] inherent in the male in all animals; women show but a rudiment of it.

Isolated instances may be shown of some special malevolence of woman to woman, easily capped a thousand times by that of men to one another and to women, too. But in the broad path of history, from the savage brutally abusing his overburdened squaw or the peasant woman yoked with the ox to the schoolteachers of America demanding equal pay for equal work or protesting against laws which forbid their marrying, the principal cruelty and injustice under which women have labored comes from men.

Even with the worst of intentions and every opportunity, women could not in the nature of things ever bring upon women the shame and agony and lifelong ruin which they have so often had to bear from their natural protectors.

COLUMN 29

July 30, 1904

In the first two parts of this column Gilman again applauds the increase of women in the industrial labor market. In the final section she acclaims women leaders in civic improvement.

Is the Woman's Movement Slow?

A correspondent writes: "You must have an unfailing well-spring of hope and faith in your breast not to despair at the slow movement of reforms of woman in which woman as a rule takes such languid interest." Is it true that ours is a slow movement? Does it need hope and faith unlimited to see it go?

On the contrary, it seems to me that one must be blind and deaf not to thrill with excitement at the gathering rush of this swiftest of social changes.

Of course speed, like any other quality, is relative. A fast glacier would make a very slow express train and the fastest train compare ill with lightning. Moreover, we are now given to understand that the electrons in our atoms are bounding about far more swiftly than light travels!

In order to estimate the speed of a social movement we must have something to measure it by, something in its own class. To the student of ancient history, the changes in modern national relations are convulsive; to the sociologist, all historic events are but incidental details; and to the geologist even sociology is a trifling modern science. As for the astronomer—but his measurements are as dizzying as those of the electrons.

Social movements have to be measured by social movements. The change in the position of women must be compared with other changes affecting similar classes, and as there is but one similar class, i.e., men, we must compare it to that.

Men were once, socially considered, in the position of women a hundred years ago. That is to say they were totally unorganized, unspecialized, uneducated; they lived in the narrow circle of their own interests, their immediate and physical relationships, their personal activities.

Each man of them "did his own work." Whatever was necessary for him to do to maintain himself, he did alone and his duties and interests ceased with those of a wolf—self, mate, and young. He may have had some tribal affiliation—but so has a wolf. The woman a century ago had none save that of her church.

The "man's movement" has brought him forward from this position into that degree of civilization in which he now stands. He has developed the arts of peace in a high degree and even his wars are highly organized and somewhat ameliorated in their worst features.

The difference between man the individual hunter and man the intricately connected manufacturer, transporter, merchant, artist, scientist, jurist, and so on is a vast one. To reach his present position, the man's movement has been going on for uncounted thousands of years. We can trace him historically for several thousands, and the earlier steps were longer than the later ones.

If anyone were going to despair of anything, it might well have been of the man's movement, yet even that has attained enormous proportions and increases in speed so that in these later years it is quite appreciable to the naked eye.

Now how does the woman's movement compare with this? A hundred years ago the women of the world were almost wholly isolated house servants with the small superior class who were housekeeper and the rare exceptions who were sufficiently noble, wealthy, or talented to show personal achievement. They were unorganized save for a few religious groups. Their capacities were those of their remotest ancestors; their duties, interests, and ambitions the same.

In one century (and a century viewed historically is but a day, sociologically but a moment) they have sprung forward in almost every line of progress and risen in many instances to full race-equality with men.

The June *World's Work* in a brief account of "Some Women at Work" quotes from the census of 1900 that there are of "hunters, trappers, guides, and scouts, male 10,020, female 1,320," "authors and scientists, male 3,442, female 2,616."[1] There are other figures as surprising but these are quite enough to measure the movement.

The hunters and trappers are but a survival of the earliest human industries and of these a little over a tenth are women. Authors and scientists stand in the front rank of civilization and there women are over two-thirds.

To "move" in one hundred years from the grade of house service to the grade of literature and science is a sociological phenomenon calling not for hope and faith but for self-restraint in the face of such dizzying achievement. The "man's movement" took nearer a hundred thousand to cover the same ground.

To this it will be replied that it is not a fair comparison—that the woman has shared in the advance of man, profited by his gains, inherited his progress. This is true in a sense, mainly in the inheritance. She has not had to develop the brain capacity as she went along as he did, but has inherited it from her civilized fathers.

I am the last to deny that women all along have been the potential equals of men, that they could at any time have manifested equal ability if given equal opportunity, but as a matter of fact this ability remained only potential; actually, the women were grossly inferior in all lines of civilized progress.

Their shooting forward in this miraculous manner is, of course, due to the eternal equality at last finding freedom to manifest itself, but the shooting remains in evidence.

No step in human development has ever approached in length and breadth and height and universal value the woman's movement of our time.

Feminine Occupations

The census figures of 1900 concerning the work of women are quite instructive; they might be called eye-openers. We find the fair sex engaged in the following lines of activity to these numbers:

Stock raisers and drovers	1,947
Lumbermen	100
Woodchoppers	113
Civil engineers and surveyors	84
Longshoremen	18
Stevedores	21
Watchmen and policemen	879
Boatmen and sailors	154
Pilots	5
Carriage and hack-drivers	43
Blacksmiths	196
Railway baggagemen	10
Brakemen	31
Conductors	7
Switchmen and yardmen	26
Ship carpenters	6
Masons	167
Plumbers and fitters	126
Fishermen and oystermen	1,805
Miners and quarrymen	1,370

It would be interesting to know something of the personal lives of these women, if they are happier and more contented than their sisters who do only housework, and it would be most important to know how their feminine position is held, if they are wives and mothers as normal women should be. There are plenty of exceptions, many women who prefer not to marry, but the average, the normal, should and does. No final answer to the woman question can be accepted that does not give to the woman full development of *all* her functions, not sacrificing sex to race, but being a strong, proud, successful human creature and a happy woman, too.

Natural Feelings

Why do we speak so admiringly of certain feelings as "natural" and condemn others so severely as "unnatural"?

It is no doubt because of an underlying and legitimate reverence for the way the world works, which is all right if applied with care, but the way we do apply it is a most narrow one.

Nature is many things, but one this she is not and that is stationary. When a trait is described as "natural" it needs to be carefully connoted with what, where, and when.

Now it is "natural" to fight but not admirable. All through nature we find a fluctuating state of general warfare, dog eat dog, quite "natural"—in its place. But hold—we find in a beehive peace and industry only, no warfare, only an occasional massacre of undesirable bachelor uncles.

In an anthill also is peace and industry, though outside it they make war.

One thing is as natural as another so that it exists in the economy of nature, and we have no other field of study.

Society is a natural form of life, just as much so as savagery. It is natural to social beings, such as ants, bees, and men, to live in peace and industry. War in a beehive would be "unnatural."

Cannibalism in civilization is unnatural, though there was a time when it was natural enough. Times change, conditions change, feelings change. When we talk so admiringly of "the natural feelings of a mother," for instance, let us inquire further as to whether the mother is a bee, a whale, a savage, or a civilized woman. Nature varies.

The whole value, use, and, therefore, existence of maternal feelings is simply to promote the advantage of the young. If the advantage of the young requires different conditions and the different conditions require different feelings on the part of the mother, then those feelings will appear.

If the modern mother realizes that the good of her children is inseparably bound up with the good of other children and that their common good requires better schools, better teachers, better books, better houses, better streets, better government, and if she finds these things are to be obtained by united public action and further that such action requires a new set of feelings on her part, then the modern mother must develop a new range of sentiments, ambitions, and duties, which are maternal because they are necessary to the good of the child and which are just as natural as the feelings of a hen.

Village Improvement

It appears that a woman started the first village improvement society in Stockbridge, Mass., some sixty years ago,[2] and the work has spread and grown to a wonderful extent. Even cities are affected by it; the wish, the hope, the dawning demand for more beautiful living rises higher every day. It is a very healthy feeling, one proper to our times and of legitimate nature.

To wish beauty for one's own body is natural, too—natural to savages, who will undergo more torture in the line of decoration than even the foot-bound women of China or the waist-bound Christian. To wish beauty for one's own house is also an ancient instinct. From the totem poles of the Alaskan Indian to the frescoes of Pompeii[3] we find this natural impulse. But the highest beauty sense and its fullest expression ever known to us was in old Greece, where the body was clad in ideal simplicity and the home equally modest in decoration, but the heart of the people was poured out in public works.

Democracy, if deep and genuine, must bear that fruit. Ours is far more thorough than that of Greece. We have partly freed our helots and even begun to free our women; therefore, with us the sense of common good must increase and does visibly from year to year. Nowhere is it more beautifully shown than in our public parks and gardens, spreading so rapidly and widely, better loved and more used all the time.

As we grow to understand that human life is essentially collective, that Christian life is essentially collective, that it is *our* daily bread for which we are to pray, so shall we more rapidly attain the peace and wealth and beauty which belong to us of right today. The last men to appreciate the advantage of collective action are farmers because their business is so separate, so self-centered, so entirely with and for their own families; and behind the last men are the women—for the same reason.[4]

But a woman in Stockbridge started the Village Improvement Society! Yes. All farmers are not alike, either.

COLUMN 30

August 6, 1904

Gilman praises another progressive editorial in the *New York Evening Post*—a proposal to establish children's cars on trollies and trains.

A Children's Car

There is an editorial writer on the *New York Evening Post* of a far-seeing and dauntless spirit. A year or so ago he put forth the most briefly complete exposition of the nature of our present house-service difficulties which I have ever seen under the title of "What We Are Coming To."[1] Now in the issue of Saturday, July 23, he demands for the convenience of the traveling public a children's car.[2]

As he justly observes, we have eating cars, smoking cars, sleeping cars, observation cars, and all manner of minor conveniences for adults, but no special provision for that part of the traveling public which is of such tender years as to need different accommodations. The Rev. E. E. Hale in the Utopian attractions of his *Sybaris* proposed that transportation companies should charge children double-price instead of half-price—so as to keep them at home.[3]

The *Post* writer recognizes that a certain proportion of our children must—or at least do—travel and proposes to provide for them a sort of ambulatory *crèche*, with a qualified attendant, where care and amusement could be offered to the little ones. The parents are free to accompany them if they prefer, but by paying a slight extra fee they can simply entrust them to the superintendent established.

The important side of this proposition is not in its immediate value or likelihood of fulfillment but as another instance of our growing recognition of *children as a class*.

Children need the individual love and care of their parents in addition to all proper public love and care from the State. The public school is not a substitute for parental instruction but an addition to it. No just thinker would wish to rob a child of the affectionate devotion of its mother and father, but many just thinkers are coming to recognize the child's need of something more.

So long as we think no one has any responsibility but the parent, so long we leave these most valuable members of society to a grade of protection totally insufficient. The great mass of our population is unable individually to give to its children the education needed to fit them for modern citizenship. We recognize this and the State provides the education. From the kindergarten and even the *crèche* in some instances up through every step of schooling to the college graduation, the collective parent—i.e., the State—today provides for its children what the parents separately could never supply. Education is the prime necessity, the most immediate and easily attained, but there are others.

A proper environment is as essential to the child's right growth as its schooling. The individual parent is unable to supply this, and little by little the collective parent, the State, is beginning to do so. The park, the playground, the roof garden of the school, certain statutes with regard to house-building and sanitation, modification of our penal system, new ways to care for orphans and foundlings and defective children—in these and other ways we see the steady gain of the idea that we, the people, must care for our children over and above the care they get from their parents.

"Me two boys is in the country," says my cheery washerwoman during the last "hot week" in New York, "the two little ones. The nursery took thim. I don't know where they are. 'Tis a good thing for thim, this hot weather."

It was a good thing and she could not have compassed it by herself.

But it is not only the children of the poor who need more than their parents give.

As I ride up the long avenues in the best part of New York, I see plenty of children playing in the street these hot evenings, children dressed daintily and fashionably, children whose parents are kept in town for part of the summer yet who pay large rents and keep maids and nurses. Yet if they have air and exercise at all—and children must have them—it is only in the street that they can get it. The boys play ball and hockey and tip-cat and tag; the girls play hop-scotch and jump-rope and whatever they can—and the street is their playground.

There are parks, of course, but all homes do not abut on parks—and they, too, are provided by the public.

Now comes a grumbler in the *Times* and says parents are to blame for their children being run over by trolley cars! Says they should keep them off the street![4] And where would the good man suggest that the parents keep them? Under the bed? A large city has thousands, yes, hundreds of thousands of children and it should make safe and advantageous provision for these growing citizens. The parents individually cannot.

Who will pay for it?

The children, of course. They are the next set of citizens, and if we improve their value they will pay for it.

COLUMN 31

August 13, 1904

Gilman contemplates here the virtues of long-range planning and locates the source of American exceptionalism in the assimilation of "the noble races who have come to us" from other nations.

Prospects

Do you remember when you were little and Christmas was coming? Or 4th of July? Or even some picnic or party—when there was light and color and movement ahead, when there was "something to look forward to."

The sense of that approaching event was an uplift and stimulus in the routine of every day; you went to bed content because tomorrow was coming and woke joyous to be one day nearer.

I told a woman once of a lot of things I meant to do in the next five years—or ten. It was a large program, full of strange and expansive doings, and quite took her breath away. "O!" sighed she. "I wish I could look forward to anything like that!"

I grinned cordially. "You can! Why don't you? It doesn't cost anything!"

Why didn't she, and why do not we, all of us, all the time, have something to look forward to a little this side of Heaven? No one likes to live in a blind alley—to stand in a corner facing the wall. We build our houses or select them with an eye to the prospect; we walk miles for a splendid view. But your real living is done in your own head mostly; no matter what is around you, you only see what is painted on the retina and recognized by the brain. The form and color does not make you see it. "What *is* that?" You puzzle and do not really see it till you know. Similarly, if you are delirious or drug-haunted, you "see" with terrible accuracy things which are not there.

This being common fact, and a good text backing it up—"As a man thinketh, so is he"[1]—why do we not take advantage of the measureless outlook afforded by our own brains? This does not mean simply to store the mind with varied knowledge or "expand" it by traveling. Many people have vast treasuries of information locked like any other treasury, have seen sea and mountain, cathedral and river, picture and statue, and yet when they sit still alone there is nothing "in the mind's eye."

It is not what is shown to the mind; it is not mere memory, power to recall what has been seen; it is the active, conscious looking ahead that gives the big prospect. We are so used to handling our brains as if they were vats and bins for storage that we fail to find the natural power of the organ to show us things, to build, unbuild, and rebuild for our pleasure and profit.

What we do know of this power we scoff at as "castle-building" or "mere theorizing" and tell our children moral tales to discourage the tendency, as of "The Barber's Second Brother" (or whichever brother it was) who dreamed of spurning the Sultan's daughter and broke his tray of pottery—his only stock in trade.[2]

Of course, if one uses this great faculty of making brain pictures merely to gratify low tastes, it is as bad as the real indulgence, and if one contents one's self with looking ahead and never goes ahead—that makes life a failure, too.

The good thing is to look ahead as far as one can see and then go. If you look without going, you never get anywhere. If you go without looking, you never get where you want to go.

We all live in such and such an environment; some of us are unable to change it; at least we cannot change it quickly; and day by day that environment gets in its deadly work on us.

There is such a thing conceivable as being in absolute accord with one's environment and such a condition is called by some Happiness. They might better call it Death. But even Death would be insulted for nothing changes more promptly than a disused body. No sooner are we out of it than the whole conglomerate assembly of matter in which we lived so pompously and said "I!" breaks up and goes home like a disbanded army.

Life does not consist of things stationary and contented but is one wide, stirring field of changeful growth.

If we settle down into contentment with any sort of environment, it may be conducive to our happiness—the happiness of a mud-bound clam!—but it is not conducive to our growth. All nature has the heavy down drag of passive inertia to overcome; and the evolution of species has gone on in spite of it; but we have set ourselves at work to cultivate inertia as a value and check any tendency toward something better by teaching people to be contented as they are.

What we should do is to take a wide and careful survey of our position, personal and general; see how far it is conducive to our best growth; and wherever it is not, change it.

There are two factors in conscious life—you and the environment. If there were you and no environment, there would be nothing to be conscious of. If there were environment and no you, there'd be nothing conscious. But here are both. Usually they do not fit. A living soul must grow and the environment does not keep pace with it. A sick, crippled soul does not grow much and perhaps its environment goes too fast for it.

The live, conscious, modern woman grows faster than her environment and is always seeking to change it. The inert, stationary woman finds her environment changing over her head faster than she likes it.

The wise and practical attitude is to keep what helps and discard what hinders, and to do this successfully needs a long-range view of the possibilities. That is why it is so good to look ahead, to look at the splendid things that lie before us, to be strong and happy because of the beautiful days to come, and so better able to bear our troubles when we must—and overcome them sooner.

What Can the Present Woman Do?

There is a very general desire among many earnest women of today to do something to promote progress and an equally general uncertainty as to what to do.

A heroic minority rush out at cost of great personal sacrifice and do what they can alone, and their necessary suffering and too frequent failure deter others from similar efforts.

Most remain as they are, doing the duties that must be done but suffering still under the consciousness of how much more needs doing, of the futility of their daily exertion.

The first step we should take to find a solution of this difficulty is recognize the social nature of the reforms we advocate, to see that whereas a far-seeing Russian might believe in democracy he could not practice it by himself nor change Russia in a day. Let us formulate to ourselves clearly the kind of life we wish to live, compare it faithfully with the one we are living, recognize that from here to there is quite a distance requiring many steps, and then proceed to take those steps—one at a time.

We must have a clearly determined end in view or we may waver sadly, go backwards, sideways, or in a circle; but while seeing the whole way, it is only to be reached by successive steps. Take, for instance, the desirability of economic independence for women. One may be wholly convinced of this and anxious to bring it about and yet, with no special training and a family of little children, be unable to reconcile the new-seen duty with the undeniable old one. One may recognize the wasteful, ineffectual, mischievous methods of domestic industry and yet find it better to serve our children with our own hands than to leave them unserved. There is such an essential difference between theory and practice.

Theory is most valuable—it is the step of the soul, swift, far-reaching, going upward. You see your mountain peak, you desire to go, you form a theory as to its ascent—whether to go this way or that, alone or in company—and then you start climbing. If your theory is incorrect, make another, but do not rush blindly against unscalable precipices or over them. Have theories, big ones, fearless and broad, then practice, slow, cautious, making safe progress from the known to the unknown.

Now the woman of today lives in an old-established system of household labor which does keep people alive—some of them. She has thriven and endured and filled the world with people, even in economic dependence. Before her lies a fuller, broader, freer life at once easier and more strenuous, a life in which the children of tomorrow shall grow to larger humanness and the men and women of tomorrow know a happiness now inconceivable.

But she cannot leap from this to that nor come sooner to that by neglecting this. This housework, which has been done by all women for all time and which we are now outgrowing with increasing throes, is made an unnecessary bugaboo by many modern women.

It is true that electricity is better than steam, steam better than wind, and wind than oars, but that is no reason that one should now row well on little lakes and rivers.

If a Hill or Harriman[3] had to drive mule-trains, it would be much to the world's loss, but they would probably make excellent muleteers.

We women should place our household business in right perspective and proportion; see over, around, and beyond it, but meanwhile show some capacity in doing it.

No man would rest content with this poor trade but, while he had it to do, he would do it as one capable of more—not incapable of this.

The new perspective is what we need most. We can keep on doing the things we have to, eating the bread that is given us, knowing that it is too late for us personally to learn new trades, but we can read, study, think, and talk; we can steadily change our minds on this subject and work constantly to change other people's, too.

The younger generation of girls, who are growing up to work as becomes the age they live in, we older ones can in all ways encourage and assist.

And presently when our children are married and we have—after twenty years—learned how to manage one house in less than twelve hours a day, then we can begin to do more things. The position of the mother is still absorbing, but that of *mater emeritus* [sic] ought not to clog the feet of an able-bodied woman of forty-five.

The Making of Americans

It is a wonderful spectacle, the mingling of peoples that goes to make up our people, not only by the slow, restricted process of physical inheritance through the ceaseless intermarriage of all stocks going on among us with great results; but the far more rapid and efficacious process of social transformation. Here now are there strong men from the north coming to us—the Finns—driven out by poor, mad Russia and out of misery, oppression, and exile coming here to help build a world people.[4] We complain too much of our low-grade immigration and are not sufficiently thankful for the value of the noble races who have come to us of whom our best are made. America, like Boston, is not a locality but a state of mind.

Coming here and entering our "institutions," all men become Americans, and that is how America comes to be the home of the world's greatest growth.

COLUMN 32

August 20, 1904

In the first two parts of this column Gilman ponders the plight of the "bachelor maid" who refuses to marry and bear children—unsought duties Gilman nevertheless considered biological imperatives.[1] She also discusses the idea of "social heredity" or the transmission of social values.

The "Bachelor Maid's" Objections to Marriage

The *Independent* recently gave a most interesting statement by a young woman, holding a chair of something in some college, of her reasons for refusing to marry.[2]

Her position is one of which we hear much from the educated girls of today and which in its very revolt against certain features of our general concept of the married state is a confession of weakness.

One of the objections raised is not against marriage at all but against housework. The power of associative idea is great and well-known, yet it is still hard to comprehend how love, marriage, and maternity, things psychological and physiological, should be absolutely confused with a plain matter of industry, a trade which is open to maid, wife, or widow, bachelor, husband, or widower.

"I will not marry," says the protesting modern woman, "because I do not wish to be a cook and chambermaid—or even to be a managing housekeeper. I prefer another business!"

But marriage is not cooking—nor housekeeping. Marriage is a union of man and woman, primarily for the best rearing of children and secondarily for the mutual happiness of the two irrespective of children. By what long oversight have we allowed these two great purposes to be so unfortunately confounded with domestic industry that "to refuse to cook is held the same as to refuse wifehood and motherhood"? "I do not wish to cook—therefore, I will not marry!" says the girl. There is no logic in this sentence unless cooking and marrying are identical—and they are not.

A man may make a wife of his housekeeper—if he likes; we usually criticize him for it. Also he may make a housekeeper of his wife—if *she likes*—but it is not in the marriage contract! No woman need follow the business unless she chooses. It is quite open to her to provide other and different methods of contributing her share to the care of the family.

"I do so hate to darn stockings!" cries the protesting modern wife. Protesting imbecile! Stockings—male or female—can be bought for twenty-five cents. The woman who cannot earn twenty-five cents in the time it takes her to darn those stockings—all the darnings that go to one paid—is so feeble that she has no right to protest.

There is no compulsion, legal or moral, to make women do work they dislike—*if they can do better*. And if they cannot do better, they have no right to complain—a self-respecting woman must do *some* work. This college professor was evidently able to far better work, work of more value and better paid.

Why then did she refuse marriage on account of this unessential and unnecessary condition of housework? Because she had not given her trained mind to the subject and was not prepared to offer to the would-be husband a better proposition than his.

We ought not to blame men for expecting us to work at home in the traditional manner while we ourselves expect the same thing and have nothing better to offer. Do we imagine that men—who do all the other kinds of work—are going to take hold of this old profession of ours and improve it over our protesting heads?

Is it not rather to our discredit that we carp at the limitations of the work we have so long kept limited, carp at the men who naturally expect us to do it as we always have done, and fail to present anything better?

If our attractive, young professor had a definite plan to propose and was prepared to abide by it, and if her lover was sufficiently in love, something might have been arranged which would have included love and marriage and excluded housework. The terms are *not* synonymous, and we should exert ourselves to prove this. I have known cases of very happy married people with children, where both parents had professions of their own and neither of them was a cook.

In these days of rapid development, where so much is being done to make modern civilized industries of "the belated trades," it seems particularly futile to give up marrying because of an aversion to housekeeping. Then comes the Bachelor Maid's next objection—the sanctified brutality of married life. Marion Harland in answering her quite fails to get this point and speaks only of children.[3] Too many children are not desirable; the care of them—also a pitifully neglected profession—is a great burden to many women; but it was neither the bearing nor rearing of children which made the friend of the Bachelor Maid call her married life "Hell." But granting that there are cases of that sort—and too many of them—it is no reason for not marrying! Because a shoe pinches, because many shoes pinch, must one then go barefoot?

Some marriages are gloriously happy; some love has reverence and restraint, comradeship as well as passion; could not this refined and educated woman command such? I do not underrate in the least the degradation, the misery, the ruin which is so often found in "holy matrimony," but that is no reason for not marrying! If nine-tenths of our food is bad, it is an excellent reason for bestirring ourselves to improve it but no reason at all for going without.

There are many of our educated women nowadays who take this position, and it seems very like that of the angry child who cries, "I won't eat my supper!" It is "biting off one's nose to spite one's face." Then there is the objection to children, or at least to children too numerous and undesired. That calls for a chapter by itself.

A Certain Attitude Toward Maternity

The "Bachelor Maid"—and many other women today, mothers actual or potential or past—have assumed an attitude toward maternity which is so false, so feeble, so cowardly that only the knowledge of our piteous history enables us to have patience with it.

In the protest of this young woman against marriage we get the new note, sharp, clear, strong, and most disagreeable.

The iron of long bondage has indeed entered our souls if the eternal mother can, under any fear or loathing, abjure her motherhood.

Yet this is what some women are doing today in the first fierce revolt against old injustice. The very magnitude of the sacrifice involved ought to be a convincing proof of our past misery to those who underrate it.

What we need most to reclaim these piteously mistaken ones is a clear apprehension of the real nature and status of motherhood and an equally clear one of the superficial, transient, wholly unnecessary nature of their grounds of objection. Because for a brief period of biological history, the human mother has been in a state of subjection to the male of her species, she has lost her splendid pride and consciousness of power based on a maternal preeminence as old as life.

Because during this androcentric period the man has been the active representative of race, has considered the child as his and the woman merely as the means of "bearing him children" (a phrase of exquisite absurdity!), she has forgotten the real relation of mother to child—primal, indissoluble, unquestionable, compared to which the relation of man to woman is of yesterday—shallow and fleeting.

In the true perception of motherhood, we see that she is the original and dominant factor while the father, long a minor contributor, has only been the principal figure for a little while and that only in his own mistaken assumption.

No matter what he thought, no matter what he did, so long as life is born on earth, the mother *is* the greater power in heredity. Her present position of relative incapacity is due to her economic inferiority—while he provides the necessaries of life for her and for the child, she naturally counts for less. In the human species, great as is heredity, environment and education are greater—and these powers the man has wholly assumed. The environment, domestic and social, he chooses and makes; and the education, although the mother administers it during infancy—*is the result of social progress made by him.*

Thus in immediate external fact the father is in the place of power, and the mother, impressed by this, does not realize that under it all she is still the main factor. Therefore—seeing the pain and shame of her recent subjection and not seeing the unquenchable glory of her original position, the modern woman renounces that which is hers by right because it has been wrongly claimed as his. She fears the physical risk and suffering of childbearing—not seeing that these are but the results of her pitiful position and its false habits—that to the free, strong, natural woman they are as nothing.

To think that in a race whose dauntless courage has met and conquered so many perils, the dominant race on earth, the female should cringe and retreat before a simple functional process common to all creation!—and not only *a* process but *the* process for which she is especially built! As human beings, men and women do not differ—the social processes are open to them equally; but as animals, male and female, she is made for motherhood and to be afraid of it is contemptible.

Then to justify her fear, she points to the ghastly facts of life about us, to maternity undesired—forced upon an unwilling woman; to the exhaustion, the care, the ceaseless effort, the physical agony—disease, death—and says she has cause to fear! Now if one were a cowering female savage in the Australian bush—this would be true. She is still in the position of helpless victim. But an American college professor is not. Has she not the knowledge of her power, her right, her duty as mother, to protect her? Is she going to be knocked down and beaten? Is she going to marry some Kaffir[4] or brutal peasant? There is something surprising in the picture of a full-grown, healthy, educated modern woman being afraid of what the gentleman she might marry might do to her! Our "new woman," with all her rapid and beautiful progress, does not realize her own power. The mistaken man, understanding nothing of the new development, says to her, "I do not approve of what you are doing. If you do this, I will not marry you. Choose between Love—Home—Motherhood—and a career." And the poor thing thought she had to—and chose the career. The choice is not necessary.

The woman—fully awake, strong, wise, and beautiful, having ordered the industries now "domestic" so that they no longer confine her to the house, having ordered the care and training of children so that it is no longer an overwhelming and often unsuccessful task but a well-understood and splendidly handled profession, doing her share in the social duties and taking her share of the social rights and privileges—is still *the woman*—the eternal mother. Her gain as a human being is no loss to her motherhood but a thousandfold added attraction. Men will not love them? Whom will they love then—when all women are like that?

Social Heredity

Some there are specially endowed who do great work for the world as individuals without contributing to the stock by physical heredity. This social heredity is the more valuable of the two. We may steadily inherit our flesh and bones from thousands of devoted mothers and remain monkeys!

The human gain—knowledge, arts, crafts, inventions, discoveries—these are taught, not born to us. These are the social inheritance, a psychological transmission that does not wait for the slow accretion of generations but leaps from brain to brain and lifts an age in the time it takes to rear one child.

If we *had to choose*, if the one excluded the other, if some had to be mothers like queen bees and the rest workers, co-mothers[5] in truth yet personally sterile, then there are more and more of us who would prefer to lift the world to nobler heights rather than to fill it with food for guns.

Napoleon's measure of motherhood was a poor one; men are not made merely to kill and be killed. But what our modern women ought to realize is that the greater includes the less, that to be a full human being by no means prevents but especially requires being a healthy animal, too.

We women, long accustomed to sacrifice and denial, having been required up to this time to give up all social functions for the sake of our physical ones, are now in the large joy of being human giving up the physical for the social.

But this is so needless! I do not mean that in certain personal cases and notably in the first steps of the woman's movement it was needless; many a glorious woman has suffered and renounced in her personal life that she might serve the world. But it is no longer necessary nor advisable. We need to have our free, human, women mothers, successful mothers, too, in order to encourage the ultra and exclusively maternal women to be human, too. We need to incorporate the racial gain in the living stock through body as well as brain, through mothers as well as fathers. We need to lift all women from their dull inertia and hasten the progress of mankind—the spectacle of splendid women, vigorous, beautiful, intelligent, independent, able, respected citizens and happy mothers, too.

COLUMN 33

August 27, 1904

Gilman celebrates Woman's Day at Lilydale, in upstate New York, a center of the spiritualist movement. Gilman "was one of the speakers" there "and fully one thousand people were in the afternoon audience" when she spoke.[1] She also discusses the merits of cremation and, in fact, at her death her body was cremated as she stipulated in her will.

Woman's Day

LILYDALE, N.Y., AUG. 17, 1904.

For the second time I am at Lilydale on Woman's Day. Last year Miss Anthony, Miss Shaw, Mrs. Upton, Miss Mills,[2] and many other well-known suffragists were here, and they were missed much this year. But the enthusiasm for "the cause" is no less and the very name of Miss Anthony meets warm applause.

The auditorium is blazing with yellow, the grounds draped with it, the women's dresses gay with it, the men wear it, the children blossom like dandelions, and the golden flowers are everywhere. A dance in the evening is a sort of leap year affair,[3] and even the band does honor to the day by masquerading in women's clothes.

One may or may not be in sympathy with the special beliefs that dominate this place, but one can hardly fail to recognize among the spirits the spirit of progress, manifesting itself in many lines and keenly alive to the value of the woman's movement.

To one who cares for human good, for the increase of happiness, and the advancement of the race, there is much to study in such an assembly as this.

The first noticeable fact is that the majority of the persons present are women—the vast majority. There are men, a good many, but mostly they are women. Some children, too, but not very many as most of the women are middle-aged, elderly, or old. The men, too, are not young—it seems to be an assembly of elderly people in the main. Why? Because the most general attraction of spiritualism is communication with the dead and old people have more dead than young ones.

But why should women be more appealed to by this hope than men? Or is it that men feel it as much as women but fewer of them can leave their business for such gatherings? Partly both. Women are more confined to personal relations than men—not by nature, not by sex, but by the conditions of their state of industry. They work alone all their lives for a few people and naturally if those people die, they have nothing else to live for.

Similarly, because they work alone in a low-grade, universal business for a few people, they can more easily temporarily adjust their affairs—put in a substitute and leave for a while—than a more specialized man in his higher grade of business.

So for these two reasons they come to a place like this more than men.

The general interest here in the larger movements of the day is very healthy and hopeful. One cannot follow truth in any form without finding more truth—so that one is brave and honest and willing to grow.

But this atmosphere of loss and heartache and longing for "the touch of a vanquished hand and the sound of a voice that is still"[4] hangs heavily over all. Is it right? Is it necessary? Is it the real law of life? Or like most human pain is it the result of mistaken action? We touch here on one of the deepest springs in the human heart and that means one of the oldest. At the very bottom of the earliest religions lies the belief in ghosts—and it is with us yet. The love, the longing, the worship for the departed spirit is to the human race an ancient instinct, and like all ancient instincts it is strong to rush forth and clothe itself in whatever form of new doctrine and new phrasing we may find.

But is it good for us, for the world as a whole and the growth thereof? Is it a kind of feeling we should approve of and maintain or one we ought rather to discourage and outgrow?

Must women always follow the dreary round described so poignantly by Jean Ingelow?

> Thy mother's lot, my dear,
> She doth in naught accuse—
> Her lot to bear, to nurse, to rear,
> To love, and then to lose.[5]

The same feeling is in a poem on "Motherhood" in the August *Scribner's*—about hugging her baby and crushing down her own heartache so, as her mother had done before her and her child would do after her—as if motherhood had been and was and would be merely a succession of heartaches![6]

The golden radiance over everything here on Woman's Day is the light of a new hope for the world. These sad-eyed, tired women, whose hearts are buried with their little ones and are now lightened somewhat by the "communications" from the lost, feel even where they do not fully understand the great new hope and joy for the world which is to come through the higher development of women. In so many ways at once it will lift our cloud of sorrow and make us strong to bear what pain is really necessary in life!

First, the new woman is to be a strong, healthy creature, recognizing motherhood as the splendid power and privilege it is and coming to it with such full preparation through years of wise young womanhood that children shall be healthy from their birth—the first check to death.

Second, the new woman will learn her business as a trainer of children; they will have wisdom and experience as well as love and instinct to guard and rear them in safety—the next check to death.

An enormous proportion of our deaths—all except those who die of old age and accident (and even some of the accidents!)—are due merely to our own ignorance of right living. Especially is the death of little children a needless pain—an inexcusable wrong of ours. If the women of the world were what they might be—what they should be, what they could be now if they choose to work for it—their children need not die as they do now.

Third, the new woman, recognizing her duty to the world as a mother, will choose her husband more wisely than she does now. This choice of the best father is the primordial duty of the female—and we women grossly fail in it.

See, for instance, the frontispiece poem in that same August *Scribner's*—a girl is considering whether she shall marry a hypothetical proposer, and not one thought does she give to the basic reason for the whole thing—if he is a desirable father. She thinks of "the legion of joys I should give" and is very uncertain as to the joys he might give her, but not a dream of the duties involved.[7]

Motherhood is a grander thing than the average girl ever thinks of; she approaches it ignorantly, often falsely, suffers needlessly, and fails pitifully—in large measure. So that even "as women" the new development to which we are rapidly coming will do much, very much, to lighten the pains now supposed to be "a mother's lot." Far beyond that comes the growth of the *humanness* in women—a thing quite aside from motherhood, and greater.

A mother whale, when her baby is harpooned, stays by the little body until she is herself destroyed—she has no other duties. The animal cycle is complete in reproduction; there is no other end for it. But to be human is quite another thing, involving a psychic relation between the constituent animals, and that relation is established by social service—by our human work. When women take the place that belongs to them in the specialized functions of our civilization, they will have a range of life, a strength of soul, a vivid, ceaseless interest in the immortal race of which we are a part, so that the pain of the personal loss, when it does come, can be borne as a little thing.

Why Graves?

Our mind—not "minds" but mind, the great, slow-growing, unbroken, racial mind which is our common inheritance, is full of old stumps that need uprooting.

Everything that was ever planted there and had time to grow lingers on through the ages, even if neglected, and some which we have consciously endeavored to hew down still resist our efforts and send up vigorous new roots in unlooked for places.

Religions show this very clearly; some new doctrine, widely adopted, turns out to have beneath it the emotions and behavior which belong with the old doctrine laid aside. In familiar instances our Christian religion, with its great central truths of human unity and mutual love, has but scantily covered the strong currents of Hebraism and Paganism with which the minds of its converts were already filled. Many a battle has been fought by "Christians" under not only the sayings but the feelings of the most dark and bloodthirsty period of the ancient Hebrews.

We need not only to accept new truth and act on it but to diligently reject old falsehood and cease to act on it.

Graves are a relic of the most remote dim savagery, of a time when the body was the only part of humanity known and men strove to preserve and honor it. They buried it or build cairns of stones over it to prevent its being eaten by wild beasts, which would have been an ignominy. To the savage of that day the other animals were very respectful rivals constantly in mind. It was an even thing which of them ate the other and an undeserved disgrace to leave the dead warrior to fatten the common foe, so they hid or destroyed the body.

Then in the dim, blind beginnings of religion, they worshipped these relics, the bones, the ashes, and the associated ghosts.

In China we have this still in force, a religion of dead grandfathers, and preserved in our literature we find at least an echo of it—

> Fight for your altars and your fires,
> Fight for the green graves of your sires.[8]

We have Shakespeare concerned lest anyone disturb his bones[9]—though why it should matter to him is not easy to show—and we have people still doing what they call "honoring the dead" by carefully preserving "the remains" and putting up monuments as permanent as they can make 'em. Cheops did that very successfully.[10] We all know Cheops' monument but what good does it do him—or us? A pyramid at its best is not equal to a very ordinary mountain and the gentleman under it is absolutely immaterial. Those Egyptians carried this body-worship to its logical extreme. They were so successful in their ingenious methods of preserving carcasses that we have them yet, much withered, black, and unattractive in expression but practically eternal—the human body—of a man whose real personality departed four thousand years ago and whose contribution to society, if he made any, remains forever in the trade or science he helped develop—quite irrespective of these bones.

One way to decide on the virtue of a given line of action is to carry it to its logical extreme and see how that would work. Let us suppose then that we had managed to preserve the bones of *all* our ancestors and had them in a neat pile somewhere. This would be an enormous pyramid, for ancestors increase in number as we count them backward and become very common, too.

A sense of unity in the remote past would thus be established, in the dark, brutal past until we all gathered under, not Adam, indeed, but let us say one valley-full of osseous ancestry.

What gain would be in any such laborious maintenance of our anything but glorious past? It is now pretty well-established that man appeared in one original spot and spread therefrom, in widening range, over the habitable globe. If all his bones remained to us, they would make a very respectful top dressing for our fruitful mother but would be of small use to the thin cousinship of their immediate descendants.

No, all the graves of our ancestors in a state of pious preservation is not what we desire.

Let us then take not the logical but the practical extreme, as we see it in some old church where the local nobility proudly point to eleven generations of Sir Marmadukes in stiff-legged statuary.

In this practical achievement, possible to very few of us, we have the narrowest skimming of ancestors, but one spoke in the widening wheel of grandparents. One has two parents, four grandparents, eight great-grandparents, sixteen great-greats, and the eleventh removed give us two thousand and forty-eight. It would take quite a church to hold all one's ancestors even for eleven generations! And on a modest basis of four to a family, that two thousand and forty-eight would belong in ten generations to one billion, eighty-three million, three hundred and forty-one thousand, eight hundred and twenty-three descendants, besides yourself? And what is the good of it all? Why erect this untenable single line of descent and brag of "my" ancestors when they are *our* ancestors so confusedly? If they gave you anything real, you have it about you, in your bones—not theirs!

If they gave the world anything, it is with us in picture, statue, or book; in iron or stone; or, most valuable and most imperishable, in our vast stock of knowledge, power, and skill to which the undying human soul has contributed from age to age—but all this has no connection with that undistinguishable calcareous deposit!

Why graves then? Why urns even? Why seek to preserve physical identity when in the very act of death it ceases? Souls are not in graves.

But we love them, you cry; we honor them; we wish to preserve their memory!

Of course you love and honor *them*—but "they" are not the mass of dissociating chemicals we have so noisomely checked in its healthy and rapid separation. Your love and honor was not—it is to be hoped—for your father's ribs and shoulder blades but for his work—the only human thing that counts.

What people do—that is their life's measure. What they do wins honor or contempt and lives on to our hurt or helping, but their muscular and osseous tissues are no more a part of that than their cotton and woolen clothing.

Besides—love and honor are too valuable to waste in looking behind us!

If the consciousness of our great fathers and mothers urges us to better deeds, that is well, but it is only the better deeds that give it value. Those who need our love and honor are here—and yet to come—it does no earthly good to dead folks. If they are in heaven, they don't need it but we do!

Therefore, again, why graves? Let us burn our dead, the only beautiful, healthful, and cleanly way to dispose of them, and scatter the ashes, thus helping nature's disbanding instead of checking it.

Bury their memory in our hearts—where it may enrich us and bring forth beautiful fruits. If it cannot do that, let them be swiftly and mercifully forgotten and the world move on.

COLUMN 34

September 3, 1904

Gilman is critical of Thomas Malthus's theorizing and asserts here that the "fears of the Race Suicide school"—that is, the more advanced the race, the lower its birth rate—"are founded on facts." She also reports on her visit to Chautauqua, New York, the center of the Chautauqua movement.

Malthusianism and Race Suicide

Here are the names of two schools of thought, two views of our human problem, both pointing to better conditions—in exactly opposite directions. The first is filled with horror of over-population and insufficient food and proposes a scientific system of stirpiculture or eugenics to check the birth rate.[1] The second is equally horrified with a decreasing birth rate and seeks to encourage large families.[2] And a lover of the human race, a student of sociology, is filled not with horror or amazement but with a patient wonder that we earnest people can see so far and fail to see further.

There are in human life certain natural laws working smoothly and certainly to admirable ends without any effort or sacrifice of ours. Some things we have to attend to consciously and with effort; others are best promoted by physiological and sociological forces.

Our habit has been from the earliest times to appeal wholly to the individual conscience and will and ignore, even oppose, natural laws. Some of these we do not know; others we misunderstand and misapply.

Now Mr. Malthus, gazing at the troublous field of human life, saw that population increased at such and such a ratio and that the world's food supply did not increase as swiftly. Here was a dreadful prospect! It was a simple arithmetical problem to show that in so many years the population would be three deep all over the earth, as it were—and nothing to eat! Or to view it a little more rationally, that the food and the people would simply balance and the rest of the world's life be a frantic struggle for existence to which our previous experience would be as a polite banquet.

There are two "ifs" in the dreadful vision of Malthus—his arithmetic was good but his judgment of facts poor.[3]

If the food supply was stationary and *if* the increase in population was certain, then his result is an evil future to be dreaded. But our recent discoveries in intensive agriculture and other scientific suggestions for improving human nutrition have so multiplied the potential productivity of the earth as to remove its limits to the dimmest of far futures.

Still, if like the cooling of the earth it would come, we should reach the end someday, so if the population continues an invariable rate of increase, we should ultimately come to that dreadful balance between food and folks. But this last "if" is the weakest point in the Malthusian argument.

The fears of the Race Suicide school are founded on facts that prove that humanity does not increase at an invariable ratio, that on the contrary it varies from twelve and twenty to a family to none at all and that in some nations the *decrease* in the birth rate is a public danger. This contradictory situation reminds one of the various Kilkenny arguments against woman suffrage.[4]

Here is England fretting about checking its population and here is France equally concerned about increasing it. Visibly there are differences in our rate of increase.

The American fear is that some people will increase faster than others—as indeed they perceptibly do. We complain that our "American stock" does not increase fast enough and that the "foreign stock" does. This is an amusing distinction—as if none were Americans save those whose foreign stock came over in a certain century, charter members, as it were—all later additions inferior!

America was "settled" by Spaniards, French, Dutch, English, and other folks and has been settling ever since with every kind of people. This is what makes us the splendid world-people we are; this blended blood is America. Let us say then that after living here a few generations our birth rate decreases, that Americanization acts as a check on population. What does that show?

It shows in the human race that great biological law Spencer phrased thus: "Individuation is in inverse proportion to reproduction"[5] and which Galton has pointed out in his work on heredity as a decrease in birth rate proportionate to improved conditions.[6] The practical ideal for the world is to have it all, the whole round globe, safe, habitable, beautiful, comfortably filled with noble human beings who had overcome all the primitive problems of life and were exercising themselves on the higher ones.

Such a comfortable filling would mean a stationary population, one which replaced itself but did not indefinitely multiply. And it is exactly to such a balance of population that we are tending under the orderly working of natural law.

The lower the grade of life the higher the rate of increase—bacteria have the largest families! Insects, oysters, fish—these are the mothers of millions, no race suicide for them. Oysters would make the sea solid in a few years if they all lived, but in nature's balance of power they are destroyed by millions, too. Small beasts and vermin of any kind—rats, rabbits, guinea pigs—thus multiply at a prodigious rate. As you go higher and higher in the line of evolution, you come to *"unum, sed leonem"*[7]—though, by the way, Mrs. Leonem usually has two.

The reason is clear. When any kind of creature has to exercise complex abilities to keep alive, when its energies must be used in lines of extreme specialization, it does not spend itself so lavishly in mere reproduction but in personal development; it becomes a finer and more able creature, less numerous, more efficient.

This is precisely what happens to the human creature. The lower the grade, the more children; the higher the grade, the less children. A complex personal development such as accompanies high civilization means a lower birth rate.

Thus beautifully, quietly, naturally does society balance itself, rising from the profuse fecundity of the lower races and their struggle for mere existence to the peace, comfort, and culture of the higher social grades, replenishing but not needlessly multiplying their numbers.

There is no fear of any extinction of the race; mother nature is quite equal to her business; we need not be so alarmed. Neither is there any fear of a higher but smaller society being overwhelmed by a lower and more numerous. Social power lies not in quantity but in quality—even in warfare, intellect and wealth count for more than numbers.

What we have to do to check population is simply *to elevate it*. As fast as we learn to eliminate gross poverty, ignorance, and the accompanying low habits, so fast will the swarming masses of inferior people give place to a lesser number of superior people.

It is a beautiful prospect. Improve the world as fast as we can, make things right for all of us, give good conditions to every child that is born, cultivate humanity to its highest, and the birth rate will take care of itself. This is better than eugenics.

From Chautauqua[8]

A week's lecturing in Chautauqua is an experience worth having. There are so many evil conditions in our cities, and so many also, though different, in the country, that it is an exhilarating thing to visit a social group where there is so much good and so little evil.

Here is beauty, health, order, peace, safety, friendliness. Here is no glaring evil of any sort, nothing to shock and pain and wring the heart. And here is such a wealth of wise provision for human happiness and improvement that one's enjoyment is only marred by the underlying wish that all the others could have it, too.

The prime condition of these useful and beautiful summer cities is *association*—free and continuous association. And the outward expression of this is in the great assembly hall, the amphitheater, where the people flock together morning, noon, and night. There are plenty of smaller places for smaller groups, that is instruction and amusement general and special, and during the season the fortunate citizens of the little City of the Future can follow their personal lives of growth and drink freely where they will. The stimulus, the enrichment, the multiform gain are testified to by thousands. "It keeps me up the whole year," said one woman to me, a happy wife and mother with a charming family group—husband and children—and no doubt a pleasant home. "It keeps me up all through the winter, and when I begin to get low—why, it is almost time to come again!"

Figure 4. The grounds of the Chautauqua Institution, Chautauqua, New York, 1908. Library of Congress, LC-USZ62-115140.

This is what Chautauqua is—a great feeding place for mind and heart and soul, and not the least of the nourishment is in the free contact of so many nice people—quite aside from the courses of instruction.

One of the bitterest evils of our present life is the lack of free association on lines of common interest. In the country we have geographical restrictions and impositions. We cannot associate with those far away and we must to a certain degree associate with those nearby. Now geographical association is not the true social ground. In our cities we are isolated also, hemmed in by brick and mortar, separated by distances we call long, and we associate on lines of financial equality—which is no more legitimate as a human base of attraction than is geography. Human beings are normally drawn together by a similarity of brain structure, which means a response to similar stimuli, that is by common tastes, interests, desires, and work.

This is what our ordinary manner of living does not furnish and what these summer schools do furnish to a great extent. To have the necessary labors of life so lightened, shared, arranged that one has time and strength to spare, and then to have a constant flow of instruction and entertainment from which each may take according to ability, this makes the season at Chautauqua a stimulus lasting through the year. The question then arises why should we not have more of this in our daily lives, why do we not recognize this need of the soul and meet it all the time?

Wherever there is the smallest human group—and real human life demands at least the village—we ought to provide the meeting place for the inhabitants on more than religious ground.

"Meeting-house" is a good name, but we should meet oftener than once a week and for many purposes. With right education to bring out the full growth of the child, with an organized industry no longer "domestic" which shall leave the woman free to grow all her life, with men relieved of much of the load that now weighs upon them, we human beings everywhere would rise to a much larger, fuller life than we now know.

These summer schools teach us both directly and indirectly.

But they have possibilities not yet fulfilled. A place like Chautauqua is *the* place of all others, where we should find an object lesson in advanced living. To the women from remote country homes, it is much to learn of the rest of the world, but it will be more when they can learn also how permanently to enlarge and improve their methods of living. Chautauqua should have a model laundry carefully arranged on the smallest paying basis, perfect in its appointments yet simple and sustainable, wherein two workers could wash for a hundred reasonable people, and also the larger, better developed one where the economy of numbers was shown. They should have in connection with the study of "domestic science" a food laboratory in operation and show what specialized skill, knowledge, and experience can do, together with the economy of numbers again.

They should have their corps of trained cleaners to preserve the whole place in exquisite antiseptic cleanliness with the newest appliances, and they should have a baby-garden as well as a kindergarten where mothers could learn by observation what the nurse, the doctor, and the teacher can do to preserve health and promote happiness in babyhood.

There could not be a better place to carry on these specimen industries, not only immediately valuable to the patrons but endlessly valuable to all the community to which they return.

So much is done already that it would be easy to add these further steps—far easier than in the ordinary community.

COLUMN 35

September 10, 1904

Gilman again expounds on her ideas about communal responsibilities and then excoriates David Starr Jordan (1851–1931), the founding president of Stanford University and leader of the eugenics movement in the United States, for his controversial opinions about women.

Alone in the World

Recently I heard an elderly woman mournfully proclaim that she was "all alone in the world!" "I have lost my husband," said she sadly, "and the young girl that I had to live with me and even my little dog!" And the bereaved one found her chief comfort in spiritualism, in communication with the dear departed.

This is but one concrete instance of our unnatural confinement to a tiny group of people. The lady was all alone in the home—but the world is as full of people as it ever was. The home is *not* the world and those who make it so live narrowly, enjoy selfishly, and suffer needlessly. When the husband, the young lady, and the little dog were all alive—was that the world? Were these the only inhabitants of the planet? Were they all to whom she owed love and service? One may suffer grievously, indeed one must suffer grievously, in losing one's closest heart companions, whether relatives by blood or marriage, or in that close relationship of soul which may coexist with these or exist without them. To lose every relative and every friend would be a bitter and paralyzing grief, but it does not leave one alone in the world.

I call an exclusive affection for one's own family "unnatural" because it is not natural to our present stage of civilization—or socialization, a broader and truer term. Cities, to be sure, are centers of socialization, but that grand process also goes on outside them. The development of commerce and navigation, for instance, are part of socialization but not wholly due to cities. As we become socialized, we enter into wider human relation; we know more people, care for more people, serve more people; become useful, valuable, desirable to more people; and it is less and less possible to become "alone in the world."

A remote, isolated family, say that of a fox-farmer on one of our Alaskan islands, must necessarily depend much on each other, and if all the members died but one, that one would be alone in his home, alone on his island, but only a break in connection—the destruction of his line of boats or other accident—could cut him off completely from the world. His business, remote and solitary as it is, depends on the fur market of London and Paris—he is doing part of the work of the world.

Sometimes we hear of a man who so idolizes wife or son or daughter that their loss leaves him a wreck, but such men are fortunately rare. If we were all so exclusively wrapped up in these personal relations, the larger, later, more exclusively valuable social relations would suffer.

We all dimly recognize the scale of values by praising the stern virtue of Brutus sacrificing his sons to the law.[1] Law is a form of social relation and higher than the physical one of paternity. We recognize it also in the soldier—always an easy type of public virtue from the sublime heights of impersonal heroism—that would sacrifice every "hostage to fortune" in service to country—to that familiar lover who explained, "I could not love thee, dear, so much love I not honor more."[2] The real spirit of that "honor" is not personal glorification but the public duty which stands always first.

And the statement is sociologically correct. Those races or those stages in history where the citizens do not love honor more also love their relatives less. They love them all they are able; they love them exclusively, having nothing else to love; but their love is of a lower grade. As in China, where there is so little of our larger conception of citizenship, where the family occupies a man's whole heart and the State has little sway yet where the wife is "the mean one"—he is insulted if you inquire of her. When China wakens, grows, lets the dead past bury its dead,[3] lets its heart spread to the limits of the whole great country and then to the world as a whole, then that larger range of exercise will enable them to love their wives more—much more. And their wives will be more worth loving, having themselves a wider field for honor, affection, duty.

It is hard to see how we can have so long remained blind to the order of duties in human life, and yet not hard when one learns the inertia of race habit and the petrifying effect of a closed religion. All early religions asserted that their truth was the whole truth—there were to be further developments. And yet each one of them successfully held down the human mind for long ages. Then when it grew too big and burst through, pouring out into some new phase of religious perception, there were usually some features of the older thought untouched.

Thus Christianity, with all its blaze of human love, has failed to wholly clear up the dark places of patriarchal Hebraism with its connection with still older family worship.

If you look at love from a "natural" point of view, you find that everywhere in nature love is evolved and developed to meet certain ends, and only so, ceasing completely when its ends are reached, as in the passionate devotion of the animal mother for its young, which completely disappears when those same young are grown up. Naturally love is a means to an end.

With us, the longer period of immaturity develops a longer flow of paternal affection, necessary for the maintenance of the dependent creature and extending through our social customs of private property and inheritance throughout the entire life of the planet. Also, together with these customs, we have developed many close and tender family ties, all of which are useful, beautiful, and good—like all natural developments.

But our later centuries have brought forward with tremendous swiftness those general ties of social service which make our maintenance itself, as well as every degree of safety, progress, happiness, depend far more on these broad social relations than on the narrower personal ones.

The advances in public sanitation, for instance, save more lives than the love of a thousand mothers. Mothers always loved their children when the wolves ate them or when they died of the black death. They love them now while they die of "the white death"—consumption—but their love has not contributed largely to the extinction of the disease. The State is now undertaking this with wonderful promise of success. We need new eyes to see these relations. We need to see that our lives are in each other's hands, every day and always, and that it is as "natural" for us highly civilized creatures to love each other in general as it is for a fox to love her family.

Moreover, if we are Christians—how *can* a Christian be "alone in the world"?

Another of President Jordan's Views

Here is President Jordan of Stanford University committing himself to posterity again, in a recent *Harper's Weekly*.[4] Usually scientific men are most careful as to how they express themselves in fields of study outside their own specialty, but President Jordan has never feared to launch out in many directions as cheerfully as if he held a chair in each of a dozen sciences. Perhaps as President one learns to generalize and, as head of a coeducational college, learns especially to generalize on sex differentiation. At any rate we are told by this authority that "only men, broadly speaking, are capable of objective study. Only men can learn to face fact without flinching, unswayed by feeling or preference. The reality with woman is the way the fact affects her. Original investigation, creative art, the resolute facing of the world as it is belong to a man's world, not at all to that of the average women."

This reminds me first of the little Canadian-French physician who once told me decisively that women could never hope to equal men on account of the inferiority of their brains. I asked him if he as a biologist had observed any other animal species where there was a difference in brain development in favor of the male. Not being as thoroughly versed in biology as President Jordan he was unable at the moment to think of any. Then I asked him further if he did not consider it fair, when he found a condition so unique among species, to attribute it to some special environment and education rather than to sex distinction. To this he made no satisfactory reply but seemed to meditate.

Now will not Dr. Jordan take up the matter with his wider knowledge and show that throughout the animal kingdom there is a marked and increasing difference in brain power and brain action between the sexes.

That in lower forms, where we find little to call brain, there is little difference; but that in the higher mammalia, in the animals of special intelligence as in the horse, fox, dog, or elephant, the males only can face fact without flinching—the females are purely subjective.

Dr. Jordan does state in this article that "women in college do as good work as men." But he asserts that "in the university they do not, for this difference exists, the rare exception only proving the rule that women excel in technique, men in actual achievement." "The rare exceptions" such as Madame Curie,[5] for instance, prove something more than the rule, it seems to me. They are not so rare as they were and that in itself proves something. Let us grant to begin with that the mass of women face life differently from the mass of men. Then let us place beside that fact this one, that the Oriental faces life differently from the Latin and the Latin from the Teuton. There are race differences in mind.

Again, that the nobleman faces life differently from the serf. There are class differences in mind. Again, that the soldier faces life differently from the tradesman. There are professional differences in mind. Again, that the Mohammedan faces life differently from the Christian. There are religious differences in mind. Again, that the citizens of our time face life differently—very differently—from the citizens of five hundred or a thousand years ago. There are historical differences in mind. All of these differences will be found in the female of race, class, time, religion, etc., as in the male—establishing that much identity in brain activity.

Now if we find in lower species no difference in brain action between male and female, and if we find in the human species a marked identity on some lines; if we find also a marked distinction, should we not seek to account for it by other causes than mere distinction of sex? To go further: Do we find in the alleged "feminine" brain qualities alike exhibited by all women of all races and times? Does the female Turk or Italian react under given conditions as does the English or American woman?

Does the English woman of today "face life" as did her maternal ancestor of the dark ages? Do we not, on the contrary, find that the environment of the harem produces one sort of "feminine" mind and that of the free school and college another?

Would not even President Jordan admit that the college-bred girl of today flinches a little less in facing a fact than her estimable great-grandmother?

The truth of the matter is this: The female of our species has for so long been confined to the narrowest of environments, to the most primitive of labors, to the earliest and least developed emotions that a generation or two of partial education has not yet removed the different mental attitude necessarily bred by her condition. If men had been isolated, uneducated house servants from the beginning of history, they, too, would flinch somewhat on facing facts hitherto unfamiliar. To establish this truth, it remains but to show that in proportion as the woman's environment changes does she change her mental attitude, and this is most overwhelmingly shown by the evidence of the last few decades. No more impressive and sudden development was ever seen in humanity than the incredible uplifting of this great class of house servants into those numerous "exceptions" which prove not President Jordan's alleged "rule" but that women are human beings and that the brain is a human organ—not one of sex.

A Correction

A correspondent writes to ask if there is not an error in the article "Is the Woman's Movement Slow?" in our issue of July 30th.

I stated there that there are by the last census of authors and scientists, male 3,442, female 2,616, and then further stated that these stand in the front rank of civilization and women are two-thirds of them. This sounds as if the 2,616 women were part of the 3,442, whereas it is an additional number—two-thirds as great as the other.

There are two-thirds as many women scientists and authors as there are men—that is the point; and thanks for the correction.

COLUMN 36

September 17, 1904

Gilman again suggests that women are obliged by the laws of nature to marry and endorses robust enforcement of libel laws against irresponsible journalists, no doubt an opinion shaped by the libel she once suffered in the yellow press.

The Refusal to Marry

Among the many difficulties which confront women in this period of change and progress, any honestly chosen and bravely held position is worthy of careful attention. Some women, fully convinced of the need for economic independence, trained in specialized labor and loving it and keenly aware of the difficulties of married life, both mentionable and unmentionable, have cut the knot by simply refusing to marry.

Is this the wisest way to improve the objectionable conditions? If it is, if it is the best form of protest, the most powerful and effective method of advancement, or if it is even necessary, it should be upheld by every thoughtful woman.

In discussing the question, let us say a word first for those who are by nature or by circumstance disinclined to wed. Probably there will always be in humanity a certain scant margin of persons of this sort, and they are as likely to be above as below the average—different, not inferior. For such there is no possible criticism. They lose much, very much, of the ordinary human happiness and escape much of the ordinary human pain; but if they are devoted to the social service, if they are so superabundantly human as not to greatly feel the force of sex, they may find joy enough in the full freedom of work to counterbalance their loss. And in any case, if the work is great and the devotion fruitful enough, it does not matter what they personally lose if, by so doing, they thereby serve society the better.

This magnificent sacrifice of the personal to the social relation is happily not often called for. On the contrary, our best work usually depends on our personal health and comfort, and that health and comfort depend more on a right marriage than on any other thing—after the animal essentials such as air, food, and warmth.

It would be a pity, a great pity, for any of us wrongly to assume that our duty to the world requires us to deprive ourselves of what after all is necessary to that duty—a fully developed, normal personal life.

Laying aside then the small number of consecrated souls who are crippled in one way only to be divinely strong in others, and the other small number who are crippled with no compensation, we then confront the normal woman who would enjoy love and marriage, who desires maternity, yet who is so sickened by the conditions of low-grade industry supposed to go with these and even more by the ignorant brutality so often found in marriage that she gives up the whole thing.

Is this to be commended? If the position were clearly defined and honestly put before the proposer of marriage, if the woman had prepared a working plan on which she would marry as well as a wholesome detestation of the plan on which she would not, then it seems not only a commendable but a necessary position.

"Will you marry me?" says the man. "Certainly," replies the woman, "if you recognize my position and meet its needs. I must be free to follow my profession as you are to follow yours, but with the money I earn I will contribute half toward our maintenance. We shall not conform to the ordinary housekeeping ideals but we shall be helping to make new ones. At any rate, we shall be no worse off than we are now—and we shall have each other."

Then if the man does not love the woman enough to marry her on her own terms, she is under no reproach. He stands convicted of wanting a wageless housekeeper with marital duties included—a very old functionary but one no longer honored by the woman of today.

If the professions of the two lovers are, so to speak, incompatible, if one or the other must be given up, that should be talked over and decided on grounds of economic advantage and personal capacity. If the man is a useful physician, having invested years of study and work and slowly built up a practice, and the woman a stenographer on a salary, she could far more easily change her place of work than he; and if one or the other must really give up working, she would be least missed by the world they serve.

But if, on the contrary, she is a teacher, a real teacher by birth, training, and experience, and he merely a dry-goods clerk—why, he could more easily make the change or even give up his work if need be—hers is the more valuable to society. We could spare several clerks better than one good teacher. It is *by the service to society* that work is to be judged—not personal profit. One other element enters into this choice—strong personal specialization. If one of them is so perfectly fitted to his or her work as to suffer intensely in losing it and be unable to do any other well, then the other should surrender. The value to society and the relative pain to the individual are the guides in this decision. At present, in most cases, the man's work is more valuable to society and more dear to himself, but there are many exceptions. The woman doctor or lawyer or the real teacher cares more for her profession than the man who is merely a wage-earner and thinks only of what he is paid.

As to the more intimate questions involved, these again require a definite position on the part of the woman to which the man must accede or withdraw. It is true that we cannot tell beforehand—by the looks—what sort of a husband a man will make. But it takes two to make a marriage, and the woman as the party most concerned must make her own terms and make them clearly.

Are any revolted at the thought of such discussion between man and maid? Surely what is doable is discussable. Where a binding contract for life is proposed, not only is it wise and fair to be precise in understanding the exact terms but it is criminally negligent not to. When the wife protests after marriage, the husband has a right to ask why she never mentioned her objections before. "I thought you understood," says he, "that this is what I married you for." She didn't. She understood something quite otherwise. Both were to blame in not making the terms of the contract clear, but she is the more to blame because as the potential mother it is not only her right to protect herself but her duty to protect her children. Our women are not convent-bred *ingenues*; they are not purchased harem beauties; they are free to make their own contracts and should make them carefully.

Furthermore, in refusing to do any longer the menial service of the world, we should not therefore drop the enormous load forthwith on the overburdened shoulders of men. It is right that we should stop this everlasting round of domestic industry, but it is also right that we should be ready with some better way of doing it. The mother must care for her children—the man is right in expecting it of her—and if she is able to recognize the failure of the old method, she must be ready to do better with the new.

Simply to refuse marriage does not improve it. Marriage we must have but on different terms. The normal woman should marry, should be a mother, but she should also be a human creature.

Each happy wife and mother who is also serving society in special work does more to promote human happiness than a thousand negations.

A Limit to Newspaper License

The Court of Appeals in New York has reversed the decision of the Appellate Division and affirmed that of the Special Term, holding the N.Y. *Sun* to be guilty of libel against Professor Oscar L. Triggs.[1]

The *Sun* must now show that it did not publish the libelous articles, which are in the files where all may read them, or that they are true, which cannot be proved, or it must pay costs and damages.

This is a most gratifying decision. The freedom of the press is the bulwark of liberty—but being free the press has no more right to offend against society than has any other form of man's activity.

"The Press" is a great social organ, illimitable in power for good and quite open to most evil uses. One of these evil uses is that of making this vast engine serve personal ends, either in malicious injury to individuals or merely as a medium of expression for vicious emotion. It is so easy to be funny at another's expense and so safe in unsigned editorials and so cheap—not only cheap but distinctly profitable—when one's fun is salable stuff. When a paper makes a specialty of caustic wit, that specialty tends to excess; and the writer, being well paid, forgets the common laws of honesty, of decency, of fair play and mercilessly makes sport of whomsoever he chooses. This particular case is more flagrant than usual because there was no evil, no danger public or private, in the work of the man selected for derision.

Merely because the literary tastes of this newspaper or some of its staff were different from those of those of the Chicagoan, it took pleasure in ridiculing him not once nor twice but repeatedly with what seems a deliberate malice. What is the meanest feature in the attacks is that, as the opinion of the court shows, "They also ridicule his private life by charging that he was unable to select a name for his baby until after a year of solemn deliberation." Now when a man, secure in anonymity, sheltered by a great newspaper, uses the enormous power of his position to sneer at a baby—or to a man's relation to his baby—it does seem time to do something. The only means of redress were those taken—suit for libel against the paper.

And this is just, for after all if the dominant spirit of the paper had not been in accord with those articles, they would not have been printed. But it would be gratifying to one's sense of justice if the particular man who so delighted to revile another man safely, secretly, and at so much a word could be made to realize how his pleasantries are regarded by the community. Unfortunately—and this is the most crippling clause in any purpose of suitable punishment—the meaner a person is the more incapable he is of realizing it! You would visit upon him a thousand-ton vengeance—and he is conscious only of an ounce-and-a-half offense! There should be some way of educating offenders so see how bad they are and then no punishment would be needed. No further punishment perhaps, we might say.

A Life-Saver

> Paterson, N.J., Aug. 27.—Sarah Caslander, the two-year-old daughter of Mrs. Peter Caslander of 285 Getty Avenue, toddled over to a cup of carbolic acid which her mother had been using for cleaning purposes and drank it. The mother ran with the child to St. Joseph's Hospital a few blocks away. The doctors worked over the infant for almost an hour and succeeded in saving its life.[2]

Here is another instance of the sublimity of the maternal instinct—the unfailing security of a mother's care—and the suitability of the home as a place for children.

Here is a mother who for some inexplicable reason was apparently engaged as a charwoman. The connection between the care of children and the cleaning of houses is not clear but seems to be common. A home, being at present a place for much dirty work and also a place for babies to grow up in, of course the house must be cleaned. And the mother, being by custom the house servant, must clean it. Being busy in this sacred task, she leaves a cup of agonizing poison in reach of a two-year-old baby.

Maternal instinct was apparently subservient to house-cleaning instinct—temporarily. But what is one to do? The house must be cleaned—the mother must clean it—the baby must be in the house and therefore, well, accidents will happen. If we brought up our babies in iron foundries or gas works instead of kitchens and laundries, they might be worse off.

Perhaps—someday—we may make a safe place for them.

COLUMN 37

September 24, 1904

In this column Gilman implicitly compares a citizen who acts in violation of his civic obligations (e.g., an environmental polluter) and an "anti" who opposes such a progressive policy as women's suffrage. Each is complicit in the commission of a social sin.

Private Sins and Public Indifference

There is in the city of New York a long, lovely park, a green, irregular, sloping margin of beauty, bright in the western sunshine, lying for miles along one of the world's noblest rivers. In this park is a monument of white marble, tall, beautiful, rich with carving, rising grandly from wide marble steps and terraces, graced by a finely-mounted towering staff where flies our flag.[1] The monument and the flag commemorate our soldiers and sailors who lived to serve our country and died in its service; the park is for the health and pleasure of the public.

Across the river, about opposite Ninety-third street, is a huge manufactory, pile on pile of brick built at the water's edge, looming large and ugly against the defaced grandeur of the Palisades.[2]

It is one of many, but to be singled out for size and special evil. From its high chimney pours continually a long, thick stream of pitchy smoke, smoke of soft coal, smoke of chemical poison and heavy mineral deposit.

Held in the moist air of a site so near the sea, borne across the river by the prevailing winds, this steady flood of defilement drifts down upon the smiling park, blighting, withering, poisoning the air, soiling the clothes, injuring the health and pleasure of all who go there. It spreads duskily along the house fronts on Riverside Drive, making work harder and life less beautiful. Most conspicuous of all, it is turning the white monument that is an honor to the dead and a joy to the living from white to gray—in time from gray to black. And all this damage because the man who owns the factory will not spend the small sum needful for a smoke-consumer.

He knows, though the suffering public do not, that it is quite possible to consume every floating blot of soot—to keep the air clean—and that at very little cost. Rather than pay that cost, he is willing to scatter soot over the beauties of nature and the beauties of art, to poison the air, to deliberately lower the health of the community. He is indifferent, thinking only of himself; we are indifferent, thinking only of ourselves. It is our private selfishness which allows public sin.

We are so little-minded in our tiny circle of domestic virtues guided by the domestic conscience that we cannot grasp a public injury nor prevent it. See what it does in London, this positive and negative egoism between which the world lies bleeding.

We learn from the calculations of Sir William Thistleton-Dyer, curator of Kew Gardens,[3] that in London six tons of solid matter—soot and tarry hydrocarbons—are deposited every week on every quarter of a square mile in and about that city. This would amount to twenty-four tons per week or 1,248 tons per week to the square mile. If any man came in one night and deposited six tons of soot in one man's yard, how gallantly the British householder would fight him!

If this American manufacturer came over and defiled the monument with his own hands, how quickly the policeman would arrest him!

Is the offense any less because it is done slowly?

But the householder, British or American, is not aroused by a common injury, the fraction touching him being a small one. More and more do the large, widespread, subtle sins of modern life call for the modern conscience—the social conscience—that broad sensitiveness to wrong as wrong and not merely to what hurts one's self.

The evils from which the world suffers most today are public evils. The good by which we rise the fastest is public good. Our sins are not wholly conscious because the ethical and legal codes do not condemn them but they do their deadly work just the same.

We are rather proud in our small section of "the New England conscience," but it is a little backyard conscience after all. The New England cotton manufacturer goes gaily down to Georgia and kills little children in the mills slowly—very slowly—not by one clean, merciful blow. It does not touch his conscience—*nor his wife's*.

The law—the poor, old, stiff, slow-lumbering law—can never keep ahead of the ramifying, ingenious devices of our electric time, more especially as each social sinner carefully hires a good lawyer to tell him exactly where the limits are. He is able to hire the best legal talent to keep him posted and other talent—legal and legislative—to make such little alterations as he needs in his business; all this we know well enough. But why do we not care? And in especial why do not women care?

Because of our continual disproportionate exaltation of the private and personal. Because of our fond idolatry of simple, primitive instincts and our gross neglect of higher development.

Because while the majority of women spend their whole lives caring solely for their immediate families, and not only that but serving them in the methods of a long past age, so long will the majority of men also care only for their private families, private interests, private gain and neglect the common good.

We who are suffragists are familiar with this dull egoistic inertia, this "I have all the rights I want" attitude.

We who care for the Armenian, for the African, for the poor, the vicious, the dejected, for any *general* cause are continually thwarted by limitations of the domestic conscience. These people we seek to move, perfectly good people, respectable, educated, and virtuous in their limits, do not care for the general cause.

The same people, were they but reared in the constant atmosphere of social service, social duty, social relation as they are now forever re-immersed in ancient egoism and familism, would feel a keen rising resistless horror of these public evils of our day—and stop them.

Now fancy this manufacturer who is poisoning and defiling upper New York, as many more are poisoning and defiling lower New York and other places without end, fancy him meeting a nice girl and her asking him quietly, "Are you the Mr. Smith who has blackened the soldiers' and sailors' monument?" "Yes." "Why do you do it? Why don't you stop it?" One girl would make little difference (unless it was *the* girl) but if all his women friends protested similarly it would have some effect. It would have more effect no doubt if these women could elect—and manage—the city government, but the reason they do not is due to this same stunted, ancient, and dishonorable conscience of the year one.

Why This Insistence?

"I saw a pleasant sight the other day which ought to have been instructive to those who oppose the further extension of suffrage to women.... It was a man sitting by his dining-room table putting into glasses, sealing and labeling, the most delicious strawberry preserve it has ever been my good fortune to taste or smell. The expression of his face as he worked told plainly of keen enjoyment in his occupation, pride in his preserves, anticipation of the pleasure the eating of them would give his guests, and words of appreciation which would follow."

The above is a quotation save that I have told the tale of a man and it was a woman—a woman who had been a kindergartner, was an amateur photographer, and by profession a physician and surgeon. She was also a radical woman, a reformer and lover of reformers, and this special skill in the preserving of strawberries is advanced to prove that the new woman will not lose her domesticity.

I take this instance of a very common position to serve as basis for a protest, a three-fold protest.

First—it is no more noble or excellent for a woman physician to be expert in jam than for a male physician. If she made jam like the great Scotchman whose marmalade is a joy to the world,[4] that would be a profession, a social service, something for a human being to be proud of. But why boast of amateur jam any more than of amateur photographs—which this same woman also made? It is no harm for any human being, man or woman, to find rest and pleasure in a turning lathe, a sewing machine, a poultry yard, or a cook stove; but it is no special credit, either. There is no inherent virtue in making one's own clothes or cooking one's own food any more than in making one's own shoes, and it does not prove any superiority in the expert amateur over other amateurs.

The things to be proud of in one's work are these: its essential value to society, as an electrician's work is today more valuable to the world than that of a stage-driver, and one's exceptional merit in it. To make the best that is made—be it soap, velvet, or tomato catsup; to have one's product a standard and used all over the world; to improve its processes, increase its sales, feel that one is continually giving a better article and more of it for less money—that is cause for human pride.

This woman's work as a physician was her real world service and her joy in her jam was no more worthy than a man's delight in catching fish—not a fisherman who catches fish for us all but a business man going fishing for fun. It is neither cause for pride nor shame but an amusement. It is restful, too, being a relapse from advanced social exertion to primitive individual exertion. That is why it is an amusement and a rest to a woman in real work to drop back for a while into "domestic industry" as the man drops to the lake-dweller's level when he goes fishing.

The second protest is against the continuous insistence on the food trade as part of domesticity. Domesticity—houseness. "The domestic virtues"—virtues belonging to a house. What do we really want in the way of virtues from the woman in the house? The virtues of a wife: health; a normal development; pure, passionate, loyal love; an equal comradeship. The virtues of a mother: health; a normal development; the ability to provide proper care and education for the child; the example of a noble human life.

These are the domestic virtues. The virtues of a cook belong to the cook-shop, not the dwelling house; the mother has no more need of the cook's virtues than has the father. One may be a cook and a father or a cook and a mother; sex has no relation to social service; but the father's and mother's virtues in their relation to each other and to the children have nothing to do with their virtues in their several trades.

"Domesticity" as it applies to the industrial system whereby work is done at home is the mark of a stage of civilization which men have passed and women ought to have passed also.

The third protest is against this catering to the prejudices of the huge, slow-minded, inert majority. The position of one who sees and speaks the truth needs no defense. We have not even the justification of danger to warrant our conciliatory timidity. We are no longer persecuted and vilified; we are in no danger of [risking] body or business interests.

The brave woman who is really in advance needs to spend her courage and ingenuity in making good her future position—not in trying to show that she still reveres the past.

The woman who helps develop the profession of preparing food, standard food, healthful, appetizing, dainty, and cheap food, to be conscientiously and artistically prepared and served to the hungry whenever they wish to have it, she is doing more for her sex and the other sex, too, than any number of super-excellent amateur jammists.

COLUMN 38

October 1, 1904

Gilman long advocated stricter food laws, such as in, for example, "The Pure Food Exposition," *Impress*, January 12, 1895, 7; "Pure Food is Fashionable," *Impress*, January 19, 1895, 3; and "The Pure Food Exposition," *Impress*, February 2, 1905, 3. She also befriended Upton Sinclair (1878–1968), author of the muckraking novel *The Jungle* (1906), which sparked support for passage of the Pure Food and Drug Act. Sinclair reprinted some of Gilman's writings in *The Cry for Justice: An Anthology of the Literature of Social Protest* (Philadelphia: Winston, 1915), 200, where he declared her "America's most brilliant woman poet and critic."

"Over-Marriage"

Here is a new term in regard to matrimony. According to General Corbin,[1] the officers in our army are "over-married," not in the Mormon sense of too many wives to the husband but in the sense of too many married men.

It would be better for the army, thinks this public-spirited general, if more officers were single. This he does not advance on the ground of any degrading or injurious effects in marriage itself but purely from an economic standpoint—the pay of the young officer is insufficient to maintain a wife of his class as the pay of a private is similarly insufficient; therefore, they should not marry.

Kipling has drawn the veil (if ever there was a veil!) from the life of the army; he has shown us with a lingering attention to detail which marks close acquaintance and keen interest how "single men in barracks don't turn into plaster saints" either as officers or privates from the gay amours of the cheerful subaltern to the hideous warning in "Love o' Women."[2] When General Corbin therefore thinks it is better for young men not to marry, he either has more faith in plaster saints than the discerning author or he frankly accepts the other alternative.

Two possible arrangements are to be suggested that would promote virtue, health, and happiness. One is to increase the pay of our soldiers. If their work is as noble, as indispensable as we are told, if they are heroic defenders of all our peace and plenty, surely they are entitled to as much payment as men in business life. Why should the soldier be punished, in health or morals, for being a soldier? Something of the money now spent in pensioning those mercenary women who marry aged veterans for the sake of this wage—camp followers a long way off without even the courage of the present kind, who face some of the hardships of war and earn their shameful wage most arduously—might be given to the existing men.

But if our government cannot afford to pay its brave and faithful servants enough to marry on, there is another way out of the difficulty.

Here is the woman in the case, contemptibly helpless, waiting to be "supported." If marriage is that profitable partnership that so many fondly maintain, why may not the soldier share its advantages?

If it is not, if Mrs. Soldier or Mrs. Officer is frankly a consumer and not in any way a contributor to the family income, is there any reason she must remain so? Why should she not earn her keep? Then of course we are told that she is so occupied with the care of her children that she cannot possibly do any other work—that old claim of inefficient women, which is unshaken by the fourteen-hour labors of the toiling millions of housewives the world over.

Women can, women do, women always have worked at trades which have nothing to do with the care of children, and very little care their children get—beyond that of some prematurely exhausted older sister.

These soldiers' wives must necessarily live in groups; there is no reason whatever why they should not organize their efforts so as to reduce the living expenses to a minimum and leave plenty of spare time for productive labor.

What labor? In the business of feeding, clothing, nursing, and generally taking care of large numbers of men, there must be work for women.

The commissariat department—the most important and generally the weakest in army management—this has been supposed to be women's special field. Let us see how well she can manage it for large numbers.

To care for the children would employ many—real, trained, expert teaching—not the care that merely hires a nurse.

Some will say that if all the soldiers had wives with them—and children—it would make an army a mere mass of families—it would spoil the fighting spirit—it would put an end to war!

Well?

School for Wives

From the *New York Times* comes this quotation: "Teaching Young Women the Science of the Home. Domestic training for daughters of professional men in the West End school. Household management and all home duties. Address X—*From the London Mail*."[3]

Among the reasons adduced for the growing reluctance evinced by the average bachelor to enter the state of matrimony are:

The impracticability of the modern girl.
The decline of professional incomes.

The author of the above advertisement has just embarked on a novel scheme which aims at removing these obstacles. She takes young women to reside with her in a large house in Ealing, allows them a sum of money equivalent to a young professional man's salary—say £250 per annum—and shows them how to make the best of it. Rent, rates, and taxes are paid out of the total; butchers, bakers, grocers, tailors, dressmakers, and other items of household management are settled with; even life insurance and annual holidays are taken into account. Only half a guinea a head per week is allotted for food.

"Modest though that sum is, the girls after a little tuition can work wonders with it," said the initiator of the scheme, Mrs. A. Hockly. "It allows of a substantial breakfast for husband and wife consisting of two or three courses. In the absence of the husband in the city, the wife contents herself with a light luncheon but prepares a good dinner in readiness for his return home. The girls are taught to make most of their own clothes but in addition are granted £20 a year for their best frocks and hats. The supposititious husband takes another £20 for a like purpose."

Weekly price lists from provision dealers are carefully studied by the young women, who base their daily menus on the existing state of the market. On certain days the pupils are taken round the grocery stores and shown how to spend money to the best advantage.

This is sensible. The more women study the ancient system of housekeeping by modern business methods, the sooner they will learn to improve it.

From the same English paper we have a burst of pained protest against the "hatless irreverence of women" who it seems are beginning to be sensible enough in Cornwall to go to church bare-headed. In real distress the agitated Vicar of Crantock beseeches these thoughtless women to cover their heads as men uncover theirs on entering God's house.[4]

Now why should God—Eternal, All-wise, All-powerful, All-good—be interested in women's hats? Is the sight of men's hair or their bald heads agreeable to God and women's hair disagreeable? What earthly or heavenly difference does it make to Him? What has a hat to do with reverence, on or off? If it has any connection with respect, it is in the age-long custom of removing it, but that is only a habit. If we analyze it, however, we surely find this basis for uncovering—that the human head, the seat of the intelligence, the noblest part of the noblest race of creatures, made we are told in the image of God, is a finer thing than any flimsy structure of straw and feathers and artificial flowers or than those black, ugly shapes of felt which we wear on our heads.

If it is not God who is to be considered but men, if the custom is justified by its discreditable old Oriental cause when a woman must needs be veiled lest men's eyes wander from their prayers, then we should consider that our huge, gorgeous, modern hats are expressly intended to adorn the wearer and attract attention—and do attract it, woefully, as well as obstructing the view of the priest and the altar. Much better exclude women's hats if men are to be more free for their devotions.

If, however, we are told that the Bible says so and that is enough, we will merely quote a few other sayings from the Bible. For instance, there is a good, plain, strong statement, unequivocal, unqualified—"Thou shalt not kill."[5] Yet our most Christian nations kill continually in both legal and military measures and the Church makes small protest.

Again we are especially told *not to make long prayers in public*—when we pray to pray secretly—yet every clergyman stands up calmly and makes long prayers in public in the supposed service of Him who forbade it!

It does not do to base conduct too closely on Scripture texts—our daily lives will not stand it.

Impure Food

Dr. Lederle of New York, formerly Commissioner of Health, says in a paper read before the International Congress of Arts and Sciences in St. Louis: "The extent to which commercial adulteration and substitution is now practiced would be absolutely incomprehensible to the layman. Competition in trade has become so keen and the substitution of inferior constituents in food so general that the honest manufacturer has hardly a chance to succeed." Against this evil, Dr. Lederle urges official control but shows how, though a federal pure food law was before Congress, "in the absence of an aroused public opinion" it was killed by those interested.[6]

Now here is a thing that ought to appeal to women. Here is a matter intensely "practical," "domestic," "maternal," in line with every oldest virtue supposed to be intrinsically ours.

We that prepare the food for the world, who serve our beloved husbands and children with such tender devotion, we—solemnly pouring down their defenseless throats all manner of inferior, deleterious, often poisonous substances because we don't know any better and then, if we do know better, if we have to our own horror painfully learned what is sold us for tea, coffee, spices, and so on, then we are helpless because of our limited time, strength, and money—in a word, our isolation. Now the women of the world should be in the business of preparing food from the first step to the last—as men are. Halve the work, divide the pay, lessen the family expenses, reduce the pressure that drives the heavy-laden man to these nefarious methods, and by mingling with him in the work diminish that "competitive tendency" which is mainly a form of masculine belligerence.

When an evil as large as this exists, when all over the world the health of the helpless children is being steadily undermined by these "business methods" of preparing food, it is surely time that women woke up, crawled out of their contented retirement—their little Holy City of a home—and fell to protect and defend that home. Holy means healthy. Only a clean and wholesome world can keep the homes clean and wholesome. Public sanitation and public honesty are the only means of safety for the baby at home.

COLUMN 39

October 8, 1904

This column epitomizes Gilman's ability to discuss in a single space two or three topics that at first glance seem unrelated; for example, the resolution of combat, including sexual combat, through organization.

World Peace and Sex Combat

As we grow to understand more clearly the nature of human development, to know what are human qualities and how they grow, what is social progress and how it is achieved, we see with increasing certainty the inhuman, un-human, sub-human, pre-human nature of war.

See first the loose flux of savage life—a disconnected, thinly-spread, uncertain stream of men; that stream settles and thickens in fat-soiled river valleys, produces abundantly, learns new arts and crafts, and then by the overflow of surplus product through a thousand widening, deepening, lengthening channels of trade and commerce these centers of productivity connect with others and the knitting of the nations begins.

Step by step or stitch by stitch as we might say, the great web thickens and stretches, taking in more and more peoples, weaving them together in indispensable connection, developing every human faculty, enriching, educating, enlarging, making the savage human by contact and exchange.

The process has been going on from the beginning of history to our time but its beautiful, orderly development has been continually thwarted by eruptions of the sub-human nature, of the fierce, predatory, combative brute below. These outbursts, whether in personal selfishness and passion or in the same selfishness and passion on the part of nations, we have hitherto characterized as "human nature." They are not human but pre-human, belonging to the animal of which humanity is made but not to that humanity itself. This we also recognize, inconsistently enough, by our words "humane," "inhuman," and others, but have not rid ourselves of the older and mistaken idea.

If we were studying human history from the point of view of some remote and superior stage of being, we should wonder at the continuance of war in a grade of social progress where it is so obviously out of place.

The antiquated nature of its organization, the extremely primitive emotions on which it rests, the injury caused the social body by an army in peace as well as the more active and terrible injury of war, these would prove to the student of comparative sociology that this was a "vestigial rudiment" of the most mischievous character. And he would seek the more earnestly with keen scientific enthusiasm for what strange conditions might combine to maintain in an advanced society, a "Christian civilization," this incredible anachronism.[1]

To that student of future centuries and to the dully resisting mind of today, I offer this suggestion. There is a double base for the war spirit, one of which is the predatory instinct common to carnivora, to those whose food is evasive and resistant—a spirit born of strenuous pursuit and active opposition and reaching a remorseless greed, a gnashing frenzy to devour, which is not developed by the unobstructed eating of acquiescent vegetation.

As soon as human profit was proven to lie in production and distribution, this predatory spirit should have disappeared in natural elimination; that it did not is due to certain economic conditions which I will not here touch upon for I wish rather to show the presence and influence of the other element in war, that of sex-combativeness.

So far as war is predatory in its nature, the female shares in it; female carnivora are fully as fierce and gluttonous as male, but in this other base the female has no share. Inter-masculine combat is purely a feature of sex, a "secondary sex-characteristic." It is found in all higher animals, even the mildest, as sheep, deer, or rabbits.

This masculine belligerence does not require the presence of the female to be competed for but is an ingrained tendency leading to combat wherever males are together. Indeed, among a great number of males without females it is far worse than when the combatants are mated; in more human terms, there would be less quarreling among a number of married men than among the same number of celibate men. This fighting spirit has nothing to do with predation; it is pure competitive fury coming from very old physiological conditions.

Now why should this spirit, so frankly animal, so far below the range of reason, the laws of human association, still rage among us to such an extent as to predispose our men to war in the face of every higher consideration, either of noblest virtue or plainest common sense? Here comes in the responsibility of women for war.

Women up to this time have taken almost no part in the civilizing processes of production and distribution, in the specialized functions of an advanced society, but have been confined to their general animal functions and the lowest grade of primitive industry. This position necessarily maintains in the woman the emotions and sentiments proper to that grade of development and as necessarily retards the emergence of the emotions and sentiments proper to civilization. Not only so, but as the advance of society goes on through the work of man and the woman inherits the power attained by him, the new social power, mistakenly confined to the same old channels, results in an inordinate development of the only side of her nature she is allowed to use. Hence we have in our highly socialized modern life this singular phenomenon of a carefully preserved primitive relation abnormally developed—the unsocialized woman, ultra-feminine, sub-human. It is this illegitimate position of the woman which checks the smooth and noble ascent of human motherhood, leaving us still unhealthy and inadequate, unable perfectly to care for even our own children in a state of neglect which needs no epithets.

It is this illegitimate position of the woman which keeps the relation of the sexes so offensively prominent in human life, in all its feverish agitation, dissatisfaction, and disease, both physical and social, and hinders the quiet, natural happiness of a true monogamy, which in this age all of us should have and none of us need talk about. When happy marriage is the common lot of civilized man, we shall not be so sensitive about it nor will literature be so surcharged with one passion. A morbid consciousness always proves disease.

It is this illegitimate position of the woman, to reach our special subject, which keeps man also in an illegitimate position, which maintains in him an abnormal degree of brute instinct which is not essential to human love, to harmonious marriage, to healthy parentage but directly injurious to them, a strange, anachronistic, monstrous growth as of some looming dinotherium in the peaceful waters of today, a group of warring passions which civilized man struggles vainly to subdue because they are born and bred in him, nursed and fed in him, steadily maintained in him from age to age by uncivilized woman.

It is this forced maintenance of primitive passions which every social process tends to eliminate that makes us helplessly burst forth in this tragic absurdity of modern war. Man is a brute, we say, "under a thin veneer of civilization." It is not true. Our civilization is no veneer; it is a deep, true, orderly growth. We are not brutes but men; and the modern man, in spite of the choking glory of slaughter, the uprush of old currents strong and fierce, has grown ashamed of war. Alexander did not say, "War is hell"; Sherman did.[2]

The weak spot in our nature through which this generally subordinate stream of passions bursts is that of abnormal sex-development and all its tangled train of consequences. As soon as our women are civilized, too—civilized wives happy and content with the man they love but not expecting to make that happiness the end of human life; civilized mothers bringing to their children the ordered wisdom of many consecrated lives instead of the unbridled maternal passion of one only and so expanding that maternal passion in its true social channels that no mother's heart on earth can rest in peace while one human child suffers neglect; most of all, civilized workers taking part in those processes which make civilization, friends, comrades, fellow-workers with men everywhere, full human creatures at last instead of too fully feminine ones—then the human spirit can rule smoothly in all walks of life. Personal love and happiness will be common to all, but social love and happiness is what we need to ensure the personal. The strong, wide, dominant human spirit, the spirit of civilized society, the divine spirit working its own ends through our vast web of social development—this is what will enable us finally to forget these sins of racial ignorance.

Universal peace calls for a general, active humanness among women as well as men. The mother of the world, when she rises to her true place, can put an end to war.

Women and World Organization

In the September *Atlantic* is a strong, hopeful article on how world organization secures world peace by R. L. Bridgman, a clear, strong, sensible article leaving the reader stirred with a deep enthusiasm.[3]

The writer shows how commercial forces are working to unify the nations, "every producer trying to enlarge his market and to bring the world closer to himself—except where statesmen are using the tremendous powers of government to put obstructions in the way of trade and to make each country an isolated economic factor." "People in incalculable numbers in every quarter of the earth wish to do business with other people in every other part of the earth." "World unity is a fact today. But unity of the world under a government of men is not a fact. Narrowness of view, conservative ideas of progress, timidity regarding the future, selfish jealousy lest others get more than we," these factors keep us back. I wish to take these words as a text to illustrate anew how the position of women affects these world-problems.[4]

It is a truism that commercial relations make for peace, but it is here brought out with specific clearness—in the producer trying to enlarge his market and bring the world nearer to himself. This is the natural development of production—the specialized producer creates an increasing supply of goods and that supply must spread to find those who need it. We say "to find a market," seeing only the price of the goods as the thing desired, but the fact is there, whatever we call it.

It is clear that if half our men were not producers but merely fished for a living, eating the fish they caught, they would contribute nothing to this growing tendency toward unity. It is the producers and distributors, the world's workers, who bring the nations together—not the isolated non-productive consumers. Women are isolated non-productive consumers—the great mass of them. They take no part in human work and so add nothing to the commercial demand for peace. But beyond this comes their share in the opposing factors mentioned by this writer: "Narrowness of view, conservative ideas of progress, timidity regarding the future, selfish jealousy lest others get more than we."

I do not mean that women as a sex are more given to these hindering things but that women in the domestic stage of industry are necessarily thus affected. To live and work alone in one's own small circle tends to create and maintain narrowness of view. To live as one's foremothers have lived from the dawn of history, piously upholding the most venerable traditions, keeps us conservative in our ideas of progress—not only the women who thus live but the men who are so enormously influenced by them.

Timidity regarding the future is the natural product of dependence on another—no anxiety so grinding as that of the helpless.

The woman feels this with terrible force because of the natural dependence of her children on her and the unnatural dependence of herself on the man. She is between the upper and nether millstone and is anxious and timid accordingly. Her only means of assisting is in careful expenditure and rigid economy; thus we see in women a small, self-sacrificing parsimony and its occasional reaction in rash and careless expenditure, but we do not see the large foresight of the good business man.

Thus a woman earning her living in a good day's work will still endeavor to make her own clothes like her domestic ancestors, weakening herself and lowering her market value, a short-sighted policy bred of long dependence. Dickens in *Great Expectations* shows the escaped convict carefully mopping up every drop of gravy with his bread and eating it all—he came from where they lived on rations.[5]

The "selfish jealousy lest others get more than we" is not in most housewives personal but embraces the family. It is well-expressed in the story of the Western senator who spent so much to promote education in his State while his good wife protested that he had no right to spend his children's money on other people! Said he, "My dear, I would rather my children grew up poor in an educated community than rich in a community of ignorant blackguards."[6] The woman's whole life being spent in the exclusive contemplation of her own family and the service of their daily needs, she is naturally unable so to enlarge her focus of the public.

It is the littleness of mind bred by domestic industry which acts as the most general check on progress today. The larger mind sees the good of the world—the claims of all humanity. The small mind sees only its personal duty to its personal relatives and exaggerates that to a size which shuts out all others.

The gentleness and sensitiveness of our sheltered homebound women makes them shrink from war; their recent education makes them see its evils, its incredible waste, its foolish wickedness; and their mother-hearts make them long for the peace we ought to have; but their business, their inexorable, ceaseless, lifelong task of personal home service prevents the growth of that general intelligence and breadth of mind which will not only cry out against war but find the way to stop it.

Love means service. If we love the world, we must serve it. World service is not best done by a detached half of the world slowly struggling up toward public virtue while the other half, sublime in domestic virtues, is in public spirit but a primeval savage in comparison. When our women are occupied in a grade of business which develops what we call the world-mind, their world-progress will be more swift. The kitchenmindedness of half of us is a great drawback to our best advance.

COLUMN 40

October 15, 1904

Gilman celebrates maternal love and reviews a recent magazine essay on "The American Woman."

The Mother-Heart

The extreme beauty of feeling and expression in Ellis Meredith's picture of motherhood in her charming book *Heart of My Heart* will be felt and enjoyed by many a reader.[1] Here is devotion as absolute, self-surrender as complete, and a subtle play of tenderness as exquisite as anyone could wish, and it will no doubt seem harsh and unreasonable to wish for more.

At the risk of offending (which indeed is one of the unavoidable risks of any honest moving life) let us from the very height of this so loving, lovely, and lovable book point out the further growth of the mother-heart for which the world waits.

We have on earth a vast population of mothers—half the world. A continuous half are mothers, future, present, and past, and the other half are their children. Mothers make mothers in endless line from the first dawn of life and also fathers from a later period.

We have on earth a vast population of children born of these mothers and fathers and, according to our general belief, owing most to their mothers' love. Now if we are to judge the power and beauty of the mother's love, it must be by its effect on the children—is not that fair? Look then with clear, faithful scrutiny at the children of any city on earth; look as the school teacher looks at the hundreds and thousands of little ones pass through her hands; look as the police officer looks at the teeming streets of the crowded quarters where there are the most children; look as the specialist looks at the terrible numbers of diseased, defective, degenerate babies; look as the health officer looks at the lamentable lists of sick and dead; and then, to be a little more cheerful, look in the best parts of the city at the scanter children of the rich, also in the streets and parks, but in the charge of that undesirable child-herd, the nurse. Thus taking the great bulk of our children in survey, does their condition satisfy the mother-heart of any civilized woman?

"No," she will admit, "but the condition of mine is satisfactory." Then if you seek to rouse her to interest in these other children, these hundreds of thousands of other children, she refuses to accept any responsibility for their care, holding that they have mothers and that each mother should care for her own. This is the key to this painful problem, this question which affronts our civilization so continually and the shame of which we are unable to escape: How can a civilized community allow children to suffer?

That children do suffer, suffer all manner of deprivation and injury, suffer till they die in thousands, suffer through stunted, thwarted, distorted lives, is not to be denied. And all these children have mothers. And all mothers, according to the creed of the matriolator, love their children. And a mother's love is the best thing the child can have. Perhaps it is the best of any one thing; but by all the horrors of child-ruin with which the world is full, *it is not enough*.

Now this is what this beautiful book about a mother's heart leaves untouched. It is the apotheosis of the personal mother, exquisite and true. I have no fault to find with it in commission but much in omission. This might have been as true of any mother in any age, of any mother in any race, sweet, deep, delicate, all-absorbing—it is the maternal passion at its height and all imbued with adoration of her husband, as is right—but have all our ages of progress brought in nothing more?

This is the foundation; this is the world-old feeling of her who brings forth young and suckles it; this is that feeling infinitely extended, made intelligent, made vocal, decorated with a wealth of illustration and gem-work of poetry—but it is the same feeling. It is a perfectly right and proper feeling, necessary and honorable and beautiful, but it is not enough.

The children of the world today suffer because their mothers do not give them the great, all-embracing, social mother-heart as well as this one-embracing personal mother-heart.

Think now of a mother who, when she felt the mystic touch of life in life—that marvelous consciousness that connect us all through our unbroken line of foremothers—should by that same sweet token feel the kindling in her heart of love for that long line of life behind her, the longer line before her, and the wide wale of life all around her—children *all, all*, at first and to be loved because they are children and she is a mother.

Then as the new life grows and strengthens and her heart swells and deepens with the rising flood of love, she feels then for the myriad others who have that infinite joy within them and find it a burden or a curse because of their ignorance, of the shame which is carried where should be glorious pride, of all the folly and lies which hide heaven from them and blight their lives and the lives they bring forth; to think of them and for them with new love and care because they are mothers and she is a mother.

To think then, as this deep ocean of pride and power swells larger, of what that power of motherhood has meant to life on earth; of how through motherhood species have risen and risen even to humanity; of how humanity, with its one root sin of degrading its mother, has had such ages of suffering and shame to struggle through; and then with a radiant blaze of new hope for the world to see how she, the mother, can remake life on earth by this, her undeniable, resistless power—if she will do it.

Love? Love that rises and pushes in her heart till she can scarce wait to express it; love that can give her little child such perfect gentle justice, such unerring care, such alluring freedom and subtle stimulus to upward growth as no child ever had before because it is the love of myriad mothers, blended, complementing one another, permanent, tireless, fully-equipped, educated—the human mother-love.

Her child? Yes, her child, now fully loved by a heart that leaves no child unloved on earth. Now someone is going to say that this is unnatural. By no means. It is distinctly natural for a human creature. We are by nature social and that implies the power to love one another.

We are by religion Christians and that implies the duty to love one another. Would Christ have commanded an impossibility? Not He. Great sociologist that He was, He knew the nature of the heart and urged it to recognize its noblest impulses and fulfill them.

And did He, does anyone think, point out this great sociological law, "Thou shalt love one another,"[2] to men only and to women leave but the primal physiological law—thou shalt love thy own young? Not He.

The animal mother loves her own young—and none other. The human mother loves her own young—*and all others*. That is what it is to be human. Our children—our human children—are crying for their mothers.

An Englishman on American Women

Here is Mr. H. B. Marriott-Watson again constructing a creature he calls "the American woman" and then making animadversions on the same.[3]

Mr. Watson should, in the first place, consider the point of view of the intelligent Italian quoted by John Foster Carr in the *World's Work* for October: "Americans are not a race. They are a society of men of different races."[4]

They are indeed, and so recently associated that there is no possibility as yet of race characteristics in the legitimate sense. Incidentally, they are a society of women of different races, too, which the intelligent Italian failed to mention.

The fundamental error in Mr. Watson's article is the usual one—the commonplace one, the one that shows the author wholly unacquainted with recent scientific development on this line and blind to conspicuous facts in life. "The foundations of feminine nature are as simple and as easily traced as those of male nature. They take their rise in physical facts and are responsible for all the moral and mental properties appertaining to the sex." Thus Mr. Watson.

This is true enough and applies with equal cogency to the ewe and ram, cow and bull, doe and buck! To use this law of sex-distinction as sufficient to account for the characteristics of women is the mistake so general among shallow thinkers.

Having chosen to confine women to her feminine functions solely for so many ages, seeing her only as a female, thinking of her only as a female, treating her only as a female, it is natural enough that men should unconsciously assume that she is nothing else. And almost as natural is it that, having monopolized all human functions for himself, the man should assume them to be "masculine." So extremely light is Mr. Watson's study of this matter that he errs even physiologically, speaking of the woman's love of jewels and colors, her "inordinate vanity," as a sex-characteristic. Whereas every biologist knows that sex-decoration and its accompanying vanity are inherently masculine as shown by every prancing stag and strutting cock the world over. As a sex the female is modest and plain; that women are not so is an arbitrary condition recently developed in them by their economic dependence.

The female has power enough to attract the male without wasting any of her energies on decoration. It is the business of the male to plume himself to please her—and he does it naturally. But with us, the woman has not only to attract the male in the natural relation but to get her living from him—so for the first time in biologic history we have a specially decorated female. It is no mark of femininity, quite the contrary; it is a falsely assumed masculinity due to her abnormal position of dependence.

With false premises like these, it is no wonder that Mr. Watson's conclusions wander strangely. "A woman's possessions are rather the fruit of her vanity than her taste," he says, and goes on to attribute various results to her vanity—which was never a feminine sex-characteristic at all. Claiming that there is a certain clearly-marked, fixed type of American woman, "almost as national in her individuality as, say, the German woman or English woman," he proceeds to "attempt to define her with some care." "An unstable nervous equilibrium" is the main feature of this type it appears.

"Women have always been the drag on evolution in every age and clime," owing to the natural conservatism of the sex. American women so far have apparently broken loose from this conservatism—to his horror. But if conservatism is a sex-characteristic of all women—"in every age and clime"—and American women manifest a lack of it, how then can American women be explained on a sex-basis merely? This he meets by the old masculine argument—"Women are a sex. They are nothing else. If they insist on being anything else, they unsex themselves."

This is precisely what Mr. Watson objects to. The American woman, according to him, "is proverbially careless of the male of her race."

The American male seems to get on fairly well under this neglect and by no means repudiates his female. Mr. Watson is a bit puzzled by the undeniable beauty and attractiveness of the "handsome clothes-horse" he describes, but explains it to be but a passing show. "She has the outward signs and rite of muliebrity," he admits, but has lost the essence. And then, quoting from our vigorous president[5] and the deep and scholarly researches of the three-week's experiment made by Mrs. and Miss van Vorst,[6] he brings out the core and essence of the whole matter.

The American woman does not have enough children! Now the African woman does. The Italian woman does. There are plenty of women who have quantities of children—and nothing else. Are there not enough of these to satisfy the anxious male? Why should he be so concerned over an evil which inevitably leads to its own extinction? Women are plenty.

Let the American women go their suicidal way—men are not compelled to imperil their paternal ambitions by marrying her. Perhaps the American woman, free, wise, strong, as attractive as any woman in the world, is too exacting in her choice of a husband—too high in her standard of what kind of children she is willing to have and when and how.

If so, she is obeying the deepest law of her sex—to improve the species by rigid and exclusive selection.

COLUMN 41

October 22, 1904

Gilman detested children's clothing fashions because, as she noted, they were designed to emphasize their sex distinction. Here she elaborates on her observation in *The Home*: "If some cartoonist would give us a copy of the Sistine Mother and Child in the costume of our mothers and children, showing those immortal cherub faces blinking obliquely from under flopping hat brims and rich plumes, perhaps we might in sudden shocked perception see with what coarse irreverence we disfigure our blessed little ones."[1]

The Clothing of Children

If anyone demands proof, plain, constant, convincing proof of the arrested development of the average woman, it is to be found in the clothing of children.

Her own clothing is to be accounted for by her dependent position. She alone of all female creation carries the burden of decorated appendages, else exclusively a masculine prerogative, and that condition we cannot expect to escape so long as the male carries all the burden of economic effort.

If stags took to agriculture, they could hardly afford to waste energy on a yearly set of antlers for no purpose whatever except to outrival another stag and win favor of the female. If the female had no part in agriculture and did not even browse for herself but was fed by the stag, her energies might afford this new expense—especially as he no longer had to compete normally for her favor but she most despicably for his.

All this is clear enough and in a sense unavoidable. But why should children be hampered and injured by this shameful profusion of untimely decoration? They do not have to compete for anyone's favor. Surely mother love and father love are enough to ensure the child's life, even if it were personally unattractive; and it is not to be supposed that the tormenting superfluity of ornament we load upon our little girls is to win favor of little boys—they do not need that, surely? Perhaps this is not so sure, however. If the observation of those who write the present-day stories of children is correct, this is precisely what is wanted.

In the October *McClure's*, Miss Marion Hill describes the attire of small girls in Sunday school thus: "But today her raiment was blue silk, her long hair was flowing in ripples till it looked like a golden washboard, and her hat was as big as a parasol and was made all out of pink and white daisies." Of another she says: "To describe her were impossible. She was just a bewitching bunch of curls, coquetry, dimples, and smiles. Everything about her floated, from the butterfly bows in her halo of curls to the tassels on her shoes. Rex felt a warm, religious fervor growing upon him as he caught her flying smiles." At the close of the tale we are told that this small boy decided to go to Sunday school, "drawn to the throne of grace solely by his desire and intention of sitting next to the dimpling Angela."[2] Josephine Dodge Daskam had this same element in her "Dicky and the Little God."[3] It is commonly exploited in current literature.

If this be true "infant psychology," which I gravely doubt, then there is a whole separate chapter of evils involved in such painful precocity of sex-attraction at an age when healthy children should have none of it. But quite aside from this is the spirit I am considering, which makes young mothers-to-be say, "Oh, I'd rather have a girl—they are so much prettier to dress!"

In another story I read lately, an unmarried woman almost stole a little girl to gratify the maternal longing of her thwarted life, and in her musings on other women who had little girls she dwelt with lingering delight on their walking by their mothers' sides in many much-beruffled white skirts looking "like double white carnations." This is a very delicate and clear expression of the misplaced, unhealthy feeling which generally governs the clothing of children whenever means allow and which proves the low-grade civilization of our women.

Here is the mainspring of mother-love stained and poisoned by sex-vanity—a vanity which is misplaced in the first instance by being transferred from the male to the female and far worse in its second distortion by being forced upon the child.

A full education and social growth would check this tendency by constant consideration of the needs of healthy childhood, but our women are not fully educated and socially grown; they are in a semi-civilized condition, maintaining in our foremost van of progress the decorative habits of low savagery.

Even the sense of beauty with which women are commonly credited fails to show them the glaring ugliness of disproportionate, precocious decoration on the beautiful body of a child. It is not the beauty sense by any means—that exquisite characteristic of our humanhood—which marks the dress of women but solely that of sex-decoration, which has little to do with true aesthetics. Conspicuous appendages, wattles, dangling bunches, gaudy callosities appear in this form of attraction as naturally as lovely plumage; and so, in the dress of women, ugly colors and monstrous shapes are as readily adopted as those which are beautiful. Beauty has no hold on fashion.

Apart from this, one would think that the hygienic knowledge of modern days would prevent our loading down little children with heavy and useless ornament, but this knowledge, too, is lacking in the average woman or is so inadequate as to weigh little against her taste for physical adornment.

One more feeling we might expect to act in defense of the helpless baby—the sympathy of the mother's heart for the child's sufferings. But no such sympathy appears. The Flathead Indian[4] mother ties up her baby's head between boards to distort its shape; the Chinese mother ties up her baby's feet to cripple and stunt them. Mother-love has absolutely no weight against the influence of fashion in these stages of social development and in our own women it has little more.

We do not so grossly injure the child's body because our fashions no longer demand it (though it is but a few years since the rigid corset and even the "backboard" were applied to little girls) but whatever the fashion demands we still apply with no regard whatever to the feelings of the child.

Some women there are who are more civilized—some few. These progressive souls allow the little bodies freedom and comfort, do not obtrude precocious sex-distinctions, and subordinate decoration to the laws of beauty and to the dominant simplicity of childhood. But a walk in the street, a ride in the cars, a visit to the park on a fair day will show no apparent diminution in the uncivilized kind of mother.

The first error is to differentiate the dress of little boys and girls at all. Their needs as children are precisely similar; they should have precisely the same advantages of free action and physical education; there is nothing whatever *from the child's point of view* to call for a difference in dress.

The strut of the wee male child who puts on his tiny trousers and becomes "a man!" is as pitifully out of place as the mincing air of the tiny female child who is set up in elaborately-trimmed skirts and told to be "a lady!" He is not a man nor she a woman and neither should have the difference forced upon them.

The second error is in the excess of ornament and its accompanying restriction. Boy baby or girl baby, dressed in white velvet coat and gaiters or any other rich material and then restricted in free action lest they soil their clothes, suffer alike under the low-grade civilization of the mother. By what right does she thus cramp a child's activities to please her savage taste in dress?

Then follow all the ill effects on growing mind and soul of the inordinate attention fixed on dress, the self-consciousness, the ridiculous centering of the beauty sense upon clothing which the boy gradually outgrows, at least in part, and the girl carries through life.

Bodily beauty is first lost sight of under a load of unnecessary and inartistic clothing, then distorted and injured by the weight and pressure of the clothing and the restricted activity consequent upon it, and then forgotten in the perversion of mind following necessarily upon the physical falsities.

A small girl with face expressing sulkiness, self-consciousness, and irritation is yet full of vanity over her pretty clothes; and her mother—who has thus injured her—is also content in the dress. The face she does not consider of equal importance nor does she think at all of the kind of spirit which speaks in the unhappy little countenance. This general condition of misguided mother-love, of ignorance, of a conservatism and slavishness to fashion which marks with daily accuracy a low savage state of development shows to any thoughtful observer how much our women need to come forward into the world's life and be *human*.

Their sheltered, stagnant, ultra-feminine position fosters undisturbed through the moving ages primitive traits which should have been long since outgrown. Men have largely outgrown them, but in their profound conviction that women ought not to share in human progress they are actually pleased with the continuance of glaring traits of savagery in them and even that they should wreck the same upon their little ones.

The boy they comfort with the assurance that he will soon be a man and outgrow all these furbelows, not realizing that the furbelow business is in its origin distinctly masculine and that what the boy triumphantly grows into is not masculinity but the front of advancing civilization. No wonder he is proud. No wonder he looks down upon his sister as "only a girl" and then learns to say "only mother." He thinks this splendid swelling sense of growth and power within him is due to his being a man. Not at all. He was "a man"—i.e., a male—when he was in the small parasitic stage and his wife ate him; it is not sex, it is civilization which he feels and which he has so long denied to her. If his sister had been reared in identical conditions with himself, equal in every study and sport, victor in many a rough-and-tumble combat—girls are larger and stronger than boys up to about the twelfth year—and looking forward as he did to doing full human service in the world, the fact that she was "a girl" would be an added power and glory, if anything—in no sense a reproach. Civilized mothers will bring up their children so.

Women who are fully human, who belong to the utmost to our age of growth, who are conscious, active citizens, social instead of domestic servants, will learn to understand what Beauty is, what Sex-decoration is, and what Fashion is and to choose wisely between them. They themselves will be athletic and beautiful as the chitoned Greek, and their children will show us the exquisite grace of the sturdy cherub instead of the helpless, awkward rebellion of these poor, waddling, little cloth-bearers.

Now the conscientious, intelligent, educated women who read this and are angry at being called lower in development than men—than the men whom some of them have been looking down on and perhaps refusing to marry because they were less "refined" and "cultured"—will demand to know what is this civilization they are charged with lacking.

It is the degree of social development which distinguishes our age from others—above others. Its distinctive features are in certain high attainments in special arts, sciences, business, and the like, as for instance our electric connection, our educational system, our growth in transportation, and furthermore by certain forms of organization as a democratic government. Civilization has moved a long way, and its most distinctive line of progress is in the form of its organic relation, from the utter lack of it in a loose savage horde period up through the order of governmental progression, from the patriarchal to the universally representative or democratic.

The distinctive business development which characterizes our age is almost wholly in the hands of men, and the distinctive governmental development also. In America our men live in a democracy—our women in a patriarchate: a poor, demoralized patriarchate as inefficacious and lacking in authority as a paralyzed megatherium but still a patriarchate.

Not until women accept full citizenship, claim and fulfill its duties and enjoy its privileges, will they be as civilized as men are today. Not until they are civilized can they be civilized mothers. Not until they are civilized mothers can their children be clothed as befits members of our stage of social growth.

COLUMN 42

October 29, 1904

Gilman traces the evolution of the sitting room into parlor into drawing room into living room. She equates the terms "living" and "doing," which explains why she titled her autobiography *The Living of Charlotte Perkins Gilman*, and mocks both the popular notion of men as natural protectors of women and the coming out of another debutante, Jane Norton Morgan Nichols (1893–1981), daughter of the financier J. P. Morgan (1837–1913).

The Living-Room

There is a certain reasonable sentiment as to the use of the term "living-room" instead of "parlor" and in favor of simple fittings, comfortable and restful rather than decorative.

This a place to live in, say these reasoners, not a mere reception room, and it should meet the wants of daily living for its inmates.

True enough as far as it goes, but resting wholly on a further question—what is "living"? Is sitting down in a warm, pleasant room with a good fire, an easy chair, a clear light, a pleasant book, and one's family about one—is this "living"?

Most of us would say yes at once. So strong, so deep, so interknit with our oldest and tenderest sentiments is this domestic ideal that we exalt it as life itself—referring to the work of the world as "business," a thing to be done in order to maintain this comfortable living; and to the play of the world as "excitement," "pleasure," "recreation," something one needs from time to time perhaps but not living.

On the other hand, we have that grotesquely narrow view, diseased and aborted, which calls a certain range of vicious indulgence "life," taking the boy to "see life" by showing him gambling dens, wild banquets and dancers, and various forms of licentiousness.

One might as well exhibit feline "life" by showing a cat in a fit. Then we have that very natural outburst of the soul when thrilled and borne along by some great excitement, some tremendous force, physical or psychic, which makes us cry, "This is life!"

But generally, when we speak of living, we mean eating, drinking, sleeping and wearing clothes, reading, talking, and otherwise enjoying ourselves; and the phrases "getting a living," "a comfortable living," "working for a living," and the like refer to these domestic processes. From this point of view the poor man works for a living and the rich man lives, the man in general works for the family living and the family lives—in the living-room.

In the Orient, where the women are more wholly secluded, the living ideal is more secluded also; a perfumed garden to drowse in beneath roses, to the music of the fountain and the nightingale, with bare, fat babies and veiled beauty of maids and mothers—this is the desired attainment. Our harem is monogamous and unbarred; our women walk free-faced and unashamed. We mingle freely in what we call "society," but still the vast majority of women pass the vast majority of their hours at homes and call it living. Against this racial age-old habit of feeling struggle two great forces, the divine truth of Christian love and the rushing uplift of social progress.

The universal love and service which is the spirit of our religion can never be manifested while we prefer to spend our whole time in loving and serving ourselves. Ascetic reaction, blindly lumping the whole group of domestic relations together, forswore them all and demanded a celibate priesthood, the renunciation of all private love, for the service of God and man.

Wiser religious thought, seeing the truth and beauty of the smaller as well as of the larger relation, has a married clergy and strives to have a consecrated laity, but all men know the strain that comes when devotion to one's family is crossed by the call to public service.

So we strive and waver between them with the general conclusion that men shall serve the public needs and women the private, that men shall build roads and ships, machines and houses, manage government, religion, art, science, and business, meet all the social, all the psychic needs of the world, while the women meet the personal physical needs of the individual at home.

Against the man's specialization in social service, against the slow and costly development of talent and genius, the consecrated calling of the true artist, scientist, or any great social servant comes the constant pressure of the great unspecialized mass of humanity at home.

Against the man who wants to do leans the woman who wants to have.

Against the great, slow-growing ideals of a nobly free society with its endless, rising stages of achievement is the heavy pressure of the old domestic ideals of personal comfort, of that small-measured family selfishness which bounds its ambitions by the living-room. To live for a human creature is to serve humanity in one special industry, to serve to the fullest, a life's long output of splendid workmanship, and *in order to live* we must have homes.

We must have love; we must have marriage; we must have children; we must be warmed and sheltered, clothed and fed; we must be educated to our utmost; we must have rest and recreation and all healthy pleasure—that we may Live. Living is Working.

Living is Doing—not Having or Getting or merely Being, as some paradoxically maintain, but Doing. The only way to tell whether a thing is alive or not is by what it *does*.

As to Being—if these sentimentalists can point out any living thing that can Be—and not Do—I should like to see it.

Stones can Be for a long time without any activity visible to the naked eye. But even in stones the atoms are up and doing at a great rate. "Pure Being" is only a metaphysical abstraction, but let there be "doing" enough and you get your "being" thrown in. Our women need to outgrow this Living-Room ideal.

There is no room for a human being to fully live in save the whole world.

All the washing and feeding and sewing and teaching of manners and morals to one's family are but the barest preliminaries to living.

As to the maternal duties, so reverently defined by Mr. H. B. Marriott-Watson in the *Nineteenth Century* of last September in his article on "The American Woman" as "those functions which alone excuse or explain her existence," these are the eternal bases of physical life—but not human living.[1]

An unmarried schoolteacher does far more "living" than the prolific negress bearing and burying her babies with the unprogressive profusion of fruit trees.

To be a mother is the splendid primal power of every female thing on earth, but in the *human* sense it is not "living." The poor, dumb brutes, our slaves, our meat fulfill their maternal functions as well as she, sometimes better.

But education—to give one's trained powers to the elevation of the human race—that is living indeed.

By whatever line of work we choose or are resistlessly called to and therein serve the world, we live.

If we in no way serve the world—contribute nothing—make no thought clearer—no road easier—no wheel swifter—add nothing to the smooth upbuilding of our human life—we do not "live."

"Is it nothing to make people?" cries the mother-and-nothing-else. It is a great deal. If we who boast so of our motherhood stood free and strong and, using that primal power in all its majesty, steadily filled the world with healthy, beautiful, good people—better and better in each generation—then we might indeed make boast of the mother-power.

But when we look at the people in the street—and the little gravestones standing so thickly in our cemeteries—it should teach us not to boast much as yet of mere motherhood. Mothers made all those people who are killing each other in Manchuria,[2] but we might have spared some of the motherhood in favor of a social progress which would save such slaughter. The world's life today calls for large minds, strong, active, healthy, and above all *broad*—the minds that can grasp social needs, social laws, social duties, and fulfill them. Such minds are not bred in living-rooms.

Two "Natural Protectors"

Man, we are often told with fond pride, is the natural protector of woman. As a matter of fact, there is no creature she fears so acutely or with such good reason. Other beasts may kill and eat her; no other can inflict such lasting pain and shame.

A particularly vivid instance of masculine protection has just occurred in the neighborhood of Cold Spring Harbor, Long Island, and is reported this morning in the *New York Times*. A woman carrying a two-year-old baby was knocked down by a negro, and while she was struggling to defend herself and her child, one Warren Thomas, a carpenter, came along on his bicycle. He acknowledged that he saw the woman struggling with her assailant, her child in her arms. He admitted that he heard the baby's cries and that the woman called out to him, "For God's sake, help me!" Then, he said, he turned and rode away on his bicycle and when asked to explain his conduct he replied, "I didn't want to interfere."[3]

Poor woman! Her jaw was dislocated, her face cut, her eye blackened, the marks of strangling fingers were on her throat, and the shock of terror—a worse terror than that inspired by a lion or tiger—must have worked grave injury besides. But that natural protector, Mr. Warren Thomas, speeds away on his bicycle "not wishing to interfere."

The only real basis for the natural protector theory is the defense of the female by the male when she is his particular property. Any general defense of females by males, either in the lower animals or in humanity, is not found until the age of chivalry, and this narrow class custom is in no sense "natural" nor has it ever changed the general attitude of men to women. The utmost that can fairly be said is that in those races and classes where the chivalric ideal has weight, men in general will protect women in general from some things—but not from others.

In no part of our country, for instance, is the chivalric sentiment so strong as in the Southern States, yet it is precisely here that women suffer most frequently from masculine attack. Not by the same men, of course, but by men of a lower grade of civilization to which no idea of chivalry has yet penetrated, men in a far more "natural" relation to women than those of an artificially cultivated period, and the "protective" attempts of the gallant gentlemen who do seek to defend their women result in most cruel vengeance on the assailants—and others—but do not protect their women.

Revenge is not protection. The word "natural" is always misleading because it varies so in regard to ages, races, and localities.

If we consider the "natural" relation of the sexes throughout the whole long gynaecocentric period—which is that of all life up to quite recent human times—we find a free female, often much larger and stronger than the male and never looking to him for defense. He often needs it—against her. The unmeasured cruelty of early female types to their helpless males is far beyond anything which women have ever had to suffer.

Then if we consider the androcentric period, which is all our conscious human history, we find the male subjugating the female and treating her with every dignity and abuse.

This condition is gradually giving way to the beautiful modern movement of sex equality, which promises more good to the world than any change yet known.

But in no case, at no time, has the male in any general sense been the "natural protector" of the female, from Abraham casting out poor Hagar into the wilderness[4] to Mr. Warren Thomas "not wishing to interfere."

This also from the *N.Y. Times*, Sunday, Oct. 23rd:

> Such astonishment as may be caused by the announcement that the daughter of a Philadelphia financier has secured official authorization to command her father's yacht, and 'on all oceans' at that, will be kept within very moderate bounds if those who feel it carefully bear in mind just what a "master's certificate" proves in regard to its possessor. As a matter of fact, to a vessel-owner in need of a Captain, an applicant's certificate tells practically nothing about what the owner wants to know. It shows that the man has the sort of information that is, indeed, the foundation of a master's competency, but information of that sort can easily be obtained by anybody with some slight knowledge of elementary mathematics and intelligence enough to commit to memory the essential contents of any one of several "epitomes"

which are neither hard to understand nor hard to get. Such a person, whether man or woman, might with just a little luck in the allotment of examiners pass a brilliant examination and secure a certificate as good as that carried by any Captain that sails the seas. But that person wouldn't be at all likely to "get a ship" except in the somewhat rare instance that the ship was a yacht owned by the candidate's father, and even then the chances are that the real master of the vessel would be a first officer who, besides a certificate quite as good as that of the nominal superior, would have the priceless, unpurchasable, and unexaminable wisdom that comes and only comes from years of actual experience at sea. Provided with her "papers," Miss Jane Morgan of Philadelphia[5] will be able to do a few things that would be illegal if she did not have them, but they will not help a bit in meeting any one of the thousand emergencies which diversity a Captain's life, and in almost every one of those emergencies her sex will count against her competency vastly more than her certificate counts for it. There have been women masters before this and a few of them, according to history—it's rather legendary history—have really performed enough of the duties of the position to serve practical ends for a voyage or two, but it will be many and many a day before the much-discussed sphere of woman widens enough to bring her nearer than in sight of actual command on vessels that work for a living.[5]

The above is interesting only as a gratuitous expression of contempt for women the moment they venture on any exhibition of capacity other than feminine. This editor does not know one thing against Miss Morgan's ability. She may be as competent a sailing master as any man, she may not, but without any knowledge on the subject this commentator lays himself out to belittle her attainments.

"Her sex will count against her competency vastly more than her certificate counts for it" in almost any emergency, asserts the writer. Why will it? How will it? What has sex to do with sailing? The idea, or rather the tradition which underlies this attitude of mind, is that which fondly assumes everything a man does to be masculine and that for a woman to do any of these things is to "unsex" herself.

There is no faintest touch of sex characteristic, primary or secondary, in a distinctly human process, and it is time these biological terms were better understood. If Miss Morgan has no experience, she is necessarily less capable than a man who has it, but if she had years of experience and was therefore superior to some young man who had just passed his examination, would this writer on the *Times* say his sex was against him?

Navigation is not a sex function.

COLUMN 43

November 5, 1904

Gilman further refines her argument for passage of the Pure Food and Drug Act.

Changes in Food

There is a lively agitation in the public mind in these later years on the subject of food. It is shown, now that we have public sanitation and health statistics, that whereas our death rate from dirt diseases has been greatly lowered, yet we die from food diseases in increasing ratio.

Whatever might have been the mischievous effects of food in earlier times, the eaters had less of it—wherefore its evils were lesser.

But we, the "best fed" nation on earth in quantity, are also in some ways the worst fed in quality. The medical profession has done much to enlighten us; the sanitary scientists have done more. Religion has had a hand. Even fashion has helped a little, and under the repeated attacks of all these and other outside forces that ancient fortress of hereditary habits, the home, with its sacred citadel, the kitchen, shows signs of yielding at last. The dear woman who did the cooking was far too busy doing it ever to think of improving the process, and the improvements made by professional cooks were but slowly adopted and not always as good for the stomach as for the palate. But the cooking schools, the Domestic Science Associations, and their kindred movements, with the more radical researches of science, are now slowly awakening us to the importance of what we eat, how much, and when and where.

It is not astonishing that the lower animals, who have nothing to do but eat and digest, should give their whole minds to getting dinner; nor is it astonishing that, with this single-hearted devotion and millions of years to become adjusted to conditions, they should have worked out a dietary which agrees with them. The animal has to adapt himself to the food nature provides.

The only beasts which show a list of alimentary diseases at all comparable to ours are the dog, the horse, and other domestic animals—which we feed! More especially the dog, who eats our food.

The human race, so progressive in most ways, shows no gain to be proud of in this line. But now we are really waking up. Civilized man is beginning to wonder whether his cherished private female cook is after all capable of safeguarding the health of the world. No one questions her good will but does she know enough? It begins to look as if she didn't, and the first effort of the awakened dyspeptic is to teach her.

Hence this amusing phenomenon of the twentieth century—societies and classes of all sorts to teach women their business—their one business, which they have carried on in a stolid and stationary manner from the earliest times without criticism.

This effort to teach women how to cook will have valuable results, one of which is the discovery that many women cannot and still more do not want to. This will lead us straight to specialization, which is all right. It is a pity such a vital process as the nourishment of the world cannot have as much time, skill, and training devoted to it as our clothing or sheltering. Still further, beyond the cooking and serving of the food, comes the inquiry into its constituents. This is something wholly outside the province of the housewife or her more ignorant subordinate and is receiving, as it should, the attention of first-class scientific research. In its light we are beginning to learn something of what food is for and how it does its work, and when that knowledge is general and is carried into action, a new people will rise up among us—on our ashes, as it were—far sounder and stronger than any people before.

While the first sporadic studies are being made in the new field, the faddish flourishes. Dozens of theories confront us, from the long hours of slow cooking that are to convert all the "starch" into "dextrine" or some such panacea, to those headlong reversionists who would have us cook nothing at all and from the dietary of clear meat and hot water to that of nuts and fruits and nothing else. I heard the other day of two Nebuchadnezzars[1] who advocated grass—nothing but grass—as a cure-all. Among all these warring wavelets one main current seems to be discernable, that toward vegetable food and less of it. Not the fetish vegetarianism with its sentimental collaterals, but a recognition that less meat and more vegetables in our menu is an advantage. The October *Pearson's* has an article showing in brief that in fifty years our meat food "decreased 36 per cent and our vegetable food has increased by 80 per cent."[2]

Most of us, looking at the food question from a narrow kitchen-bred viewpoint, go no further than to consider how this or that viand may "agree" with us and with our little group of table-mates.

Across this low-grade interest flutter occasional ideas of how the general public may be benefited, but these make no deep impression.

What we need to see—and don't see, notably we women whose business it is—is that we can change the bone and sinew of the world, its brain power and muscle quality, its rate of death and joy of life, by right feeding.

Like all human questions, this must be studied in the large—for all. It needs the social grasp, the broad, general view, the ability to hold the whole of a question.

This is precisely the ability which is not raised in the kitchen and which the world will never have while nearly half its population are [sic] kitchen-minded. To feed John may be the business of one woman but to feed the world is the business of all women, and they cannot "prove it by John." You may say, "If each woman feeds John properly, the world will be properly fed." That is kitchen-philosophy. It is false in that it postulates an impossibility. As well say, "If each man builds his own house nobly, we shall have noble architecture" or "If each man makes his own boat, we shall have fine shipbuilding."

It is precisely this limitation to private effort and personal taste, judgment, knowledge, and affection which prevents progress in this business. It will be a great day for the world when a wise, progressive people first recognize the importance of this great social function and prepare to fulfill it properly.

In the recent studies of physical degeneration in England, it is found that one enormous factor is improper food. Whole classes, and those the largest, are ill fed and die because of it, are sick and crippled because of it, are weak, puny, inefficient because of it. Is England to wait for a change until she can build brains in millions of low-bred women and then teach them severally all that it is necessary to know on right nutrition? She can use her public machinery to change the building laws; she can cleanse the air by enforcing smoke-consumption and removing nuisances; she can cleanse the food supply by rigid inspection; but then come in the millions of ignorant women and buy what they please as far as their poor funds go to feed their helpless families. It is not solely poverty that is responsible, for the rich people die of food diseases, too, albeit of different sorts.

Now let us suppose by no unreasonable effort of the imagination the opening of more and more food laboratories, the purpose of which should be to provide absolutely pure and nourishing food with such skill and art as to make it delicious and such wisdom as to make it cheap—cheaper than the wretched stuff now bought by these poor people.

Rigid inspection could prevent the selling of bad materials, and the good ones bought at wholesale could be sold by these larger establishments cheaper than at retail raw. The people would not like it? Give good food like this to the children in the nurseries and schools and they'd learn to like it quick enough. A proper code of city laws and a proper enforcement of them would clear our streets of their flagrant crimes in the sale of unhealthy and adulterated food supplies.

A cooked-food establishment of a certain size with scientific attention could, as I have said, sell its cooked food—nourishing and delicious—below the cost of retail buying. The children could easily be taught to like it—and the rest is easy. This applies to our own country as well as England, to any and every country where the human stock is injured by improper feeding.

And who is to do it?

The women, of course—women who are wide-awake to their world-duty; women who are citizens; women who will vie with one another city by city to have a higher standard of purity in their milk supply, their meat supply, the vegetable and fruit supply than any other; women who will learn the art, science, business, and handicraft of cooking—one in a hundred of them—and apply it to the food of the city, including their own especial family; women who as citizens will help to make proper laws as to the care of human life and its essential processes and help to enforce them; women who will wake up and come out of their ancestral seclusion, see what ails the world, and take hold and help.

We need women like that and we are gradually getting them, but they need to hurry for these great, needless, wasteful evils go on and on, and the children sicken and die by thousands, the people by hundreds, and those left are hopelessly inferior because we have not this body of large-minded, free, intelligent, active, independent citizen women. We have instead our immense body of good, pious, dutiful, domestic, smally-loving, kitchen-minded women, who mean so well and do so little.

COLUMN 44

November 12, 1904

Gilman first expands on her Lamarckian theories, particularly the importance of "physical heredity" and the transmissibility of acquired characteristics, then endorses the installation of air filters at the luxury St. Regis Hotel in New York.

Brain Growth

We are told by some scientists that the human brain has made no progress since it could first be called a brain, that our gains are in brain-products and methods of education, but that the organ itself is the same.

This position is buttressed by reference to the intellectual power of the Greeks or to the more remote Hindus and Chinese, and many hold it with sincere conviction. One man writing recently on the subject instances the universal delight in predatory and combative games as proof that we are still governed by the same impulses and tastes as our earliest progenitors. The subject is one of vital importance, whichever side of the argument is established, for if the brain does grow, it behooves us before anything else to learn how it grows—and forthwith to apply the means and make it grow. There is plenty of room!

If, on the contrary, it does not grow but is potentially the same in all of us, black, white, and yellow, only differing as it has access to our social store of knowledge and mechanical achievement plus the benefits of education, then it behooves us still more to give that access and those benefits to every human soul as rapidly as possible that all may be equally intelligent and the world at peace.

To women the question appeals direct for we, whatever else we are, are men-makers and on us rests the chief responsibility for the kind of human stock with which the world is filled.

In that position of isolation, ignorance, dependence, and low development which has been ours so long, we have failed to grasp this essentially feminine duty; and the movement of women today rests not only on individual justice to women as persons but sex-justice to woman the mother. As the mother, the maker of people, we are responsible for the kind of people we make, and if their brains as well as their lungs and stomachs may be made healthy and vigorous by any action of ours, it is an inescapable duty so to make them. If, on the other hand, they are all born alike and show no improvement in the ages, if there is no difference between the greatest of our social servants and the most detrimental of our social parasites except in external advantages, then even more is it our unescapable duty to arouse and obtain those advantages for our children as a whole.

Now let us consider for a moment that game argument. It is true that man still responds to the same stimuli that affected him as a savage, but this is not saying half the truth. He also has many points in common with the animal—even the vegetable—kingdom and, still further, is under the action of physical laws like a mere mineral. That we are in such and such things like our progenitors by no means proves that we have made no advance.

That we still enjoy hunting, fishing, fighting, and games based on these ancient instincts is true but it is also true, and much more to the point, that we enjoy constructive games—refined and subtle combinations governed by an elaborate special ethics, and not only games but economic processes of this nature.[1] If anyone wishes to prove that modern man has made no progress in brain growth over primitive man, he must show not that both can accomplish and enjoy the same things but that there are no mental processes and powers in which one excels the other.

Surely the difference between those low savages who cannot count above three or five or, in more advanced instances, up to the sum of their fingers and toes and those highly developed men who delight in the vast computations of astronomy or the subtle and intricate combinations of the higher mathematics is a difference in mental structure.

The argument from the Greeks and Hindus is equally beside the point.

Each stood high in civilization, not low. The comparison should be made between the Athenian and his remote ancestors in the Aryan tablelands,[2] and far, far back of them to the hairy cave-dweller, or between the writers of Sanskrit literature[3] and the same aboriginal ancestors. It is true, most hopefully and comfortingly true, that our human gain is largely embodied in various forms of art and so made free to us from age to age. It is as reassuringly true that education—real education—and free access to society's vast stores of truth and beauty, knowledge and achievement will "even up" our varying brains with wonderful speed—but the variation is there—not only that between individuals and between races but between stages of racial growth.

Both means of improving the human brain are open to us and both are especially incumbent upon women.

So far as the physical structure and functional capacity of the brain can be changed to our advantage, it must be done through physical heredity.

Physical heredity is the original line of improvement in all created things—modification through environment or through variation, seized upon and incorporated in the racial stock by heredity.

This is first, last, and always the mother's function. It was her function when she was lower than the reptiles, it is yet, and always will be while we are in physical form. And singularly enough, in her complete surrender to the much-vaunted "duties of maternity," she has completely lost sight of the very core and center of those duties—an inexorable standard of selection.

We extol the "wifely devotion" which puts up with any kind of evil in the husband and the "mother's devotion" which bears and condones every evil in the child, but we say nothing—think nothing—feel nothing—about a womanhood which shall insist on making better children and refuse to be a mother to inferior ones.

We are sentimental about the mother who loves the deformed or idiot child the best. We need a strong sentiment of condemnation for any mother who bears such.

If it be some avoidable accident, there is need only for pity, but if she continues to bring them forth, there is need of blame.

Then having learned how to do all she can for the race through this basic physical process by selecting always the best of the race to wed and by a conscientious self-development before marriage, she should further how to bring to bear on the world's children all the splendid enginery of improvement through educational advantages of the largest and deepest kind.

This again can only be considered collectively. All human problems must be so studied; all human needs so met—for man is a collective animal. It is the separateness of women, the hopeless isolation and self-centered littleness of their ancient and unprogressive occupations which keeps them back. It prevents in them the brain-growth which they need to incorporate and educate in their children.

The Hotel and the Home

The St. Regis Hotel, which aspires to stand in a class by itself at the head of all human habitations and to give the best to those who can afford to pay for it, has at last undertaken to civilize our barbarian habits in the matter of air.[4]

We have with advancing civilization grown very particular about personal cleanliness. We must bathe, forsooth, not only daily but bi- and tri-daily, dressing and re-dressing our well-washed bodies in continual clean clothes. From this height of superiority we look down with scorn on the poor brother whose clothes reek with many odors and who is washed mainly by the natural functions of the skin. Yet doctors tell us that the hard-working man, who earns his bread in a sweat only poetically confined to his brow, is cleaner than the much-soaked millionaire. There is less dirt in him—it comes out.

We are also most particular about cleanliness in our houses; many servants must keep them swept and garnished for us; and about cleanliness in our food, eating only of first-class materials daintily prepared. But with all this delicacy of habit, the most greasy savage is seraph-clean compared to us in the matter of air. He breathes pure air, rich in oxygen. We get together in vast herds, defile the air with all manner of disagreeable and revolting matter—including disease germs—and then contentedly breathe it.

We have cultivated an extreme sensitiveness to heat and cold, and if any person with a trained perception of relative purity in air demands more ventilation, the others say, surprised, "Does it seem too warm?" Even where some recognition of the needs of ventilation has been given, there remains this complete indifference as to the quality of the air obtained. Only in places where delicate machinery must be preserved from defilement have we learned to take elaborate precautions as to the nature of the air admitted.

Now comes this great hotel advancing the standard of human living and installs a costly and elaborate system for cleaning the air its patrons are to breathe. It is first filtered and barrels of dust are cast out daily—whole barrelsful that would else be gradually clogging the lungs of the residents and adding to the labors of the servants. Then it is washed and dried and warmed to any desired degree so that varieties of air can be served to guests as desired. This can only be done in immense establishments, and I am far from wishing to suggest that our homes be saddled with any such additional labor and expense. No, the example of this great hotel cannot often or easily be imitated; its value lies mainly in the standard established.

When those of refined and luxurious tastes begin to spend some attention on their air as well as their wine; when the habit is formed of breathing pure air, recognizing it, valuing it, demanding it, and getting it; when we begin to imitate this line of luxury as we imitate others and to look down with scorn on the soiled lung tissues of the uneducated as we now do on a soiled shirt or unwashed hands, then we shall see a universal improvement in this particular.

No longer shall we see richly-dressed persons in sumptuous parlor cars fairly wallowing in foul air, contentedly inhaling a thick mixture of coal gas, dust, bacteria, and many mingled breaths; or the same Sybarite at a steamship table being wastefully served with every kind of edible luxury in an atmosphere of such condensed impurity it could almost be leaned against.

We need the refined and cultivated taste to notice this form of dirt, and only this costly and fashionable method can give it to us, apparently. For we have long had pure air in the country—every summer our rich people have it and at other times occasionally; the point is that we do not know it when we have it, do not appreciate it, do not demand it, do not object to the lack of it.

We pay $2 for a seat in a first-class theater. Everything that art and wealth can do to please us is done—except in pure air. We enjoy the light, the color, the sound, the acting or singing or whatever we are entertained with; and we wave our fans in a heavy atmosphere of most vile constituents and never notice it.

There are serious points to be followed up in this matter. When we have learned what sort of air is essential to human health, then we may study the question of whether a city can allow such processes, industrial or other, as defile that air. We cannot in the separate home spend millions to laboriously clean our air but can, by the influence of the collective homes, the combined intelligence and force of the citizens, insist on keeping the air clean.

This is work for women—the rearers of children, the keepers of our homes.

COLUMN 45

November 19, 1904

Gilman again discusses the implications of the Russo-Japanese war. Never a pacifist, even arguing that the Civil War in the United States advanced the cause of women, she considered the Asian war an opportunity for the Japanese to reform their androcentric culture.

Japan's Reserve

Fortunate is that army which has behind its fighting force a large and strong reserve on which to draw if necessary. Fortunate is that nation which, when it sends its armies to the front, has other armies in the rear, a home guard, equal to carrying on the productive processes of the nation while the soldier carries on the destructive. War is an evil thing, wasteful, painful, costly to all good work, but at present war *is*. And while we should all work to end the fighting period of human life as soon as possible, we should also take advantage as we may of some of the side issues of war.

For instance, in our own fearful struggle of the sixties, one of the most noticeable consequences was the swift and enormous advance of the women of America.

The "head of the family" went to fight—the woman became the head and stayed at home to work. Out of that headless home she came and *joined the other women* in common work for a common cause. That great association of women who toiled together to help the soldier crossed several centuries of social growth at a jump. They came out like coiled springs and snapped to the front of their period of civilization. They developed families they never thought they had, did work they never dreamed they could; they *grew*. And having come out, they couldn't go back—having grown they couldn't un-grow. Having learned the joy and power of world work, they could never again be wholly content with housework.

The Civil War in America marked a new stage in the growth of women, and the growth of women is the growth of the world. They learned, under that terrible pressure, the great human advantage of organization, and in the fierce heat of their pain they were welded together. A common grief, a common loss, flooded the hearts of our women and united them. Always women have suffered from war but before this they had suffered alone. And they hadn't *done* anything about it—just suffered. These women did things and did them together, and that is what gave the development. Moreover, there was a second factor in the case: full of agony for the individual woman, full of good for the world.

They lost by the thousands their male relatives—husbands, brothers, sons, those they had always lived for, worked for, loved. Now women have to love, have to work—it is the sex-instinct with them as fighting is sex-instinct with men.

At one stroke the women lost their "support," the men who stood between them and the world and enabled them to say, "I do not have to work!"; and also lost the thing they worked for—the men they served. A double pressure drove them on. They "had to work" now because there was no man to pay their bills, and they had to work because a woman must—being a woman.

So they learned to work—in the world, for the world—and in working they grew. Organized, specialized world-work breeds a very different character from housework. This larger, stronger, wiser womanhood has done marvels for the men of this generation, the big-brained men who are beginning to get a hold on social problems. Up to this stage the active forces of society have been men—women were the passive forces, the reserves.

Half the people of the world were reserved—the "better half."[1] That vast body of world-people is just awakening to their possibilities, their responsibilities, their duties. When these are rightly apprehended we shall see an advance most cheering to anticipate. Now see the opportunity of Japan.

Here is a nation of noble people, clean-fleshed, clear-brained, high-hearted. Never in all our history has a more splendid proof been given of the noblest human powers.

It is not only in martial heroism and willing martyrdom—the world has had heroes and martyrs many—the early Christians fairly ran about begging to be martyred, the frenzied Mohammedans—"Fuzzy Wuzzies"—sacrificed their lives as freely as the Japanese.

All honor to Japan for her heroism but more for her unerring intelligence. The marvelous wisdom of the last fifty years of national development in that fair island kingdom is without precedent or parallel. They deliberately went to other countries and asked to learn of them—taking the best from each—and then having learned, they went back and did things, put in practice what they had learned. Short-sighted people called them "imitative." If it was imitation, how could they discriminate so finely? While they were imitating, why not imitate our vices and follies and mistakes? European civilization had some things better than Japanese and with unfailing judgment they selected our best—and bettered it!

With the fresh, unprejudiced mind of an utterly different culture, they studied ours and selected its good points: the vital principles of constitutional government as far as they could safely be connected with an old imperialism, the scientific attitude of mind and its invaluable products, and the tremendous aid of mechanical inventions—these this wonderful race of men have learned from us and made their own. But they have left us our intemperance, our gross habits of body and pig-like feeding. That sounds rather severe, but when you compare our heavy masses of blood and grease and sugar—a "course dinner" which should be recognized as the "coarse dinner" it is—with the clean, slight menu of rice and fish and tea, it is like comparing a turkey-buzzard with a hummingbird.

They have learned our best and avoided our worst, and if we want to keep at the head of the class in the international competition for race superiority, we had best be considering our errors.

Now it remains to be seen if Japan with her daring foresight, with that peculiar strength of mind that is willing to change, can see the most vital step in the world's progress—the advance of women. They have read Spencer and profited by him. Will they read Ward—Lester F. Ward, the great

American sociologist, and consider his gynaecocentric theory? They have studied biology and profited by it.

Will they recognize the biological value of a free, strong, fully-developed mother—a mother who is a full race-type as well as a sex-type? They have studied democratic government and adopted many of its principles and methods.

Will they see that democracy has to be universal to be sound, must be loved and understood and practiced by *all* the people? They have studied economic progress—its organization, its mechanical facilities—its prodigious multiplication of wealth.

Will they be able to avoid that vicious individual appropriation of this new volume of socially-produced wealth with its hotbed of evil consequences? Not consequences of the new processes of collective production, which lighten labor, shorten working hours, multiply production a thousand-fold; but consequences of the old method of individual appropriation of profits—which does more harm than it used to because the profits are larger.

They have studied what gains we have made in the freedom and development of women, and they are educating their women and letting them grow in wider ways than of old.

But will they go further—will they go beyond us? Will they be the first nation on earth to recognize this vast reserve of power—*and use it?*

The marvelous free-mindedness they have already shown may hold good still further and allow this, too. And the sharp, cruel pressure of a great war may force them, as it forced us, to even more than they fully understand. If they can so see and so do, the result is past measuring in good. Take the economic side of it. While the men fight, the country is weakened in productive labor. Turn loose the productive labor of the women and you double the economic reserve.

The intelligence is the same; the power—with the mechanical service of our engines—is the same. Give the same training and you have the same productive capacity. But there are advantages far beyond the merely economic. War fills a land with widows—empty-hearted—robbed.

It makes sonless mothers and maidens left unmarried perforce. Only polygamy can absorb the "surplus women"[2] war makes, and polygamy is not good for any nation of our times. It is an outworn method of the past like slavery. But let these women become active members of society, pouring the love of wife and mother into social service, and they are not "surplus" anymore.

So long as the woman has only her private family relationship, when the man to whom she is related is gone, she is "unattached." In primitive times these leftovers were quickly appropriated in polygamous marriage and so rapidly repopulated the land—a useful enough process when only numerical strength was wanted.

In modern times war is usually followed by an immense increase in prostitution—an unalloyed evil. The alternative to this social evil is social service.

If the woman who has no one to take care of her learns to take care of herself, if the woman who has no husband to serve learns to serve the world, if the woman who has no children to love learns to love all children, then you have that greatest biological force, maternal energy, turned loose in society—to society's immense advantage. Here is Japan's opportunity. She will conquer in this war and so serve not only her own ends but those of the world. The defeat of Russia will benefit not only the rest of Europe but Russia herself.[3] That great sleeping nation whose splendid prophets have been vainly seeking to rouse to noble living will be thrilled to life by pain and shame.

That so great a people in so great a land can be conquered is due to errors in the national life, and these errors are being ruthlessly exposed. Russia will be checked in wrong-doing and roused to right action to her immense advantage and the world's. The pitiful sacrifice of hundreds of thousands of helpless peasants will not be in vain if the whole population becomes freer, wiser, stronger under better conditions. Japan will then have to face the dangers of victory, the evils which follow on great wars and which are so closely connected with the Western civilization she has so largely adopted. If she can rise above this as she has above other perils, she will indeed make history—of a higher sort than we have ever known.

As against the depleted manhood incident to war, she can show this army of newly-grown women—women wiser, stronger, freer, more capable as citizens.

From such advance of womanhood shared by all, those who are mothers will transmit to the coming generation greater capacity than ever—a race of larger, wiser men.

So shall the splendid gains and progress of modern Japan be most rapidly incorporated in the racial stock, the strength of the present be doubled and of the future increased beyond counting.

Any nation can do this if it will. The secrets of science are open to the student and its benefits free to all. The secrets of economic progress are equally open—and its benefits should be also. But back of all this lies the race itself—the human stock—and the best way of all to improve the human race is by improving its mothers. The nation that shall first recognize the citizen mother will lead the world.

COLUMN 46

November 26, 1904

Gilman approves in theory the merger of the "society and clubs" department on the woman's page of newspapers, though in practice the column merely covered marriages.

"Society and Clubs"

This department heading in a Chicago newspaper marks a real step forward.

The word "society" in this sense is always pathetic, and to have its pitiful abortiveness strengthened by the addition of a genuine social movement is very comforting. The "woman's paper" or "woman's column" has always had a strong flavor of what the unfledged homelings called "society" because the isolated primitive life of the domestic calls desperately for some touch with real human life, and the only form of that great mingling open to them was the contact found in "society."

They also had the church and have fully used and enjoyed its social privileges, but that was by no means enough.

Men do not care as much for "society" as women because they have real social life—the daily contact and interchange of their specialized labor. They have always rather chafed under the arbitrary form of "social life" so-called, resenting its conventions and caring little for its triumphs. They had the real thing and small respect for the little game of imitation.

But the woman, from the small continuous restrictions of her life, found in "social" opportunities a real relief and grasped eagerly after them. The more free she was from the absolute pressure of domestic labor, the more her husband was able to impress a second, third, or fourth woman to do the work formerly hers, the more eagerly she gave herself to what was called "society." This has been so long common to women that it was duly accepted as "feminine" and no one thought of blaming them for it unless it was carried to a glaring excess that involved unnatural injury to the family life.

So habitual has this "social life" become to women that you find in fiction—that running reflection of custom—a frank acceptance of it as essentially a feminine medium.

A short story I read not long since describes a heroine, a quiet, domestic character, boarding for a while in New York and being by accident invited to a ball by an attractive young man. She proceeds to spend all her small capital on dancing lessons and costume for the occasion, and the young man fulfilled his part of the engagement royally. The little old maid blossomed out in sudden rapture. She looked beautiful in her unusual splendor of raiment and roses. The youth provided flowers, carriage, and was all devotion during the evening.

It was a rapturous dream of glory all too brief, and as she went back to her original obscurity and domesticity she praised God that for once—even for once—she has tasted Life!

Think of it! An adult human being, in this splendid rushing century full of growth and hope, full of pain and shame, needing every one of us to hasten the good days coming and offering to every one of us a world to work in and a world to love—this human creature calls going to a ball "life"!

No sharper comment could be made on the aborted growth of women, on the influence of their arrested position and its petty industries.

Now at last in the resistless rush of the age we live in, this so long stationary creature is moving. She comes out of her snail-shell and her long loneliness and begins to unite with her kind for some better purpose than to dance or play games. This coming together of women finds its widest expression in the club movement, and that movement has at last won for itself enough acceptance and esteem to be considered sufficiently important and sufficiently feminine to be classed with "Society."

When the women who had no form of meeting but "Society" begin to find society in their club life; when they habitually come together to study and to work, it will develop far better qualities in the world-mother than any number of ballrooms. The club is a step between the home and the world—a step that leads onward, outward, upward and that teaches women to "lend a hand."

Marriages

Nevertheless, I was grieved to find on carefully reading one of these "Society and Clubs" departments that there was nothing in it to speak of except announcements of marriages. At the very end were one or two small paragraphs announcing club meetings, but most of it gave but too patent proof of the main purpose of what we call "Society"—i.e., to bring about marriages.

So long as marriage is a profession, a means of livelihood, and the only esteemed profession among women, it is but natural that they should class the permanent attainment of a suitable position in life as of dominating importance.

With a man it is, of course, of extreme importance to his personal life that he choose a right wife, but to his human life it is of far more importance that he choose a right profession. To the man personally it matters much whether his marriage be successful, whether he is happy in it. But to the world it matters more whether he is successful in his profession. If Mr. Edison[1] or Mr. Marconi[2] is happily married, we are glad for his sake. If he supplies the world with new power and comfort by electrical inventions, we are glad for our sakes—with more reason. It is of far more importance to the world that the man built for work in electricity should choose that work and do it than that he will marry well or ill, save indeed if his marriage seriously affects his work. In that sense marriage is an important social factor.

But to make it the principal incident of a life—the one culminating celebration with a great flourish of trumpets—simply shows how painfully limited are the lives of women. Men as a rule dislike and dread the elaborate ceremonies of a wedding. They have passed that stage of civilization. But the women delight in the mass of detail, exult in that peculiar survival of ancient custom—the bestowal of wealth upon the bride—and are in no way ashamed to make a public exhibition of this so exquisitely private matter.

That marriage has its true social importance I do not deny; it simply concerns the welfare of the State and should be far more rigidly guarded than it is. No person having a contagious disease, for instance, should be allowed to marry. If an intelligent community demanded and enforced proper consideration of public policy in marriages, we should have far less trouble with the afterclap.[3]

The careful legal recognition of the union and its record in the official archives is [sic] the legitimate social side of the affair and quite different from the public spectacle we now make of it.

That two serious human beings should wish to establish and record their contract in the same way that other important contracts are recorded is well, but that they should wish to make a show of the performance is owing to quite other lines of social tradition.

There is no more exquisite and important moment, personally speaking, than that when two lives unite—when the man and the woman leave their several families and form a new one—but why brand the bride with a conspicuous costume so that any stranger may comment and observe?

So far this is our custom, and for this one crowning act we arrange the great game we call "society" and strive to give our girls "advantages" therein.

Men rather despise it; they see through it; they know that in "society" the "eligible" man is fair prey; they perfectly recognize the "managing momma" and the "designing young woman," but since they prefer to have their women engage in no other business they cannot logically object to this one—and the game goes on.

To marry, men and women must meet. In original freedom they met in the field and forest; then, secluded in Oriental harems, they were married by parents and go-betweens; later, in transition stages, they met by stealth or by chance; and with growing frequency they met in places of entertainment. So have slowly grown among us all manner of games and exhibitions, feasts and dances, the underlying reason of which is to bring together young men and women. Hence it is not surprising that a department called "Society" should consist mainly of announcements of marriages. All the other announcements were but preliminary to this grand event.

When our women all take part in the work of the world, they will meet men naturally and rightly, in working clothes and working manners, and each will know the other far more fully and wisely than is possible now.

This will make for better marriages by far. Man and woman will know what it is they are getting beforehand. The woman will be far more developed as an individual character and the attraction of sex will be strongly augmented or fortunately nullified by the attraction or repulsion of real personality. Then the woman being a larger-minded and more valuable citizen, she will welcome and appreciate a true marriage but she will not act as if it was the one solitary event of a lifetime.

———

Mrs. Roosevelt about this time organized her "Social Cabinet" in Washington,[4] a sort of Court, doing in democratic circles by election plus matrimony what is done in Europe by royalty.

Why not? If these things are of the importance the time, labor, and money we spend on them would indicate, why not give our minds to them seriously? It appears that this social cabinet will determine social standing, precedence, and similar matters; and if one is not recognized by this body, one is thereby shown to be of no recognized position in society. In all the trouble and heartburning involved in "social" ambition in America, some authoritative body like this should be welcome. To some it will mean peace of mind—the calm of perfect assurance such as the "well-born" of old aristocracies may feel. And others may be promptly and mercifully put out of their misery—convinced at once that it is no use to strive.

A thought occurs to me—will these mandates take color from parties? Shall we have a Republican and a Democratic "society"—alternating in power—with a possible Prohibition—Populist—even Socialist "society" waiting its chance? Perhaps.

If so, what an added zest to elections! What a new interest in politics for women! Good again. They will perhaps see cause to vote when the turn of the ballot marks their social standing for four years.

———

Against women's clubs in England we have grave charges. That they are failures—financially. That they have been obliged to sell out to a Company—Limited—even though Duchesses were on their lists of members. That they weaken family life and disrupt the home—and so on. Studying these charges more closely, it appears that these were social clubs—like the ordinary men's clubs—not at all the American idea of a woman's club, which exists mainly for study and work.

So the vast and growing body of our clubwomen need not mind if some clubs fail in England—it is not the kind of club nor the kind of failure we have here. In ours, speaking generally, is a very healthy upward tendency. They generally begin in hitherto clubless towns, either for charitable purposes or the improvement of the mind. Then step by step they grow until we find the leading clubs all over the country taking active steps in civic study and civic improvement.

The woman's club in America is a school of citizenship and of noble usefulness. May they increase daily! And they do.

———

Incident to exactly the line of progress spoken of above, a split is reported in one large woman's club because the majority decided to change the word "philanthropical" in their constitution to "sociological."[5]

Some hadn't grown to it but most of them had and the change was made.

COLUMN 47

December 3, 1904

Gilman reluctantly concludes to cancel her column a month before the end of the year because it failed to attract a wider audience and more subscribers.

To My Readers in Especial

As this year's experiment draws to a close, it seems fair to preface that close with a word of explanation.

Many readers of the *Woman's Journal* do not yet understand—and some seem persistently to disbelieve—that its writers *give* their work.

The clerical and office part has to be paid for, of course, not sufficient people of independent means or other sources of income being forthcoming to do that work.

Some, again, not readers of the *Journal*—if they were, they would perhaps have more sense—even believe that this paper is a source of income to its owners, who have made it a high-priced paper for their own advantage.

If these ignorant persons would inform themselves as to the cost of typesetting and printing, if they would simply inquire the price of other weeklies, as *Collier's* at $5.20, others at $4, some less well-printed at $3, they would see that the *Journal*'s price, $2.50, has been low to the verge of charity and that its "new subscriber" offer of $1.50 for the first year on trial has been a gift to widen the subscription list.

Cheap papers with "patent inside," stereotyped plates of poor stuff bought by the yard and with inferior paper and workmanship may be offered for less, but no such weekly as this.

The "dollar monthlies" are what mislead the public mind; but they are first, monthlies; second, popular; and third, they are supported by advertisements. The subscription list is merely useful as bait for advertisers. To quote *Collier's* again, it is ten cents a week whether you buy it weekly or by the year. Yet they are offering this year a fine set of Poe's complete works and a reduction for cash payment in advance.

"What is there in it for you?" asks the intending subscriber. And the agent enlightens his ignorance to the effect that if they can show a greatly enlarged paid subscription list, they can get more advertising and raise the price of what they have. But this method does not apply to a "reform paper."

The woman's movement is not yet sufficiently "popular"—or those who consider it important are not yet sufficiently interested or sufficiently beyond poverty—to have its organ attract advertisers.[1] A paper with a special purpose like this one must always depend for its support on those interested in that purpose and interested also in the best method for advancing it.

Any great world-movement of today is dumb and helpless without an "organ"—a voice. The woman's movement, including the demand for suffrage, is as important as any step ever made in human progress.

The *Woman's Journal* is the most representative organ of that movement in America and I know of none better anywhere.

It has a world circulation, exchanging with similar papers wherever there are such, and with all manner of other progressive periodicals besides as well as many not particularly progressive.

It represents not only the suffrage question but all the lines of advance for women—educational, industrial, and other. Not only that but it has space and enthusiasm for other world-movements, recognizing that none can work alone and that all together constitute the vanguard of the age.

All of this work it could do more and better if it were supported by a large as well as an intelligent and appreciative mass of readers, and if the volume of readers increased sufficiently, there would follow enough advertising to enable the management to engage its writers on fair terms. At present the work done on this paper represents the constant bestowal of unpaid labor for the good of the cause.

It is quite right that those who care enough for these great upward steps of the world, those who through all history have led and pushed and dragged and driven the reluctant mind of the masses should give their work freely. They are fortunate to get off with that! In earlier times they were promptly killed or continuously persecuted at the best. But today, when the public mind is so far enlightened, when we move not so much by the frenzied strain of heroic martyrdom as by the large and growing force of many people together, so rational and beneficent a movement as that represented by this paper should have a very solid background of support.

Suppose now that there are in this country among its seventy millions, reducing that to its two-fifths of adults, twenty-eight millions, reducing that by standards of education and progress—say ten million intelligent readers. Divide that to get the women (though men have a deep interest in the question, too), we have five million. Reducing that by incomes above a thousand dollars, call it one million. One million intelligent, progressive women readers with over a thousand dollars a year.

Now if one-tenth of these, one hundred thousand women, care enough for the advance of humanity to be interested in one of its important aids to the extent of five cents a week—that would mean by the year $2.60 in cash from each, in total at the *Journal*'s price of $2.50 a year $250,000. That would enable this paper to engage the best writers from every land, to have working agencies everywhere to keep it in touch with every step of advance along its many lines, to give to its readers a clear, full, carefully-arranged record of the progress of women in every country and the progress of every allied movement in politics, education, industry, science, art. It is hard to find one step of the world which does not connect with all the others.

Such a paper could afford to carry also a body of literature of the highest quality, which should attract and amuse and carry on the good work in wider and subtler channels than any mere record or exhortation.

The world should have such a paper. To my mind it should be illustrated, full of attractions, alive with progress, and only a "woman's magazine" in that it kept steadily before the reader in special departments the position of women as it has been, as it is, as it is becoming and what that position means to the world.

Most of the existing "women's papers" and magazines of the "popular" kind, of the kind that find unlimited half-opened minds to nibble them, treat this position as stationary. They cater to the primitive woman, to all her littlenesses and prejudices, to her special virtues and her special perplexities, like the little shops that sell slate-pencils and cookies to school children. They treat things as they are and as they have been and weigh heavily to keep them there. They may be harmless, amusing, instructive in many ways—there is no reason they should not meet existing wants—while they exist, but they are not in the same class as a publication whose purpose is to seek, to build, to smooth, to lighten the upward path of half the world—not excluding the other half.

This thing will be done and done soon. Those who can read the signs of the times, who watch the rise and fall and swift succession of the would-be women's papers, and the change in character even in the most reactionary can see this kind of publication shaping itself dimly in the minds of the promoters and failing again and again because they have not yet fully met the needs of the situation. If the *Woman's Journal* is one of these, it must give way to a successor; but if not, if it has been true to the noble purpose of its founder and yet has grown continually with the growing movement it represents—then it can succeed itself.

Now this paper has a subscription list in many lands. It is long and honorably known. It has many friends both old and new. But it has not enough to make it even self-supporting, still requiring gratuitous labor of contributors and heavy sacrifice from its financial backers. Now are these subscribers willing to have this paper stop and take their chances of a better one?

Are they willing to support the paper as it is?

Are they willing to help make it better?

If the subscription list should increase by 3,000, then the paper could go on easily as it is. By 6,000, it could enlarge. A substantial gain would mean larger advertising, larger capital, power to engage the best writers and add many attractive features.

My own work closes with the year, being a contribution of time and labor equal to about three thousand dollars if placed in paying magazines at my present rate.

If the *Journal* goes on and grows as it should grow, I should be proud and glad to work with it still; but in my view of human labor, it is not legitimate to continually give *what is not wanted* to people who could easily pay for it if they did want it. The same work through other channels reaches a wider audience and does full as much—if not more—good.

It is the business of the teacher or preacher to reach his hearers, to make them listen, to rouse and stimulate, instruct and inspire. He is quite justified in doing this for nothing and glorying in it. All true work is "giving" in the deepest sense, but if he preaches to empty houses, why maintain the fruitless sacrifice?

Now if throngs of people read this paper who could not afford to pay for it, gladly would every true-hearted worker for humanity in this line contribute his or her share of the good work. But the crucial point in this case is that there are more than enough earnest women in our country to whom one car fare a week would be absolutely imperceptible. The difficulty is to reach them. I do not mean to reach their homes but to reach their brains!

There are plenty of good suffragists, even, who know this paper, who approve of it, who even read it occasionally, but to whom it never occurs as right that they should each and all put up five cents a week rather than let half a dozen people put up thousands a year. And these same good ladies would be sorry to have the *Journal* discontinued and would attribute it, probably, to incapacity in management.

Now for a bit of interpretation on special lines.

Why is it that out of so many women, competent and intelligent all over the country, so few take this five cents' worth of interest in maintaining the best voice of the woman's movement?

> 1. Because "personally" they do not care for the paper enough to pay for it. They care for the movement and like to see it promoted but do not want to do the promoting or at least to do it that way.
> 2. Because they have never in their own minds considered the question as a whole, never have seen the invariable need of a representative organ for a great question, never have weighed and considered the advantages of this special organ, both in our country and abroad, and whether *apart from personal preference* it is not worth supporting as a "campaign document." This last is the spirit in which men pay their contributions to a political

campaign—not that they care *personally* for its literature but they have sense enough to see the need of it.

3. Because five cents is bigger to most women than five dollars is to most men. Because most women do not *own* any money. They expend the family funds, it may be, for the family interests, but as to indulging a purely personal choice, acting from their own private judgment and in a matter so remote as reform literature, it is quite beyond their range.

4. Because the whole foreground of most women's minds is like a country store—full and running over with dry goods and groceries. If we could look into the chart of this dear, common mother-brain, we should see it platted out something like this: eight-tenths of the area, John—the children—the housework. Three-twentieths—Heaven. One-twentieth—all the rest of the world's affairs.

It is this disproportionate space occupied by our separate affairs that prevents our giving any sort of proportionate attention to the world's affairs, and we think it is right! We honest believe that this is the best way to take care of the world—each one doing it alone.

Now fancy, in the birth-throes of our great Revolutionary War, each man saying, "If I support my own family—at my own doorstone—the country will be safe."

Fancy, when chattel slavery threatened to wreck our young nation irretrievably, that men had said: "If I do not keep slaves—if my family is free from this evil—there is nothing else to do; all will be well."

Or to take industrial instead of martial illustrations, suppose each man said: "If I make shoes for my family, build a home for them with my own hands, keep sheep and raise corn for them, nothing else needs to be done. There is no world. The family is the world. I will care for it and my whole duty is performed."

We have remained at this level of action, trusting the whole progress of the world to men and sharing in it as we were allowed. Their books, their pictures, their newspapers, their buildings, their great businesses, their peace and their wars, we have profited and suffered by but done little to assist.

Surely we do not expect them to support a woman's paper? Surely the women must be the first to recognize the world-value, the world-duty, the world-honor of the greatest movement in all history—the advance of women to full and equal civilization?

Unfortunately, the men have a far wider field of thought and action. They in business and in politics are used to handling large questions, common interests. They can far better grasp the immense content of the woman question. And it would be asking superhuman intelligence of the average man to see, as indeed many great men have seen, that this growth of women means the growth of the whole world. So the average man sees, but only enough to disapprove, and the specially intelligent woman sees indeed but as a small, dim, distant thing. She does not see clearly, her vision being obscured by the looming bulk of the five-cent piece and the opacity of the kitchen door.

COLUMN 48

December 10, 1904

Gilman defends her proposal to establish childcare centers and kindergartens that would enable young mothers to seek employment outside the home.[1]

These "Municipal Nurseries"

When the Russian government wants to incite a massacre of Jews, we are told, it circulates stories about the sacrifice of Christian babies in Jewish religious rites; and when a newspaper wishes to incite condemnation of the Russian government, it circulates similar accounts of its methods, though to be sure we have facts enough about that systemized oppression to form our opinions without need of fiction. The old saying on this method of warfare, the method of our political campaigns, is "Give a dog a bad name and hang him."

Anyone familiar with the workings of the human mind on the average is not surprised by its ordinary actions; they are foretold, expected. The Abolitionists were, in the Southern States, formerly believed to advocate marriage between whites and blacks and to incite slaves to massacre their masters; the early woman suffragists were firmly believed to hate men and yet—confusing mixture—to maintain "free love" doctrines.[2]

When we do not approve another person's doctrine, we are all too apt to imagine it to comprise evil views it never included.

Knowing all this and not objecting to it especially (why object to water's being wet or fire hot?), it does not surprise those who are advancing any late step of progress to have that step generally misconstrued and made to mean things it never dreamed of. So a little while ago, speaking in Chicago on the advance of educational ideas in regard to the care of infants, I was not surprised to see the reporter for the *Tribune* describe the proposition as "the segregation of babies in municipal nurseries."[3]

This phrase to the average mind calls up a vague and repellant image of big, noisy, dusty places full of neglected babies howling and tumbling about under the care of cold, indifferent public functionaries who do not care whether they live or die.

Even to the more thoughtful, who might see in it at least a guarantee of cleanliness, safety, and scientific care, it would seem cold and heartless enough—a desolate, scientific, wholesale sort of service—not in any way comparable to the love of the displaced mother.

This impression is produced by the ingenious use of terms. "Segregation"—babies in a heap, babies torn from their homes and herded indiscriminately—clear separate babies with no mothers. "Municipal"—that word to our shame is synonymous with political rascality and mismanagement. The people of Chicago, familiar with municipal management as it is, have reason to be shy of trusting things most precious and beloved to such cold care.

And even "nurseries"—the only nurseries we know that treat groups of babies are those charitable establishments to provide for the children of the poorest women, who must work and who are willing to admit that the nursery is better than the street or the locked-up room, where the baby is so often burned to death.

But these charitable nurseries for the ignorant poor are not pleasant to the thought of the cultivated rich. To "send a baby to the nursery" suggests being a scrubwoman.

So my friend on the *Tribune* with well-chosen words succeeds in arousing three complete sets of prejudices in one headline—a good deal to do even for a newspaper.

Using this merely as an illustrative incident, typical of the methods of modern journalism and the effect of the reportorial position on the brain of the reporter, let us proceed to a consideration of what it is that is recommended by some of those who love more babies than their own and who believe that the care of babies, like any other field of human life, is open to improvement.

We have always had before us the great primal function of motherhood. We loved and honored it before we were at all civilized—in that vast and world-embracing cult, the matriarchate. It is now found that the savage races we have still with us are decadent races, that language and custom point unerringly to an antecedent period when they were far better off, more highly developed, more prosperous, under the matriarchate.

That great period passed, and with the subjection of the mother, the world sank low indeed. In some few instances, however, a given race rose from that downfall, gave some recognition to its women, and became civilized; and as we now see, the position of woman is the surest measure of human progress. The higher the woman, the higher the race; the lower the woman, the lower the race; these are truisms.

Through all vicissitudes we have perforce respected motherhood—else we died. And the mother, sure of some consideration on account of this one function and having *no other*, quite naturally grew to have a high idea of herself in this regard. Being worshiped as a mother during the long era of the matriarchate, being spared as a mother when she had no other protection, being rewarded as a mother when it was her only guarantee of a livelihood—when the barren woman was cast off like a garment—and then in these later years, having a vast flood of emotion and sentiment, poetry, painting, and religious enthusiasm poured forth on motherhood—it is small wonder that we women think a great deal of ourselves in this capacity.

There is the underlying foundation of fact, of natural law—the great life process we represent—and then the superimposed structure of custom, tradition, sentiment, and religion. How could we avoid matrimony?

So here we all are worshiping motherhood, and while people worship they can't *think*.

We don't think, we don't observe, we merely feel and naturally we make small progress. The human mother of today has little more to offer to her young than the savage mother of the far past or the brute mother behind that. In some things she has less.

The gain of the child of our times comes through the father, not the mother.

There are mothers enough—in all lands and peoples—Comanche

mothers, Patagonian mothers, Madagascan mothers, mothers French and German, Arab, Mongol, Japanese. They are all mothers, one as much as another. They all bear children, nurse them, love them, serve them as they know how. But what they know—the standard of their civilization—comes from the attainments of the fathers. Mrs. Comanche may love her papoose as well as Mrs. Boston, but the baby Comanche has little to ensure and develop his life; the Boston baby has the best fruit of the world.

The advantage has been gained by the father, and the mother and child share in it.

Now the animal mother does all for her child, sometimes assisted by the father. The human mother, while savage, does far more than the father; the civilized mother does far less.

Education has been carried down the ages in growing volume almost exclusively by men; only lately are women sweeping forward to learn and teach and grow.

Education—the most ennobling and beneficent influence of our lives—has spread and grown in its range from the college and university for youths to the schools for children and very recently to the kindergartens for the little ones. This last step is still but partially accepted by the most ancient, undeveloped, prejudiced, and arrogant functionary in human life—the mother.

She who is truly the greatest power in life, she whose love is the fountain of all our human affection, she whose creative force is the base of all industry and art, she who once led and ruled the world by virtue of her womanhood—she now holds back the world *by that very motherhood*—because she will not let it grow.

Of course, it will be said that man has oppressed her and refused her education and freedom and all that, which is true enough in its way, but she has room enough now, education enough now, freedom enough now (enough to get more, at any rate) and she still remains motionless and inert.

Education is creeping to the highest place at last, the true place—at the very headwaters of life—the first years of the child. At first it merely told what things were known to the already tangled brains of grown youths. As it grew wiser and wider and learned that *the brain* was the thing to be educated, it went on to younger and younger children. Now we are seeing at last that the impressions of the first years are the most important, and that even love is not enough for the right education of the little child.

So the demand has arisen for expert care for our babies, care from the wisest, best-trained minds, from practiced hands, from large hearts full of human love—love for all children—instead of what we now give our babies, the care of ignorant, low-grade hired servants.

We are just beginning to see, some of us, that motherhood is a great, common animal function open to every kind of female animal, but that education is a very high, recent, special human function for which some few persons are fit—most persons are not.

Every woman—speaking generally—can be a mother; not every woman can be an educator. And if the average mother with all her "mother love" and "mother instinct" is not therefore an educator, how much less than we look for that special talent in the nursemaid—lower class, lower training, and *not even a mother!*

The best single proof for the failure of the average mother to appreciate the importance of the care of babies is her willingness to depute it to others.

We engage to teach our grown children a college faculty—the best brains trained by long special study for the important work. We engage to teach our younger children schoolteachers who must also fit for their profession by years of special study. We engage for our little children kindergartners who must also study their business thoroughly. We engage to teach our babies half-grown "mother's helpers," colored girls or "mammys," young Irish or German peasants—persons such as we should never think fit company, to say of fit instructors, for our older children.

This is because we do not think of the care of babies as a process of education. Education to us has meant the school studies, "book learning," and the baby could not read therefore could not be educated. Herein is shown the pitiful ignorance of mothers, their incapacity for their business; they do not even know that the first years are years of supreme importance in education, the real education of the growing brain.

The impressions which throng in upon that brain through every eager sense are each and all important. It is largely because the early impressions of all of us are so incoherent, discordant, illogical, unfit that we continue to grow up with the muddleheadedness of all our ancestors. There is progress, great progress, thanks to the school and college and general gain of later years. We inherit better brains—but the more highly-developed is the mental machinery of the baby, the more injury he is likely to receive from the senseless surroundings of his infancy.

The modern baby needs the modern mother—but she is slow to awaken. All the baby gets is the primal mother—and very much weakened at that. Our long civilization has greatly reduced the force and clarity of primitive instincts, and unless we supplement that loss with the greater gain of intelligence we have but a poor motherhood to offer.

As soon as we do recognize the need of the baby for exquisitely selected educational environment, highbred specialized training and care, then we must also see that not only is the nurse-maid unequal to this demand but that the mother herself is. We see the need of teachers as wise and experienced as those to whose care we entrust our older children—or even more so.

When we see that, we realize that these teachers are not to hired for five dollars a week. Even if they would take that wage, *there are not enough of them to go around.* That is the crux of the whole matter. Our babies need a kind of care that cannot be given by the average woman. It needs the special woman, the born teacher, and one of long training and experience.

To have this advantage, the babies must be brought together in small groups just as the little ones in the kindergarten are. There is nothing more offensive or degrading in a group of babies in a scientifically-managed nursery than in a group of young men and women in a college or boys and girls in a school.

These nurseries need not be "municipal" any more than our other educational institutions are. The public school is the school of the future—it sprang from the private school, which came first. The private nursery, small, select, local, expensive, may be to many far more desirable than the public nursery; but gradually, as the kindergarten is added to our primary grades, so will nurseries be added to kindergartens—so that every baby, however poor his parents, may have the advantage of civilized care.

And as to "segregation"—even if the mother worked for eight hours, she would have eight waking hours a day left to devote to her baby and the other children. How many of these so sensitive mothers, who are pained and shocked at the "segregation" of babies, spend eight hours a day with their children?

The poor can't; the rich won't; scarcely anyone does.

When the mother has done a fair day's work and the baby has had his day of peace and happiness in his own place, perhaps they would really be more to each other than they are now.

At present you see them, the babies, "segregated" in our parks and streets or asleep or tucked away in the single "nursery" such as the private home can offer, and you see the mothers working at house service or other trades if they are poor or playing at "society" if they are rich.

But you do not see the average mother glued to her baby in constant, though intelligent, devotion for eight hours a day. It would be a bad thing for baby if you did.

Too much mother—clear, concentrated, unalloyed mother—is no great advantage. We want to think and study about this matter, not just feel.

COLUMN 49

December 17, 1904

Related by birth or marriage to the famous Beecher, Hale, and Stowe families, Gilman harbored an ambition to serve humanity her entire life. Here she defends similar aspirations in other women, predictably incurring criticism from her detractors.

This "Craving for Notoriety"

One of the things essentially hard to understand is the difference between the world of facts and the mental picture of those facts in which we live. Living—consciousness—is a mental condition; an idiot lives as far as his physical functions go, but he is not actually conscious of it.

The world we *live* in is the world of brain pictures; the real world may or may not agree with our ideas. Our lives and deaths go on remorselessly under the action of what is; but our happiness or unhappiness, our sense of vice or virtue, depends on what we think.

We have lived in our physical bodies all this time and died, but we have only just begun to learn the laws of those bodies, the real facts concerning them, and how to treat them properly. The bodies went right on living according to their own laws, peacefully indifferent to what we thought about it.

So we have lived in cities, sharing their advantages and disadvantages, loving or hating or indifferent, proud or ashamed, helping or hindering, but the cities went right on according to their laws quite regardless of our point of view.

Now human nature in general has its laws and processes; it works on along lines of its own; and we in our conscious minds are as ignorant of these laws and processes of social life as we have been of physical life or civic life.

We have in our minds certain accepted views—always very old and inadequate—and those "views" stand to us for the real landscape.

Along this line of study is to be found the explanation of the phrase at the head of this chapter. A certain phenomenon of social life forced itself upon our attention; and we, having no correct data whereby to interpret it, fetched out a little label from our dusty heirlooms of old labels and labeled it. As the phenomenon varied, cropping out in different circumstances, we varied the label. We did not recognize it as the same because the circumstances were different. When we saw this universal tendency of human nature in the soldier, we called it "a thirst for glory." When we saw it in the statesman, artist, or even the millionaire, we called it "the desire for fame." When we saw it in kings and queens and priests, we called it "the love of power." When we see it in women, we call it "the craving for notoriety."

What is this common tendency in human nature which crops out everywhere in all kinds of people? What is the governing impulse behind the pictured desire ahead, the pressure which drives people on and on *and is never satisfied?*

What kind of appetite had Alexander, sighing for new worlds to conquer?[1]

Nordau—having a brain set hard in one line of thought—calls it megalomania, a disease.[2] We know this disease in common life and call it "the big head." Is there nothing in this worldwide and age-long phenomenon of human nature except disease? May we not rather suspect the brain which sees all things in one light and that abnormal, of disease, and look for a healthier explanation of the facts?

Try this one. Human nature is essentially collective—man is one thing. Men, the separate animals, as they become human through ages of development, are drawn into larger and larger social relation. This relation develops in us all an increasing capacity for social service; we are able to be useful to more people and *conscious of that ability*. The new functions, the social functions, bring with them like all conscious activities, their pleasures and their pains. Given any necessary conscious physical process and it is a pleasure to fulfill it—a pain to deny it. It is a pleasure to see—a pain to see too much or to be blind. It is a pleasure to eat—a pain to eat too much or to starve.

A normal, conscious process is led by pleasure—driven by pain. Whatever we have to do for our own good is given a stout manager called an appetite to continually call us on to action. To get something to eat is often much trouble, even perhaps dangerous, but the longing within draws us on to exertion, a longing which is at first only a pleasant titillation, then an irritation, then a passion, then an agony, then, if ungratified, death. Social nature has its laws as absolute as those of physical culture. Sociology is no abstract field of metaphysics—it is a definite science about definite facts.

It is a baby science yet—the youngest of all. We know very little of its laws, though for all these years we have lived under them.

When societies understand themselves, they will be able to maintain social health with its virtue and happiness; but so far they merely live and die without understanding.

One of the first conditions of social life is, on the face of it, association. Hence human beings draw together. This association is not mere congregation of particles like a heap of sand; it is a vital relation, an organic relation, the heap is alive! This calls for communication between the parts that it may act, and under that social necessity have [sic] developed language, literature, and the arts.

Further than this lies the great governing condition of organic life—the interchange of service. An organ is not a separate life; it is part of something. Its existence as an organ depends on the existence of other organs. One organ breathes, one sees, one pumps the blood about.

No heart could run about pumping for its own purposes; he has to have something to get the blood from, something to pump it to; he is an organ, not an entity.

In the organic relation of human beings called society, we serve one another in our special work. The farmer, grazier, carrier, and distributor feed us; the teacher teaches us, and so on. As society advances, its widening growth calls for a larger and larger range of service; our corn, our machinery, our books go round the world.

This large circle of exchange of large services is a vital necessity of human life today. Human life is conscious; these world activities are not yet relegated to the field of automatic action. We have to do these great duties consciously, often under great difficulty and sometimes danger. To meet this need, Nature as usual provides her two great forces, pleasure and pain, to lead and drive us, to reward and punish us.

We being social creatures, our largest consciousness being collective, our human activities being collective, we receive our highest pleasure collectively. To be *known*, felt, recognized with love and honor is humanity's sweetest gratification; to be despised and condemned is our bitterest, most crushing pain.

In small civic communities of old time, this common consciousness was limited but strong and found its highest honor in a statue in the marketplace, its worst punishment in ostracism and exile.

Today we are bigger—far bigger. Our social consciousness has spread from family to tribe, from tribe to city, from city to nation, from nation—in these tremendous days—even to the world. World-consciousness is growing now and growing fast.

We have in human life today far larger need of service, far larger power of service, and—by beautiful necessity—far larger appetite for service and for its natural reward—recognition. This natural appetite of the social being, man, for social service and social reward is the underlying fact which we have called all these names and by worse ones. It is a right thing, a noble thing, a useful thing, but open to misuse and disease as is the appetite for food.

The physical appetite—*in right conditions*—is a guide, teacher, and friend. In wrong conditions it may become a vicious tyrant.

The natural desire for social service and social recognition should lead only to a constant enlargement of human usefulness, power, and joy. But in our blind ignorance of the nature of the thing we live in, in our perverse and arbitrary insistence on the oldest kind of foolish misconceptions, we seldom find a free field for normal growth. Therefore, this great social appetite only too often works wrong instead of right.

Its one widest, truest field, that of plain industry, has been cut off completely in our minds by our primeval superstitions about work (see Veblen's

Theory of the Leisure Class—a classic),³ and in consequence much of the noblest human ambition has been forced to fizzle off unduly in games and sports or to do positive evil in the deadly foolishness of war.

In the arts and sciences we allowed it freer way, and a most useful thing it has proven in the great field of social service. No field is great enough, however, except the whole field; and it is to our wholesale injury that people should think it more honorable to paint pictures than to teach school, or to teach school than to make dresses, or to make dresses than to cook.

All social service is social service. The only dishonorable thing is personal service—to work for self or a few extra selves, alone, to serve the part instead of the whole.

The line of honorable advancement, of rising dignity and worthiness, is the larger and larger range of service.

To learn that such a drug is anesthetic and to use it on one's self is not wicked—it is perfectly right in its way—but it is a little thing to do, a paltry, pathetically little thing. To give that anesthetic to a suffering world is a great thing to do, and the more widely its use can be extended the greater is that service and the greater should be the reward of *recognition*—love and honor from our great Self—Society.

To make good orange marmalade—and eat it—is not wicked; it is ingenious, clever, skillful, but of small consequence. To make good orange marmalade and have one's family eat it is bigger by six—or ten. But to make good orange marmalade for the whole world—that is social service and so more honorable.

The manufacturer—sitting blindly inside of his own mind—that little close room artificially lit and hung with antediluvian "views" in place of open windows—he may think he is making marmalade for himself and for his own family. He may even cheat the public by charging more than his marmalade is worth—taking to himself an extortionate share of what we call "profits"—and by so doing, he loses utterly the real reward, the loving honor of millions.

He might be known and praised everywhere as a great social servant; he prefers to take his pay in cash and we, knowing that, do not honor him, but the work he does is social service just the same. He helps to feed the world and that is a greater, better thing than merely to feed ten people.

The demand of the modern world is for large-brained, large-hearted, capable, efficient social servants in every line of human work. The supply is here—we have the people with the power.

But they are hindered and misled by false ideas; and we, watching the push and surge of the great impulse in the soldier, artist, statesman, say he loves fame; but seeing the same in a woman we say she "craves notoriety." We blame and belittle in the woman precisely the same impulse we extol in the man because in the popular mind we consider men only as people—women are just women.

"What's fame for a woman?" cries Mrs. Browning passionately,[4] and goes on to show how it lies all in the range of a mother's devotion. Now the mother is all right and so is the father—neither of these functionaries has anything to do with "fame."

Fame is public recognition; it is a social condition rightly desired by a human being, a member of society; and women are human beings—by nature.

They are, unfortunately, not human beings by practice, being content to be female beings mostly; their humanness, their social service, generally remaining on the scale of primitive exertion called "domestic industry."

When a woman does feel the rush and sweep of the great social impulse; the desire to live out, wide and full; to rise to the upper limits of capacity; to work in the great range of world activity; and naturally to feel the large recognition that should meet large service, she is accused of a morbid "craving for notoriety."

We are so sure that women, differing from men in the essential distinction of sex, must therefore remain a race apart, another set of beings, animal if you please but never Human!

So misinterpreting, we blame; and the woman, cowed and weakened by long dependence, fights down the splendid impulse toward world service and world power and tries to satisfy a human heart with the functions of a sex and the occupations of a servant.

One recourse remains to us, one supreme call which women have always recognized and in the mass obeyed—the voice of Duty.

So long as we thought our duty lay only in the kitchen, dining room, bedroom, and parlor, we have stayed there and suffered there.

We have fed the heart of humanity with the small, small praises of a little circle and wrung the sweetness out of love by trying to make that blessed little god a man-of-all-work.

We need not any longer be frightened with the jumping-jacks of our childhood—we are older, wiser, braver now. We should think out for ourselves this great open road before us, this call to serve the noble race to which we belong.

The highest human duty is the fullest social service, and there is no perfect peace, no perfect joy without it.

No amount of fulfillment of lesser duties can excuse us from fulfilling the greater.

We are members of society and as such owe our life's service to society—first.

What is social service?

The largest possible development of any social process—to make shoes, to paint houses, to teach children, to do any kind of human work in the best way for the most people. There is little service and big, but it is the nature of the human being to long ceaselessly to do bigger and bigger work and to bask in the appreciation of a wider and wider circle of beneficiaries.

If I have grown old as a teacher in one city, if I have been a civic mother to thousands of growing boys, it is a deep and natural joy to have a hundred hats lifted to me by the men of that city as I come and go, the men who were my boys. It is just as "natural" a feeling as a mother's feeling and *higher*. Higher because it is more human. Humanity is a higher thing than motherhood even. So when our hearts swell with the desire to lead big, useful lives and to be known and appreciated in the larger work, let us recognize it as a healthy human impulse and obey it.

Let us not be frightened off from a dominant line of duty by the criticism of old-world ignorance.

To love the world, to serve the world, and to long for the world's love, this is natural to a human being and it is not a "craving for notoriety."

COLUMN 50

December 24, 1904

In her Christmas Eve column Gilman celebrates the birth of Christ and scorns the Santa Claus myth.

"Even Mother"

"Yes," said the sober-faced little boy, recounting his Christmas gifts, "everybody gave me something—even mother!" But there was a twinkle in his eye.

Strange indeed would be the Christmas where a mother forgot her little son. What is Christmas but the Baby's Birthday—the everlasting birthday of the Child who loved the world and taught the world to love? Here came One with a new religion. Others had taught sacrifice, worship, obedience. He taught love. To love mankind, *all* mankind, and to serve them continually—this is the vital spirit of Christianity; this is what Christ taught as the will of God.

We are very slow to do it. We are still wrapped up almost wholly in lesser love and lesser service; and though we give at a pinch to the crying need of the stranger, yet our whole life's devotion is for our own close relatives. We fear that they will suffer if we give our lives to the world's help, that if we do not care for our own no one will.

This attitude we defend as being "natural" and consider the person who frankly puts the whole world before the part, who would prefer to lift a nation an inch to lifting his family a yard, as "unnatural." "Whoso careth not for his own," we solemnly quote, "is worse than an infidel," and fail to see the corollary, "and whoso careth only for his own is no better."[1]

That word "natural" is a most misleading one. So long as we supposed nature to be stationary, a fixed status below humanity yet of which humanity partook, it served as a distinction; but now that we find all nature, including our own, to be in a constant state of flux and progress, the word "natural" must have its place and date to make it definite.

There was a time, and a very long time, when mankind had no families at all, when fatherhood was unknown and motherhood scarce more than among brutes. This family affection was not "natural" then.

There was a time when we had no nations, no ties of common country to bind us together by thousands and millions, but now patriotism is "natural" as familism and the man who will not defend his country is considered as unnatural as he who will not defend his child. Even the mother surrenders her son to the service of her country and is not called "unnatural" for the sacrifice.

We live in nations as we live in families, and the same laws of nature which developed family affection out of the family relation have developed love of country out of the national relation. Hearts thrill and eyes glisten at sight of the flag, at sound of the National Hymn, as they do at "Home, Sweet Home."[2] Both these feelings are natural. So now that we are becoming daily more conscious of international relation, of economic ties which bind us together all around the earth, we are developing also a larger love than ever before. In our own lands we are feeling it, in our own cities—a growing sense of common responsibility, common care, common duty, and the love which always "naturally" follows upon these. This gives promise of a better Christmas for the world than it has ever had before.

The love which Christ preached as the first and all-embracing duty of man we have set aside heretofore as a remote and difficult virtue attainable only by a few consecrated souls, whereas in fact it is as natural to humanity so to love one another as to love its close kindred. Indeed, it is *more natural* today because it is the distinctive characteristic of our times, whereas the lower forms of love had their leading place in lower stages of civilization.

The immense spread of our interdependence today and its accompanying spread of intelligent consciousness brings with it perforce the love that nature, or say God, always provides to accomplish its own ends. If any associate action is required by differing entities, it must be provided either through an unconscious mutual service, as where bees fertilize flowers, seeking only their own ends, or by conscious mutual service, as where the same bees serve each other and their common ends in the hive.

Man has been led far in the ascending line of social relation by his own blind self-interest, as unconscious of mutual obligation as the blundering bee butting his thick head into the pollen, brushing stamen and stigma with like indifference; but the vast web of his worldwide interservice is so complicated that it needs a conscious devotion to forward still higher development—and that conscious devotion is forthcoming.

It has taken us two thousand years to see the sense of Christ's teaching—two thousand slow, black, painful years to find out practically and prove to our own minds that "no man liveth to himself nor dieth to himself."[3] All this time we have been busy maintaining that it was "natural" for man to be brutal and fierce and selfish and to care only for his own.

Two thousand years is not much in social development, however. It took far longer than that to produce national sentiment or even a feeling so "natural" as the love of the father for his child. Even as late as in Roman days, fathers cast out to death their own children if they didn't like their looks; they are still doing it—with girls—in China, we are told. But China, even China, is moving today! There is a splendid stir of broad humanitarian reform in that old, old land. If ever the Chinese brain, so simple, so subtle, powerful, and clear comes to really appreciate this law of human love and *apply* it—apply it as we Christians have never done—why, the last may be first; the tortoise beats the hare after all.

In China, more plainly than anywhere on earth, stands out this old-world obstacle to human growth, the limitation of the family. They fully and frankly worship as well as love the family, especially the dead ones.

No fabled ostrich with its head in the sand is blinder than a people with its heart in the grave.

So long as the family was the only human group for mutual support, so long was its cult the highest, its affections complete and satisfying.

No history goes back to that period, but we can study in the scattered tents of the Bedouin something of its limitation. So soon as life and liberty and progress call for, evolve, and depend on a larger relation, that relation calls for our love and service by the same law that brought out family affection.

We today know, publicly and commonly know, who it is that is more than father, more than mother, more than child, far more than one's own uncounted self. It is no secret, no mystery or enigma.

Food is raised for us, brought to us, prepared for us; clothes are woven and cut and sewed and distributed for us; homes are built for us; books are written for us; all—all that we have is given to us not by the family but by the big working world. What we get, how much we get, our safety, our peace, our hard-won heights of education and prosperity—these are ours by virtue of our mutual service worldwide and not by virtue of the skill and industry of our father the carpenter or our mother the cook.

We believe that these things are ours by the efforts of the individual parent moved by love for the individual offspring. We really believe this in face of facts as plain and huge as the Rocky Mountains.

Can we not see this individual love and service pegging away busily in every country on earth—with results so glaringly different as to show a child of ten that there must be some other cause at work to give one nation composed of families such vast advantages over another nation also composed of families?

What we have here in America of peace and power and wealth today is due not to our loving our own families better than do the people of other nations but to our offering better conditions to all people. It is the height and beauty of our national institutions which give us our great place, and it is the gross defects of those same institutions and our sins and failures in them which so threaten and shame us today. We need more strongly and immediately than ever before the general recognition of this public honor, of duty and truth and courage and devotion in public service.

We are good at home, most of us—sufficiently good at home—but not good enough abroad. Here is this rich, big land, full of fertility and power.

Here are these eager millions of people thronging in from other countries, born even thicker and faster in this one, striving in their primitive selfishness to profit each for himself and his own family at the expense of anyone or everyone else and his family!

And here is the slow uprising of national ideals, the slow development of those free institutions for which our ancestors so sternly fought.

This is where the heart and head of the nation is wanted—our best brains, our best consciences, our best and bravest service.

We need more people and better people to maintain and carry further our public honor and our public work. There is no stopping place in social growth.

It is not enough that we are richer than other nations. Have we still slums? Still sweatshops? Still child labor? Still too long hours, too little pay, too wearing tasks?

It is not enough that our railroads are swifter, better, and more numerous than in other countries; have we still a yearly sacrifice of dead and wounded, of maimed and crippled employees and slaughtered passengers? And have we still the railroad crimes?—the discrimination in rebates,[4] whereby the common carrier is false to his public trust as a postman who could be hired to carry one man's letters and refuse another's?

It is not enough that our schools are in some ways the best in the world and growing better—not nearly enough! Are they the best that America can make? Are they loved and honored and *served* as our most important social function—the great work of race improvement in the hands of the common parent—the Nation?

We have in every city numbers of comfortable, intelligent, and "good" people, but we have also greater numbers of uncomfortable, stupid, and defective people—and we need not have them.

It is not enough that each mother gathers her little ones about a Christmas tree—what has she done the year through to provide the same for the thousands of children who have none? At Christmas time, if at no other, for the sake of the Child who loved all children—if you cannot feel it directly yourself, for the sake of the children themselves—no mother should be content while any child on earth is ill-fed, ill-housed, ill-clothed, ill-taught, denied aught of all that is needed to make the very best kind of people. We know what we want for our own children—what we do our best to give to them. Why do we not want it for all? We do we not give it to all?

Is there not enough with this great, rich world and all the strength and skill of all these parents?

There is no question of their earning it first—children are not confronted with that fallacy. The child comes helpless, needing all things, and to him must be given fully, freely, richly that he may grow.

Here is Christmas upon us again. Here are children with us always.

Here are mothers, millions of mothers, wishing to give all the joy they can to their own children.

Wish it *wider*, deeper, higher; wish it for all children—and do not stop at wishing! The world's children need the world's mothers united and organized.

When we have that, when the mother joins the father in his public service, adds her love to his, her strength to his, her big, bounteous mother-heart to his laborious father-toil, then indeed will there be no hungry child on earth at Christmas time or any other time.

Santa Claus

More talk about the myth of Santa Claus.[5] Shall we teach it to our children or shall we not? Some call it lying and say it affronts the child's intelligence and weakens his faith in us. Some call it cultivating the imagination and a good thing for the child. The real wonder is that in a Christian country this particular myth ever obtained a foothold and has still a defender.

What is Christmas?

The birthday of Jesus.

It is a celebration of an event believed by Christians to be of measureless importance and good to the world. They hold that in this child's birth dawned the salvation of the world. Their whole religion rests on him. A Child-God with a mother. A Baby worshiped by kings. Then the growing Christ child with all the sweet stories of that childhood, its love and duty.

Built on this is as stirring and sweet a group of stories as a child's heart could wish. Here is the fountain of human love, the mother; the center of human care, the child; and the main thread of human behavior, religion.

Here is the love beyond mother-love—the new teacher of the world, the giver of the great doctrine of love and service to all mankind. So great was this love that it flows on yet through all our widening hearts—feeding, teaching, healing, helping, doing more and more for more people from year to year. Because of this love and its accompanying service we have grown on and on, richer, wiser, stronger, nearer to peace.

All this we may teach our children with beautiful legends of the Talmud,[6] with beautiful stories from the Gospels, with lovely true tales of people who have lived sweetly and died bravely because that Child was born that day.

And we Christians, who have this at the very foundation of our religion, this gloriously beautiful story, the main fact of which is true—we have picked up from medieval barbarism this Arctic kobold with his hybrid name, this preposterous, fat hobgoblin with his one annual appearance to distribute prizes to good children by way of the chimney—and teach that to our children instead of the child Jesus!

It is no wonder that Christmas has grown selfish. What should be the festival of universal love, opening our hearts to the widest, has become a mere family festival when the child is taught, carefully and particularly taught, that the main thing is the getting of presents from a hypothetically yearly distributor!

Let us teach our children beautiful and appropriate stories, myths if we must, but why leave out Heaven for sake of Santa Claus?

COLUMN 51

December 31, 1904

Controversial even among feminists for advocating broad social and cultural reforms, Gilman ends her weekly department after only one year. In her final column she summarizes the trials and tribulations of the experience.

A Valedictory

A cheerful good-bye to my friends with gratitude for their interest, their appreciation, their words of approval.

Reassurances to those who disapprove—it is not really as bad as they think, this doctrine of a new world for women.

Who would have supposed, some half a century or more ago, when the demand for the ballot shocked and astounded the most "advanced," that those who but sought equal suffrage would become by now conservative in their turn?

"There is no cure for the ills of freedom but more freedom." Wasn't that what Emerson said?[1]

The woman, long repressed, has been rising since her first escape like the genii from the jar. Given education, she would have the ballot. Given the ballot (or not), she would have industrial freedom. Given industrial freedom, she therein develops and begins now to see that her own old cradle is the one thing that needs moving most today.

That dear old cradle, the Home, which we thought need never move though all the rest of the world needs must! We imagined that the woman of this century, spread and grown beyond recognition, filling a larger and larger space with every year, could continue to fill the identical place at home with the same content and pride that her revered grandmama had contentedly and proudly filled before her. Now that it appears she cannot, that this place, too, must wake up and step forward, that the woman of this century needs the home of this century and cannot be satisfied with anything else, we are alarmed.

We persist in spelling "ruin" when all that is urged is "reform." We are as ignorant, as timid, as prejudiced in regard to these latter-day propositions as were our forebears in matters as novel to their time. We are as sure that the world will be un-homed if the kitchen is expunged and the baby better placed as people used to be sure women would be unsexed if they voted.

All of which is perfectly natural and not to be feared or much condemned. To be sure, one always wonders why those who see so far cannot or will not see a little further, but then they never do.

It is hard for women, naturally, to free themselves even in a hundred years from the views and thought-forms trained into them for a hundred thousand.

Even in the long and peaceful age of the matriarchate, we were still primitive as mothers and in but the first steps of industry. We had developed the rudiments of many a trade and art but only the rudiments. We were unspecialized, unorganized, undifferentiated then, and we are yet.

Now that we emerge after long subjection into the equal light of this bright day, we find a world quite different from what it was when we went in.

All these ages while we were patiently doing the same thing, men were impatiently doing different things and growing thereby.

When we went in, we could swim as well as men or paddle a canoe; now we come out to find the whole world's oceans threaded with colossal enterprises of shipping lines in which we have had no part.

Save for the stewardess to wait on women passengers and the pretty girl to break a bottle over the bow when the great thing is christened, no woman has aught to do with this, one of the world's greatest industries.

When we went in, we were ourselves the beasts of burden, sinewy and strong, dignified, beautiful; we were the carriers of what small goods we had. Now we come out, behold what huge and fire-fed engines haul immeasured loads of wealth from sea to sea!

Such as it is, with all its joy and pain, its riches and poverty, its good and evil—the world has been made by men *since they left us at home.*

A good lady sought to contradict this position in a recent issue and spoke with fond enthusiasm of the "civilizing influence of women." She instances the men who go to a mining camp and revert to barbaric habits, then being joined by their women, promptly becoming civilized again.[2]

But it was a lack of *civilization* that ailed these men—not lack of women. When their women came, the men produced the civilization to set the women in. If women in themselves civilized men, then *there would be no uncivilized races!* For lo! there are women among all peoples—to the very lowest.

Civilization, such as we have, is a masculine achievement and the women share in it to a certain extent.

Civilization consists externally in the products of our arts and crafts, our buildings, tools, fabrics, and all other manufacturers. Little enough do women contribute to these. It consists internally in those traits and attributes of the modern man which differentiate him from the savage, most distinctively in the power of highly specialized production, far-reaching and complicated distribution, and that broad-minded capacity for organization which marks the foremost nation. In all these things women are behind. They enjoy the fruits of civilization as far as they can reach them but contribute little to the process of making that fruit.

Now that the woman is at last awakening from her long stupor, coming forward into the world as an honorable human being to fill her rightful place there, she is much handicapped by her own misconceptions as well as the active opposition of men. Most women are still inert, still subhuman, still content to be a female auxiliary to the representative human being—the man. They are willing that he shall divide and subdivide into the vast, fine-woven fabric of world-industries, working lifelong at a thousand special tasks whereby the modern world moves as it does; eats and drinks as it does; wears the clothes and jewels as it does; reads, learns, hears, sees what it does. And while men do all these myriad things, they, these half-made women, are content in their millions and millions, each and all do the same thing.

And this thing which they do is not done well. This is where grief and pain strike deep to the heart of the average woman—and many more above the average; this is where horror is felt, and fierce resentment, at such an allegation. They, being each alone in her task—either all alone as the working housewife or in company with hired subordinates and generally born subordinates, the helpless children—each woman thinks she does her work well and there is none to contradict her! Children cannot criticize parents. Servants cannot criticize mistresses. Husbands can praise what pleases them and blame what offends them, but they cannot intelligently criticize a business they have never learned.

They despise the business as women's work. Women being feeble, ineffective creatures, they must be borne with by man, the superior! And then seeing the inefficiency of the work, they despise the woman further because of the business.

We are not human enough yet, we women, to see that no human work can be successfully brought up to civilized standards while it is done by universal amateurs. There is no trade on earth but what would sink to the kitchen-maid level if it was performed by every man, just because he was a man and it was thought to be a masculine occupation. Even fighting—that essentially masculine function—had to be specialized to become successful; nowhere is organization more elaborate and more vital.

To fight is common to every male, but the male does not seek to defend wife and child with his unaided arm against what foes may chance—not he! He unites, he specializes, he organizes, he subdues the enemies, he makes peace and maintains it—till his fighting instinct is too much for him and he makes war again! Meanwhile, the woman—cooking and serving as best she might for the Egyptian husband, the Chaldean, Persian, Roman, Greek, European through all the Dark Ages—is still cooking and serving as best she may for the American of 1904—most of the women.

This is the thing that must move at last if the world is to swing forward smoothly and in unison on its broad upward path. It is not enough that we have women teachers and women lawyers, women doctors and women ministers, women in every business, art, and trade—these are all necessary, all valuable, all helping to show the way—but they are not enough.

It is not the success of women who leave home, nor even of those who by some miracle do world-work and "keep house," too, that matters; it is the fact that the vast body of our women are still engaged in this so utterly outgrown and left-behind grade of industry and can do nothing else. It is that industry itself which keeps us back.

We must marry; we must have children; we must have homes. So long as the women who do modern, civilized work have to give up love, marriage, home, and children, so long the advance of women is not established. It is all women who must be equal to all men, not here and there one. And it is the mother who must be equal to the father, not the maiden aunt. For the child's sake—and that is the one great reason for all evolution—for the child's sake, who is born of woman and brought up at home, we need a new woman and a new home.

To this, of course, the ready answer is "We are satisfied. We like our homes as they are, our children as they are, our mothers as they are. We have sat still lo! these thousands and thousands of years and we will not move now."

Yes, you will. You may not want to but you'll have to. Human progress, the swift, sure, cumulative vanguard of civilization, has attained such force at last that the very oldest, slowest, most immovable thing that we had to hold to is being swept forward willy-nilly. The home itself, last of all institutions to be stirred, is moving now. What is the nature of the change? It is this:

First: A clear distinction between the relation of husband and wife and the relation of master and servant. When this change is fully established, a man would no more think of having his wife become his house servant than a woman would think of marrying her butler *and retaining him in that capacity.*

It is as revolting as it is ridiculous—and ridiculous as it is revolting—that half the world should be the private servants of the other half.

Let the married pair follow any trade or trades they will; let them both be cooks if they please or one cook and one wait on tables; but one should not be the servant of the other. No amount of poetry, sentiment, or devotion alters the industrial fact; to "keep house" is a trade and when a man does it we call him a janitor.

Second: a clear distinction between the psychical function of maternity and the social function of education. Every normal woman should be a mother and glory in it. But no woman should be allowed to take care of children *unless she is competent.*

We assume that all mothers are competent. They are not. Visibly, glaringly, awfully, they are not.

Their little ones sicken, their little ones die, their little ones grow up—such as survive—and make the poor, confused, stupid, unhappy people the world is full of.

Children could be far happier, healthier, wiser, stronger, better in all ways than they are now. The character of humanity has changed enormously in these long ages; the possibilities of care and education have changed enormously—but the mother has not changed.

Young, inexperienced, uneducated, she takes at the hands of the skilled gynaecologist the intricate, marvelous mechanism of a little child with no more preparation of such a charge than had her far-off ancestress who stepped into the bushes with no doctor or nurse and presently rejoined the line of march, her baby on her back. That woman was in some essentials a better mother; she gave health, vitality, love, nursing on strong milk. The modern baby is the product of modern civilization and he needs civilized care. The relation of mother to child should keep its primal power and purity: a strong, free, splendid motherhood, glad and proud, cheerful and unafraid. We should have big, well-grown women, no frail girls, looking forward to this as the crown of personal life—their glorious distinction and first power. Each mother would love her own children best—each child would have its own dear mother—but the years of infancy and early childhood would be given a care worthy of the age we live in instead of being left to the irresponsible ignorance of variously deficient parents.

There are some who urge State regulation of parenthood—as if being born was all that mattered! Recent study and conscientious effort of trained specialists have shown that foundlings—children of the lowest, most depraved parents, even defectives and degenerates—respond to intelligent care with wonderful improvement. It is not opinion, belief, tradition, superstition, emotion, habit, or instinct—it is fact. Even positively defective children under the loving, enthusiastic care of scientific teachers (not parents) respond to an astonishing degree. What then can be done for the human race in general when all children have expert care and training!

This is the unbounded hope of the new century. This the work of the new woman.

She is to be human at last; that is, she is to take part in those great, modern, social processes which make civilization. She is to be free as women never were since that dim, matriarchal past and use her freedom solemnly and joyfully—as a human being in the best social service, as a woman in choosing for her husband only the best for the child's sake.

If there aren't enough best men to go around—well, the others can be spared! And if the inferior women were immoral enough to marry inferior men, they would tend to die out, too.

This great new hope for humanity absolutely requires the civilizing of the home industries—both the care of children and the preparation of food. A civilized industry is one performed by specialized experts in organized business. Now this is the change that so terrifies the ancients: they who were once wildly radical, desiring the ballot for women, and are now fearsome and conservative, dreading to lose "the home." We shall lose nothing that is necessary to our welfare. We shall gain what the weary world most needs—better people! There is no stopping place in social evolution. We go on, on, on, higher and higher.

Today there are plenty of us loving, caring, sympathizing, willing to do all they can to serve the world but not fully seeing how.

This is only one step in that great onward march of man toward God, but it is one of vast and immediate importance.

As a last word for the present to this circle of readers, let it be understood that the "views" some fear so much are very honestly believed to be views of a more lovely, healthful, and happy life for us all.

Afterword

IN THE END GILMAN'S unconventional beliefs about the roles women should assume in social evolution were more progressive than many readers of the *Woman's Journal* could tolerate. She became an increasingly divisive figure over the course of her year-long "experiment." As early as February 1904 she was addressing in Vital Issues some "inquiries" sent her. In mid-March the editor of the *Woman's Journal* began to run a disclaimer to the effect that Gilman was "solely responsible" for what appeared in her department.[1] A week later the paper published a complaint from Louise Norcross, a suffragist and Emily Dickinson's cousin, begging Gilman "not to run down housekeeping anymore!"[2] Gilman addressed a steamer letter while en route to Germany in May to her "Gentle Readers, Enraged Readers, or any kind of readers interested in these columns."[3] In October she conceded that giving offense to readers was "one of the unavoidable risks" of speaking the truth.[4] So controversial were some of her essays that Alice Stone Blackwell was forced to intervene, as when Gilman criticized an article that praised the culinary skills of a woman physician[5] or defended women who sought notoriety and fame. "One must emphatically dissent," Blackwell averred, "when Mrs. Gilman says that 'fame is rightly desired'" by some women and that it is "a healthy social impulse" to wish for "large recognition."[6] Toward the close of her year-long experiment, Gilman admitted that she had been rash "to continually give *what is not wanted* [italics in original] to people who could easily pay for it if they did want it. The same work through other channels reaches a wider audience and does full as much—if not more—good."[7] Even in her final piece for the paper in 1904 she tried to reassure readers who disapproved of her progressive "doctrine of a new world for women" that it was "not really as bad as they think."[8] More to the point, Gilman refused to surrender to her detractors. She published dozens of articles over the next several years in such venues as *Harper's Bazar, Critic, Grand Magazine, Independent, Success, Delineator, Collier's Weekly*, and even *National Home Journal, Woman's Home Companion*, and *Good Housekeeping*. Blackwell occasionally excerpted or reprinted some of these pieces. Then in November 1909, less than five years after suspending her column in the *Woman's Journal*, Gilman launched her monthly magazine, *The Forerunner*, which she single-handedly wrote and edited for more than seven years, and which contained some of her most important work.

Notes

Introduction

1. Carl Degler, "Introduction" to Gilman, *Women and Economics* (New York: Harper and Row, 1966), xiii.
2. Charlotte Perkins Gilman, "Comment and Review," *Forerunner* 3 (April 1912), 111.
3. Gilman, *The Living of Charlotte Perkins Gilman* (New York: D. Appleton-Century, 1935), 216.
4. Agnes E. Ryan, *The Torch Bearer: A Look Forward and Back at the Woman's Journal* (Boston: Woman's Journal and Suffrage News, 1916), 12, 15, 17.
5. Quoted in Cynthia J. Davis, *Charlotte Perkins Gilman: A Biography* (Stanford, CA: Stanford University Press, 2010), 266.
6. Denise D. Knight and Jennifer S. Tuttle, eds., *The Selected Letters of Charlotte Perkins Gilman* (Tuscaloosa: University of Alabama Press, 2009), 216.
7. "A New Department," *Woman's Journal*, December 26, 1903, 409; Gilman, "To My Readers in Especial," *Woman's Journal*, December 3, 1904, 386.
8. *Selected Letters of Charlotte Perkins Gilman*, 216.
9. Gilman, *Concerning Children* (Boston: Small, Maynard, 1900), 4. See also Gilman, *The Home* (New York: McClure, Phillips, 1903), 135: "A child is fed by his mother, who transmits remote ancestral customs, unchanged by time." Mark Twain expressed a similar view in "A Family Sketch," written in the late 1890s, in which he suggested that breast milk "imparts to the child certain details of the mother's make-up . . . such as character, disposition, tastes, inclination, traces of nationality, and so on." Twain, *A Family Sketch and Other Private Writings* (Berkeley: University of California Press, 2014), 31.
10. Gilman, "Brain Growth," *Woman's Journal*, November 12, 1904, 362.
11. Gilman, *Women and Economics*, 147.
12. See also Gilman, *The Home*, 79: "When a peasant family from Hungary comes to America, they establish a Hungarian home. As they become Americanised the home changes and improves. The credit is not due to the home, but to the country."
13. Gilman, "Brain Growth," 362.
14. Gilman, "Herland," *Forerunner* 6 (June 1915), 153.
15. Gilman, "Is America Too Hospitable?," *Forum* 70 (October 1923), 1983–84.
16. Gilman, "The Mother-Heart," *Woman's Journal*, October 15, 1904, 330.

17. Gilman deploys the term "race" to mean either a species or a racial type.
18. Lester Frank Ward, *Pure Sociology* (New York: Macmillan, 1903), 313–14.
19. Ward, "Our Better Halves," *Forum* 6 (November 1888), 275. In chapter 2 of *Herland*, Gilman dramatizes this image of women as the "trunk" of a "genealogic tree." The first Herlanders depicted in the novel cling "close to the great trunk" of a tree.
20. *Selected Letters of Charlotte Perkins Gilman*, 251–53.
21. Gilman, *Living*, 187.

A Note on the Text

1. See Gary Scharnhorst, *Charlotte Perkins Gilman: A Bibliography* (Lanham, MD: Scarecrow, 1985); and Scharnhorst and Knight, eds., *Charlotte Perkins Gilman's In This Our World and Uncollected Poems* (Syracuse: Syracuse University Press, 2012).

Column 1

1. From the elegy "In Memoriam" (1850) by the British poet laureate Alfred, Lord Tennyson (1809–1892).
2. A limerick by British poet William Cosmo Monkhouse (1840–1901).
3. The American sociologist Lester Frank Ward (1841–1913).

Column 2

1. June 19, 1920, 72–74.
2. See Gilman, "The New Generation of Women," *Current History*, 735–36: "In our great cities especially . . . women have shown an unmistakable tendency to imitate the vices of men" in "this lowering of standards in sex relationship."
3. *Wanderjahr* = A wander year or a year spent traveling.
4. More than five thousand Boer prisoners were transported by the British to concentration camps in Bermuda during the Anglo-Boer War of 1899–1902.
5. The Peter and Paul Fortress, built early in the eighteenth century on an island in the Neva River in St. Petersburg, Russia, on orders of Peter the Great (1672–1725), confined political criminals until the 1917.
6. *gage d'amour* = pledge of love.

Column 3

1. Gilman often discussed the distinctions among these terms, as in "Masculine, Feminine, and Human," *Kate Field's Washington*, July 6, 1892, 6–7; *Woman's Journal*, July 9, 1892, 220.
2. Amanda Carolyn Northrup (d. 1955), "Successful Women of America," *Popular*

Science Monthly, 64 (January 1904), 239–44. Gilman was a regular reader of *Popular Science Monthly*. See also Gilman, *Living*, 36.

3. Gilman misplaces a decimal point. The actual percentage of women among the "successful" people is 11.8 or about twelve in a hundred.

4. The English philosopher and sociologist Herbert Spencer (1820–1903).

5. See "Servant Girls' Union Forming," *New York Sun*, January 9, 1904, 7.

6. Frederic Dan Huntington (1819–1904), bishop of the Episcopal diocese of Central New York from 1869 until his death. See "Worldliness of Mind," *Washington Star*, December 1, 1903, 18.

7. The Iroquois Theater fire in Chicago in late December 1903, the deadliest theater fire in US history, killed more than six hundred people.

8. Gilman apparently refers to an explosion at a hotel in Keasbey, New Jersey, that injured twenty-eight people and panicked some five hundred others, many of them trampled, though there were no initial reports of fatalities. See "28 Hurt by Explosion at a New Jersey Inn," *New York Times*, January 4, 1904, 1.

9. On January 10, 1860, the Pemberton textile mill in Lawrence, Massachusetts, collapsed and caught fire, killing as many as 145 workers, most of them young women and children—the second-worst industrial fire in American history after the Triangle Shirtwaist fire in 1911.

10. Mrs. William Douglas Sloane, aka Emily Thorn Vanderbilt (1852–1946), was the wife of the businessman and philanthropist William Douglas Sloane (1844–1915).

11. "Dance for Miss Twombly," *New York Times*, January 5, 1904, 9. Ruth Twombly (1885–1954) was descended from the Vanderbilts through her mother. The invitation list to the dance included the names of about two hundred persons prominent in New York and Newport society, including Ethel Roosevelt, Eleanor Roosevelt, Stuyvesant Fish, Cornelius Vanderbilt, W. K. Vanderbilt, Ethel Barrymore, Mary and Cornelia Harriman, August Belmont, Ogden Codman Jr., William Sloane Coffin, George W. Smalley, and former US senator Edward O. Wolcott of Colorado.

12. Japan declared war on Russia on February 8, 1904, only three weeks after the publication of this column.

13. A bloody anti-Jewish pogrom known as the Kishinev Massacre erupted across Russia on Easter 1903 and was followed by a wave of anti-Jewish violence that continued until 1906.

14. Gilman refers to the resolution through arbitration in 1899 of a long-standing border dispute between Venezuela and British Guiana.

Column 4

1. The Italian explorer Christopher Columbus (1451–1506); Revolutionary Army general and US president George Washington (1732–1799); Protestant reformer Martin Luther (1483–1546); German composer Ludwig van Beethoven (1770–1827); French microbiologist Louis Pasteur (1822–1895); English scientist Isaac Newton (1643–1727);

Scottish author Robert Louis Stevenson (1850–1894); Italian Renaissance artist Michelangelo (1475–1564); and Abraham Lincoln (1809–1865), sixteenth president of the United States.

2. Albert B. Cummins (1850–1926), governor of Iowa.
3. The thesis of Gilman's *Women and Economics* (Boston: Small, Maynard, 1898).
4. "Suicides and Murders of 1903," *Chicago Tribune*, January 1, 1904, 20.

Column 5

1. "antis" = anti-suffragists
2. The National American Woman Suffrage Association, founded in 1890 under the leadership of Susan B. Anthony (1820–1906). Gilman refers to Anthony in her autobiography as "that grand leader of the Equal Suffrage Movement" (*Living*, 174).
3. Lady Isabel Margesson (1863–1946), "On the Ethical Training of Children," *Woman's Library* 3 (1903).
4. The American writer Josephine Dodge Daskam (1876–1961).
5. Adèle Marie Shaw (1866–1942), "Evening Schools for Foreigners," *World's Work*, 9 (January 1904), 5738–44.
6. Belle Smith Bruce (d. 1924), principal of school No. 3 in Yonkers, New York, from 1893 to 1922, organized the first Parents-Teacher Association in the city circa 1899.
7. Eohippus, a primitive ancestor of the horse.
8. Beginning in 1902, the Chicago Teachers' Union was affiliated with the Chicago Federation of Labor, the first group of teachers in the United States to join a local labor organization.
9. From the lecture-essay "Traffic" by the English writer and art historian John Ruskin (1819–1900), first published in *The Crown of Wild Olive* (New York: Wiley, 1866), 49.

Column 6

1. The American journalist Ernest Poole (1880–1950), author of *The Plague in Its Stronghold: Tuberculosis in the New York Tenements* (New York: University Settlement, 1903).
2. The Black Death was a pandemic of bubonic plague in Europe in the mid-fourteenth century.
3. The physician Addison M. Baird, author of *Consumption* (1903).
4. Reprinted in the *New York Times*, February 8, 1904, 2.
5. "Topics of the Times," *New York Times*, January 29, 1904, 8.
6. The English economist and reformer Helen Bosanquet (1860–1925), "The Poverty Line and Physical Degeneration," *Contemporary Review* 85 (January 1904), 65–75.
7. William Booth (1829–1912), founder of the Salvation Army.

Column 7

1. The American journalist and dramatist Jesse Lynch Williams (1871–1929), author of *The Stolen Story and Other Newspaper Stories* (New York: Scribner, 1899).
2. See "Fighting Standard Oil," *New York Times*, January 20, 1904, 1.
3. This anecdote, attributed to Samuel Johnson (1709–1784) but of dubious authenticity, originally appeared in *Boswell's Life of Johnson* (1791). See George Birkbeck Hill, ed., *Life*, vol. 1 (New York: Harper & Bros., 1891), 535.
4. Mrs. Partington was a comic character popularized by the American editor and humorist B. P. Shillaber (1814–1890).
5. "Footpads in Williamsburg," *New York Sun*, January 29, 1904, 2.

Column 8

1. See, for example, "Stetson Objects to Reform," *San Francisco Examiner*, December 20, 1892, 1; and "Women of Brains as Wives," *San Francisco Examiner*, December 25, 1892, 6.
2. Gilman, *Living*, 143.
3. The German archeologist Theodor Mommsen (1817–1903).
4. Ambrose Bierce (1842–ca. 1914) often ridiculed the Pacific Coast Women's Press Association in general and Gilman in particular in his weekly Prattle column in the *San Francisco Examiner*. See also Lawrence J. Oliver and Scharnhorst, "Charlotte Perkins Gilman versus Ambrose Bierce," in *Charlotte Perkins Gilman and Her Contemporaries*, eds. Davis and Knight (Tuscaloosa: University of Alabama Press, 2004), 32–45.
5. The National Convention of Women Suffragists convened in Washington, DC, February 11–17, 1904. See also Gilman, "An Advancing Cause," *Current Literature*, 36 (April 1904), 388–89.
6. Annie Watson-Lister of Australia.
7. King James of Scotland (1567–1625), sponsor of the King James Version of the Bible.
8. Katharine Seymour Day (1870–1964), a resident of the Nook Farm neighborhood in Hartford and, like Gilman, a grandniece of Harriet Beecher Stowe (1811–1896), was active in the Women's Municipal League of New York.
9. The National Convention of Women Suffragists convened in New Orleans March 15–19, 1903.

Column 9

1. "Conservatism of Feminine Sentiment," *New York Sun*, February 12, 1904, 6.
2. victoria = a four-wheeled, horse-drawn carriage.
3. The American social scientist Thorstein Veblen (1857–1929) discusses this tendency by trophy wives to exhibit "pecuniary canons of taste," particularly

"conspicuous leisure," in *The Theory of the Leisure Class* (New York: Macmillan, 1899). For example: "The exemption from pecuniary stress has been carried farther in the case of the leisure-class women of the advanced industrial communities than in that of any other considerable group of persons" (338). Gilman also commends Veblen's "classic" several times in *Human Work* (New York: McClure, Phillips, 1904), 72, 179, 219, 309, 323; in *The Home* (119, 134, 220), and his "unforgettable" theory in "The Dress of Women," *Forerunner* 6 (July 1915), 192.

4. "Court Orders Wife to Cook," *New York Times*, February 21, 1904, 1.

5. The initial letter to the editor of the *New York Times* titled "Men Reluctant to Marry" (February 16, 1904, 8) elicited several responses in the paper ("Bachelor Called Selfish" and "Comforts of Some Bachelors," February 17, 1904, 8; "Topics of the Times," February 18, 1904, 8; "Topics of the Times," February 20, 1904, 8), including one from the original writer: "A Protest from 'Bachelor,'" February 21, 1904, 12.

6. "When Lovely Woman Stoops to Politics," *New York Times*, February 20, 1904, 9.

7. "Defends Women Voters," *New York Times*, February 20, 1904, 5. Colorado became an equal suffrage state in 1893.

8. Former US congressman John L. Shafroth of Colorado (1854–1922).

Column 10

1. Colorado approved women's suffrage by popular referendum in 1893.

2. "Changes in the Woman Suffrage Movement," *New York Evening Post*, February 20, 1904, 4. Gilman not only commended this editorial but she also later contributed a piece to the *New York Evening Post*: "Housing for the Poor," November 18, 1905, 24.

3. See also Gilman's *Human Work*, 33 ("That superstitious respect for the aged which distinguishes China is giving way to a respect for wisdom, for knowledge, for judgment and ability") and *The Home*, 20 ("ancestor-worship" was "made a religion" in "some of our oldest, *i.e.*, most primitive civilizations, as the Chinese").

4. Acts 7:4.

5. The reformer Kang Youwei (1858–1927), advisor to Emperor Guangxu (1871–1908) and author of *A Study of Confucius as a Reformer of Institutions* (1897).

6. Empress Dowager Cixi (1835–1908).

7. Kang Tongwei (1878–1974), cofounder of the *Journal of Women* in Shanghai in 1898.

8. Kang Tongbi (1887–1969) attended Hartford High School and graduated from Barnard College in 1909.

9. Gilman, *Women and Economics*, 164. No frail Victorian, Gilman was an unapologetic advocate of women's physical exercise and the work of woman's clubs throughout her career. While residing in the Bay Area in the 1890s, for example, she "joined dozens of clubs" (Davis, *Charlotte Perkins Gilman*, 145).

Column 11

1. In his *Republic*, Plato (ca. 427–347 BC) described an ideal state composed of artisans, guardians, and philosopher-kings.
2. Jesus's command "Let the dead bury their own dead" (Luke 9:60) was echoed in "A Psalm of Life" (1838) by the American poet Henry Wadsworth Longfellow (1807–1882).
3. Probably Hristina Tapchileshtova (b. 1864), the wife of Konstantin Stoilov (1853–1901), the prime minister of Bulgaria from 1894 until 1899.
4. Thomas Arnold (1795–1842), headmaster of Rugby School in England from 1828 to 1841.
5. The French novelist George Sand, aka Amantine Lucile Aurore Dupin (1804–1876).
6. "Women in Panic in Blazing Car," *New York Times*, February 7, 1904, 1.

Column 12

1. The Egyptian pharaoh Rameses II (ca. 1303–1213 BC).
2. The Russian novelist Leo Tolstoy (1828–1910).
3. Czar Alexander II freed the Russian serfs in 1861.
4. The millennium was the thousand-year reign of Christ on earth prophesied in the biblical Book of Revelation.
5. Romans 8:19.
6. Shaw, "The Ideal Schools of Menomonie," *World's Work* 7 (March 1904), 4540–53.
7. James H. Stout of Wisconsin (1848–1910), Wisconsin state senator from 1895 until 1910.
8. N. J. MacArthur of the Menomonie Public Schools.
9. The plutocrat Andrew Carnegie (1835–1919) donated the 76-acre Pittencrieff Park to his hometown of Dunfermline, Scotland, in 1903.
10. The British artist and writer William Morris (1834–1896), author of the utopian novel *News from Nowhere* (1890).

Column 13

1. Matthew 13:12.
2. John J. Jegi (d. 1904), professor of physiology and psychology at the Milwaukee Normal School.
3. Gilman addresses the same issue later in "Women Teachers, Married and Unmarried," *Forerunner* 1 (November 1910), 8–10.
4. Gilman cites "Wants Children to Hate War," *New York Times*, March 1, 1904, 2:

"The Syndic of the Paris Municipal Council recently invited the Education Department of the Seine to request the teachers to explain to the pupils the alliance between France and Russia.... The children, said the Syndic, would be enlightened in regard to the Russo-Japanese campaign, would learn how the Hague Conference came about, and would be inspired with a horror for war."

5. Between 1892 and 1917 France and Russia observed a joint foreign policy.
6. The Hague Peace Convention of 1899.

Column 14

1. Louise Norcross (d. 1919), "Housework Defended," *Woman's Journal*, March 26, 1904, 98.
2. Florence M. Atkinson (1861–1928), one of the associate editors of the *Woman's Journal*.
3. Robert Webster Jones, *Housekeeper* 28 (March 1904). Gilman also cites Jones in "Domestic Economy," *Independent*, June 16, 1904, 1359; Larry Ceplair, ed., *Charlotte Perkins Gilman: A Nonfiction Reader* (New York: Columbia Univ. Press, 1991), 157.
4. Gilman echoed this Lamarckian idea that "racial habits of unbroken centuries" such as hunting "are not to be offset by one lifetime's change" in *Human Work* (26).
5. See Gilman, *Women and Economics*, 242, 267. She also touches on this subject in *Human Work*: "You cannot build right houses for modern humanity on the basis of a kitchen, on the service of the belly of a beast" (387).

Column 15

1. Gilman, *Living*, 284. See also Gilman, "The New Generation of Women," *Current History* 18 (August 1923), 736: "The special demand of women for a permanent name of their own is wholly right."
2. "Mrs. Everard Cotes," *Current Literature* 36 (April 1904), 404. The journalist Sara Jeannette Duncan (1861–1922) married the entomologist Everard Charles Cotes in 1890. See also Gilman, "The Honor of Bearing His Name," *Forerunner* 7 (February 1916), 46–47.
3. Gilman offers a hypothetical example and plays on the name of Anna Sewall (1820–1878), author of the children's novel *Black Beauty* (1877).
4. The short-lived *Women's Welfare*, published in Dayton, Ohio, from 1903 until 1905.
5. The Woman's Century Club of the National Cash Register Company of Dayton was affiliated with the General Federation of Women's Clubs.
6. Louise Catherine Hinck of Montclair, New Jersey. See also "What Some Women are Doing," *City and State*, May 5, 1904, 275.
7. Mrs. Ira E. Tutt, an electrical and mechanical engineer and a native of Minnesota (not Michigan), supervised the construction of electrical plants in Long Beach, California, and Globe, Arizona. Her husband became the manager of the Long Beach

plant. Gilman fails to identify the woman electrical engineer by name because in all the news coverage she is known only as "Mrs. Ira W. Tutt." See also "This Will Interest Women," *Brooklyn Eagle*, August 1, 1900, 12; and "What Some Women are Doing," *City and State*, May 5, 1904, 275.

Column 16

1. *Ajax*, a classical Greek tragedy about a warrior in the Trojan War by Sophocles (ca. 476–405 BC).
2. Jane Addams (1860–1935), founder of Hull House in Chicago and a leader in the settlement house movement in the United States. In her autobiography Gilman remarked that "Jane Addams was a truly great woman" (*Living*, 184).
3. Lillian Wald (1867–1940), founder of the Henry Street Settlement in New York. See also *Living*, 248–49.
4. "East Side Has Its Waldorf," *New York Times*, March 1, 1904, 9.
5. The lead actor in both the Chicago and New York productions of *Ajax* was Georgias Mettalas, a Chicago bookkeeper.
6. Alexander the Great (356–323 BC), military ruler of ancient Greek kingdom of Macedonia.
7. The French military commander Napoleon Bonaparte (1769–1821) was leader of the First French Republic and First French Empire from 1799 to 1815.
8. A member of an elite, old New England family.
9. Ward, *Pure Sociology: A Treatise on the Origin and Spontaneous Development of Society* (New York: Macmillan 1903). See especially chapter 14, "The Phylogenetic Forces," 290–416.
10. The biologist Charles Darwin (1809–1882) had published *On the Origin of Species* (1859).
11. In Gilman's utopian novel *Herland* (1915) a race of women reproduces parthenogenetically.
12. "Hearst's 'Examiner,'" *Woman's Journal*, April 9, 1904, 114.
13. Hearst was twice elected to the US Congress from New York as a Democrat but left the party in 1904 to found the Municipal Ownership League.

Column 17

1. Gilman considered the phrase "Christian Science" an oxymoron. See *Human Work*, 316. Her opinion was no doubt influenced by reading "Mark Twain's splendid article on Xian science" in the December 1902 issue of the *North American Review*. See Knight, ed., *The Diaries of Charlotte Perkins Gilman* (Charlottesville: University of Virginia Press, 1994), 829.
2. "Enemies of the Republic," *McClure's*, 22 (April 1904), 587–99, by the muckraking journalist Lincoln Steffens (1866–1936).

3. The Italian humanist Giovanni Boccaccio (1313–1375) recounts the tale of Griselda, a peasant woman repeatedly tested by her rich husband, in *The Decameron* (1349–1353). Gilman also mentions the tale in *The Home* (326).

4. "What Are We Coming To?," *New York Evening Post*, February 28, 1903, 4.

5. "Future Housekeeping: Woman's Unorganized Work to be Done Commercially," *New York Evening Post*, April 13, 1904, 12.

6. American botanist Luther Burbank (1849–1926).

7. American civil engineer George E. Waring Jr. (1833–1896).

8. Emil Reich (1854–1910), "The Future of the Latin Nations/France," *Contemporary Review* 85 (March 1904), 402–12. See also Gilman's reply to Reich's essay, "The Future Influence of American Women," in "Foreign Critic and American Women," *Success*, 8 (September 1905), 614–16.

9. *jeune fille* = young girl.

10. "Annie Laurie" was a Scottish folksong ostensibly based on a poem by William Douglas (1682?–1748).

11. Beatrice guides Dante Alighieri (ca. 1265–1321) through hell and purgatory to heaven in *La Divina Commedia* (ca. 1308–1320).

Column 18

1. The German dramatist Frank Wedekind (1864–1918), author of the play *Erdgeist* or *Earth Spirit* (1895).

2. Grant Allen (1848–1899), "Woman's Place in Nature," *Forum* 7 (May 1889), 258–63. Gilman had discussed this exchange in *Women and Economics*, 172. In her autobiography she would accuse Allen of "social treason" (*Living*, 206).

3. Lulu, the snake woman or femme fatale in Wedekind's plays *Erdgeist* and *Die Büchse der Pandora* (1904).

4. Gilman also alludes to this painting in *Human Work*, 315: It "typifies well man's opinion" of the femme fatale.

5. On the treatment of women in the writings of the Anglo-Indian novelist, poet, and journalist Rudyard Kipling (1865–1936), see Dieter Petzold, "The Female of the Species: Frauenfiguren in Kiplings Werk," *Arbeiten aus Anglistik und Amerikanistik* 14, i (1989), 3–18; and the "Women and Kipling" special issue of the *Kipling Journal* 93 (March 2019), 1–64.

6. "The Letter L" (1863) by the English poet Jean Ingelow (1820–1897). Gilman quotes the same lines in "The New Generation of Women," *Current History* 18 (August 1923), 737; and different lines from the same poem in *Women and Economics*, 112.

7. A Greek myth about the release of evil into the world.

8. "Woman and the Spirit of Earth: A German Drama of Power," *Literary Digest*, April 23, 1904, 585.

Column 19

1. In chapter 6 of his novel *A Hazard of New Fortunes* (1889), Howells estimates that "women form three-fourths of the reading public in this country." See also Joanne Karpinski, "When the Marriage of True Minds Admits Impediments: Charlotte Perkins Gilman and William Dean Howells," in *Charlotte Perkins Gilman and Her Contemporaries*, eds. Davis and Knight (Tuscaloosa: University of Alabama Press, 2004), 17–31.
2. Eros and Psyche, the Greek goddesses of love and the soul.
3. A slight misquotation of the essay "Love" (1841) by Ralph Waldo Emerson (1803–1882): "All mankind love a lover." Gilman was an avid reader of Emerson. See Gilman to Martha Luther Lane, August 1, 1881: "*I was right*, I read Emerson's incomprehensible conundrums! My mind was his for a moment?" *Selected Letters of Charlotte Perkins Gilman*, eds. Knight and Tuttle (Tuscaloosa: University of Alabama Press, 2009), 15.
4. A slight misquotation of Shakespeare's *Troilus and Cressida*, III, iii: "a touch of nature makes the whole world kin."
5. Canto I of *Don Juan* (1819) by the English romantic poet Lord Byron (1788–1824).
6. Jennie L. Vandewater (b. 1878) had been dismissed from her teaching position in New York in December 1903. After filing suit against the Board of Education, she was reinstated four months later. See "Will Permit Women Teachers to Marry," *New York Times*, April 28, 1904, 16.
7. The Board of Education retained the substance of the regulation in its bylaws. It merely deleted the phrase "which may direct that charges be preferred against such a teacher by reason of such marriage." Gilman quotes M. Dwight Collier, member of the Committee on Elementary Schools, who is cited in the *New York Times* article.
8. Eliza Burt Gamble (1841–1920), author of *The Evolution of Woman* (New York: Putnam's Sons, 1894).
9. Ward, "Our Better Halves," *Forum* 6 (November 1888), 266–75. In this essay, as Gilman asserted, Ward "clearly [proved] the biological supremacy of the female sex." See Gilman's *Women and Economics* (Boston: Small, Maynard, 1898), 171.

Column 20

1. The American novelist and poet Flora MacDonald Thompson (1878–1962), "The Truth About Women in Industry," *North American Review* 178 (May 1904), 751–60.
2. "Ivy and Oak" by American poet Mary Quinlan Laughlin (1860–1929).
3. The Iroquois Theater fire in Chicago in late December 1903, the deadliest theater fire in US history, killed more than six hundred people.

4. Proctor's Theater in New York caught fire during a performance the evening of May 6, 1904. See "Saved from Theater Panic," *New York Sun*, May 7, 1904, 1.
5. Harry Brunelle (1861–1922), manager of Proctor's Theater.
6. Captain John J. McNally (1857–1937) of the New York Police Department.

Column 21

1. See "Hazing at West Point," *New York Tribune*, December 19, 1900, 4; and "Hazing at Annapolis," *Washington Times*, May 2, 1904, 6.
2. St. Stephen's College, an Episcopal boys' school in Annandale, New York, today Bard College.
3. Edwin Bedell (b. 1850). His son, Archer Wilsey Bedell (1885–1976), graduated from Trinity College in Hartford in 1908 and became a major in the army engineering corps during World War II. See also "St. Stephen's College Sued for a Hazing," *New York Times*, May 9, 1904, 1. The suit was apparently settled out of court.
4. Gilman similarly referred in *Human Work* to the "Happy Hunting Grounds of our American savages" (8).
5. The Mandan are a Great Plains Indian tribe located today mostly in North Dakota.
6. After a "looking over," the man-cub Mowgli is admitted to the wolf band in Kipling's *The Jungle Book* (Garden City: Doubleday, 1894), 68.
7. According to this antiquated anthropological theory, children during maturation recapitulate the evolution of the species. See, for example, the first chapter of Stephen Crane's *Maggie*, in which "little boys ran to and fro, dodging, hurling stones, and swearing in barbaric trebles" and "fighting in the modes of four thousand years ago." Crane, *Maggie* (New York: Appleton, 1896), 2, 7.
8. The character Harold Skimpole in Charles Dickens's novel *Bleak House* (1853).
9. The character Wilkins Micawber in Dickens's novel *David Copperfield* (1850).

Column 22

1. The Greek classical poet Théocrite (ca. 310–ca. 250 BC).
2. "A Musical Instrument" (1860) by the English poet Elizabeth Barrett Browning (1806–1861).

Column 23

1. See Jennifer S. Tuttle, "Introduction" to *The Crux* (Newark: University of Delaware Press, 2002), 42–42; Tuttle, "Gilman's *The Crux* and Owen Wister's *The Virginian*: Intertextuality and 'Woman's Manifest Destiny,'" in *Charlotte Perkins Gilman and Her Contemporaries*, eds. Davis and Knight (Tuscaloosa: University of Alabama Press, 2004), 127–38; and Tuttle and Scharnhorst, "Charlotte Perkins Gilman and the US

West," in *Charlotte Perkins Gilman and a Woman's Place in America*, ed. Jill Bergman (Tuscaloosa: University of Alabama Press, 2017), 21–24.

2. See also the reply by Emma Harriman, "Shall Women Go West?," *Woman's Journal*, July 2, 1904, 215.

3. An admonition usually credited to the American newspaper publisher Horace Greeley (1811–1872).

Column 24

1. "With a homogeneous nature bred of two parents in the same degree of social development, we shall be able to feel simply, to see clearly, to agree with ourselves, to be one person and master of our own lives, instead of wrestling in such hopeless perplexity with what we have called 'man's dual nature.' Marry a civilized man to a primitive savage, and their child will naturally have a dual nature. Marry an Anglo-Saxon to an African or Oriental, and their child has a dual nature." Gilman, *Women and Economics*, 332.

2. The artist George du Maurier (1834–1896) repeatedly satirized the British nouveau riche in the humor magazine *Punch* in the character of the snobbish Mrs. Ponsonby de Tomkyns. Gilman apparently alludes in particular to his sketch titled "Killing Two Birds with One Stone" (1879), reproduced in *English Society at Home* (London: Bradbury, Agnew, 1880), in which the singer Jenkins meets the Duchess of Stilton, a patron of the arts.

3. Many state laws at this time stipulated that the ballot was forbidden to "minors, aliens, paupers, idiots, lunatics, criminals, and women."

Column 25

1. Gilman sailed from Hoboken, New Jersey, across the Hudson River from New York, on May 19 for Bremen via Plymouth and Cherbourg aboard the Norddeutscher Lloyd steamship *Friedrich der Grosse*.
2. The third-century AD Roman emperor Heliogabalus.
3. The first-century AD Roman emperor Vitellius.
4. Matthew 7:14.
5. Proverbs 13:15.
6. In 1887 Gilman underwent the so-called "rest cure" for neurasthenia, which required total bed rest and was prescribed by the nerve specialist S. Weir Mitchell (1829–1914), "with what I considered the inevitable result, progressive insanity" (*Living*, 119).
7. A traditional rug design.
8. *Zutritt verboden* = entrance forbidden.
9. H_2SO_4 or sulfuric acid.
10. Gilman traveled with the suffragists Susan B. Anthony, her sister Mary

Stafford Anthony (1827–1907), Ida Husted Harper (1851–1931), Lydia Kingsmill Commander (1869–1940), Elizabeth Grannis (1840–1926), May Wright Sewall (1844–1920), Hannah G. Solomon (1858–1942), Mary Wood Swift (1841–1927), and Kate Waller Barrett (1857–1925). At the dock Gilman was also "greeted with applause from deck and pier and a waving of yellow banners. 'What are you to talk about at the quinquennial?' Mrs. Gilman was asked. 'Ward's Theory' came the answer. . . . 'If you knew anything about suffrage or social purity, you'd know what Ward's Theory is. Read the fourteenth chapter'" of *Pure Sociology* ("Women Off to Rouse Europe," *New York Sun*, May 20, 1904, 7). See also "Congress Ends," *Boston Globe*, June 19, 1904, 21: "The leading speaker in the main hall was Mrs. Perkins Gilman, who discussed Prof. Lester F. Ward's theory of the biological origin of the sex, according to which the female became the established type prior to the male. Mrs. Gilman turned the theory to account, discussing in a brilliant way the relations between the sexes today, claiming that society will not be perfect till woman participates in all human interests equally with men." As Gilman reminisced in her autobiography, she received a "warm welcome" in Germany and "So popular was I that great crowds followed me from one hall to another" (*Living*, 298).

11. The American suffragist Lucretia Longshore Blankenburg (1845–1937).

12. The American suffragist and peace activist Carrie Chapman Catt (1859–1947), one of the leaders of the National American Woman Suffrage Association, was elected the first president of the International Woman's Suffrage League in Berlin. Catt reported in a letter from Europe that "Mrs. Gilman had an army of delighted admirers about her all the time" ("Editorial Notes," *Woman's Journal*, September 3, 1904, 281).

13. During the campaign for women's voting rights in Kansas in 1867, the suffragists adopted yellow as the color of their cause after the sunflower, the Kansas state flower.

14. The short-lived *Southern Woman's Magazine* was published from February 1904 until August 1905.

Column 26

1. The confusion likely was the result of the similarity of the German words for "fifty" (*fünfzig*) and "fifteen" (*fünfzehn*).

2. Hillman's Hotel, built in 1847 in Bremen by Johann Heinrich Hillmann (1808–1866).

3. The medieval St. Peter's Cathedral located in the market square in Bremen.

4. The Parkhaus in Burgerpark, Bremen.

5. John H. Klosterman (1857–1937) of Nebraska, the US consul at Bremen.

6. Isabella Napier (1876–1930) of New Zealand.

7. Rudolf Breitscheid (1874–1944), a prominent member of the Social Democratic Party of Germany.

8. The British suffragist Sophia Rodger-Cunliffe.

9. Daniel J. Sully (1861–1930) cornered the American cotton market in 1903.
10. The physician and feminist activist Aletta Jacobs (1854–1929) also translated Gilman's *Women and Economics* into Dutch in 1900.
11. Anna Howard Shaw (1847–1919), president of the National American Woman Suffrage Association and an ordained Methodist minister, closed the exercises ("Dr. Shaw and Berlin," *Montgomery Advertiser*, June 28, 1904, 9).
12. Shaw's sermon at the interdenominational American Church on Motzstrasse near Nollendorfplatz in Berlin marked "the first time a woman" had preached "from a German pulpit" (Malcolm Clarke, "Germans in Constant Fear of War with the Other Great Powers," *Pittsburgh Press*, June 5, 1904, 5).
13. See note 6 to column 25.
14. The Greek mathematician Archimedes (ca. 287–ca. 212 BC).

Column 27

1. According to the *Woman's Journal* ("Editorial Notes," September 3, 1904, 281), Carrie Chapman Catt sent at least one private letter to the United States about the Berlin meeting.
2. *Mitglied* = member.
3. Charlemagne Tower Jr. (1848–1923), US ambassador to Germany. His wife, Helen Tower (1859–1931), also hosted a reception for the American delegation during the conference (*Living*, 299).
4. Kipling's "The Ballad of East and West" (1889).
5. *Grafin* = Countess.
6. Probably the women's rights activist Friederike Zeileis, aka Friederike Mekler von Traunwies (1872–1954), one of the founders of the International Women's Suffrage Alliance in Berlin.
7. The Palast Hotel on Potsdamer Platz in Berlin, completed in 1893.

Column 28

1. Gilman, *Living*, 299; *New York Sun*, July 14, 1904, 5. The first part of this column was reprinted in the *Woman's Exponent* (Salt Lake City), July 1, 1904, 3; and in the Elmira *Star-Gazette*, August 8, 1904, 6. Gilman also reported on the meeting in "The Growing Power of Woman: Impressions of the Congress in Berlin," *Booklovers*, no. 4 (September 1904), 385–90.
2. The *Prinzess Irene* was built in 1899 for the North German Lloyd steamship line.
3. *Frauenstimmrecht* = women's suffrage.
4. Empress Augusta Victoria of Schleswig-Holstein (1858–1921), wife of Kaiser Wilhelm II (1859–1941).
5. Lady Aberdeen Ishbel Maria Hamilton-Gordon, Marchioness of Aberdeen and Temair (*née* Isabel Maria Marjoribanks (1857–1939)).

392 Notes

6. Probably the Norwegian suffragist Gina Krog (1847–1916).
7. See also L. F. C.'s response to this column in "Stealing a Servant," *Woman's Journal*, December 3, 1904, 386.
8. Kate Thyson Marr (d. 1907), "Are Women More Cruel Than Men?," *Minneapolis Star Tribune*, June 5, 1904, 30.
9. From the hymn "From Greenland's Icy Mountains" (1821) by Bishop Reginald Heber (1783–1826).
10. "Man was Made to Mourn" (1784) by the Scottish poet Robert Burns (1759–1796).
11. King David murdered Uriah the Hittite, Bathsheba's husband (2 Samuel 11).

Column 29

1. "Some Women at Work," *World's Work* 8 (June 1904), 4938. See also "A Correction," in column 35.
2. The "parent village improvement society" in the nation was founded in Stockbridge, Massachusetts, in 1853. See Clark W. Bryan, *The Book of Berkshire* (Great Barrington: Bryan, 1886), 69.
3. The Italian village of Pompeii was destroyed in the eruption of Mount Vesuvius in 79 AD.
4. Gilman developed this notion at greater length in *Human Work*, 137: "The farmer is engaged in our most remote and ancient industry, the one nearest the bottom; in fact it is the bottom of real social growth; only the cattle-keeper stands between the farmer and the savage."

Column 30

1. See note 3 to column 17.
2. "Why Not a Children's Car?," *New York Evening Post*, July 23, 1904, 4.
3. The American Unitarian minister Edward Everett Hale (1822–1909), Gilman's uncle and author of the utopian romance "My Visit to Sybaris," collected in *Sybaris and Other Homes* (1869).
4. "How Gaminland Finds Its Summer Joys," *New York Times*, July 24, 1904, 19.

Column 31

1. Proverbs 23:7.
2. "The Barber's Tale of His Second Brother," from the *Arabian Nights* or *A Thousand and One Nights*. In "Stories About Women" (*Lima Republican-Gazette*, March 7, 1920, 10) Gilman cites the 1840 translation by Edward William Lane (1801–1876).
3. The American railroad barons James J. Hill (1838–1916) and E. H. Harriman (1848–1909).

4. A series of Russian manifestoes between 1899 and 1903 introduced obligatory Russian language instruction in Finnish schools, abolished the Finnish army, and challenged the authority of the constitution of the "Grand Duchy of Finland."

Column 32

1. Gilman reiterated in 1923 that "wifehood and motherhood are the normal status of women, and whatever is right in woman's new position must not mitigate against these essentials" ("The New Generation of Women," 735).
2. "Why I Do Not Marry by a Bachelor Maid," *Independent*, June 30, 1904, 1482–86.
3. The American author Marion Harland, aka Mary Virginia Terhune (1830–1922), "'A Bachelor Maid' and Common Sense," *Independent*, July 7, 1904, 34–38.
4. *Kaffir* = a racist slur for black South Africans.
5. Gilman considered Grace Ellery Channing (1862–1937), her friend and Charles Walter Stetson's second wife, the "co-mother" of her daughter, Katharine.

Column 33

1. See also "National Column," *Woman's Journal*, September 3, 1904, 288.
2. Suffragists Harriet Taylor Upton (1853–1945) and Harriet May Mills (1857–1935).
3. The year 1904 was, in fact, an intercalary or leap year containing an additional day (February 29). In leap years, by folk custom, women may propose to men.
4. Alfred, Lord Tennyson's "To E.L. [the painter Edward Lear], on His Travels in Greece" (1853).
5. Jean Ingelow's "Seven Times Six. Giving in Marriage" (1864).
6. The American poet and Emily Dickinson's niece Martha Gilbert Dickinson Bianchi (1866–1943), author of "Song of Motherhood," *Scribner's* 36 (August 1904), 181.
7. The American journalist and editor, E. S. Martin (1856–1939), author of the poem "Diagnosis," *Scribner's* 36 (August 1904), 140.
8. "Marco Bozzaris" (1825) by American poet Fitz-Greene Halleck (1790–1867).
9. The inscription on the gravestone of William Shakespeare (1564–1616) in Stratford-upon-Avon: "Good friend, for Jesus' sake forebeare, / To digg the dust enclosed heare; / Bleste be the man that spares thes stones, / And curst be he that moves my bones."
10. Cheops, twenty-sixth century BC Egyptian monarch.

Column 34

1. The English political economist Thomas Malthus (1766–1834) theorized that population increases exponentially while food supplies increase arithmetically, leading inevitably to widespread hunger and starvation.

2. The notion of race suicide, originally promulgated in 1900 by the sociologist Edward A. Ross (1866–1951), Lester Ward's nephew, and popularized by Theodore Roosevelt (1858–1919), US president from 1901 to 1909, foreshadowed the contemporary racist "replacement theory" and argued that the "native" American stock would gradually become extinct, and an immigrant or "unfit" population would supersede it.

3. Gilman makes essentially the same argument in *Human Work*, 378.

4. Kilkenny, Ireland, was a hotbed of opposition to women's suffrage early in the twentieth century.

5. Gilman rephrased or even misquoted Spencer, who in fact wrote: "This inverse variation of Individuation and Genesis is exact" in *Principles of Biology* (New York: Appleton, 1867), II: 410. Nevertheless, Gilman repeated her own formulation of the idea in *Human Work*, 365, 378; *Moving the Mountain* (New York: Charlton, 1911), 58; *Herland* (1915), chapter 6; and "Back of Birth Control," *Birth Control Review* 6 (March 1922), 31–33.

6. Francis Galton (1822–1911), English eugenicist and author of *Heredity Genius* (1869).

7. *unum, sed leonem* = one, but a lion.

8. A town in western New York, birthplace of the Chautauqua movement. Gilman published five articles, including one of her lectures during the week, in the *Chautauqua Assembly Herald* in August 1904 (Scharnhorst, *Gilman: A Bibliography*, 116).

Column 35

1. Lucius Junius Brutus (d. ca. 509 BC), who reputedly founded the Roman Republic, ordered the deaths of his sons for conspiring against the Republic.

2. "To Lucasta, Going to the Wars" (1649) by the English poet Richard Lovelace (1617–1657).

3. See note 2 to column 11.

4. Jordan is quoted in Ely Van de Warker, "Is the Education of Women with Men a Failure?" *Harper's Weekly*, August 20, 1904, 1288. Gilman omits the conclusion attributed to Jordan by Van de Warker apparently for reasons of space: "Shall we give the girls the same education as our boys? Yes and no. If we mean by the same an equal degree of breadth and thoroughness, an equal fitness for high thinking and wise acting, yes, let it be the same. If we mean this: shall we reach this end by exactly the same course of study, then the answer must be no, for the same course of study will not yield the same results with different persons."

5. The naturalized French scientist Marie Curie (1867–1934) was awarded a Nobel Prize in Physics in 1903 for her pioneering research in radioactivity.

Column 36

1. Oscar L. Triggs (1865–1930), professor of English at the University of Chicago, sued the *New York Sun* for libeling him in its reports on his scholarship. See also

"Literary Criticism and the Law of Libel," *Michigan Law Review* 3 (November 1904), 64–66. Though his suit was initially successful, it was dismissed on appeal.
    2. "Child Drinks Carbolic Acid," *New York Sun*, August 28, 1904, 10.

Column 37

    1. Riverside Park in New York runs along the Hudson River from West 62nd Street to the south to West 126th Street to the north. It was not far from Gilman's apartment at 179 W. 76th Street.
    2. Probably the Schwarzenbach-Huber silk factory in Union City, New Jersey.
    3. Sir William Turner Thistleton-Dyer (1843–1928), curator of Kew Gardens.
    4. Probably the Scottish grocer James Robertson (ca. 1831–1914), who created and marketed Golden Shred marmalade in 1864.

Column 38

    1. Henry Clark Corbin (1842–1909), adjunct general in the US Army.
    2. Kipling's story "Love-o'-Women" (1893).
    3. "School for Wives," *New York Times*, September 22, 1904, 8.
    4. The Vicar of Crantock, Reverend George Metford Parsons (d. 1924).
    5. Exodus 20:13.
    6. Ernst J. Lederle (1865–1921), quoted in "Much Impure Food," *New York Times*, September 22, 1904, 9.

Column 39

    1. Gilman contradicts her point about the anachronism here in her comments on "Santa Claus" (see column 50), where she refers to the United States as "a Christian country."
    2. William Tecumseh Sherman (1820–1891), Union general during the American Civil War.
    3. The American journalist Raymond L. Bridgman (1848–1925), "World Organization Secures World Peace," *Atlantic Monthly* 94 (September 1904), 349–64.
    4. Gilman was a consistent globalist. As Davis notes, "When Congress rejected the treaty [ratifying US membership in the League of Nations in March 1920], Charlotte could scarcely contain her outrage" (*Charlotte Perkins Gilman*, 335).
    5. Dickens's novel *Great Expectations* (1861).
    6. Wisconsin state senator Stout. See note 7 to column 12.

Column 40

    1. American novelist Ellis Meredith (1865–1955), author of *Heart of My Heart* (1904).

2. Matthew 22:39.

3. British writer H. B. Marriott-Watson (1863–1921), "The American Woman—An Analysis," *Nineteenth Century and After* 56 (September 1904), 433–42.

4. American author John Foster Carr (1869–1939), author of "The Italian in the United States," *World's Work* 8 (October 1904), 5401, advocated for the education of immigrants.

5. President Theodore Roosevelt.

6. American writer and journalist Bessie van Vorst (1873–1928) and her sister-in-law, the author and artist Marie van Vorst (1867–1936). The affluent van Vorsts briefly worked as factory hands in Pennsylvania, Massachusetts, and North Carolina, experiences they chronicled in a five-part series titled "The Woman Who Toils" in *Everybody's Magazine* in 1902.

Column 41

1. Gilman, *The Home*, 240.

2. American author Marion Hill (1870–1918), "A Fruit of the Fair," *McClure's* 23 (October 1904), 623–29.

3. Josephine Dodge Daskam, "The Little God and Dicky," *McClure's* 17 (August 1901), 338–47.

4. The Bitterroot Salish, Kootenai, and Pend d'Oreilles tribes who reside on the Flathead Indian Reservation in western Montana.

Column 42

1. Marriott-Watson, "The American Woman—An Analysis," *Nineteenth Century and After* 56 (September 1904), 433–42.

2. The Russo-Japanese War fought in 1904–1905 over rival claims to Manchuria.

3. "Negro Attacks Woman, Witness Rides Away," *New York Times*, October 23, 1904, 8. The race of neither her assailant nor would-be rescuer is relevant to Gilman's point, of course.

4. Genesis 16:4–6.

5. "Topics of the Times," *New York Times*, October 23, 1904, 6.

Column 43

1. According to Daniel 4:33, Nebuchadnezzar II (ca. 632–562 BC), ruler of Babylon, suffered from mental illness and "ate grass like oxen."

2. F. W. Hews, "How the American is Changing His Food," *Pearson's* 12 (October 1904), 397.

Column 44

1. Gilman similarly discusses the ameliorating influence of play in *Human Work*: "Children's games show the natural development" of "social consciousness.... The game involving a contest of team with team is more enjoyed than the older sport of individual race and contest, both by spectator and player" (132). See also chapter 4 of *Herland*, where the women of the country defeat the male interlopers at a game of skill.
2. For information on the "Aryan tablelands" in central Asia, the ostensible "cradle of the Aryan race," see E. P. Evans, "The Aryan Homestead," *Atlantic Monthly* 57 (May 1886), 633–43. Gilman also notes that the citizens of Herland were "of Aryan stock" in her utopian novel. See *Forerunner* 6 (May 1915), 125.
3. Sanskrit is a classical, South Asian written language.
4. The luxurious St. Regis Hotel on Fifth Avenue in New York opened in 1904.

Column 45

1. Ward, "Our Better Halves," *Forum* 6 (November 1888), 266–75. In this essay, as Gilman asserted, Ward "clearly [proved] the biological supremacy of the female sex." See Gilman's *Women and Economics* (Boston: Small, Maynard, 1898), 171.
2. "Surplus women" were the abundance of unmarried women of marriageable age, particularly after a war decimated the population of single men. See also Gilman, "Superfluous Women," *Women's Journal*, April 7, 1900, 105.
3. Like Mark Twain and others who sided with Japan in the war, Gilman expected the defeat of Russia to precipitate an anti-czarist revolution.

Column 46

1. The American inventor and industrialist Thomas Edison (1847–1931).
2. Guglielmo Marconi (1874–1937), Italian inventor and engineer.
3. Gilman puns on gonorrhea or the "clap."
4. First Lady Edith Kermit Roosevelt (1861–1948) organized a "Social Cabinet" consisting of the wives of cabinet members.
5. "Clubwomen Vainly Oppose Proposal to Admit Unions," *Chicago Tribune*, October 21, 1904, 1.

Column 47

1. Each issue of the *Woman's Journal* contained a modest number of ads—two or three columns per four-page issue.

Column 48

1. See Gilman, *Women and Economics*, 242.
2. Gilman refers to the American suffragist Victoria Woodhull (1838–1927).
3. In "Tilts at Child Labor: Mrs. Charlotte Gilman Startles Consumers' League," *Chicago Tribune*, November 22, 1904, 5, Gilman is described as the "mother of the plan of segregating babies in municipal nurseries." Jane Addams, founder of Hull House in Chicago, reportedly "challenged the statements of Mrs. Gilman. She took exception to the declaration that a woman can go out into the industrial world without sacrifice to the home."

Column 49

1. Alexander the Great supposedly yearned "for new worlds to conquer." See note 6 to column 16.
2. Max Nordau (1849–1923) was a Zionist leader, physician, and author of *Degeneration* (1892).
3. The American social scientist Thorstein Veblen (1857–1929), author of *The Theory of the Leisure Class* (New York: Macmillan, 1899).
4. A rephrasing of the line "What's art for a woman?" in "Mother and Poet" (1861) by Elizabeth Barrett Browning.

Column 50

1. Timothy 5:8.
2. "Home, Sweet Home" (1823), with lyrics by the American actor and playwright John Howard Payne (1791–1852).
3. Romans 14:7. Gilman also quoted this biblical text in *Human Work*, 81.
4. The Standard Oil Company extorted rebates or reduced freight rates from railroad companies in exchange for its business.
5. Gilman often demythologized Santa Claus in her writings. See her "The Santa Claus Story," *Impress*, December 22, 1894, 3; "Better Than Santa Claus," *Christian Register*, December 12, 1907, 1402–3; "Santa Claus," *Forerunner* 7 (December 1916), 325; "Better Than Santa Claus," *Louisville Herald*, December 25, 1919, 15; and "Cross-Examining Santa Claus," *Century* 105 (December 1922), 169–74.
6. The Talmud is a source of Jewish law in Rabbinic Judaism.

Column 51

1. While a plausible paraphrase of passages in Emerson's essay "Self-Reliance" (1841), this exact quotation nowhere appears in his writings.
2. The civilizing influence of women in the mining camps was a recurring topic

in western American literature. See, for example, Bret Harte's "The Luck of Roaring Camp" (1868), "The Outcasts of Poker Flat" (1869), "The Idyl of Red Gulch," (1869), and "Miggles" (1869). Gilman likely refers here to one of many western tales, specifically perhaps "The Trumpeter" (1894), by the American author Mary Hallock Foote (1847–1938). See Scharnhorst and Knight, "Charlotte Perkins Gilman's Library: A Reconstruction," *Resources for American Literary Study* 23, no. 2 (1997), 196.

Afterword

1. *Woman's Journal*, March 19, 1904, 90.
2. L[ouise] N[orcross], "Housework Defended," *Woman's Journal*, March 26, 1904, 98. Norcross's letter complaining about Gilman's denigration of housekeeping also contains the only first-hand account known to scholarship of Emily Dickinson reciting her poetry aloud in the pantry of her home: "I know that Emily Dickinson wrote most emphatic things in the pantry, so cool and quiet, while she skimmed the milk; because I sat on the footstool behind the door, in delight, as she read them to me." See also Scharnhorst, "A Glimpse of Dickinson at Work," *American Literature* 57 (October 1985), 483–85.
3. Gilman, "A Steamer Letter," *Woman's Journal*, June 18, 1904, 194.
4. Gilman, "The Mother-Heart," *Woman's Journal*, October 15, 1904, 330.
5. A[lice] S[tone] B[lackwell], "Mrs. Gilman on Strawberry Jam," *Woman's Journal*, September 24, 1904, 308.
6. A[lice] S[tone] B[lackwell], "The Thirst for Fame," *Woman's Journal*, December 24, 1904, 412.
7. Gilman, "To My Readers in Especial," *Woman's Journal*, December 3, 1904, 386.
8. Gilman, "Valedictory," *Woman's Journal*, December 31, 1904, 418.

Index

Aberdeen, Lady, 212, 391n5
Addams, Jane, 135, 385n2, 398n3
Aesop's Fables, 5
Ajax (Sophocles), 135, 385n1
Alexander II, Czar, 383n3
Alexander the Great, 138, 286, 352, 385n6, 398n1
Allen, Grant, 151, 386n2
American College for Girls at Constantinople, 91, 93
androcentric period, 6, 139, 217, 240, 308
Anglo-American Lyceum Club, London, 88
Anthony, Mary Stafford, 198, 389–90n10
Anthony, Susan B., 73–74, 198, 199, 203, 208, 211, 212, 245, 380n2, 389–90n10
anti-Semitism, 35, 101–2, 343, 379n13
anti-suffragists, 43, 75, 147, 165, 271, 380n1
Arabian Nights, 5, 392n2
Archimedes, 206, 391n14
Arnold, Thomas, 94, 383n4
athletics, 88–90, 188
Atkinson, Florence M., 118, 119, 384n2
Atlantic Monthly, 287
Augusta Victoria, Empress, 391n4
Australia, 64, 72, 171, 202

baby gardens, 124
Baird, Addison M., 56, 380n3
Barrett, Kate Waller, 389–90n10
Barrows, Mabel Hay, 135–37, 138

Barrymore, Ethel, 379n11
Bedell, Archer Wilsey, 388n3
Bedell, Edwin, 171, 388n3
Beecher, Henry Ward, 5
Beethoven, Ludwig van, 38, 379n1
Belmont, August, 379n11
Bergman, Jill, 388–89n1
Berlin, Germany, 3, 195, 202, 207–9, 211–13, 391n1, 391nn6–7
Bible, 5, 280–81, 381n7
Bierce, Ambrose, 67, 381n4
Black Death, 261, 380n2
Black Plague, 54–55
Blackwell, Alice Stone, 375–76, 399n5
Blackwell, Henry B., 1
Blankenburg, Lucretia Longshore, 198
Boccaccio, 148, 386n3
Boer War, 21, 378n4
Bonaparte, Napoleon, 138, 242, 385n7
Booth, William, 57, 380n7
Bosanquet, Helen, 57–58, 380n6
Boston, Mass., 236
Breitscheid, Rudolf, 202, 390n7
Bremen, Germany, 201–2, 389n1, 390nn3–5
Bridgman, Raymond L., 287, 395n3
Browning, Elizabeth Barrett, 5, 180, 356, 388n2, 398n4
Bruce, Belle Smith, 46, 380n6
Brunelle, Henry, 170, 388n5
Brutus, Lucius Junius, 260, 394n1
Bulgaria, 91, 383n3
Burbank, Luther, 148, 157, 386n6

401

Burne-Jones, Philip, 151
Burns, Robert, 5, 392n9
Byron, Lord, 5, 387n5

Carnegie, Andrew, 105, 383n9
Carr, John Foster, 294, 396n4
Caslander, Sarah, 270
Catt, Carrie Chapman, 198, 203–4, 207, 391n1
centralized kitchens, 2, 124, 311, 313, 314
Chamberlin, Katharine, 211, 393n5
Channing, Grace Ellery, 393n5
Chautauqua, N.Y., 3, 253, 256–58, 394n8
Cheops, 249, 393n10
Chicago, Ill., 48, 329, 344, 385n2, 398n3
Chicago Tribune, 344, 398n3
childcare, 109, 314, 343–49, 398n3
child labor, 2, 131, 363, 398n2
China, 48, 86–87, 160, 249, 299, 361, 382n3
Christian Science, 144, 385n1
City Beautiful, 105
civil service, 110
Civil War, 323–24, 395n2
Cixi, Empress, 87, 382n6
Codman, Ogden, Jr., 379n11
Coffin, William Sloane, 379n11
Cold Spring Harbor, N.Y., 307
Collier, M. Dwight, 387n7
Collier's, 335, 336, 376
Colorado, 72, 81, 83, 382n7, 382n1
Columbus, Christopher, 38, 379n1
Commander, Lydia Kingsmill, 389–90n10
Confucius, 86
consumption, 51, 54–56, 107, 261, 380n1, 380n3
Contemporary Review, 57, 148
Corbin, Henry Clark, 277, 395n1
Coshocton, Oh., 79
Cotes, Everard, 127, 384n2
Crane, Stephen, 388n7
cremation, 2, 245, 249–51

Critic, 376
Cummins, Albert B., 40, 380n2
Curie, Marie, 263, 394n5
Current History, 378n2, 384n1, 386n6
Current Literature, 127, 381n5

Darwin, Charles, 385n10
Daskam, Josephine Dodge, 45, 298, 380n4, 396n3
Davis, Cynthia, 395n4
Day, Katharine, 73, 381n8
Dayton, Oh., 129
debutantes, 2, 23, 35–36, 303
Degler, Carl, 1
Delineator, 376
Denver, Col., 81
Dickens, Charles, 5, 128, 288, 388nn8–9, 395n5
Dickinson, Emily, 375, 393n6, 399n2
Dickinson, Martha Gilbert, 393n6
Domestic Science Associations, 311
Douglas, William, 386n10
dress reform, 2, 23, 29–30
du Maurier, George, 189–90, 389n2
Duncan, Sara Jeannette, 127, 384n2
Dunfermline, Scotland, 105, 383n9

economic independence of women, 109, 110, 234, 265
Edison, Thomas, 331, 397n1
Elmira, N.Y., *Star-Gazette*, 391n1
Emerson, Ralph Waldo, 5, 367, 387n3, 398n1
Eohippus, 47, 380n7
Equal Suffrage League, 64
Erdgeist (Wedekind), 151, 153–54, 386n1, 386n3
eugenics, 4, 253, 256, 259, 394n6
Evans, E. P., 397n2
Evening Post (New York), 3, 85, 143, 147, 227, 382n2
Everybody's Magazine, 396n6
exceptionalism, American, 4, 231

exhaust sweeping, 155–56

Farmington School for Girls in Connecticut, 91, 93–94
Fish, Stuyvesant, 379n11
Foote, Mary Hallock, 398–99n2
Forerunner, 376
Forum, 164
Franco-Russian alliance, 115
"free love," 343

Galton, Francis, 255, 394n6
Gamble, Eliza Burt, 164, 387n8
General Federation of Women's Clubs, 384n5
Gilman, Charlotte Perkins, writings of: fiction, *Crux, The*, 185, 388n1; *Herland*, 1, 378n19, 385n11, 394n5, 397n1; *Moving the Mountain*, 394n5; "Yellow Wallpaper, The," 1; non-fiction, "Advancing Cause, An," 381n5; "Back of Birth Control," 394n5; "Better Than Santa Claus," 398n5; *Concerning Children*, 3; "Cross-Examining Santa Claus," 398n5; *Diaries of Charlotte Perkins Gilman, The*, 385n1; "Domestic Economy," 384n3; "Dress of Women, The," 23, 381–82n3; "Future Influence of American Woman, The," 386n8; "Growing Power of Woman, The," 391n1; *Home, The*, 2, 117, 122, 179, 297, 377n9, 377n12, 381–82n3, 386n3, 396n1; "Honor of Bearing His Name, The," 384n2; *Human Work*, 2, 381–82n3, 384n4, 384n5, 386n4, 388n4, 392n4, 394nn3–5, 397n2, 398n3; "Is America Too Hospitable?" 4; *Living of Charlotte Perkins Gilman, The*, 303, 385n2, 386n2, 385n3; "New Generation of Women, The," 378n2, 384n1, 386n6, 393n1; "Pure Food Exposition, The," 277; "Pure Food is Fashionable," 277; "Santa Claus Story, The," 398n5; "Shape of Her Dress, The," 7; "Time to Read for the Housekeeper," 7; "Whatever Else We Lose, We Must Keep the Home," 17; *Women and Economics*, 1, 3, 189, 380n3, 386n2, 386n6, 387n9, 389n1, 391n10, 397n2, 398n1; "Women Teachers, Married and Unmarried," 383n3; poetry, "Two Callings," 179
Good Housekeeping, 376
Grand Magazine, 376
Grannis, Elizabeth, 389–90n10
Greece, 89, 92, 136, 137, 159, 224
Greeley, Horace, 389n3
gynaecocentric theory, 6, 135, 138–40, 153, 169, 239, 308, 326

Hague, 115, 383–84n4, 384n6
Hale, Edward Everett, 227, 392n3
Halleck, Fitz-Greene, 393n8
Hamilton-Gordon, Lady Aberdeen, 212, 391n5
Harland, Marion, 239, 393n3
Harper, Ida Husted, 389–90n10
Harper's Bazar, 376
Harper's Weekly, 262, 394n4
Harriman, E. H., 235, 392n3
Harriman, Emma, 389n2
Harriman, Mary, 379n11
Harrison, Cornelia, 379n11
Harte, Bret, 398–99n2
Hartford, Conn., 381n8
hazing, 2, 171–75, 388n1
Hearst, William Randolph, 2, 67, 71, 141, 385n13
Heber, Reginald, 392n9
Hebrew Orphan Asylum, 56
Heliogabalus, 196, 389n2
Hews, F. W., 396n2

Hill, James J., 235, 392n3
Hill, Marion, 298, 396n2
Hillmann, Johann Heinrich, 390n2
Hinck, Louise Catherine, 130, 384n6
housework, 40, 46, 77, 79, 80, 88, 89, 96, 113, 117, 121–24, 166, 222, 235, 237–39, 324, 340
Houston, Tex., *Chronicle*, 64
Howells, W. D., 159, 387n1
Hull House, Chicago, 135, 385n2, 398n3
Huntington, Frederic Dan, 30–31, 379n6

immigration, 2, 4, 100, 110, 138, 231, 236, 394n2, 396n4
Independent, 237, 376
Ingelow, Jean, 247, 386n6, 393n5
Institute of Social Services, New York, 106
International Congress of Arts and Sciences, 281
International Woman Suffrage Alliance, 202, 204, 212, 312, 391n6
Iroquois Theater fire, 3, 32–34, 170, 387n3, 379n7

Jacobs, Aletta, 203, 391n10
James VI of Scotland, King, 72, 381n7
Japan, 87, 100, 101
Jegi, James J., 113, 383n2
Johnson, Samuel, 64, 381, 3
Jones, Robert Webster, 118, 119, 384n3
Jordan, David Starr, 259, 262–64, 394n4

Kang Tongwei, 87, 382n5
Kang Youwei, 87, 382n7
Kansas, 390nn12–13
Karpinski, Joanne, 387n1
Keasbey, New Jersey, 379n8
Kew Gardens, London, 172
Kilkenny, Ireland, 254, 394n4
kindergartens, 103, 124, 182, 228, 258, 274, 343, 346, 347, 348
Kipling, Rudyard, 5, 151, 172, 209, 277, 386n5, 388n6, 391n4, 395n2

Kishinev Massacre, 379n13
Klosterman, John H., 390n5
Knickerbocker Athletic Club, New York, 87, 88
Knight, Denise D., 378n1, 385n1, 398–99n2
Krog, Gina, 212, 392n6

labor unions, 2, 3, 30, 48, 157, 379n5, 380n8, 397n5
Lamarckianism, 3, 9, 189, 384n4
Lane, Edward William, 392n2
Lane, Martha Luther, 387n3
Laughlin, Mary Quinlan, 168, 387n2
Lawrence, Mass., 379n9
Lear, Edward, 393n4
Lederle, Ernst J., 281, 395n6
libel laws, 265, 268, 269, 394–95n1
Lilydale, N.Y., 3, 245
Lincoln, Abraham, 38, 379–80n1
Literary Digest, 386n8
London, England, 54, 88, 260, 272
London Mail, 279
Longfellow, Henry Wadsworth, 5, 383n2
Los Angeles, Cal., 130
Lovelace, Richard, 394n2
Luther, Martin, 38, 379n1

MacArthur, N. J., 104, 383n8
Malthus, Thomas, 253–54, 393n1
manual training, 45, 103, 182
Marconi, Guglielmo, 331, 397n2
Margesson, Lady Isabel, 44, 380n3
Marr, Kate Thyson, 216, 392n8
Marriott-Watson, H. B., 294–96, 306, 396n1, 396n3
Martin, E. S., 393n7
Master Carpenters' Association, 130
matriarchate, 6, 94, 217, 345, 368
Mattalas, Georgias, 385n5
McClure's, 145, 298, 385n2, 396nn2–3
McNally, John J., 170, 388n6
Menomonie, Wisc., 102, 104–5

Meredith, Ellis, 291, 395n1
Mexico, 202
Michelangelo, 38, 379–80n1
Mills, Harriet May, 245, 393n2
Mitchell, S. Weir, 201, 389n6
Mommsen, Theodor, 67–68, 381n3
Monkhouse, William Cosmo, 378n2
Montclair, N.J., 45, 384n6
Morgan, J. P., 303
Morgan, Jane, 303, 309–10
Morris, William, 105, 383n10
motherhood, 15, 19, 47, 57, 69, 80, 96, 110, 115, 146, 151, 238, 240, 241, 242, 247–48, 285, 290, 293, 306, 345, 346, 347, 348, 357, 360, 372, 393n1, 393n6
Mussey, Mabel Hay Barrows, 135–37, 138

Napier, Isabella, 202, 390n6, 390n6
Naples, Italy, 211
National American Woman Suffrage Association, 44, 380n2, 391n11
National Convention of Women Suffragists, 67, 85–86, 381n5, 381n9
National Home Journal, 376
Native Americans, 101, 121, 197, 224, 299, 345–46, 388nn4–5, 396n4
Nebuchadnezzar, 313, 396n1
New Orleans, La., 74, 381n9
News from Nowhere (Morris), 105
Newton, Isaac, 38, 379n1
New Year's resolutions, 9–13
New York City Federation of Women's Clubs, 87
New York Exchange for Women's Work, 93–94
New York Times, 3, 35, 56, 80–81, 279, 307, 308–10, 382n5, 383n4, 388n3, 396n3, 396n5
New Zealand, 64, 202, 390n6
Nichols, Jane Morgan, 303, 309–10
Nineteenth Century, 306, 396n1
Norcross, Louise, 117, 375, 384n1, 399n2

Nordau, Max, 398n2
North American Review, 165, 385n1
Northrup, Amanda Carolyn, 27–28, 378n2
nurseries, 109, 314, 343–49, 398n3
Nurses' Settlement, New York, 135

Oliver, Lawrence, 381n4
Orange, N.J., 30
"Our Better Halves" (Ward), 6, 164, 387n9, 397n1

Pacific Coast Woman's Press Association, 71, 381n4
Palast Hotel, Berlin, 210, 391n7
Paris, France, 115, 260, 383–84n4
Parsons, George Metford, 280, 395n4
Pasteur, Louis, 38, 379n1
Paterson, N.J., 269–70
patriarchy, 261, 302
Patrick, Mary Mills, 91–92
Payne, John Howard, 398n1
Pearson's, 313
Peter the Great, 378n4
Philadelphia, Pa., 309
Plato, 86, 91, 383n1
pollution, 271, 273
Pompeii, 224, 392n3
Poole, Ernest, 54, 380n1
Popular Science Monthly, 27, 378–79n2
Porter, Sarah, 91, 93–94
prohibition, 213, 333
Punch, 389n2
Pure Food and Drug Act, 2, 277, 311
Pure Sociology (Ward), 6, 138–40

Quinquennial Congress of the International Council of Women, 195–213

race suicide, 4, 253–54, 394n2
Rameses II, 99, 383n1
Reich, Emil, 148, 386n8
rest cure, 3, 197, 201, 204–6, 389n6
Robertson, James, 274, 395n4

Rodger-Cunliffe, Sophia, 202–3, 390n8
Roosevelt, Edith, 333, 397n4
Roosevelt, Eleanor, 379n11
Roosevelt, Ethel, 379n11
Roosevelt, Theodore, 394n2, 396n5
Ross, Edward A., 394n2
Ruskin, John, 5, 49, 380n9
Russia, 99–101, 234, 236, 343, 383–84n4, 393n4
Russo-Japanese War, 3, 35, 99, 115, 306, 323, 325, 327, 379n12, 383–84n4, 396n2, 397n3

Sand, George, 95, 383n5
San Francisco Examiner, 67, 71, 140–41
Scharnhorst, Gary, 381n4, 388n1, 394n8, 398–99n2, 399n2
Scribner's, 247, 248, 393nn6–7
Sewall, Anna, 212, 384n3
Sewall, May Wright, 207, 208, 212, 384n3, 389–90n10
sex combat, 218, 283–84
sexual selection, 6, 186
Shafroth, John L., 81, 382n8
Shakespeare, William, 5, 249, 387n4, 393n9
Shaw, Adèle Marie, 45–46, 102, 104, 380n5
Shaw, Anna Howard, 203, 245, 391nn11–12
Sherman, William T., 286, 395n2
Shillaber, B. P., 65, 381n4
Sinclair, Upton, 277
Sloane, William Douglas, 35–36, 379n10
Smalley, George W., 379n11
Social Hall Association, New York, 135
socialism, 84–85, 213
Solomon, Hannah G., 389–90n10
Sophocles, 135, 137
Southern Woman's Magazine, 390n14
Sparta, 89, 136
Spencer, Herbert, 5, 255, 325, 379n4, 394n5

Standard Oil Co., 64, 398n4
Steffens, Lincoln, 5, 145, 385n2
Stetson, Charles Walter, 67, 393n5
St. Louis, Mo., 281
Stevenson, Robert Louis, 38, 379n1
Stockbridge, Mass., 224–25, 392n2
Stoilov, Kanstantin, 91, 383n3
Stone, Lucy, 1
Stout, James H., 103, 104, 383n7, 395n6
Stowe, Harriet Beecher Stowe, 5, 381n8
St. Petersburg, Russia, 378n4
St. Regis Hotel, New York, 317, 320–22, 397n3
struggle for existence, 187, 254
Sturgis, Roderick H., 128
Success, 376, 386n8
suffrage, women's, 1–2, 43–44, 46, 49–50, 53, 55–56, 64, 67, 75, 81, 83–86, 106, 111, 168, 211, 213, 245, 247, 254, 271, 273, 394n4
suicide, 41
Sully, Daniel J., 203, 391n9
Sun (New York), 3, 268
"surplus women" 326–27
Sweden, 202
Swift, Mary Wood, 208, 389–90n10

Talmud, 365, 398n6
Tapchileshtova, Hristina, 91, 383n4
tattooing, 2, 30
Tennyson, Alfred, Lord, 5, 378n1, 393n4
Terhune, Mary Virginia, 239, 393n3
Texas, 64
Théocrite, 180, 388n1
Theory of the Leisure Class, The (Veblen), 354–55, 381–82n3, 398n3
Thistleton-Dyer, William, 272, 395n3
Thomas, Warren, 307–8
Thompson, Flora MacDonald, 165–67, 387n1
Tolstoy, Leo, 100, 383n2
Tower, Charlemagne, Jr., 208, 391n3, 391n3

Tower, Helen, 391n3
trade schools, 103
Trenton, N.J., 45
Triangle Shirtwaist fire, 379n9
Triggs, Oscar L., 268, 394n1
tuberculosis, 51, 54–56, 107, 261, 380n1, 380n3
Turkey, 92, 148
Tutt, Mrs. Ira E., 130, 384–85n7
Tuttle, Jennifer, 388n1
Twain, Mark, 377n9, 385n1, 397n3
Twombly, Ruth, 35–36, 379n11

Union City, N.J., 395n2
Upton, Harriet Taylor, 245, 393n2

Vanderbilt, Cornelius, 379n11
Vanderbilt, Emily Thorn, 379n10
Vanderbilt, W. K., 379n11
Van de Warker, Ely, 394n4
Vandewater, Jennie L., 162, 387n6
van Vorst, Bessie, 396n6
van Vorst, Marie, 396n6
Veblen, Thorstein, 354–55, 381–82n3, 398n3
vegetarianism, 189, 192, 313
Villard, Oswald Garrison, 143
Vitellius, 196, 389n3
von Trauwies, Friederike Mekler, 212, 391n6
voting rights. See women's suffrage

Wald, Lillian, 135, 385n3
Ward, Lester F., 6, 9, 13, 138–40, 151, 152, 164, 170, 325–26, 378n3, 394n2

Waring, George, Jr., 148, 386n7
Washington, D.C., 3, 67, 83, 381n5
Washington, George, 38, 379n1
Watson-Lister, Annie, 72, 202, 381n6
Wedekind, Frank, 151, 386n1, 386n3
Wilhelm II, Kaiser, 391n4
Williams, Jesse Lynch, 63, 381n1
Williamsburg, N.Y., 65
Wister, Owen, 388n1
Wolcott, Edward O., 379n11
Woman's Century Club, Dayton, Oh., 129, 384n5
Woman's Exponent, 391n1
Woman's Home Companion, 376
Woman's Municipal League, New York, 91
Woman's University Club, New York, 88
Woman's Welfare, 128–30, 384n4
women teachers, 3, 109, 114–15, 159, 162–64, 218, 267, 306, 370, 383n3, 387n6
women's clubs, 2, 30, 43, 44, 59, 62–63, 87–88, 94, 106, 129, 208, 329–31, 334, 382n9, 384n5, 397n5
Women's Municipal League, New York, 91, 381n8
Woodhull, Victoria, 398n2
World's Work, 45, 102, 221, 294, 396n4

Yonkers, N.Y., 46, 380n6

Zeileis, Friederike, 212, 391n5

www.ingramcontent.com/pod-product-compliance
Lightning Source LLC
Chambersburg PA
CBHW021333230426
43666CB00006B/280